Kansas Monks

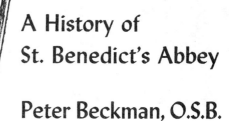

A History of
St. Benedict's Abbey

Peter Beckman, O.S.B.

BENEDICTINE COLLEGE PRESS, ATCHISON, KANSAS

NIHIL OBSTAT
Victor Gellhaus, O.S.B.
Censor Deputatus
Atchison, Kansas, die 21a Junii, 1957

IMPRIMATUR
Eduardus J. Hunkeler, D.D., LL.D.
Archiepiscopus Kansanopolitanus in Kansas
Kansanopoli, die 25a Junii, 1957

CUM PERMISSU SUPERIORUM
Cuthbertus McDonald, O.S.B.
Atchison, Kansas, Junii 1, 1957

Second printing 1979

TABLE OF CONTENTS

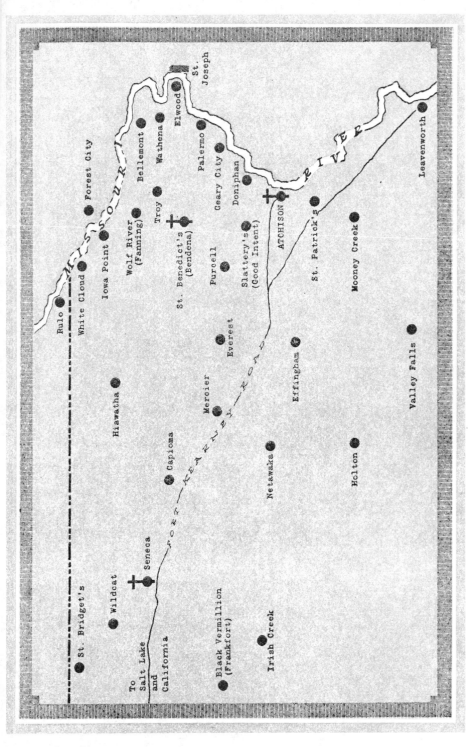

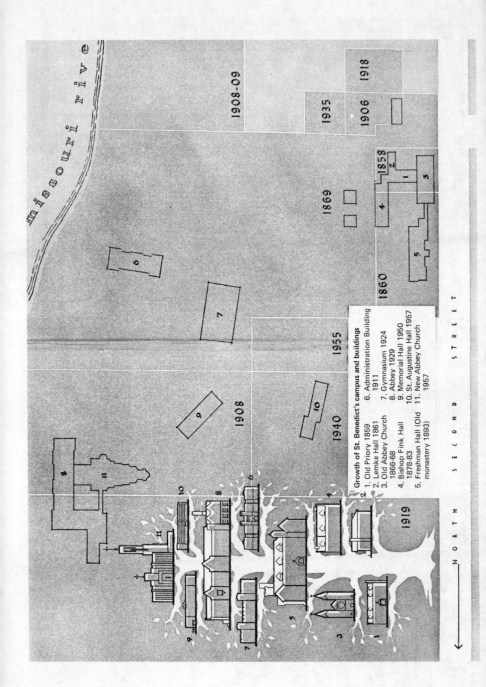

Missouri river

Growth of St. Benedict's campus and buildings

1. Old Priory 1859
2. Lemke Hall 1861
3. Old Abbey Church 1866-68
4. Bishop Fink Hall 1878-83
5. Freshman Hall (Old monastery 1893)
6. Administration Building 1911
7. Gymnasium 1924
8. Abbey 1929
9. Memorial Hall 1950
10. St. Augustine Hall 1957
11. New Abbey Church 1957

1908-09
1918
1935
1906
1858
1869
1860
1955
1908
1940
1919

NORTH SECOND STREET

Introduction

"A true history of Kansas Benedictines and missions is a sad affair and good only for archives."
—Abbot Innocent Wolf to Abbot Alexius Edelbrock, January 13, 1887.

The history of St. Benedict's Abbey is less conventional than that of many religious houses. As a matter of fact the first twenty years demonstrate how not to found a monastery. Everyone agrees that the history of a monastic community, taken as a whole, should be edifying unless the venture was a failure. But even the history of quite proper religious communities cannot possibly be uniformly edifying because it is the record of human beings plodding through life, with inevitable detours, in their search for God.

This is a family history, and like all family histories it contains a considerable quantity of treasured minutiae, unimportant to all but friends and members of the family. It is hoped, however, that some of these minutiae are the significant details that will make clear the personality of this particular Benedictine community. Every monastic community has a distinct personality, and a history of the community should describe this personality and give some account of its origins. Here it is assumed that the personality of St. Benedict's Abbey is the product of the men who founded the house, of the kind of work they did, and of the circumstances in which they lived — all as modified by the personalities, interests, work, and circumstances of their successors.

1

History is concerned largely with change, but the truly essential features of any monastic community are practically unchanging. Back in the sixth century St. Benedict founded a great family that has gone on from that day to this, seeking God through the practice of the religious vows and of the life of charity and prayer that he taught. These essentials of monastic life exhibit little change, and although they are the true life of the monastic community, they depend so little on externals, on the things that history finds tangible, that history can hardly touch them. On the other hand, the nonessentials of religious life change readily from generation to generation and probably assume a disproportionate place in history.

This long tradition of a particular form of Christian life is the greatest treasure the Benedictine has, and it was this tradition that Father Boniface Wimmer brought from Bavaria to the United States in 1846. The Bavarian Congregation of Benedictines had a long and honorable history. Temporarily wiped out by the secularization decrees of 1802-3, the congregation was restored in 1830 by Ludwig I, king of Bavaria, while old members still lived to preserve continuity. Its restoration was a part of the vigorous Catholic revival in Bavaria. The restoration of monastic life attracted a young diocesan priest, Sebastian Wimmer, and in 1833 he was one of the first to join the restored Abbey of Metten. As a Benedictine he took the name of Boniface, and throughout his life he burned with the ideals of his patron saint, the great Benedictine apostle of Germany. Boniface Wimmer believed firmly that the modern Benedictine must accept the challenge of the need for missionaries. In his own case that became a vocation to the German immigrant in the United States. His religious superiors, however, were faced with the manifold problems of the restoration in Bavaria. Wimmer could realize his dream, therefore, only after some years and after the application of considerable pressure, both diplomatic and religious.

Boniface Wimmer felt that founding an American Benedictine monastery would solve the problem of supplying missionaries to the rapidly growing numbers of German immigrants in the United States. Such a foundation, in his mind, would soon be self-supporting, would carry on the mission to the German immigrant, and at the same time would produce new missionaries and multiply mission centers throughout the new country. His plan would combine a school for the education of missionaries and typical Benedictine community life for their spiritual formation.

Father Wimmer was able, energetic, and not at all indecisive. Strongly supported by European friends, he ventured to America in 1846 with candidates rather than already trained Benedictine monks. After arriving in the United States he quickly absorbed the American technique of thinly spreading his resources of men, money, and credit to cover as much of the present and future needs as possible. He was confident that with rare exceptions the rapid growth of tomorrow would justify the gamble. These circumstances demanded that he stress rapid expansion in personnel and physical plant — the material aspects. By following these policies he developed his monastic community rapidly enough so that after ten years it began to undertake missionary activity well beyond the bounds of Pennsylvania, where he had made his first foundation.

Later in life Archabbot Wimmer seriously questioned the quality of the organization he had constructed, but the need for missionaries and mission centers had been urgent, and a slower and more deliberate development would not have met that need. American Benedictines today are the product of the past — a long past — and they can plan wisely for today and tomorrow only if they understand the past.*

* A more extensive account of the beginnings of the American Cassinese Congregation will be found in Colman Barry, O.S.B., *Worship and Work, St. John's Abbey and University 1856-1956* (Collegeville, Minn., 1956). See also the sketch of Abbot Wimmer by Felix Fellner, O.S.B. in the *Dictionary of American Biography*.

Unless otherwise indicated, the documents and letters cited are in the archives of St. Benedict's Abbey. Other archives are indicated by the following abbreviations:

(ACHS) American Catholic Historical Society of Philadelphia.
(AM) Abbey of Metten, Bavaria.
(GHA) Geheimes Hausarchiv, Munich.
(LMV) Ludwig-Missionsverein, Munich.
(SA) College of Sant' Anselmo, Rome.
(SJA) St. John's Abbey, Collegeville, Minn.
(SMA) St. Mary's Abbey, Morristown, N.J.
(SPexM) Abbey of St. Paul's outside the Walls, Rome.
(SVA) Archives of the American Cassinese Congregation, St. Vincent Archabbey, Latrobe, Pa.

The original language of letters cited is indicated by the prepositions *an* for German and *ad* for Latin.

I thank the archivists and librarians whose cooperation made this history possible. I thank also my Abbot and my confreres who generously gave me time, facilities, countless hours of editorial assistance, and encouragement so that this work could be completed.

Maps and layout are by Dennis McCarthy.

Father Henry Lemke, Missionary Extraordinary

This story begins in the troubled years preceding the Civil War. By the Kansas-Nebraska Act of May 30, 1854, Congress had created two new territories and left the status of slavery in them to be settled by squatter sovereignty. Kansas Territory, lying just west of Missouri and extending to the crest of the Rocky Mountains, promptly became a bone of contention between pro-slavery and antislavery forces. In the winter of 1855 Westport, Missouri (now a part of Kansas City), although not in neutral territory, was in many ways the frontier equivalent of the fabled wartime "neutral capital." Supplies and reinforcements for both parties struggling for control of Kansas moved through this gateway to the West. Here members of each party spied on the activities of the other. Many of the men involved were gambling their political and economic fortunes on the success of the party to which they were committed. One group of men so committed, Democrats from Pennsylvania, arrived in Westport in December, 1855, accompanied by a restless and adventurous old missionary, Father Henry Lemke, of the Order of St. Benedict.

Father Henry accompanied Dr. Aristides Rodrigue, with his son and daughter, into the territory at the end of the year. Their path crossed that of G. D. Brewerton, correspondent of the *New York Herald*, at Donaldson's house, eleven miles from Westport, on December 30. The party provided Brewerton with a page of romantic copy; the contrast of fragile young beauty as represented by the doctor's daughter and the weatherbeaten old priest who had once been a soldier lent itself easily to the reporter's need for color:

... we could not help thinking, as we gazed upon those strongly marked features, and that powerful, though now somewhat time-bowed form, that the priesthood had spoiled a good dragoon, and that the padre, like pious Friar Tuck, might still handle the quarterstaff quite as effectively as his breviary. Yet there was something touching, too — when we went to take our homely evening meal, in the fire-lighted apartment, which was both kitchen and supper-room — in the attitude of this war-worn old veteran, as he stood for a moment beside his chair, while he bent his head, and asked a silent blessing upon our food.   It was indeed just such a picture as some of the grand old masters would have loved to paint.   The man was a study in himself; and the rough cabin, with its yet more unpolished accessories, just the surroundings for a highly-finished interior of the Flemish school.

Supper was over; we had drawn our chairs nearer to the open fireplace; the winter night was dark without, and the blazing brands threw a cheerful glow upon the inmates of Donaldson's best sitting-room; the old priest had produced his short pipe, and tobacco-bag, and was now smoking placidly, with his dark eyes looking so intently the while at the glowing embers upon the hearth, that we almost fancied he must be reading some day-dream of the past in their ever-changing forms. . .[1]

Dr. Aristides Rodrigue and Father Henry were old friends. Father Henry had begun his missionary career as assistant to Father Gallitzin, the Russian prince who became the apostle of western Pennsylvania, and the doctor had been Father Gallitzin's physician. Doctor Rodrigue had come out to Kansas in the preceding year, and as a member of the Lecompton town company and contractor for the government buildings to be erected there was inevitably involved in the civil war in Kansas.[2]

[1] G. D. Brewerton, *The War in Kansas* (New York, 1856), 234-5.
[2] Lecompton, then the territorial capital, is situated between Lawrence and Topeka on the Kansas River.
The Rodrigue family's adventure in Kansas started in hope tempered with doubt and ended in tragedy. According to George W. Martin, Dr. Rodrigue and the other Pennsylvanians at Lecompton were free-state Democrats and as such were disliked by the proslavery element.—"A Kansas Pioneer

Father Henry had just arrived from Pennsylvania, was not in good standing with his ecclesiastical superiors, and so was depressed, discouraged, and convinced that the world around him was a lawless mess. All of this is reflected in his letter from Westport to his friend and attorney, Robert L. Johnston, back in Ebensburg, Pennsylvania:

You see, I am here yet, crippled up with rheumatism, hardly able to write. You will by this time have seen many and I am sure, the most contradictory accounts in the papers about the disturbances, which took place in this neighborhood. You, being no fanatic, can easily form an idea of the matter, but what all this will lead to, God only knows. I for my part think it is the commencement of dreadful convulsions — which will shake the whole Union. Our friend Rod.[rigue] is rather in a critical position, having espoused the proslavery party and being surrounded and closely watched by a set of the most bigoted abolitionists. He was just here, when word came of the rising in the territory. He hurried back and found his friends and dependents under arms and Andrew [his son] elected and acting as colonel. If it had come to open hostilities they all would have been massacred at the first onset. Govr. Shannon, who stands on screws himself, is hated and persecuted by the abolitionists and will be surely sacrificed by the proslavery men at any unfavorable turn of affairs, is his whole reliance, with him he has to stand or to fall. He has given him now the contract for the building of the state capitol and other public buildings in Lecompton. Rodr.[igue] is at present here, buying mules, oxen and provisions and engaging workmen. I have done all I could to warn him. For you are aware, that the other party have laid out a place for a Capital, Topeka, and are preparing and building with the greatest confidence. If Shannon therefore and his party go down, which is not very impossible, Lecompton will be a second Nauvoo. But if matters go, as R.[odrigue] and his friends anticipate, he will undoubtedly be one of the first men in the new State. Nothing is now to be done but to let matters take their course, it is now neck or nothing.

Merchant." *Kansas Historical Collections*, VIII, 381.
    Dr. Rodrigue died at Lecompton on the feast of Corpus Christi, 1857. His oldest son, Andrew, a graduate of Fordham, a lawyer, and for a short time postmaster of Lecompton, was killed by a border ruffian at Lecompton in 1858. —Clara Rodrigue Ruthven to Stephen Wise, O.S.B., Hollidaysburg, Pa., Jan. 8, 1912.

As for myself I have nothing to do with all these affairs and shall take care not to be involved in them. I am now a complete separatist in every respect. I am tired of the world and can not disengage myself from the opinion, that we live in the last times, near the epoch of Antichrist, for I see that a poisonous miasma has penetrated all relations of life, social, political, and religious. My creed has been reduced to a short sentence of the Apostle James, Chapt. 1, v. 27. [Religion pure and undefiled before God the Father is this: to give aid to orphans and widows in their tribulation, and to keep oneself unspotted from this world.][3]

The history of St. Benedict's Abbey begins with Peter Henry Lemke's trip to Kansas. A number of now respectable religious houses in the United States are the monuments of pioneers who moved first and had their ecclesiastical status legalized later. Father Henry is one of the genuine "characters" in American Catholic Church history, and he displayed in somewhat exaggerated form all the characteristics of the typical free lance frontier missionary. These men were with few exceptions extraordinarily individualistic. Only men who in their search for souls prized freedom of action above comfort, decent shelter, regular meals, and a reasonably well-ordered life would ordinarily accept the poverty and hardship of the frontier missionary's life. In this numerous company Father Henry yields place to few as an individualist. He was sometimes at peace with his superiors, but apparently he considered such peace bought too dearly. In keeping with their individualism, frontier missionaries were often restless, footloose men. On this test, too, Father Henry scores high marks.

Infection by the prevalent fever of land speculation is another characteristic of the frontier missionary. Whether the purpose was to get enough for the church's needs while land was still cheap, or to use the profit from rapidly rising land values to build churches, or to provide income for himself (for there was almost none from the struggling settlers), it was difficult for the missionary to resist the temptation if he could lay his hands on a few

<hr>

[3] Lemke to R. L. Johnston, Westport, Dec. 27, 1855. (ACHS)

hundred dollars. Father Henry seems to have caught the fever immediately after his arrival in the United States, and it stayed with him through much of his life. As a consequence, his financial affairs were ordinarily unsettled and became fantastically tangled at the crises of his life.

The frontier notoriously talked big and was full of grandiose plans. Father Henry bubbled over with grand designs except during his brief periods of deepest depression. Fact and fantasy tended to get inextricably mixed, not only in prospect but also in retrospect. Life to him was a melodrama, with himself always in the role of the hero. He had eccentricities and faults, but he was nevertheless an apostle. He faltered once or twice, but otherwise, in his own peculiar fashion, he pursued his vision of bearing the Word of God to the scattered peoples of the American Republic with fidelity and real sincerity. His life was unusual, and it is pointless to expect him to fit the ordinary mold.

Peter Henry Lemke

According to the account he gives of himself in an autobiography, Peter Balthasar Henry Lemke was born July 27, 1796, the youngest child of a business man, J. Martin Lemke and his wife Friederike, at Rehna in Mecklenburg. His education was haphazard. His empty-headed mother and his phlegmatic father cared little for him. His maternal grandfather taught him his prayers and an appreciation for music. A distant relative, an atheistic classicist, gave him a good start in Latin and contemporary literature. What little family life there had been in the Lemke household was destroyed in 1806 by the confusion that accompanied the French occupation of Mecklenburg after the battle of Jena. In 1811 the fifteen-year old boy decided to leave home for Schwerin, the capital of Mecklenburg, where he stayed with friends of an older brother while continuing his studies at the Lutheran cathedral school. Two years later, Lemke was caught up in the enthusiasm of the War of Liberation and joined the Mecklenburg contingent which ultimately served with the Swedes in Holstein.

After the war he matriculated at the University of Rostock to study for the Lutheran ministry. Student life there was at a low ebb, with drunkenness and duelling the order of the day. The faculty of theology was completely and often bitterly rationalistic. Two fellow students, an unnamed pietist and Dr. X. Adler, a doctor of philosophy from Goettingen, lax Catholic and universal genius, seem to have taught him more theology than did his professors. Dr. Adler's decision to return to his religion and his transfer to the Catholic center of Regensburg, whence he continued to correspond with Lemke, were an important influence in the latter's life.

In 1820 Lemke passed his theological examination and was granted a license to preach. He became tutor to the sons of the landlord of Harkensee near Dassow, and on Sundays he usually preached in neighboring churches. Only then did Lemke read Luther's works and promptly lost his faith in Lutheranism. His correspondence with Dr. Adler had kept Lemke's interest in Catholicism alive, and in 1823 he made the break and went to Regensburg, where Dr. Adler introduced him to Bishop Sailer and his circle. The saintly Willmann, rector of the seminary, instructed him in the Catholic faith. On April 21, 1824, Bishop Sailer received his profession of faith and confirmed him. Lemke immediately began his study of Catholic theology, and on April 11, 1826, he was ordained.

His first assignment was assisting Pastor Buchner at Binabiburg. A couple of months later his Bishop transferred Lemke to the vicarage of Wiesbach in the same parish. He immediately fired the sacristan and plunged into the work of improving the property. He remodeled the rectory, built new barns, and bought cattle, but his work apparently was not appreciated. He asked for a change, and the petition coincided with a request from Herr Friederich Schlosser, Goethe's wealthy nephew, for a private chaplain at his residence, Stift Neuburg near Heidelberg. Lemke insists that Bishop Sailer talked him into accepting the position.

At Neuburg he had but little priestly work to do, and so he soon drifted into managing the lands and property of the estate. The lack of priestly work, however, continued to worry him. In the autumn of 1833, a letter to Clemens Brentano, a house guest of the Schlosser's, from the new Bishop of Philadelphia, F. P. Kenrick, begging for priests, caused Brentano to remark, "Ah, Monsieur, that would be something for you, a young, strong man, well equipped in body and mind, now sticking around here as a chaplain deluxe, getting big and fat, while hundreds of poor Catholics are begging for spiritual food."[4] The others in the company took this remark as an example of Brentano's wit, but Lemke did not. He could not forget that word, chaplain deluxe. That had hit the nail on the head. He decided to go to America, and with the permission of his Bishop, he sailed for New York in 1834.[5]

After his arrival in Philadelphia in 1834, Father Lemke served briefly as assistant at Holy Trinity Church.

[4] Lemke Autobiography, MS, 80.

[5] Lemke entrusted his autobiography to a friend in Germany, Rev. Michael Forner, who died in 1902. The manuscript was thought lost until it was discovered when the Abbey of St. Boniface in Munich transferred its archives following the bombing and fire of March 10, 1943. This is not Father Lemke's original manuscript but a thoroughly scrubbed revision by Father Forner. Scant mention is made of Lemke's sojourn in Kansas. The part covering Lemke's European years has been published by Father Willibald Mathaeser, O.S.B., "P. Heinrich Lemcke's Erinnerungen an Europa," *Studien und Mitteilungen zur Geschichte des Benediktiner-Ordens und Seiner Zweige* (1946), 60, 331-371. St. Benedict's Abbey is indebted to Father Willibald for a microfilm copy of the manuscript.

Father Lemke began to publish an English version of his reminiscences in the Carrolltown, Pa., newspaper in 1878. About the time he had brought these up to his relations with Abbot Wimmer, their publication suddenly ceased. According to Flick, the completed manuscript was placed in the hands of Mr. Johnston for safe-keeping but was lost.—Lawrence F. Flick, "Biographical Sketch of Rev. Peter Henry Lemke, O.S.B., 1796-1882," *Records of the American Catholic Historical Society of Philadelphia* (June, 1898), IX, 184.

With one exception the only extant letters to which Father Lemke signed his last name are those to Mr. Johnston. In these he spelled his name Lemke, and that spelling is followed here. In the archives of the Ludwig-Missionsverein there is one letter from him in which the signature can be interpreted as being spelled Lemcke.

During the last months of that year he toured Pennsylvania, caring for the scattered Catholics, particularly the Germans, wherever he found them. In 1835 the Bishop sent him to the famous Father Gallitzin at Loretto, who assigned him as resident pastor of Ebensburg. Two years later Father Lemke bought a farm and lived at Hart's Sleeping Place. Next, following Gallitzin's example, he bought land and laid out the town of Carrolltown in 1840. Gallitzin died that same year, and so Lemke took his place and resided at Loretto.

The Diocese of Pittsburgh was created in 1843, and the following year the See was filled by the first Bishop, Michael O'Connor. From him Father Lemke received permission to go to Europe to collect money for his church. On his return in 1846 he found another pastor in residence at Loretto and so settled at Carrolltown. The Bishop demanded an account of the money collected in Europe. Father Lemke considered this demand unreasonable and so in 1848 sold his Carrolltown farm to Father Boniface Wimmer, O.S.B., and transferred to the Archdiocese of Philadelphia. He was assigned to Reading, but after about a year he announced that he and Reading were finished with each other.[6] Meanwhile he busied himself acquiring land in Cambria County,[7] and for this reason, he thought, the Bishop of Pittsburgh viewed him with suspicion.[8]

In 1852 the old missionary decided to become a Benedictine and entered the novitiate at St. Vincent Priory near Latrobe, Pennsylvania, and was given the name of Henry. This decision was apparently dictated more by the fact that Father Lemke had run out of bishops than by any real vocation to the monastic life. At any rate, Abbot Wimmer later reminded Father Henry that about 1850 he was neglecting his priesthood and leading a rustic life, useless to God and to the Church. Abbot Wimmer felt that he had reconciled Father Henry with the Bishop

---

[6] Lemke an Wimmer, Hollidaysburg, Oct. 12, 1849. (SVA)
[7] Flick, *op. cit.*, 173-4.
[8] Lemke an Wimmer, Ebensburg, Nov. 14, 1849. (SVA)

and admitted that it was ". . . true that I urged you to enter the Order. . . because only under that condition and as long as you were with us would the Bishop restore your faculties."[9]

After Father Henry had spent some months at St. Vincent, he went up to Carrolltown to complete his novitiate. There he made his vows as a Benedictine on February 2, 1853. He was fifty-six years old, had been a priest for twenty-five years, had founded the town of Carrolltown, and now found himself not prior of the house, not pastor of the congregation, but an assistant to younger men. Further frustrations developed. At one time or other Father Henry had title to almost 2400 acres of land in Cambria County.[10] In 1848 he had sold his Carrolltown farm to Father Wimmer for $3000.[11] Father Henry held a mortgage on this land, and he made his vows as a Benedictine with the understanding that he would transfer the title to St. Vincent and cancel the mortgage without further payment by Father Wimmer.[12] At the same time Father Henry possessed two other large properties, the Hopper lands and the Loop estate. Wimmer decided to leave these lands in Father Henry's name temporarily, because the titles were not clear and because Lemke would need security if Rome did not give final approval to Wimmer's foundation.[13] On the other hand, although Father Henry suffered poverty often enough, he had little understanding of the vow of poverty. As he wrote to his lawyer about another bit of land he owned, ". . . it is my last reliance for a little pocketmoney in my old age. The Benedictines are bound to feed me, but you know, man lives not by bread alone."[14]

While Father Wimmer was in Europe applying for the status of an abbey for his foundation, Father Henry's troubles at Carrolltown came to a head. In 1854-55 he

[9] Wimmer ad Lemke, St. Vincent, Jan. 3, 1856, copy. (SVA)
[10] Flick, op. cit., 189 note.
[11] Transcript from Recorder's office, Cambria County, Pa. (ACHS)
[12] Wimmer to Johnston, St. Vincent, Jan. 13, 1856, copy. (SVA)
[13] Wimmer ad Lemke, St. Vincent, Jan. 3, 1856, copy. (SVA)
[14] Lemke to Johnston, Vienna, Dec. 21, 1859. (ACHS)

was sued for debt, levy was made on some of his land, and he was sued for damages as a result of his officiating at the marriage of a minor without the permission of the parents. He was cleared in the latter case, and a settlement was reached on the debt. But at the Priory in Carrolltown he had trouble with his young confreres. He complained that no one would take his advice, all intrigued against him and blackened his name to the Bishop, and his accounts were misunderstood merely because they were rather confused. The situation was impossible, and when he had his legal affairs reasonably in order, he asked the Prior, Father Demetrius, for permission to go on a begging trip. The Prior refused permission. "That was too much for me," Father Henry wrote, "I took matters into my own hands and left, without however rightly knowing where I was going."[15]

Father Henry later gave various accounts of his intentions after leaving Carrolltown, but when he arrived in Westport, Missouri, depressed and unhappy, he thought only of retirement. His letters to his friend and attorney, Robert L. Johnston, are very different in tone from his letters to Abbot Wimmer and probably reflect his mood more accurately. At that time he wrote to Johnston: "I am now a complete separatist in every respect . . . Next week I shall go out with R.[odrigue] into the territory and see whether I can find a place where I may hope to spend the rest of my life in peace and retirement. . . I do not wish to come to any extremes with that brainless Wimmer as long as I can help it. . ."[16] And as a matter of fact he had not said Mass since leaving Carrolltown.[17]

Meanwhile Abbot Wimmer had returned from Europe in high spirits. The Holy See had made his foundation an abbey and had appointed him abbot for a period of three years. He held a chapter, January 10-12, 1856, at

[15] Lemke an Wimmer, [Lecompton], K. T., Feb. 6, 1856. (SVA) His last entry in the baptismal record at Carrolltown before leaving for Kansas was on October 5, 1855.—Fellner to Pusch, St. Vincent, June 1, 1925.
[16] Lemke to Johnston, Westport, Dec. 27, 1855. (ACHS)
[17] Lemke an Wimmer, [Lecompton], K. T., Feb. 6, 1856. (SVA)

which the creation of the abbey was officially announced, vows were renewed under the statutes of the Bavarian Congregation, and the chapter decided to accept Bishop Cretin's invitation to begin a foundation in Minnesota.[18]

Shortly before this Abbot Wimmer learned that Father Henry was in Westport, and on January 3, 1856, sent him a long paternal admonition, recalling him "formally and under holy obedience." He insisted that Father Henry must return unless sickness or other honest circumstances should detain him temporarily. The Abbot then reviewed their long and rarely smooth relations, recalling Father Henry's troubles with his Bishop, with his property, and with his confreres. Father Henry had evidently complained that he had not been made prior of the community in Carrolltown. Abbot Wimmer asked him to be honest with himself: Could he have been the guardian of discipline? Had he observed the Rule strictly, even in externals? The Abbot knew, indeed, that Father Henry had set out with the intention of abandoning the Order and feared that he might abandon even his priesthood. He pleaded with him: "Return, return as soon as you can . . . O Henry, Henry, what folly has taken possession of you! Old age is weakening your mind!"[19]

A month elapsed before Abbot Wimmer's exhortation reached Father Henry at Lecompton, because, as he wrote, "all communication between here and the States has been cut for weeks. From four to five feet of snow covered the province; there is no one to break a trail, and there are no places where freezing travelers can find quarters."[20]

---

[18] Wimmer an Archbishop Gregor Scherr, St. Vincent, Mar. 10, 1856. (AM)
   Only the first page of this *Erstes Generalcapitel* remains. The chapter of 1858 was later officially counted as the First General Chapter. (SVA)
   [19] Wimmer ad Lemke, St. Vincent, Jan. 3, 1856, copy. (SVA)
   The date on the copy is illegible, but Father Henry in his reply of February 6 refers to it as "Your kind letter of Jan. 3."
   [20] Lemke an Wimmer, [Lecompton], K. T., Feb. 6, 1856. (SVA)
   This statement was only exaggerated. The Lawrence *Herald of Freedom,* January 26, 1856, said the winter was reportedly the most severe in seven years. Snow was falling in "endless profusion," the thermometer had been ranging from ten to thirty-two above and occasionally to zero and below. The same newspaper on February 9, 1856, reported that the thermometer had gone to twenty-nine below zero on Sunday, February 3, and that there had been eight continuous weeks of cold weather.

By this time Father Henry had had some second thoughts about retirement and admitted his error — in his own way. "After reading your letter, I wished I had wings to fly to you immediately, throw myself at your feet, and beg pardon for all the heartache I caused you. In the life of a hermit which I have lived since Christmas, with nothing to eat except pork and shelled corn, with nothing to amuse myself except my breviary and Thomas a Kempis — I had both time and opportunity to think of myself and my circumstances. In the main you are right, but on many points I too am right. My mistake consisted in this that I preferred to be right, rather than practice humility." He goes on to explain why he had not written sooner: "I would long ago have written to you and not been so long without Mass and hung around without priestly duties, if circumstances had not led to it. As long as I was in civilized places I did not know whether you had returned."[21]

Rationalizing his action, Father Henry maintained that his novitiate was invalid since it had been made not in the monastery but in large part at Carrolltown. Abbot Wimmer insisted that this did not invalidate the novitiate and explained that he had not thought a strict novitiate necessary on account of Father Henry's advanced age.[22] After Father Henry was convinced of the validity of his vows, he offered other explanations of his flight. He reminded Abbot Wimmer that because circumstances in Carrolltown had become so unpleasant, the Abbot had given him permission to stay at any other place. By this the Abbot had meant of course any other of his Benedictine houses. Father Henry maintained also that at first he had made up his mind to become a Trappist, but after several long talks with one in Pittsburgh he decided that "it was no place for me." About the same time he met several acquaintances on their way to the new territory. As he explained the matter about two months later: "I went with them, and hinted that it was my purpose to

21 Ibid.
22 Wimmer ad Pescetelli, St. Vincent, Mar. 31, 1856. (SPexM)

look around for a location for a possible new Benedictine settlement. And that is really my intention. I feel I have both the strength and the courage for it, if you grant me the permission. You sent several priests to out-of-the-way places, why not me? The thought of returning now frightens me. I would be considered by all as an oddity, and to live again in O'Connor's diocese — I simply can't think of that."[23]

Abbot Wimmer's orders to return unless sickness or some other honest circumstance detained him were interpreted by Father Henry as permission to stay. He easily found plenty of honest circumstances. He was promptly full of plans, as usual. If the Abbot would only send three Brothers, the four of them could preempt a whole section of land. Father Henry had already picked the spot. He knew the Surveyor General and some of his assistants. The place was in the southern part of Miami County on the Marais des Cynges River, near the remnants of the half-civilized Miami tribe. He could found a monastery and convert Indians, all at the same time. But meanwhile: "Next week a wagon train leaves here for Missouri via Fort Leavenworth for supplies. I will go along to see Bishop Miége, who at the present time stays at Leavenworth. He knows about me through Rodrigue and others. He wrote me a friendly letter at Westport and invited me to work in his little diocese (extending from the Rocky Mountains to the boundaries of Missouri). I will show him the first part of your letter, and especially that passage about if other circumstances should reasonably detain me. . ."[24]

John Baptist Miége, S.J., had been named vicar apostolic of the territory east of the Rocky Mountains when the Vicariate was created in 1850. Members of the Society of Jesus had begun their work among the Indians in the territory in 1836. Most of these missionaries were Belgians, refugees from the religious suppression accom-

[23] Lemke an Wimmer, [Lecompton], K. T., Feb. 6, 1856. (SVA)
[24] *Ibid.*

panying the Napoleonic Wars. Their mission to the Potawatomi Indians dated from 1841 and had been located at St. Mary's Mission on the Kaw since 1848. St. Francis Mission to the Osage, the present St. Paul in southeastern Kansas, was inaugurated in 1847.

Bishop Miége was born September 18, 1815, in the parish of Chevron, La Foret, Haute-Savoie. He entered the Society of Jesus in 1836, was ordained September 12, 1847, and was sent to St. Louis, Missouri, to serve in the Indian missions the following year. After his consecration by Archbishop Kenrick in St. Louis, March 25, 1851, he took up his residence at St. Mary's Mission. When the character of his vicariate was altered by the passage of the Kansas-Nebraska Act, he journeyed as far north as Omaha, Nebraska, trying to select likely sites for future churches. Fort Leavenworth on the Missouri River was headquarters for troops controlling the Indian country, and the town of Leavenworth seemed as promising as any in the territory, so Bishop Miége chose it as his See city, moved there in August, 1855, and began erecting a small frame cathedral. At the same time he called to Leavenworth the Rev. Theodore Heimann, a diocesan priest who had been assisting the Jesuits at Osage Mission.

When Father Henry went to Leavenworth to meet the Bishop in February, 1856, the situation was substantially unchanged. Aside from the two Indian missions, the Catholic Church in Kansas had a Bishop, a little frame cathedral, one diocesan priest, a scattering of Catholics, and nothing more. Bishop Miége received Father Henry kindly, and Abbot Wimmer evidently soon removed his ecclesiastical censure, for Father Henry wrote that since Easter he had celebrated Mass daily.[25] But for some time Abbot Wimmer persisted in his decision that Father

[25] Lemke an Wimmer, Doniphan, Aug. 28, 1856. (SVA)
"On April 14th, of the same year [1856] he wrote from Independence, Missouri, where he had gone, in all probability, to assist during Holy Week. He wrote from Kansas City, Missouri, on May 6th. . ."—Flick, *op. cit.*, 180. These letters are not among the other material used by Flick at ACHS. Father Lemke does refer to Father Donnelly of Independence as a friend.—Lemke an Wimmer, n.p., Nov. 26, 1857. (SVA)

Henry must return to Pennsylvania, even though the prospect of having such a troublesome subject almost a thousand miles away was a real temptation.[26]

Bishop Miége was evidently willing to give Father Henry work in his Vicariate and had written to Abbot Wimmer inviting him to send more Benedictines to Kansas. The Abbot thought that he could send some later if the clerics persevered in their vocations, but he gave no indication of leaving Father Henry represent the Order in Kansas.[27] However, the intercession of Bishop Miége finally prevailed, and on July 4 Father Henry wrote joyously to his Abbot: "Te Deum laudamus, and I repeat it wholeheartedly, for as I came from the chapel at seven o'clock this evening at the close of our retreat, the Bishop handed me your letter. What gave me special cause for joy was the fact that I am a Benedictine and will remain such; that I may appear as a Benedictine in the beautiful West, and work as a Benedictine."[28]

The only cloud on Father Henry's joy was the condition imposed by Abbot Wimmer for his permission to stay in Kansas: Father Henry had to make another gesture of recognition to his vow of poverty by transferring some of his beloved deeds to the Order. But the Bishop made even this sacrifice seem not too difficult:

Bishop Miége regulated all matters to mutual satisfaction. He is truly one of the most amiable men I ever came in contact with. There is nothing of the Irish character about him, nor of the German pedantry. He is a real warmhearted Frenchman. He is a very learned and pious man, but at the same time as merry and guileless as a child and shows in every respect and under all circumstances the French savoir-faire. He seems to think a great deal of me When I first hesitated to enter upon the Abbot's condition, viz. to strip myself of everything in order to get his leave to stay with Bishop Miége, he said: Never mind, I make quite another man of you than they ever could, for, saith he in his playful way, did not I tell you that I would divide my diocese with you and give you a district

26 Wimmer an Archbishop Gregor Scherr, St. Vincent, Mar. 10, 1856. (AM)
27 Wimmer ad Pescetelli, St. Vincent, Mar. 21, 1856. (SPexM)
28 Lemke an Wimmer, Leavenworth, July 4, 1856. (SVA)

at least three times as large as the whole Diocese of Pittsb?
with thousands of Indians and buffaloes.[29]

Father Henry's enthusiasm for land no doubt amused
Bishop Miége, who always kept in sane perspective the
role of property in the expansion of the Church.

In stating that he had been forced to strip himself of
everything, Father Henry had, as usual, exaggerated a
little. Apparently he was to be allowed to apply to any
good use whatever he could realize from his unclear title
to the Loop lands. At any rate he complained that this
tract and twenty-five shares in a plank road were all that
were left to him.[30] With an accompaniment of grumbling
about Abbot Wimmer's lack of trust in him and labeling
the rumor that his debts would exceed the value of the
land as the gossip of envious confreres, he finally surrendered the deeds to the Carrolltown farm and the Hopper
valley lands.[31]

Bishop Miége, too, was pleased that Father Henry
was permitted to remain in Kansas. Since the Bishop
had been approached by a representative of some Catholics who had settled "in a beautiful region near Nebraska," who had promised to donate property for a
church if he would send them a priest, the Bishop decided
to send Father Henry Lémke to Doniphan. He promised
to give $500 to help build the church and assured him
that the Order could hold the property in its own name.[32]
The Bishop furnished his latest missionary with a chalice
and vestments, and even with a Jesuit breviary because
Father Henry had brought along only the winter volume
of his own breviary.[33] He had left his trunk of extra
clothing at Independence and asked the Abbot to send
some supplies. Anything sent would be welcome, but he
especially wanted a set of small breviaries, a sick-call kit,
a chalice, and some vestments. He closed with a post-

[29] Lemke to Johnston, Doniphan, Aug. 30, 1856. (ACHS)
[30] *Ibid.*
[31] Lemke an Wimmer, Leavenworth, July 4, 1856; Doniphan, Aug. 28, 1856. (SVA)
[32] *Idem*, Leavenworth, July 4, 1856. (SVA)
[33] *Idem*, Doniphan, Aug. 28, 1856. (SVA)

script on July 5, 1856, asking the prayers of all his confreres, for "tomorrow I leave for the wilderness!"[34]

Doniphan City, K. T.

Almost two months passed before Father Henry found
time to write to his Abbot, giving him his first impressions
of Doniphan and reporting his arrangements for working
and living there:

I arrived here in the beginning of July. They have started
a town here which must develop into an important place if
the progress made to date continues, perhaps another Cincinnati or St. Louis. It has the only good landing place on the
swift Missouri in the territory outside Leavenworth, and is the
farthest point up stream that heavily freighted steamers can
reach at any season of the year. Moreover the surrounding
country is both beautiful and fruitful. Water and wood in
abundance and the climate is healthful. You will not easily
find the like in any part of the world. Steamers arrive and depart daily. The commerce of this place, only fourteen months
old, amounted to a half-million dollars since last fall according
to the newspaper. The Americans recognize the importance
of this place quite well and fight for the lots, which extend from
the river over the slowly rising ground half a mile into the
prairie. Our dear Bishop strives with praiseworthy foresight
to get a firm foothold wherever new settlements are made.
He had bought three lots here. When I came here, he gave me
a recommendation to one of the members of the town company, in which he praised me as a man who could draw many
new settlers and contribute much to the growth of the city.
Thereupon he donated three additional lots to me. I purchased six more lots at the original price of $50 as a special
favor. Lots are even now selling at $200-$300, at least on
Front Street. I own therefore, a full block of twelve lots with
a frontage of 308 by 264 feet, in the most beautiful part of the
town, at an elevation of a hundred feet above the river. I immediately started building on this ground so that I might have
a roof over my head before winter sets in. Until then life will
be hard enough. An Irishman erected a shanty fourteen by
sixteen feet on his lots. He has a claim and a shanty two miles
from town where he lives with his family during the summer.
He rented his town house to me. It is not yet plastered or
floored. Near by lives a family where I can wash, bake bread

[34] *Idem*, Leavenworth, July 4, 1856. (SVA)

and get milk and water. Mornings and evenings I make a little soup, and tea or coffee. At noon I go to the local hotel so that I will have at least one good meal a day. I sleep on a straw sack which lies on a few boards nailed together.[35]

The population of Doniphan in 1856 is certain to have consisted almost entirely of speculators and bully boys just arrived from South Carolina to save the territory from the abolitionists. When Kansas Territory was opened in 1854, the inhabitants of nearby Missouri, joined by some enthusiasts from more distant parts, crossed the river and posted preemption claims in their own names and in the names of all their relatives, real and imaginary, on all desirable land within miles of the river.[36] Whereever a break in the bluff made a townsite seem plausible, a townsite was surveyed and lots were offered for sale. Then the claimants sat back to await the coming of the expected settlers.

Pastoral work in the little town of Doniphan, full of speculators and young men looking for excitement, was bound to be unusual. To make the work even more difficult, the territory was in a more or less constant uproar that summer. Toward the end of May the town of Lawrence was "pacified" by the destruction of its hotel and printing presses. John Brown retaliated with the murders on Pottawatomie Creek. Both sides had men in the field, and the rest of the summer was full of alarms. When Father Henry left Leavenworth, he hopefully thought that the measures just taken, presumably Governor Shannon's proclamation disbanding all armed bodies of men, would end the trouble.[37] But the Missourians put a strong-arm embargo on the river, seizing goods,

[35] *Idem*, Doniphan, Aug. 28, 1856. (SVA)
Garin states that when Bishop Miége visited Doniphan in the summer of 1855, he decided that its good steamboat landing promised much for the town. —J. Garin, *Notices Biographiques sur Mgr. J. B. Miege. . .* (Moutiers, 1886), 110.
[36] Preemption permitted settlers to stake claims on surveyed lands and to purchase up to 160 acres at the minimum price of $1.25 per acre.
"In present Doniphan County all the land from ten to twenty miles back, with but few exceptions, had been taken by June 26, [1854]."—Martha Caldwell, "Records of the Squatter Association of Whitehead District, Doniphan County," *Kansas Historical Quarterly,* XIII, 18.
[37] Lemke an Wimmer, Leavenworth, July 4, 1856. (SVA)

forcibly turning back would-be settlers with free-state opinions, and applying a variety of indignities to outspoken critics of slavery.

Father Henry experienced the Missouri censorship one day on a steamboat going up river on a sick call. The boat was crowded with Kentuckians and Missourians who had "lynched" (i.e., manhandled or perhaps tarred and feathered) a Methodist minister that very morning and dropped him off on a sandbar. Finding himself an object of suspicion, and finally approached directly, Father Henry announced that as a Catholic priest his platform must remain above the level of the questions generating such hatred among men at the time. His was the policy of the Church, which concerned itself not with destroying the established conditions of the world and human life but with ennobling and sanctifying them. On the slavery question he was at one with St. Paul; he would send back the slave and admonish the master that his slave was a fellow human being.[38]

Father Henry, like many of his fellow Catholics, feared that the fanaticism of the abolitionists would generate evils as great as slavery. He thought abolitionism a bad means to a good end. Furthermore, the abolitionist camp seemed to have welcomed all the former members of the Know-Nothing party. What Father Henry really thought of slavery, no matter what excuses for its existence the theologians might offer, is clear from his comment that Lecompton ". . . is the stronghold of the proslavery party and the curse of God is on it.[39]

During August the cities on the Kaw were at it again, and because travel through Missouri was so uncertain, the parties of free-state settlers came out by way of Iowa and Nebraska. A large party accompanied by James H. Lane, the self-appointed military leader of the antislavery forces, was rumored to be an army, and its arrival at Nebraska City on August 29, 1856, threw the northeast corner of Kansas into a state of excitement. Father Henry

[38] *Idem*, Doniphan, Aug. 28, 1856. (SVA)
[39] *Idem*, 'My Claim Shanty,' June 27, 1857. (SVA)

reported that the building of his house had been halted because his workmen had either fled or joined in the fighting.[40] The proslavery men went south, where D. R. Atchison and a force of Missourians were in the field around Bull Creek, southwest of Olathe, and the abolitionists went north to meet Lane. The air was full of wild rumors, and Father Henry was even certain that he had heard the distant thunder of cannon.[41] In September Governor Geary arrived in the territory and talked D. R. Atchison into taking his Missourians home. Less freebooting took place after that, and Kansas was fairly quiet.

Under these circumstances no quick development of stable parish life was to be expected. At first Father Henry said Mass in a room of the Doniphan House. It was the town's first hotel and was operated by Barney O'Driscoll, one of Father Henry's first parishioners.[42] Later he offered Mass in a wooden hut originally intended for a carpenter shop. Only three Catholic families were in Doniphan that first summer. Geographically his mission was large, extending half way to Leavenworth toward the south, to the Nebraska line on the north, and "ad infinitum to the Rocky Mountains" in the west. Father Henry found that "individual scattered families may be encountered anywhere. They are often brutalized and it will take time and effort to bring them back on the right track. Some are half Indian where Irish and Catholic Americans intermarried with Indians." Nevertheless, he expected to have a parish soon enough. He knew of five good German families in Missouri who planned to settle in Doniphan that autumn. Two men from Indiana, who planned to buy land in the town, also stopped to see him.[43]

Numbers of his acquaintances in Pennsylvania wrote enquiring about prospects in Kansas. He complained that he could not answer all these letters, and asked a confrere to tell Martin Schwamm to come on: "A good

[40] *Idem*, Doniphan, Aug. 28, 1856, P.S. Aug. 30. (SVA)
[41] Lemke to Johnston, Doniphan, Aug. 30, 1856. (ACHS)
[42] B. O'Driscoll to Wm. Rettele, O.S.B., Silverton, Colo., Mar. 31, 1884.
[43] Lemke an Wimmer, Doniphan, Aug. 28, 1856. (SVA)

plasterer receives $2.50 per day. City lots can still be bought cheaply. There will be considerable building next spring. Land claims are no longer available in the neighborhood of the city. You must go six to eight miles farther out."[44] Father Henry himself was excited about the possibility of buying for only $500 a squatter's preemption right to a quarter-section only a mile from town. He was certain that it would be worth thousands within a year,[45] but he could not raise the money and had to suffer the disappointment of seeing it go to another.[46]

Father Henry was no stranger to financial stringency, but Kansas poverty was apparently the worst he had known thus far. He was beginning all over again, as he wrote to the Johnstons, but with a difference. When he began his ministry in Pennsylvania, he was thirty-eight years old, had $1400 in his pocket, and settled down amid a large congregation. Now he was sixty, almost destitute, even his clothing badly in need of mending, and with but a few scattered Catholics for a congregation.[47] The three-family parish could not support him; in fact, for his priestly functions in the first two months he received only fifty cents for a Mass and a dollar for a baptism. He asked Abbot Wimmer to send him Mass stipends. Nevertheless he began building a combination chapel and rectory with $150 the Bishop had given him. Beyond that he used his credit, and the townspeople reciprocated with generous pledges on his subscription list. All of them counted on next year's lush promises. Catholics and non-Catholics alike had promised $700 for the church and rectory. Father Henry was full of dreams of the monastery he would found and tried to banish from his mind the evidence that Abbot Wimmer considered him temperamentally unfit for such a role.[48]

Winter set in early that year, and some of the new settlers suffered great hardship. Many could return to

44 Lemke an [Celestin Engelbrecht, O.S.B.], Doniphan, Nov. 16, 1856. (SVA)
45 Lemke an Wimmer, Doniphan, Aug. 28, 1856. (SVA)
46 Lemke to Johnston, Doniphan, June 12, 1857. (ACHS)
47 *Idem*, Aug. 30, 1856. (ACHS)
48 Lemke an Wimmer, Doniphan, Aug. 28, 1856. (SVA)

warm homes in nearby Missouri, but others, like Father Henry, who had to remain in the territory, knew the meaning of misery before the winter was over. Father Henry's combination chapel and residence was ready for plastering when the cold weather struck in November.[49] Unplastered and without windows or stove, the building stood useless until spring. The box expected from Abbot Wimmer and other supplies ordered by Father Henry failed to arrive. With the cold weather his rheumatism became so bad that he could no longer chop wood and do other necessary chores. So he moved from the shanty he had rented to a lawyer's office in the central part of town, where a stove would give him warmth, and neighbors could give him aid.[50] A bed was there too, but in a neighboring hut a young man lay dying of fever and "the French disease." Father Henry put him into his bed and went back to his pallet. Little snow had fallen, but for weeks the wind blew constantly from the northwest, "straight from the Rocky Mountains." He complained that "the cold is terrible."[51]

Even before the winter set in, Father Henry was desperate for lack of money. He learned that his letter to Abbot Wimmer at the end of August had failed to reach St. Vincent before the Abbot had left on an extended trip to Minnesota, and he feared that he would "perish" before help reached him from that quarter. Expected money from his lawyer failed to arrive. To a confrere he explained that he could not continue without help and begged him to send at least some Mass stipends.[52] He had received some money from Abbot Wimmer during the summer, but fifty dollars sent by the Abbot in November through Bishop Miége was presumably stolen from the mails between Leavenworth and Doniphan. To keep alive Father Henry "accepted the offer of the local postmaster and storekeeper, and borrowed a hundred dollars."[53]

[49] Lemke an [Engelbrecht], Doniphan, Nov. 16, 1856. (SVA)
[50] Lemke an Wimmer, Doniphan, Dec. 12, 1856. (SVA)
[51] *Idem*, Jan. 4, 1857. (SVA)
[52] Lemke an [Engelbrecht], Doniphan, Nov. 16, 1856. (SVA)
[53] Lemke an Wimmer, Doniphan, Jan. 4; Apr. 1, 1857. (SVA)

At times Father Henry was tempted to give up. His people were not only few and poor but showed "no zeal for the project." The preceding winter had been hard, too, but then when the icy blasts swept the plains, he could curl up by the fire or under a buffalo robe. This winter he was not only sick and cold but at the call of any soul needing a priest. Now, he wrote, it was ". . . hurry, hurry, the old man is dying. Well, how far is it? Oh, about fifteen miles. And when you come to it, it is twenty-five miles. There are as yet no roads, no stopping places, only now and then a miserable shanty, where you can find nothing but frozen bread and a little bacon."[54]

Father Henry had no horse, and when he could not borrow one he walked, sometimes great distances. Walking had its dangers, for getting lost in winter could be fatal. On one occasion, while answering a sick call at night, Father Henry lost his way. As he told the story, his situation seemed so desperate that he thought of asking the aid of the Blessed Virgin. Like some other converts he had never had much devotion to her and so hardly knew how to address her. He therefore prayed as follows: "Till now, O Mary, I have not called on thee, but if you help me out of this difficulty, I shall always call on thee." Then he saw a light and found himself not far from a settler's cabin. When he arrived there he recognized the place, entered, and expressed his surprise at not seeing the light sooner. The lady of the house explained that the baby had cried so hard that she arose and struck a light to see what had suddenly come over the child. Father Henry jokingly insisted that the Blessed Virgin had made the guardian angel pinch the baby to make it cry and save Father Henry's life.[55]

The old missionary was not of a contemplative nature, and he found the means of his own salvation in the active

[54] *Idem*, Dec. 12, 1856. (SVA)
[55] This story was frequently told by Father Henry and his confreres. Contemporary reference to the incident is made in Wimmer an Ludwig I, Carrolltown, Dec. 7, 1857, quoted in Mathaeser, *Bonifaz Wimmer und Koenig Ludwig I von Bayern*, Jahrbuchfolge 1937 des Priester-Missionsbundes in Bayern (Munich), 100.

apostolate. If the work and hardship sometimes made him despondent, they also convinced him that he was finally learning the real meaning of his religious vocation. During that winter he wrote to Abbot Wimmer:

Now I am ashamed of my despondency and fainthearted-ness, and see that I am here through Divine Providence, that the Lord intends to use me for important matters. Lately things have taken place which have made matters clear to me. I am more conscious from day to day that I am the prop of many souls and the intermediary of their salvation. For true pastoral care, we are really only sounding brass and tinkling cymbals, as long as we are not absolutely in earnest, and seek and desire nothing except Christ and salvation in his true Church and according to its regulations. This thought has dominated me for thirty years, but I never felt content or happy in it until now, when I live in need and oppressed, especially since I made out and sent away the last deeds.[56]

With the coming of spring, hope was renewed, and plans began to sprout in Father Henry's mind. He wrote that it was "pleasant to note how the community is growing. It would develop into a Catholic locality if I were supported, first in a material way, and then with members of the Order." He informed the Abbot that "Father Lemke is held in high esteem far and wide," and that his impartiality "gives me great influence, but not over pocket books. The pocket books of those who come here are empty or contain only sufficient for their own needs." He continued that it would be a shame to give up the place but that he could not continue as he was, an isolated Benedictine floundering around like a fish out of water. He would rather live as a hermit as he had once planned. Hoping against hope that the Abbot would finally decide to make the Doniphan mission a real monas-tic foundation and name him superior, Father Henry again asked for help. The box expected from the Abbot still had not arrived, and Father Henry was again desper-ately in need of money. He needed $200 "to escape un-pleasantness." He received a hundred dollars from the

<hr />

[56] Lemke an Wimmer, Doniphan, Dec. 12, 1856. (SVA)

28

Bishop and borrowed the other hundred from a good old German in Doniphan. Then tragi-comedy entered: he put the bank notes in the vest pocket of his old coat, forgetting that the pocket had a hole in it, and lost the money.[57] His hope of support for his foundation also ended in disappointment. Abbot Wimmer informed him that he was sending two more men to Kansas but that they were to live in some other place.[58]

Reinforcements

By 1857 Abbot Wimmer had thirty-eight priests. The latest ordinations had made it possible for him to increase the number in Minnesota to six, to found a new priory in Newark, New Jersey, to accept new places in Pennsylvania, and still have two for Kansas.[59] Bishop Miége had asked for more priests, but Kansas was something of a special problem. The need for priests was real, but outside Leavenworth there was no town with sufficient Catholics to support a priest. The Bishop welcomed the news that two monks were coming that spring. But the Abbot's insistence that they should not dwell with Father Henry presented difficulties, because Doniphan, as the only concrete beginning outside Leavenworth, was the only place that offered any promise for a new religious foundation. Still the Bishop was certain that he could find a suitable place for the monks, but frankly warned the Abbot that the beginning would be a period of privation.

They will be pioneers and as such shall go through the troubles and the privations of a new country, but our Blessed Lord helps his apostles, and gives them always the strict necessaries of life. So it is in Kansas; we have to labor now under great disadvantages; we have to create everything and the receipts never, so far at least, meet the expenses, yet I hope that matters will soon take a more agreeable and cheerful aspect.[60]

[57] *Idem*, Apr. 1, 1857. (SVA)
[58] *Idem*, June 12, 1857. (SVA)
[59] Wimmer an Ludwig I, Carrolltown, Aug. 10, 1857, in Mathaeser, *op. cit.*, 92.
[60] Miége to Wimmer, Leavenworth, Mar. 23, 1857. (SVA)

The two men sent to Kansas by Abbot Wimmer were Father Augustine Wirth and a theologian ready for ordination, Casimir Seitz. Francis Christian Wirth was born in Lohr, Bavaria, March 17, 1828. He was one of the recruits brought over by Abbot Wimmer in 1851 and was ordained December 8, 1852. He was pastor in Greensburg, Pennsylvania, and had taught dogma and canon law in St. Vincent.[61] He was an able and energetic man but very ambitious and eager to be his own boss. Casimir Willibald Seitz was born in Pirkach, Bavaria, August 13, 1829, came to the United States in 1854, and was solemnly professed at St. Vincent Abbey, August 31, 1856. These two arrived at Leavenworth on Holy Thursday, April 9, 1857.[62]

Meanwhile Father Henry had heard of the new arrivals, and on Easter Sunday he hurried down to Leavenworth. That evening he had a long talk with the Bishop and Father Augustine, but it brought him no cheer. "I noticed," he wrote, "that everything had been settled, even though the Bishop asked for my opinion."[63] The Bishop casually remarked that it would probably be best for the two newcomers to go to Doniphan immediately after Father Casimir's ordination. Father Henry countered that according to the Abbot he was to stay at Doniphan and the others were to be assigned elsewhere. If that plan was to be changed, he suggested that the Abbot's wishes be consulted. The Bishop said nothing more, but, according to Father Henry's account, on the following morning Father Augustine brusquely announced that he, Father Henry, was to go to Lecompton, while Father Augustine took over Doniphan.

Father Henry capitulated to the inevitable, and he and Father Augustine went up to Doniphan to arrange

61 Testimonial letter, Wimmer, St. Vincent, Apr. 1, 1857.
62 Wirth to Wimmer, Leavenworth, Apr. 16, 1857. (SVA)
63 Lemke an Wimmer, Doniphan, June 12, 1857. (SVA)
He was quite correct in this observation. The Bishop explained to the Abbot that since Doniphan was a much more promising town than Lecompton, he and Father Augustine agreed that the foundation should be made at Doniphan.—Miége to Wimmer, Leavenworth, June 11, 1857. (SVA)

30

matters. In his report to the Abbot, Father Henry spared
no ink in telling of his friends' shocked unbelief that he
could be discarded "like a pair of wornout wooden shoes"
after enduring such hardship; that a worthy old man was
to be sent back into the wilderness while a boy was put
in his nest. He would even have the Abbot believe that
he had sent Father Augustine back to Leavenworth for
his own safety, while the worthy old man pacified the
justly indignant parishioners.[64] Though Father Henry
made no attempt to make things easier for Father Augustine, the latter reported simply: "I went with Fath. Henry
to Doniphan to look at the place. I like it well and told
the Bishop that I would accept it."[65]

Casimir Seitz had remained with Bishop Miége. The
Bishop made a deep impression on Father Casimir, who
wrote that the Bishop was "loved and honored as a saint
by those around him." According to Father Casimir,
"he gave many proofs of his generous heart, referred to
me as his 'dear first child of Kansas,' pressed me to take
snuff from his snuffbox, presented me a relic of St. Augustine in a silver case, together with proper authentication,
and ordained me *sine examine*," that is, without a formal
examination, though Father Casimir admitted that he
had been examined informally for ordination. On the
second Sunday after Easter, April 26, 1857, Father Casimir was ordained by Bishop Miége, assisted by four
priests, in the little frame Cathedral of the Immaculate
Conception. He was the first priest ordained in Kansas.
Father Augustine's sermon, Father Casimir reported, was
loudly praised and served as an excellent recommendation for the Benedictines in Kansas.

On the following day the monks went up to Doniphan
and began a quasi monastic life in the new foundation.
During the week Father Casimir was homesick for St.
Vincent, but on Saturday he made a temporary altar
"from four fence posts and two old boards," and on Sun-

[64] *Ibid.*
[65] Wirth to Wimmer, Leavenworth, Apr. 16, 1857. (SVA)

day celebrated his First Mass. Fathers Henry and Augustine were presumably on mission, and after Mass, as Father Casimir made his own breakfast of black coffee and bacon, he decided that he felt better than at any time since his arrival in Kansas.[66]

Doniphan today is practically a ghost town, with a few houses, an empty store building, and some moldering foundations scattered between the almost lost traces of streets. But in 1857 Doniphan City was a typical riverfront town in the new territories: an unlovely conglomeration of scattered stores and shanties hastily constructed for the most part of notoriously fast-warping green cottonwood planks. This did not mean that the town was inferior; it was larger than Atchison at the time, its steamboat landing was considered better than many, and it was generally conceded to have possibilities. The town company had been organized in St. Joseph, Missouri, in 1854. The Formans opened a store, S. Collins put up his saw mill in 1855, and the Doniphan House was opened with a grand ball January 8, 1856. That year the town was overrun with South Carolinians determined to save Kansas for the South, but they proved very temporary immigrants. In 1857 Jim Lane lent the magic of his name to the town and was considered its first citizen for a couple of years. Doniphan received a government land office in March, 1857, making the town a place of importance, but Kansas politics were extremely volatile, and the office was moved to Kickapoo before the year was out.[67]

Doniphan was a lively place that summer. At the Fourth of July festivities the orator of the day, J. R. Boyd, and one Mitchell got into an argument and wanted to duel, but the authorities prevented bloodshed. Proslavery and Free-State parties then took up the argument.

[66] Seitz an Wimmer, Doniphan, June 4, 1857. (SVA)

[67] The first land office in Kansas was opened at Lecompton, May, 1856. Offices were opened at Doniphan, Fort Scott, and Ogden in March, 1857. The Doniphan office was moved to Kickapoo in December, 1857, and to Atchison in September, 1861.—Albert R. Greene, "U.S. Land Offices in Kansas," *Kansas Historical Collections*, VIII, 4-7.

Jim Lane seized thirty-seven muskets belonging to the government and declared that he was defending the town. Guards were placed round the town all night, but nevertheless the peace was not disturbed.[68] Later in the year Henry Latham was shot dead by Frank McVey. Latham was walking up the street with a Sharp's rifle under his arm and was supposedly up to no good.[69]

Father Casimir had to build a temporary altar for his First Mass because Father Henry's combination chapel and residence, begun late in the preceding summer, was still not completed. Father Casimir spoke of it rather bitterly as a shanty, without floors, windowpanes, or stove.[70] But Father Augustine noted that the building had a good foundation and thought that it would serve very well. He expected it to be finished in two weeks. It was seventy-two feet long and sixteen feet wide, with a porch running its entire length. Rather more than half the length was to be used for a church. The remainder of the house was divided into two rooms, with space for bed rooms in the half-story above, and a good cellar beneath. Located on the bluff one block east of Main Street, the building overlooked the river front. "We have the nicest view from the hill," wrote Father Augustine, "we can look down on the Missouri River and see the steamboats coming at a distance of eight miles."[71]

The immediate problem, however, was paying Father Henry's debts. According to Father Henry these were trifling. On August 4, $140 would be due on the lots, and if his claim in the country was to be held, money for that would be needed in the autumn. The debt on the chapel and rectory was covered by pledges. He admitted that payment on the pledges did not come in very rapidly, but with new Catholics immigrating daily, the debt, in his mind, was certain to be paid.[72] But according to the

[68] *Elwood Weekly Advertiser*, July 9, 1857.
[69] Gray, *Doniphan County History*, 13-14.
[70] Seitz an Wimmer, Doniphan, June 4, 1857. (SVA)
[71] Wirth to Wimmer, Leavenworth, Apr. 16, 1857. (SVA)
[72] Lemke an Wimmer, Doniphan, June 12, 1857. (SVA)

Bishop, Father Augustine found debts amounting to nearly $800.[73]

According to Father Casimir the creditors viewed the two impecunious newcomers as ousting Father Henry, the rich old gentleman from Pennsylvania, and threatened to evict them. But by vigorous campaigning Father Augustine managed to collect enough money in two weeks to satisfy the noisiest creditors. Father Casimir summarized the results:

After two weeks of labor the result was as follows: The creditors were satisfied, and the constables kept off our necks. The windows were fitted with glass, the church received a floor, bedsteads and a table arrived from St. Joseph, the sacks we had brought along were filled with prairie grass and shavings. With six bricks we built a fireplace for cooking, and I declared myself ready to function as cook. We considered ourselves gentlemen, praised God's providence for his children, gave a toast to monastic poverty, and hoped for better times.[74]

The Bishop was pleased, writing that Father Augustine "is a good manager, and will soon be a perfect one. Poor F. Henry, in the line of business, speaks much better than he acts. Yet I hope his intentions are good." The Bishop hoped the Abbot could send more priests and asked the Abbot to visit him: "I am indeed very anxious to see you, and to have a fair discussion of Kansas matters. My impression is that Kansas will be an immense field and a rich one for missionary labors; your fathers are well calculated for it, and as far as will depend on me, I shall by all means in my power, help them along, and let them perfectly free to act as directed by you or their immediate superior."[75]

Sometime before the arrival of Fathers Augustine and Casimir, Father Henry had preempted a claim about ten miles northwest of Doniphan, near the present Bendena, Kansas. The Bishop suggested that Father Henry either secure his claim or transfer it to one of his confreres and

[73] Miége to Wimmer, Leavenworth, June 11, 1857. (SVA)
[74] Seitz an Wimmer, Doniphan, June 4, 1857. (SVA)
[75] Miége to Wimmer, Leavenworth, June 11, 1857. (SVA)

then go to Lecompton.[76] But Father Henry had no faith in Lecompton and no intention of returning there. He suggested to Father Augustine that they stick together, preempt more claims, and establish something worth while at one place.[77] Father Augustine then told the Bishop that he felt pity for the old man and would keep him if that was agreeable to the Bishop. Bishop Miége left the matter to Father Augustine and Abbot Wimmer, and Father Henry stayed at Doniphan.[78]

Father Henry wrote sarcastically about Father Augustine, saying that, "As there were no saddle horses or coaches at hand for His Grace," Father Augustine sent Father Casimir out with Father Henry to preempt a claim.[79] The odd way in which the legal requirements of improvement and residence were fulfilled shocked Father Casimir, although what Father Henry bade him do was merely the usual practice on the frontier. As Father Casimir described it: "One day P. Henry took his young confrere Casimir out into the country, showed him a piece of land, ordered him to build a hut with fence rails and boards dragged to the spot, told him to take a nap in broad daylight, and sent him home."[80]

Father Henry spent most of his time on the claims and was once again master of his own domain. He was visited occasionally by Father Casimir and on one occasion by Father Augustine. Father Henry described the latter as a visitation by the "Reverend Prelate of Doniphan." Father Augustine had bought a horse with all the trimmings, even a "fashionable whip," as Father Henry described this outrageous extravagance. He commented that the money would have fenced the lots and bought a year's supply of potatoes and cabbage.[81] Abbot Wimmer had directed Fathers Augustine and Casimir to aid Father Henry with the necessary "spiritual and material

[76] Miége to Lemke, Leavenworth, Apr. 27, 1857. (SVA)
[77] Lemke an Wimmer, Doniphan, June 12, 1857. (SVA)
[78] Miége to Wimmer, Leavenworth, June 11, 1857. (SVA)
[79] Lemke an Wimmer, Doniphan, June 12, 1857. (SVA)
[80] Seitz an Wimmer, Doniphan, June 4, 1857. (SVA)
[81] Lemke an Wimmer, 'My Claim Shanty,' June 27, 1857. (SVA)

support," but the old greybeard, as Father Casimir called him, showed little inclination to seek either kind of assistance from his unwelcome confreres.[82] Father Augustine gave him small sums occasionally, as did Abbot Wimmer, and he might have received funds also from his attorney in Pennsylvania.

If Father Henry was short of money, he was not short of friendly neighbors. Two Catholics had helped him and Father Casimir locate their claims. Then he worked with a neighbor to make the necessary improvements: "I have persuaded a good, hardworking Catholic family to move their little home to the corner of their claim, where it will join our two claims, that is mine and P. Casimir's. Our little homes are erected at the corners of our claims. Casimir's is *pro forma*, mine is habitable. Seven acres of land are already under cultivation, eight more will be broken. This land extends equally into the three claims, to save some fencing. As long as I am around and work on it, as I do, no one else can take possession."[83]

By this time quite a number of Catholics were in the neighborhood, because Father Henry had the idea of establishing a Catholic settlement and directed Catholic settlers to the area. He maintained that they had taken up all the vacant claims for five miles around but that few Germans were among them. "Fritz is always too late," he said.[84] Father Augustine stated that about twenty-five Catholic families were in the neighborhood,[85] whereas Father Casimir put the number at twenty Catholics, twelve of them with families.[86] Father Henry wrote that he celebrated Mass for these people in a neighboring house that was roomier than most of the settlers' shanties.[87]

The first problem was finding money to pay for the claims. Father Henry had sought it without success from his lawyer in Pennsylvania. Father Augustine demand-

[82] Seitz an Wimmer, Doniphan, June 4, 1857. (SVA)
[83] Lemke an Wimmer, 'My Claim Shanty,' June 27, 1857. (SVA)
[84] *Idem*, Doniphan, June 12, 1857. (SVA)
[85] Wirth to Wimmer, Doniphan, May 10, 1857. (SVA)
[86] Seitz an Wimmer, Doniphan, June 4, 1857. (SVA)
[87] Lemke an Wimmer, Doniphan, June 12, 1857. (SVA)

ed that Abbot Wimmer send the necessary $400 or author-
ize him to sell their squatter's rights for what they might
bring.[88]   Father Henry was very much afraid that Father
Augustine would give up the claims and disappoint the
Catholic settlers who had come at his invitation.[89]   In the
end Father Augustine borrowed money to buy the land.
Hurrying before the land office was moved, he used the
"deposit of Mr. Tuohy, who, I hope, will not call for it,
till I can get it some place else," and bought the claims
on November 20, 1857.[90]

Father Augustine reported that the claims near Bendena were good land with plenty of water and limestone.
"There is not a stick on it, but in six years, if we keep the
fire off, we will have fine timber, hickory and oak.   The
little trees are already four feet high and timber grows
very rapidly here, but was up to this time destroyed by
prairie fire, by which the Indians burnt the old grass
every spring so as to make the young grass grow better."
Concerning the problem of fencing, he wrote that a friend
just across the river in Missouri would permit them to
cut from his timber all the rails they needed.[91]

Fathers Augustine and Casimir had meanwhile been
exploring their missionary field in and around Doniphan.
When they arrived, twenty-one Catholic families were in
Doniphan, a considerable increase over the previous year,
and this growth convinced them that Doniphan would
be a good place.[92]   Father Henry had held services ir-
regularly, a circumstance that was unavoidable, but as a
consequence attendance at the little church in Doniphan
was at first small.   Father Casimir wrote that only
seventeen people were at Mass on their first Sunday there
but that by the beginning of June attendance had grown
to seventy or eighty and that the little chapel was already too small.   The missionaries had also "explored the
land towards the south and the north.   On every occa-

[88] Wirth to Wimmer, Doniphan, May 10, 1857. (SVA)
[89] Lemke an Wimmer, 'My Claim Shanty,' June 27, 1857.   (SVA)
[90] Wirth to Wimmer, Doniphan, Nov. 20, 1857. (SVA)
[91] Idem. May 10, 1857. (SVA)
[92] Idem, Leavenworth, Apr. 16, 1857. (SVA)

sion these excursions produced favorable results. Of course the excursions through this paradise were on foot, and cost us, children of a fallen race, plenty of exertion and sweat. Poverty and misery on every side, but most of the settlers could be well established in three or four years. Three places for mission stations were located, but cannot be staffed at the present time and will have to be content with occasional visits from the missionary."[93]

Regular mission journeys began in June. In that month Cotter's (St. Patrick's) was visited twice and Atchison once.[94] Toward the end of July Father Augustine made an extended trip through the settlements as far north as Omaha. He was gone five weeks and witnessed marriages and administered baptism at Sand's Settlement (near Nebraska City) and at Omaha. At the same time he wrote that there were about 150 Catholic families in Doniphan County and about sixty in Atchison County.[95] Towards the end of August Father Casimir first visited Sonora, Missouri. Father Augustine had probably visited the place on his way to or from Omaha. Iowa Point and Geary City, Kansas, were next added to the circuit of river towns visited regularly. Other places mentioned during that first year are Herman Volmer's and Bourke's in October and O'Brien's in December.[96]

When the missionaries were at home in their little Priory, they lived a very simple life, though Father Henry insisted that it seemed positively luxurious to him. "The little people in Doniphan," he reported, "have now taken in a family with two old ladies and live quite in style."[97] But these housekeepers were only a temporary acquisition — probably an immigrant family looking for land— for the missionaries were soon importuning Abbot Wimmer for a cook. The records kept would indicate that they subsisted on coffee, cornmeal, flour, butter, eggs, an

93 Seitz an Wimmer, Doniphan, June 4, 1857. (SVA)
94 Cashbook.
95 Wirth to Wimmer, Doniphan, Aug. 31, 1857. (SVA)
96 Cashbook.
97 Lemke an Wimmer, 'My Claim Shanty,' June 27, 1857. (SVA)

occasional bit of fresh meat, quantities of ham and bacon, and generous supplies of snuff.[98]

The furnishings of the Priory were far from elaborate. In May the monks bought only a bucket, a saw, a lounge, a table, some carpeting, and ten yards of muslin. In June they added only a pitcher and a basin. In July they disposed of their straw ticks and began to sleep on mattresses and pillows, and Father Casimir received a real stove on which to practice cooking. In August parish life became more formal with the addition of a desk, along with another lounge and a Mexican grass mattress. In September there was a purchase of forty-two yards of calico and twenty-five pounds of cotton, presumably to make quilts. October with its cool nights and the threat of winter dictated the purchase of two chamber pots and two heating stoves. Other equipment added during this month included a water barrel, a lock, a hoe, and a white-wash brush. Father Augustine built a stable for his horse, and putty, glass, and nails were used to ready their house for the winter winds. At long last they invested in chairs, six of them, and two more lounges, which evidently served as cots. The missionaries spent very little on clothing. Aside from the purchase of two hats in May (western style?), only occasional repairs to trousers were entered among the expenses until the approach of winter brought a cap for Father Casimir and a pair of buffalo shoes to cope with the cold and the mud. Presumably they were ready for the winter, for their only purchase during November was a melodeon for the chapel. The instrument cost sixty dollars, but Abbot Wimmer gave twenty-five dollars and Bishop Miége thirteen dollars towards its purchase.[99] The chapel was completely bare at first, and Father Casimir asked Abbot Wimmer to send some pictures, especially one of the Blessed Virgin. At the same time he asked for more fundamental needs, such as a mold for baking hosts and another set of oil stocks.[100]

[98] Cashbook.
[99] Ibid.
[100] Seitz an Wimmer, Doniphan, June 4, 1857. (SVA)

What the missionaries wanted most was a Brother to cook for them — the usual arrangement in Benedictine houses in those days. Father Augustine had asked for a Brother cook in his first letter to Abbot Wimmer. In reply Abbot Wimmer suggested that the monks hire some elderly lady. Father Casimir, who was the acting cook and did not like the job, informed the Abbot of the exalted position of women and the demand for them on the frontier. All the people in Doniphan were gentlemen and ladies and had negroes to do the work.[101] Father Henry was reinforcing the Abbot's reluctance to send any Brothers by writing that "they cannot be of much service."[102] Nevertheless, in September Abbot Wimmer did send Brother Paul Pfeifer, who had been cook at St. Mary's in Elk County, Pennsylvania.

Abbot Wimmer's refusal at first to send a Brother to cook caused hard feelings and brought more basic problems into the open. Father Casimir wrote that the Abbot's statement, "You must help yourself," hit him like a bolt of lightning, and he accused the Abbot of abandoning his monks. Father Casimir also refers to the Abbot's "outspoken unfriendly attitude to Kansas,"[103] and Father Augustine asks: "What makes you so *embittered against* me, that you refuse to grant such a modest request of sending me a cook?"[104] These letters make it clear that Abbot Wimmer had been reluctant to send monks to Kansas. Probably only Father Augustine had been eager to come. Both Father Augustine and Father Casimir agreed that the Abbot had warned them that he could not help them with money, but they insisted that he had promised help in men. The Abbot's refusal of a cook caused Father Augustine to write that he was "treated like a stepchild. You have done more than is right for Minnesota, but nothing, nothing at all for Kansas. Minnesota got more than $2000 from St. Vincent, Kansas

101 *Ibid.*
102 Lemke an Wimmer, 'My Claim Shanty,' June 27, 1857. (SVA)
103 Seitz an Wimmer, Doniphan, June 4, 1857. (SVA)
104 Wirth to Wimmer, Doniphan, May 10, 1857. (SVA)

not a copper. Minnesota has received five brothers and you do not know whence to take one for Kansas. You are greatly mistaken about Kansas. I wish you could see it soon, and if you don't like it, I am willing to go back with you."[105]

Perhaps this outburst convinced Abbot Wimmer that he had better visit Kansas. The Bishop had invited him, and in almost every letter Father Augustine had asked the Abbot to come and see for himself the wonderful prospects in Kansas. Early in October Abbot Wimmer left St. Vincent on a long trip to visit his new foundation in Minnesota, to which he took three more Brothers, and to have a look at Kansas. After visiting St. John's in Minnesota he came to Kansas by way of St. Louis. His journey up the Missouri River did nothing to put the Abbot in a good mood. The steamboat on which he traveled from Jefferson City, the terminus of the Pacific Railroad from St. Louis, was so crowded that he had to sleep on the hard boards of the deck all four nights. He commented that the river was unreliable, the scenery unattractive, and the scattered wrecks along its banks depressing. He arrived in Leavenworth at midnight on November 2, 1857. After spending what remained of the night with the Bishop, he left for Doniphan next day and again arrived at an hour calculated to ruin any disposition, this time at one-thirty in the morning. He liked the view from the hill on which the Priory was located, and the house was comfortably furnished, but it had cost $2500, of which $300 was not yet paid, and there was no well. Father Augustine rented a buggy and took the Abbot to visit Father Henry and to see the claims. The Abbot admitted that the soil was fertile but deemed it unhealthful. He considered it full of poisonous reptiles, especially after Father Casimir had killed a rattlesnake in the house. Abbot Wimmer remained four days and arrived back in St. Vincent with almost no money and

[105] *Ibid.*

41

clothing, because "the poverty of the missionaries is often very great."[106]

While he was at Doniphan Abbot Wimmer presumably arranged for Father Henry's return to the East. On November 15 Father Augustine gave Father Henry fifteen dollars for traveling expenses, and on November 20 they paid for the claims at the land office. Three or four days later Father Henry boarded a steamboat and left Kansas. Thirty miles below Kansas City his boat was stopped by ice and frozen in. Father Henry went ashore on the north side of the river and stayed temporarily at a "miserable country inn" until he had a chance to cross the river to Independence and his "old friend" Father Bernard Donnelly. The old missionary was almost out of money, and he planned to borrow from Father Donnelly and then probably take the stage to Jefferson City and the railroad thence to Pennsylvania.[107]

Father Henry went back to Carrolltown and in the autumn of 1858 returned to Europe. There he collected money and published his life of Gallitzin. He returned to the United States in 1861 and was given a parish in Elizabeth, New Jersey. At last, at the age of sixty-four, he seems to have got most of the restlessness out of his bones, for he spent the next seventeen years in comparative peace and quiet at Elizabeth. He celebrated his golden jubilee as a priest in 1876. Having retired to Carrolltown in 1878, he died there at the age of eighty-six, November 29, 1882. He is buried there, and a simple monument honors him as the founder of the town.

Father Henry was a restless and cantankerous man. Father Alban Rudroff, another pioneer monk at St. Benedict's, reportedly said of him, "He was a Lutheran minister, and he never got over it." Nevertheless, God managed to make use of him. He accepted real hardship in his zeal for souls, and the charity he demonstrated in giving his bed to a dying syphilitic speaks for itself. As Father

106 Wimmer an Ludwig I, Carrolltown, Dec. 7, 1857, in Mathaeser, *Wimmer und Koenig Ludwig I*, 100.
107 Lemke an Wimmer, n.p., Nov. 26, 1857. (SVA)

Mathaeser points out, Father Henry urged the usefulness of Benedictines in the American missions as early as 1835, encouraged Father Wimmer to come, and was a pioneer in the technique of encouraging Catholic settlers to form colonies. He is indelibly a part of the early history of St. Vincent, of the beginning of St. Benedict's, and of the founding of St. Elizabeth Convent in New Jersey.[108]

[108] Mathaeser, "P. Heinrich Lemcke's Erinnerungen an Europa," *Studien und Mitteilungen*, 60, 331.

CHAPTER II

Prior Augustine Wirth

The foundation of St. Benedict's may be said to date
from the arrival of Fathers Augustine Wirth and Casimir
Seitz in 1857, for even in those less formal days at least
two monks were needed to make a priory.[1] The arrangement was made formal in 1858 when Father Augustine,
after attending the Second Provincial Council in St. Louis
in September,[2] returned to Pennsylvania for the meeting
of the First General Chapter of the American Cassinese
Congregation. The chapter voted to erect independent
priories in Minnesota and Kansas, and Father Augustine
was elected prior of the Kansas monastery for a three-
year term.[3] These acts were confirmed by papal decree
on December, 15, 1858. In the case of St. Benedict's
this action was an example of legislating for hopes rather
than for facts. Prior Augustine explained that distance
had dictated the action,[4] and Abbot Wimmer stated that
it was done "so that the resident priors would have more
power for free and rapid development."[5]

Now that the by-product of Father Henry Lemke's
individualism had been made a quite proper religious
house, at least on paper, there remained the usual question of the fluid frontier: Is this the right location? Will
this townsite really grow into an important town? Father

---

[1] Abbot Wimmer gives the date of foundation as 1857 in his "Prolegomenon
Historicum" in the *Album Benedictinum* (1869), 59.
[2] *Wahrheitsfreund*, Sept. 16, 1858.
[3] Records of General Chapters. (SVA)
  Before the move from Doniphan Prior Augustine signed himself "Prior
Monasterii ad St. Joannem Baptistam."—Wirth an Lebling, Doniphan, Dec.
17, 1858. (LMV Leav II 1/10)
[4] Wirth an Ludwig I, Doniphan, Dec. 18, 1858. (GHA 86/6 V)
[5] Wimmer an Ludwig I, St. Vincent, Dec. 12, 1858, in Mathaeser, *Wimmer
und Koenig Ludwig I*, 108-9.

Henry's plans had called for a school in Doniphan, supported by a monastery and farm on the claims near Bendena.[6] During his first few months in Kansas, Prior Augustine also planned to open a school at Doniphan and for this purpose asked Abbot Wimmer for two men.[7] Another quarter-section was added to the claims near Bendena, and a part of the land was at one time divided into town lots, although no town plat was ever filed with the State.[8] These claims and the Catholic settlers in the area were referred to as St. Benedict's Colony, and as late as the end of 1858 Prior Augustine could still write that it was the place "where we later plan to build the main monastery for Kansas."[9] By this time, however, he must have been convinced that the plan for a school might better be realized in Atchison than in Doniphan.

The Catholics in Atchison had been visited quite regularly, about twice a month, since Prior Augustine's first arrival in Kansas. The number of Catholic families reportedly increased from four to forty in that one year.[10]

[6] Lemke an Wimmer, 'My Claim Shanty,' June 27, 1857. (SVA)

[7] Wirth to Wimmer, Leavenworth, Apr. 16, 1857; Doniphan, May 10, 1857. (SVA)

[8] Deed: Valentine Wirth to St. Benedict's College, Nov. 1, 1870, for lots, part of NE 1/4 12-4-19 Doniphan County, "known as St. Benedict's Church property and bought of Augustine Wirth et aliis by B. O'Driscoll and assigned to the undersigned."

Father Henry Lemke located the SE 1/4 12-4-19 in the Register Office, Doniphan, K.T., Nov. 20, 1857. Father Casimir's claim was the NW 1/4 18-4-20, for which the patent was issued Apr. 10, 1860. The NE 1/4 12-4-19, on which the present St. Benedict's Church near Bendena is located, was entered (deed dated Jan. 14, 1858) by Joseph Gerig, who appears in the Priory Cashbook as Brother Henry Gehrig in May, 1858, and thereafter. He is supposed to have been accepted as a Brother by Father Henry, to have made vows to Prior Augustine, and to have left the community and the Order about 1864. —Wolf Memoranda, 1890-1894, entry between July and Sept. 16, 1894. Land records indicate that he transferred his title to Prior Augustine in 1862 and that Father Henry's quarter section was transferred to Gehrig in 1866.

Prior Augustine did considerable buying, selling, and perhaps swapping in the neighborhood during his incumbency so that the old College farm was based only in part on the original preempted claims.

[9] Wirth an Ludwig I, Doniphan, Dec. 18, 1858. (GHA 86/6 V)

In connection with the question of moving, it should be noted that Prior Augustine was not free to move to, e.g., Kansas City. The understanding with Bishop Miége was that the Benedictines were assigned to the missions of northeastern Kansas. A move out of the Vicariate would have involved abandoning him and negotiating with another bishop.

[10] *Wahrheitsfreund*, Sept. 2, 1858, from *Herold des Glaubens*.

After Samuel Pomeroy and the New England Emigrant Aid Company bought controlling interest in the town in 1857, Atchison was no longer a political stronghold of the proslavery forces. The citizens now concentrated on developing the overland trade and on improving the value of their real estate. The town already had a promising share in the Utah trade when the discovery of gold on Cherry Creek in the far western reaches of the territory (now Colorado) brought brighter visions. Prior Augustine probably saw what Sol Miller, editor of the White Cloud *Kansas Chief*, saw in 1858. Giving his impressions of a trip south, Miller wrote of Doniphan that it was "rather the largest town in Kansas above Leavenworth . . . with some thirty or forty new houses under way— most of them small, one-story buildings." Atchison, he said, "is nearly as large as Doniphan, and there are quite a number of buildings going up. We liked the looks of Atchison better than those of any other town we visited. The buildings are generally of a better class, and there is a substantial appearance about the place."[11] Doniphan, on the other hand, had already lost its land office and with it the lawyers and other hangerson. The town showed signs of decline.

Meanwhile General Benjamin F. Stringfellow donated to Prior Augustine a plot of ground, 250 by 140 feet, just beyond the north edge of Atchison for the purpose of erecting a Catholic church and school. It was not a princely gift even after Colonel Abell, his partner, added the rest of the block.[12] The General was simply trying to attract buyers for the lots in his new subdivision. The site was a mile from the main street, and in those days there was little but buckbrush between the two. It was an unhandy spot for a parish church. If a boarding school was the object, a small block, with a deep ravine taking up a good part of the land, was hardly adequate. In 1860

---

[11] May 27, 1858.
[12] Deeds: B. F. Stringfellow to Wirth, Aug. 27, 1858; P. T. Abell to Wirth, June 25, 1860.

someone inserted a letter in the Atchison *Union*, praising the "magnanimous liberality" of the citizen who had made this donation to the "Germans and Irish, who may be termed the humble order." This letter provoked a prompt reply from *Vindex*, who wrote plainly what he thought of both "magnanimous liberality" and the label "humble order."[13]

Prior Augustine, in any case, had accepted the gift, and in August, 1858, began building a frame church, fifty by twenty-five feet, on the site of the present church. Before the end of the year, although the interior was unfinished, the church was in use.[14] This small, plain, frame building was Atchison's first church. While it was still in the framing stage, the Editor of the *Champion*, with true frontier hyperbole, referred to it as "an exceedingly tasty edifice, built in the Gothic style of architecture." In the same article he commented on the Methodist church then being built and concluded his discussion of the new churches with the observation that "the morals of the place have suffered heretofore for want of church room."[15]

Prior Augustine, from the vantage point of 1861, maintained that Father Henry had used poor judgment in settling at Doniphan. The number of Catholics in Doniphan declined, whereas the Catholic population of Atchison constantly increased. By the end of 1858 Prior Augustine had decided to move the Priory to Atchison. The Prior had asked donations of both the Ludwig-Missionsverein and King Ludwig I of Bavaria for his monastery. The King's first donation in December, 1858, the Prior said, prompted him to move to Atchison.[16]

Probably the chief reason for the move from Doniphan was that Atchison offered a more promising location for a school. If Prior Augustine was to develop a community

---

[13] Atchison *Champion*, Dec. 15, 1860.
[14] Wirth an LMV, Atchison, Jan. 2, 1861. (LMV Leav II 1/17-18)
Wirth an Ludwig I, Doniphan, Dec. 18, 1858. (GHA 86/6 V)
[15] Sept. 25, 1858.
[16] Wirth an LMV, Atchison, Jan. 2, 1861. (LMV Leav II 1/17-18)

with independent powers of growth, he had to have a school for the training of its members. Furthermore, his most effective plea for aid from the missionary societies and other sources was his school to train missionaries for this frontier area. Bishop Miége also favored this project, because it would solve one of his major problems. Frontier bishops were always hard pressed for priests. Until they could inaugurate a training program these bishops had two kinds of priests, namely, a few heroic souls on the one hand, and, on the other, a small parade of failures who were willing to make a new start, sometimes successfully, wherever they could find a bishop to accept them. Although Bishop Miége doubted the Prior's chances of success,[17] he nevertheless pleaded eloquently with Abbot Wimmer to send men, or at least one man, to aid the venture.[18] "We poor people of Kansas," he wrote, "are almost tempted to believe that we are on the wrong page of your liberality. F. Augustine feels discouraged for not receiving the help he needs so badly."[19] Abbot Wimmer was not unsympathetic; he happily boasted to King Ludwig I of the classical and scientific educational venture the King's generosity had made possible in Kansas, but Prior Augustine would have to wait for an ordination before obtaining his faculty.[20]

The cornerstone of the building for the College and Priory in Atchison was laid on May 29, 1859.[21] As one of the Brothers remembered it the occasion had a touch of arcadian simplicity: "Father McGee then of Lawrence, Kansas, delivered the Oration in the frame church which had just been finished. There was a very large crowd there. Three of us walked down from Doniphan that morning. There had been a terrible rain the night before but the morning was beautiful and we picked almost an armful of wild flowers on the road with which to deck

[17] Garin, *Miége*, 122.
[18] Miége to Wimmer, Leavenworth, Jan. 4, 1859. (SVA)
[19] *Idem*, July 6, 1859. (SVA)
[20] Wimmer an Ludwig I, St. Vincent, Apr. 5, 1859, in Mathaeser, *Wimmer und Koenig Ludwig I*, 113.
[21] Atchison *Union*, June 4, 1859.

48

the altar."[22] A month later the *Champion* noted with satisfaction the arrival "of a large lot of pine lumber, shingles, lath, etc., discharged from the steamer *Meteor*" for the College.[23] About the first of September the little community abandoned Doniphan and moved into the nearly completed building. St. Benedict's College was ready to open.

The Frontier College

Although St. Benedict's College dates its origin from this time, a beginning of sorts had been made at Doniphan, even though Prior Augustine was the whole faculty and was frequently absent on his missionary journeys. William Kelley was sent to Doniphan by Bishop O'Gorman, of the new Vicariate of Nebraska, to finish his studies in theology. After residing for some time at the little Priory, Father Kelley was ordained in Omaha on June 25, 1859, and brought the total of Bishop O'Gorman's priests to three.[24] With Kelley at Doniphan were three possible candidates for the community: Joseph Wattron, Thomas Hynes, and Joseph O'Donohue.[25] What this group represented would more nearly resemble a club for self-improvement than a school. Prior Augustine wrote that one of them had even opened an elementary school for boys in Doniphan.[26]

The formal beginning of the College was made at Atchison in 1859, and the first students were entered on the books on October 12. At the end of October only four students were in attendance, but by the end of the year the enrollment was up to sixteen. Board and tuition cost $60 a semester.[27] Father Edward Hipelius, gifted,

[22] Hynes to Rettele, Axtell, Mar. 14, 1884.
[23] July 2, 1859.
[24] *Wahrheitsfreund*, Aug. 18, 1859, from *Kath. Kirchenzeitung*, July 20, 1859.
[25] Hynes to Rettele, Axtell, Mar. 14, 1884; Record drawn up by Father William Rettele, O.S.B., in 1884, substantiated by contemporary financial records.
[26] Wirth an Ludwig I, Doniphan, Dec. 18, 1858. (GHA 86/6 V)
[27] Priory accounts, 1860-62.

well-educated, but chronically dissatisfied, came from St. Vincent to organize the school. He was its vice-president and most of its faculty but stayed only one year.[28] Frater Celestin Wattron was the first prefect and professor of French.[29] Brother Francis Hynes taught English and mathematics. He was more famous for his quick temper and ready rod.[30] With the addition of the names of Father Casimir Seitz to teach German, of Father Edmund Langenfelder, undoubtedly only to make the size of the faculty seem more imposing, and of Prior Augustine as the president of the college, the roster of the first faculty was complete.[31]

The textbooks used indicate clearly that the title of college really meant a traditional classical school. Colleges in those days necessarily provided also for the elementary background if that was lacking in their students. The books listed for that first year included *The Poor Man's Catechism*, *McGuffey's* and *Christian Brothers Readers*, *Webster's* and *Carpenter's Spellers*, *Bullion's English Grammar*, *Zumpt's Latin Grammar*, *Anthon's Latin Lessons*, a *Historia Sacra*, a *Deutsches Lesebuch*, a *French Grammar*, *Reeve's Bible History*, *Shea's History of the United States*, and *Ray's Arithmetic*.[32]

St. Benedict's began its second year with twenty students. Prior Augustine wrote that ten of these wished to be priests, and of these, four were able to pay nothing for their education.[33] Bishop Miége had decided to send

[28] Edward Hipelius was born Feb. 7, 1836, in Laueringen, Bavaria, professed Jan. 14, 1855, ordained Aug. 8, 1858.—Moosmueller, *St. Vincenz in Pennsylvanien*, 344. He later left the Order and became a diocesan priest.

[29] Francis J. Wattron was born in Alsace, July 8, 1833, and came to the United States at the age of seventeen. He was one of the casualties of the visitation of 1862 (*infra*) and after leaving St. Benedict's studied theology at St. Francis Seminary in Milwaukee and was ordained by Bishop Miége for the Vicariate on Aug. 8, 1865. He was long pastor of Paola and died at Fort Scott, Dec. 19, 1904.—T. H. Kinsella, *A Centenary of Catholicity in Kansas, 1822-1922* (Kansas City, 1921), 92 ff.

[30] Francis (Thomas) Hynes' vows were declared invalid in 1862, and he left St. Benedict's in 1863. He died at his home in Axtell, Kansas, May 6, 1899.—*Abbey Student*, VIII (May, 1899), 515.

[31] *Metropolitan Catholic Almanac*, 1860, adv.

[32] School year 1859-60, inside front cover of Priory accounts, 1860-62.

[33] Wirth an LMV, Atchison, Jan. 2, 1861. (LMV Leav II 1/17-18)

his six seminarians to St. Benedict's, and Bishop O'Gorman, of the Vicariate of Nebraska, also sent two students.[34] By the autumn of 1861 twelve students were enrolled for the priesthood: four in theology, four in philosophy, and four prepared to enter philosophy in the following year.[35] St. Benedict's was a versatile place in those days. With a handful of students and a tiny faculty, it offered everything from grade school to theology.[36]

The College seemed so promising that at the end of the second year Prior Augustine added an ell (the present chemistry laboratories) of about the same size as the original building. He wrote that the two brick buildings, each about thirty by eighty feet, had cost about $16,000.[37] The *Champion* described the buildings and their arrangement when the new wing was completed:

The basement is divided into a kitchen and cellar, each thirty by fifty feet, and a cook room thirty feet square. The first story has a spacious dining room, twenty-two by forty-eight feet, four class rooms, each sixteen by twenty-two, one twenty-two by forty-eight and a hall. The second story contains two class rooms, one sixteen by twenty-two, the other twenty-two by forty-eight, an examination room, sixteen by thirty, a parlor about eighteen by twenty, and five smaller rooms. The third story is divided into a hall, thirty by fifty feet, two dormitories, one twenty by thirty, the other twenty-two by thirty, and five small rooms. The buildings are in every respect most substantially built, and though plain, everything about them is neat and in good taste.[38]

At the beginning of the school year of 1862 the College announced the opening of a day school for boys.[39] This announcement brought an important increase in enrollment, and by 1864 forty-four boarders and sixty-two day students appeared on the books. That was the peak year

[34] Garin, *Miége*, 135.
[35] Wirth an Lebling, Atchison, Nov. 10, 1861. (LMV Leav II 1/22)
[36] Students of the first few years who are known to have been ordained for the vicariates of Kansas and Nebraska are William Fitzgerald, John Cunningham, and Kilian Gunther, all of whom enrolled in 1860; Sebastian Favre and John Hays in 1861, and Anton Kuhls in 1862.
[37] Wirth an LMV, Atchison, Jan. 25, 1862. (LMV Leav II 1/23)
[38] Nov. 23, 1861.
[39] *Champion*, Aug. 23, 1862.

in Atchison's overland trade. By 1866, however, the Union Pacific Railroad had been built far enough west to put an end to wagon train freighting from the Missouri River towns. Consequently, Atchison was less prosperous, and the College enrollment declined. Furthermore, Prior Augustine concentrated on building his church. Only seventeen students enrolled in 1866. The College was closed during the year 1867-68, because the dormitory was converted into a chapel while the church was being built. The College was reopened without much advance notice in 1868, but students began to appear from October on, and during the course of the year enrollment totaled nineteen boarders and fifteen day students. In spite of the uncertain condition of the monastic community and frequent changes in the faculty, enrollment in the College grew steadily to sixty-six boarders and forty-three day students in 1873-74. The panic of 1873 and the depression that followed no doubt account for the decline to forty-two boarders in the following year. Enrollment reached a low point with only twenty-five boarders and thirty-eight day students in 1875-76 when rumors were afloat that the College was closing again.[40]

Considering the conditions in Kansas at the time, the wonder is that the school had any students at all beside priesthood students. Kansas was thinly settled, the percentage of Catholics was small, and the settlers were poor. Usually only the settlers' older sons were ready for college, and they had to help on the farm, going to school only in winter months.[41] As a consequence, many students arrived in November and left in March, and the faculty adjusted their classes as best they could. These farmers and the local merchants wanted their sons to have the rudiments of a commercial education. In its advertisements the College gave special emphasis to Professor Erickson, who was hired at twenty-five dollars a month to teach the commercial courses in 1863-64.[42] After 1867

---

[40] Record of Students, 1869-1881.
[41] Fink an LMV, Atchison, Jan. 23, 1870. (LMV Leav II 1/46)
[42] *Champion*, Jan. 28, 1864.

Father Peter Kassens, with his Master of Accounts degree from Jones Commercial, Mathematical and Telegraph College in St. Louis, was the feature attraction.

Colleges are not paying businesses, and in those days St. Benedict's was sometimes an outrageously uneconomic occupation for the community. The gross income of the College in those years reached a high of little more than $6000 in 1873 and dropped to a low of $3000 in 1875. The most important task for the College, as the monks saw it, was training badly needed priests for the western settlements. But most of the priesthood students were unable to pay board and tuition. The aid of the missionary societies was sought particularly to subsidize this work. In the depression after 1873 many bills went unpaid. Day students often paid their tuition in laundry service, coffee, beer, groceries, and sometimes money.

In those early years St. Benedict's taught not only all ages; it taught all kinds. Among the notable students in those first years was John Cunningham, who entered in 1860 and ultimately became bishop of Concordia. At the other extreme was the eldest son of one of the town's founders, whose father advertised him as simple-minded, forbidding tradesmen to sell him anything.[43] Further variety was added by Indians such as Andrew Jackson Fitzpatrick, a Cheyenne from Leavenworth, Stephen Akan Pensineau from the Kickapoo Reserve, and Joe Provaux. As soon as Abbot Martin Marty arrived at Standing Rock, Dakota Territory, he sent young Edward de Grey, who later served for many years as a teacher to his fellow Sioux.[44] The various bishops' students added touches of Irish and French. In 1865 when Atchison was sending out wagon trains in the Santa Fe trade, there were Oteros, Gallegos, Gutierrez, and Lunas from New Mexico.

But the most romantic figure of all was Jimmy King, the alumnus who was scalped by Indians. His story may be legend, but the history of a frontier college really needs

[43] *Ibid.*, July 14, 1860.
[44] Marty to Moosmueller, Standing Rock, D.T., Oct. 26, 1876.

53

a student scalped by Indians, and every college ought to have a few legends. Jimmy King attended St. Benedict's from 1859 to 1864. His home is given first as Chicago and later as Butte, Montana. Thomas Hynes, who as Brother Francis taught English and mathematics during the years when King was in school, stated in 1884 that King had been scalped by Indians at Plum Creek.[45] Father Boniface Verheyen, who had been a fellow-student for a year or two with King, wrote the following in 1922:

Jimmy King was killed by Indians in July, 1865. He, together with a companion, had secured a light team and started for Montana. Owing to the hostility of the Indians, they traveled for protection with freighting trains. These trains traveled rather slowly, making about twenty miles a day, always camping early enough to give the mules and the oxen a chance to graze before sundown, when they were coralled for the night in the circle of the wagons, lined around the camping area, with the wagon tongues turned inward. King and his companion with their light rigs could easily have doubled the distance made by the freight trains, and they thought to take advantage of the protection of trains they had heard were ahead of them, and thus got the idea of making a lap on the train ahead of them and overtake the second train ahead of them if the chance offered. It so happened that after one of these laps, something went wrong with King's team, before they had reached the train in advance. King told his companion to go on, overtake the freight train and prepare for camp. He would make his repairs and come on after. — King did not reach camp during the night, a party was sent out the next morning to investigate, and coming to the place of the breakdown they found King's outfit burned, the horses gone, and poor Jimmy dead and scalped, and his body pierced with thirteen arrows. I saw one of the steel arrow points taken from his body, in the possession of Brother Francis [Hynes], one of the profs of the College. His body was buried by the roadside.[46]

45 Hynes to Rettele, Axtell, Mar. 14, 1884.
46 Verheyen Reminiscences, 1922.
  A search for contemporary evidence unfortunately turned up only an account that one James Kean of Atchison County, a passenger from Ft. Kearney to Atchison on Nagle and Fulkerson's train, had accidentally shot himself by pulling a gun from a wagon after full warning from a teamster that the gun was loaded. This occurred on June 21, 1865, about seventeen miles west of Oketo, Marshall County. The body was buried at Guittard's Station, and an affidavit was sworn to before Justice Lanham in Seneca.—*Champion*, July 4, 1865, from the Seneca *Courier*, June 29, 1865.

By all accounts the student of the early days led a Spartan life. Bedtime came at nine, and the students were up at five in the morning. They breakfasted at six and were ready for a long morning.[47] Students and priests all ate in one refectory, and in 1875, to put an end to mischief, even the day students were brought into the common refectory to eat their lunches and to benefit by the table reading, which was intended both to edify the students and to keep them quiet.[48] The rules on leaving the campus and receiving mail were strict. "The use of tobacco is positively prohibited," said the catalog of 1870. In later catalogs it was found necessary to add: "Those who will not stop chewing will not be admitted."

From its prominence in the recollections of old alumni, one concludes that the tin wash basin should be on the coat of arms of St. Benedict's. Father Boniface tells of leaving the dormitory, snatching up a tin wash basin, dashing down the stairs to the well near the kitchen door, and lining up at the bench along the east wall of the building. In winter this ceremony was reduced to the merest gesture, followed by a dash back to the big stove in the study hall.[49] John Storm, '62, remembered a barrel and basins in the hallway outside the dorm, a more humane arrangement.[50]

Storm remembered also that his dormitory, at the east end of the second floor of the Old Priory, was unheated. One extremely cold night Merrit Murphy, of Leavenworth, filled several students' boots with water. In the morning when the students arose to dress, they found their boots filled with ice. Storm concluded that "the very primitiveness of the institute seemed to beget deviltry. In other words there was nothing for the boys to do but study, pray, and practice mischief." On the other hand, under the heading of popular sports he listed marbles, tops, kite flying, old fashioned town ball, rugby,

[47] *Champion*, June 1, 1873.
[48] Record of Visitation, May 26, 1871; Chapter Minutes, Dec. 8, 1875.
[49] Verheyen Reminiscences, 1922.
[50] *Abbey Student*, VII (May, 1898), 523-4.

fishing, swimming, shinny, archery, quoits, dominoes, checkers, and cards. But the most common form of recreation was walking — organized walking in large groups attended by a prefect. Storm remembered one occasion when the commercial and classical groups, which did not mingle much, found themselves approaching each other on the same country lane. That meeting ended in a grand fight, but it was the only such incident that he could remember. Most of the students had a vigorous interest in the political questions of the day, and in spite of the rigid discipline, they roped themselves out of the dorm to go down town to hear the big political speeches.[51] Holidays were, of course, frequent, and freedays occurred for a variety of reasons. May, with its spring fever, usually brought the big picnic of the year, often at Sugar Lake, which later grew into the institution of May Day.[52]

The first attempts at drama were occasioned in 1861 by the completion of the new wing with its hall, fifty by thirty feet, and sixteen feet high. Forty-four dollars were recklessly spent on scenery for the theatre and sundry articles for the stage.[53] The entertainment aimed specifically "to show the people of this city, that, although the institution is yet in its first stages, still it can show a rapid advancement in its inmates in the various branches of learning, that might, perhaps, be looked for in vain from other institutions, already flourishing and sanctioned by time, and patronized by thousands. No expenses have been spared towards contributing to render the performance acceptable. A new set of scenery and stage accompaniments has been purchased expressly for the occasion. . . and the performance will be enlivened by musical treats from the College Band." The public was warned that "as the institution is yet in its infancy, a finished and faultless performance cannot be expected." The program included an opening address in poetry by Master C. Creeden; *The Hidden Gem*, a drama full of

[51] Storm to Wise, St. Louis, Nov. 29, 1911.
[52] Cashbook, May, 1864; *Champion*, June 5, 1874.
[53] Cashbook, Nov., 1861.

56

Romans; *The Village Lawyer,* a skit with a storekeeper named Snarl; Henry Meurs' oration which drew the praise of the Editor, and, as the comic afterpiece, *A Game of Cards.*[54] Tickets sold for twenty-five cents, and total receipts amounted to $64.50.[55]

The band mentioned was evidently organized at about this same time.[56] Old Mr. Kathrens from town was the first director. The band preceded the Irish Brigade in a patriotic parade on July 4, 1862, but at that time the director was a certain "Rev. Mr. McMahon."[57] A year later, when Father Timothy Luber arrived in Kansas, the band was already defunct, and he heard that it had not amounted to much. In 1863 he bought the first college piano, a Gabler, and gave piano and violin lessons.[58] The band was revived by Father Urban Bayer, who was sent from St. Vincent in 1871 particularly to restore this proof of culture to St. Benedicts.[59]

As in every self-respecting school of the time, the Philomathic Society, dedicated to debate and elocution, was the oldest and longest-lived student organization. The Pioneer Chess Club had a very brief history. The Bachelors' Spontaneous Combustion Club, for the encouragement of extemporaneous speech and the publication of literary efforts in the manuscript "Semi-Monthly Banner," lasted a couple of years. When Prior Oswald Moosmueller took over the College, he continued the Philomathic Society and added a Sodality, a St. Boniface Literary Association for the encouragement of German studies, a St. Cecilia's Society to develop a student choir, and a Base Ball Club of which the catalog for 1875 says, "The design of this Club is the promotion of health, the development of the muscular system, and the encouragement of the invigorating exercise and manly pastime; justly named the American Game of Ball."

[54] *Champion,* Nov. 16, 1861.
[55] Cashbook, Nov., 1861.
[56] Cashbook, May, 1861.
[57] *Champion,* July 5, 1862.
[58] Luber to Prior, Burlington, Iowa, Apr. 6, 1897.
[59] Wolf Diary, Nov. 23, 1871.

After St. Benedict's was reorganized in 1868 it advertised a six-year classical course leading to a Bachelor of Arts degree and a four-year commercial course leading to a Master of Accounts degree. But most classical students stayed only for three or four years of the advertised course, and most commercial students were satisfied with even less. Only six Master of Accounts diplomas and no bachelor's degrees were awarded before 1876, but the annual commencements at the end of June nevertheless had long programs. They included a drama (on one occasion a play in English translated from the German, and a sketch in German translated from the English), demonstrations of competence in the arts of elocution and music, and sometimes demonstrations in spelling and mathematics as well. Every student had to receive some kind of "premium" and a number of "distinctions" in the various classes or at least for conduct or application. The list was always very long and can usually be trusted as a complete roster of the students still in attendance at the end of the year.

Such was St. Benedict's College during Atchison's frontier days and in the decade following the Civil War. Little evidence remains on the most important question concerning a school — the quality of the teaching — but apparently some of the teachers were excellent and a few of them were poor. In short, through most of this period the school was reasonably good by frontier standards, for St. Benedict's was a frontier college, with all the limitations that the frontier implied. Considering the difficulty of supplying even a handful of men to staff it and of procuring the modest sums necessary to erect its buildings, the wonder is that St. Benedict's College was opened and did somehow survive.

The Prior's Problems

Prior Augustine Wirth founded St. Benedict's College because it was essential to the future growth of the community, but in those early years the most important work of the Kansas monks was the mission to the settlers. The Prior was an able missionary with a clear understanding of the settlers' needs. He had established the first regular circuit, that of the river towns north of Doniphan, but after moving to Atchison he was fully engaged with developing his community, the College, and the local parish. The details of missionary activity are related in a later chapter. In developing his community and its work in the missions and in the College, he was harassed by two problems: the lack of men and of money. His attempts to solve these problems in his own way led to friction with Abbot Wimmer.

By 1861 Prior Augustine's problems were beginning to come into focus. He had a reasonably adequate group of buildings on a small block of ground. He had, by agreement, no financial backing from his motherhouse. How closely his notions of the personnel needed would coincide with Abbot Wimmer's ideas remained to be seen. Prior Augustine wanted to be an abbot, but Abbot Wimmer at first seemed to view the Kansas foundation as a mission house with very limited possibilities. Some of the monks sent to Kansas had very slender talents even for that kind of work. Generally speaking, Abbot Wimmer seems to have tried to supply the Kansas foundation with one man for the school and two for the missions. But Kansas was not a popular assignment; to the German and Irish immigrant everything about the state was foreign, particularly the climate with its extremes of heat and cold. To the old label of Great American Desert there were added the lurid headlines of Bleeding Kansas and the drought of 1860. The Benedictines at St. Vincent used to make grim jokes about being sent to Siberia (St. John's in Minnesota) or to the Sahara (St. Benedict's in Kansas). Many of the men sent by Abbot Wimmer came unwillingly. For this reason, and also because they often suffered with the ague, a common malady in those days, their careers in Kansas were short.

Father Casimir Seitz, who accompanied Prior Augustine to Kansas, was just under thirty years of age. He had come to the United States only in 1854 and could not preach in English.[60] He spoke of studying English along with his other duties and remarked that as few Germans were in Doniphan, he had little work there.[61] If Father Henry can be believed, Father Casimir and the Prior did not get along well.[62] And on one occasion Father Augustine complained that Father Casimir was lazy, doing nothing, and not even studying.[63] On the other hand, Father Casimir seems to have done well in organizing the German Catholics in Leavenworth and in building their first church. While there he also served as confessor to the Sisters of Charity.[64] When the College was opened in Atchison in 1859, Father Casimir was recalled from Leavenworth. Bishop Miége had meanwhile secured the services of Father Fisch for the Germans there. But Father Casimir had suffered from attacks of ague shortly after his arrival in Kansas and so returned to the East early in 1860.[65]

In 1858 two more monks were sent from Pennsylvania. They were intended to staff missions in Nebraska, but only one, Father Francis Cannon, actually went to Nebraska at this time. He also seems to have returned to the East in the spring of 1860.[66] Father Edmund Langenfelder, the other man sent out in 1858, worked the missions out of Doniphan, replacing Father Casimir.[67] He

[60] Casimir (Willibald) Seitz was born in Pirkach, Bavaria, Aug. 13, 1829, professed Aug. 31, 1856, and died July 23, 1867, at Newark, N.J.—*Necrologium Congregationis Americano-Cassinensis O.S.B.*, *1846-1946* (Collegeville, 1948), No. 43. The date given for his ordination in the *Necrologium*, April 27, 1857, is in conflict with Seitz's own statement that he was ordained on the second Sunday after Easter, i.e., April 26.—Seitz an Wimmer, Doniphan, June 4, 1857. (SVA) See his obituary in the *Catholic Telegraph*, Aug. 7, 1867.

[61] Seitz an Wimmer, Doniphan, June 4, 1857. (SVA)

[62] Lemke an Wimmer, 'My Claim Shanty,' June 27, 1857. (SVA)

[63] Wirth to Wimmer, Doniphan, Nov. 20, 1857. (SVA)

[64] [Sr. Mary (Julia) Buckner], *A History of the Sisters of Charity of Leavenworth, Kansas* (Kansas City, Mo., 1898), 64.

[65] Wimmer ad Pescetelli, St. Vincent, May 30, 1862. (SPexM)

[66] Francis Cannon was born May 19, 1811, in Killybeg, Ireland, was professed Jan. 6, 1854, ordained in Covington, Ky., Aug. 12, 1858.—Moosmueller, *St. Vincenz in Pennsylvanien*, 327. His last baptism recorded from Nebraska City in the Omaha register is dated Mar. 4, 1860. Father Cannon later left the Order and returned to Ireland.

[67] Edmund (Michael) Langenfelder was born in Laichling, Bavaria, Aug. 16, 1823, professed July 26, 1857, ordained May 29, 1858, and died April 18, 1885.—*Necrologium*, No. 121.

too suffered from the ague and language limitations. Preaching a funeral sermon in Doniphan, he reportedly said, "This man, a good man, this man gave much money to the priest — *darum steht auch ein Priester an seinem Grab.*"[68] (. . . that's why there is a priest at his grave.) He was renowned for his powerful voice, which, it was said, once frightened a dog out of church.[69] He also returned to Pennsylvania early in 1860.[70] Some years later, when apparently there was question of lending him to St. Benedict's again, Abbot Innocent demurred, saying that Father Edmund reputedly would be more annoyance than assistance.[71] Father Edward Hipelius, sent to St. Benedict's to open the new school in 1859, was a very able man, but he was in Kansas through no wish of his own, was no admirer of Prior Augustine, and left at the end of the school year. His attitude to Kansas thereafter was one of wry amusement.[72]

Thus four of the five priests sent to Kansas by Abbot Wimmer returned to the East in 1860. To replace them the Abbot sent Father Emmanuel Hartig and two clerics, Philip Vogg and Gottfried Weiss, who had apparently studied at St. Vincent for the Kansas Priory, or were, perhaps, reluctant volunteers.[73] Father Philip Vogg was ordained at Leavenworth, March 17, 1860, shortly after his arrival in Kansas — the first priest ordained specifically for the Kansas Priory. He worked in the Nebraska missions and in the northern counties of Kansas, and he collected aid for the drought victims of 1860. Then he and the Prior evidently became incompatible, and Father Vogg left.[74] The other cleric sent out in 1860 had an even

[68] Verheyen Reminiscences, 1922.
[69] Obituary in Carrolltown *News*, Apr. 24, 1885.
[70] Cashbook, Jan., 1860.
[71] Wolf to Wimmer, Atchison, Aug. 13, 1876. (SVA)
[72] Hipelius to Edelbrock, St. Mary's, Pa., May 20, 1870. (SJA)
[73] Wimmer ad Pescetelli, St. Vincent, Aug. 3, 1861. (SPexM)
[74] According to some old-timer's memory, on Ash Wednesday, 1862.—Wolf historical notes, n.d. Philip Vogg was born Oct. 2, 1827, at Oberwaldbach, Diocese of Augsburg, and came to the United States in 1858, according to the notes of Alexius Hoffman, of St. John's Abbey, quoting the German *Schematis-*

shorter career in Kansas. Gottfried Weiss had arrived with Vogg, but for some reason Prior Augustine refused to permit his ordination. Gottfried was angry and before the summer was out went off to the Trappists.[75] Father Emmanuel Hartig had also taken vows for the Kansas Priory, but he stayed at St. Vincent until after his ordination on September 21, 1860.[76] During his first year in Kansas he was, in effect, the replacement for Father Hipelius in the College. A year later he was sent to Nebraska City where he spent most of his life. Finally one had arrived who did not go back and did not quit.

The year 1861 brought two more volunteers to Kansas, neither of whom lasted long. Severin Rotter was another of the group educated at St. Vincent for St. Benedict's.[77] He was appointed the first resident pastor in the settlement on Wildcat Creek in Nemaha County (St. Mary's Church) and was to care for the surrounding missions. A year later he was back in Atchison and in November left or was sent away by Prior Augustine.[78] Father Alphonse Heimler came to Kansas apparently in a fit of pique and before the end of the year had returned to the East.[79]

The next man to come to St. Benedict's from St. Vincent was a genuine volunteer. A year after his arrival Father Emmanuel Hartig wrote to his friend Father Thomas Bartl, urging him to come to Kansas for real apostolic work.[80] The newly-ordained Father Thomas asked to be sent to Kansas, but the Abbot was only irritated.[81] However, a year later conditions had changed. Abbot Wimmer told Father Thomas that Prior Augustine

mus of 1892, 183. Vogg became a diocesan priest and died in Milwaukee, Oct. 2, 1895.—Wolf an Mueller, Atchison, Dec. 6, 1895. (SVA)
    75 Vogg and Wirth an Dr. Hueller, Atchison, Aug. 23, 1860.
    76 Emmanuel (Jacob) Hartig was born in Inchenhofen, Bavaria, May 1, 1830, professed Jan. 7, 1859, and died Sept. 1, 1910.—*Necrologium*, No. 387.
    77 Wimmer ad Pescetelli, St. Vincent, Aug. 3, 1861. (SPexM)
    78 Bartl, "Beitrag zur Geschichte der Missionen in Kansas," n.d. [probably 1884].
    79 Wimmer ad Pescetelli, St. Vincent, Aug. 3, 1861; Oct. 1, 1862. (SPexM)
    80 Hartig an Bartl, Atchison, June 6, 1861.
    81 Bartl an Hartig, n.p., n.d. [but an answer to the above].

needed a priest, "and particularly one who will keep the Holy Rule and the daily order *conscientiously*, so that the priory may become a real *cloister*. [The Prior] has too much to do. For that reason we have chosen you, because you are a lover of order, a God fearing religious, and because you earlier asked to go to Kansas."[82] Father Thomas fulfilled Abbot Wimmer's expectations. At first he was a bit disappointed with Kansas,[83] but he shortly became the outstanding missionary in the community, tireless in his rounds of the settlements. He personifies the story of St. Benedict's mission to the settlers.[84]

Prior Augustine went to St. Vincent in July, 1863, and he returned to Kansas with two clerics, Timothy Luber and Bernard Lesker.[85] Lesker evidently remained only one year, returning to St. Vincent in September, 1864.[86] Timothy Luber had been teaching at Abbot Wimmer's Canadian venture, and when that was discontinued, he was available for Kansas. He was the third foundation stone of the community at St. Benedict's. During Prior Augustine's time Father Timothy was most important in the school, but his later career was devoted to missionary work.[87]

At the beginning of 1864 Prior Augustine reported that his monastic family numbered four priests, one deacon, one subdeacon, four clerics (at St. Vincent Abbey), and five Brothers.[88] Those present at the canonical visitation of 1864 were the Prior, Fathers Emmanuel Hartig and Thomas Bartl, Fraters Timothy Luber and Bernard Lesker, and Brothers Lucas Zaeune, Anton Wirth (the Prior's brother,) and Joseph von Bragel.[89] Later in the

82 Wimmer an Bartl, St. Vincent, May 23, 1862.
83 Bartl an Mitbruder, Atchison, July 18, 1862.
84 Thomas (Michael) Bartl was born in Partenkirchen, Bavaria, Dec. 12, 1830, professed Feb. 2, 1858, ordained May 25, 1861, and died Nov. 30, 1885. —*Necrologium*, No. 131.
85 Cashbook, July, 1863.
86 Cashbook, Sept., 1864.
87 Timothy (John) Luber was born in Baltimore, Md., Oct. 29, 1842, professed July 11, 1859, ordained June 24, 1865, and died Mar. 29, 1901.—*Necrologium*, No. 283.
88 Wirth an LMV, Atchison, Jan. 6, 1864. (LMV Leav II 1/29)
89 Record of Visitation, Apr. 29, 1864.

year Lesker left, and Father Placidus Pilz was sent out from St. Vincent particularly to teach the popular commercial subjects in the school.[90] With him he brought a cleric, Pirmin Koumly, who became the fourth permanent acquisition of St. Benedict's. Father Pirmin's first years in Kansas were devoted to the school, but later he was busy with pastoral work. He spent the last years of his life as master of novices.[91] After the arrival of Father Placidus Pilz in 1864, no more priests were sent on loan from St. Vincent until after the crisis of 1868.

If the Priory was to grow and prosper, it needed not only priests but also Brothers. Father Boniface Verheyen wrote that when he was a student in the early sixties, the care of the institution was in the hands of "Brother Joseph, who did the baking and sawed the fire wood, the latter also for the Sisters. Brother Luke managed the culinary department. Brother Anton, the brother of Father Augustine, was the sacristan, and attended to some of the Fathers' rooms. Brother Lambert had charge of the kitchen and garden by turns."[92] Besides these Brothers, the old records reveal a shadowy procession of men who came and went — men like John Gehrig, who was Brother Henry for a while, or like John Schratz, who came in October, 1858, and was Brother Benedict until he left in April, 1860.[93]

From the account just given of the coming and going of Benedictines in Kansas during the first years of the

[90] Placidus (Peter) Pilz was born in Moegendorf, Bavaria, Nov. 9, 1835, professed Jan. 6, 1857, ordained Apr. 20, 1859, and died Mar. 15, 1911.—*Necrologium*, No. 396. He evidently remained in Kansas only one year at this time.
[91] Pirmin (Blaise) Koumly was born in Boozheim, Alsace, Feb. 21, 1840, professed Nov. 13, 1862, ordained Aug. 19, 1865, and died July 27, 1904. —*Necrologium*, No. 324.
[92] Verheyen Reminiscences, 1922.
Luke (Peter) Zaeune was born in Bamberg, Bavaria, Aug. 30, 1822, professed Jan. 20, 1856, and died May 15, 1907.—*Necrologium*, No. 356. He came to Kansas in 1860 with Father Emmanuel to replace Brother Paul Pfeifer and stayed the rest of his life.
Joseph (John) von Bragel was born in Kegen, Wesphalia, Mar. 3, 1837, professed Mar. 19, 1863, and died Jan. 21, 1883.—*Necrologium*, No. 103.
Brothers Anton and Lambert did not become permanent members of the community.
[93] Cashbooks, *passim*.

Priory, it is clear that Father Augustine must soon have been convinced that he could not depend upon men from St. Vincent to build his community. From the beginning he had sought to attract vocations, and for some years he evidently permitted young students to take vows after a very sketchy novitiate. These men were an important part of his faculty. Wattron and Hynes, who had joined the Prior at Doniphan, were the nucleus of this group. Frater Celestine Wattron was said to have made vows at Doniphan.[94] Prior Augustine referred to Thomas Hynes as an "Irish Brother." Like so many others he reached a parting of the ways with the Prior. Early in 1863 Hynes wrote to Father Emmanuel, "I could put up with things no longer and when I made complaint Father Prior sent me away without a single article of clothing that was fit to wear. . . I tried to get ten dollars from him but he said such charity would be sinful."[95]

One priest was also, temporarily, the product of Prior Augustine's program. John Meurs was a student in St. Benedict's from the time of its opening in Atchison in 1859. When he said his First Mass on the feast of St. Benedict, March 21, 1862, he was hailed as the first Benedictine to complete his theology at St. Benedict's.[96] Although the canonical visitation of 1862 presumably declared his vows invalid in mid-May, he and Brother Henry were sent to Nebraska City in September.[97] Two years later the *Catholic Directory* no longer lists him as a Benedictine but places him at Seneca and in 1865 gives Fort Scott as his residence.

After the canonical visitation of 1862 Prior Augustine had to send his novices to St. Vincent for their novitiate. He did this only once, but this class of novices was large for so small a priory, and it must have brightened his already optimistic outlook. In June, 1865, he sent to the novitiate in Pennsylvania Peter Kassens, Boniface Ver-

[94] Wolf, historical notes, n.d.
[95] Hynes to Hartig, Wild Cat, Feb. 16, 1863.
[96] *Wahrheitsfreund*, Apr. 2, 1862.
[97] Meurs to [Wirth?], Nebraska City, Sept. 8, 1862.

heyen, Placidus McKeever, Eugene Bode, Casimir Rudroff, and one Frater Benedict.[98] Only Frater Benedict dropped out. Prior Augustine referred to three of them as orphans whom he had accepted in St. Louis in 1861 to study for the priesthood.[99] With the addition of these names the roster of the community in the early days is almost complete. The kind of men they were and the work they did can be told later.

Prior Augustine's second major problem was that of finance, and, like the problem of personnel, it led to differences with Abbot Wimmer. The Prior admitted that when he and Father Casimir had come to Kansas, the Abbot had warned him, "I will help with men, but I cannot send you money."[100] But if claims were to be taken up and the usual landed basis for an abbey provided, the Prior had to have money. Finally he fell back on the current slogan: "Once more, *raise money* for poor bleeding Kansas."[101] But Abbot Wimmer held fast to the original agreement and sent no money. The outlook was gloomy, for as Bishop Miége had warned, it would be some time before the missions could support a priest.

Abbot Wimmer had given Father Casimir twenty dollars for expenses when he left, but no evidence indicates that he gave Father Augustine anything.[102] The latter's accounts show that when he left Pennsylvania he had $170, which he later said he had begged, and Bishop Miége gave him $60. The expenses of travel and the purchase of some modest supplies had used up half of these funds by the time the pair arrived in Doniphan. Their income for the first month in Kansas was $21.10, but this improved rapidly so that by the end of the year 1857 they had received $668.55. This came from collections at Mass, offerings from parishioners, donations from

98 Cashbook, June, 1865.
99 Wirth an LMV, Atchison, Dec. 3, 1862. (LMV Leav II 1/26-27)
100 Wirth to Wimmer, Doniphan, May 10, 1857. (SVA)
101 *Idem*, Nov. 20, 1857. (SVA)
102 Fellner, "Erzabt Bonifaz Wimmer, O.S.B., und die Anfaenge der St. Benedicts Abtei, Atchison, Kansas," *Central Blatt and Social Justice*, XXI (May, 1928), 54.

Bishop Miége and others, and Mass stipends. The usual offering for a Mass at that time was fifty cents. Mass intentions from the Bishop or from priests in St. Louis and back East were their main reliance.[103]

The Priory would have continued in poor straits for some years even if the times had been normal, but Kansas had been something less than normal from the beginning. Once the politics of the territory had been decided, there came the drought of 1860, which resulted in a complete crop failure. In the following year the outbreak of the Civil War brought business in Kansas almost to a stand-still, but the later years of the war brought something of a boom.

After the move to Atchison and the expense of building there, Prior Augustine neglected no possible source of income. He exhorted the missionaries on their rounds to collect money for the Priory and to speak plainly to their little flocks of the obligation to support the missionary.[104] He advertised in the Catholic press for donations for his Priory. He reported having received about $200 from this source and about $400 from his neighbors, both Catholic and Protestant.[105] There were the usual festivals, ordinarily advertised as college rather than parish affairs.[106] The Prior even bought town lots cheaply at tax sales. Most of these lots were raffled or sold for the benefit of the Priory, but on a few of them he built small houses for rental income.[107]

The Prior's most important benefactor was King Ludwig I of Bavaria. Prior Augustine knew that the King gave generous support to Abbot Wimmer, and as the Prior was making an independent start, just as the Abbot had, he asked the King's help. In December, 1858, he received a gift of 3000 florins ($1218.27) from the King.[108]

---

[103] Cashbook; Wirth an LMV, Atchison, Jan. 14, 1860. (LMV Leav II 1/11)
[104] Wirth an [Langenfelder], Atchison, Dec. 4, 1859.
[105] Wirth an LMV, Atchison, Jan. 2, 1861. (LMV Leav II 1/17-18)
[106] Cashbook, Nov., 1862: $159; Nov., 1863: $250.
[107] Cashbook, Oct., 1859, Raffle of two lots, $150.
[108] Wirth an Ludwig I, Doniphan, Dec. 18, 1858. (GHA 86/6 V) Wirth an Lebling, Doniphan, Dec. 17, 1858. (LMV Leav II 1/10)

Requesting further aid from the King at the end of 1859, Prior Augustine stated that he had built the Priory in Atchison with the King's gift, and on the strength of promised aid from the Society for the Propagation of the Faith in Lyons. But Lyons had disappointed him, and now the survival of the Priory depended upon his ability to meet a note for $600 on May 1, 1860.[109] The King responded with another 2000 florins ($800).[110] The Prior thanked the King in most extravagant terms. The letter gives the impression that Ludwig had saved the Catholic Church, at least in Kansas. The Prior promised prayers for the King as long as the community endured, enrolled him first on the list of the Priory's benefactors, promised an annual Mass on his nameday, and asked for his autograph.[111] The King, pleased to be hailed as founder and savior, graciously responded with a holograph note.[112] In all, King Ludwig made four donations between 1858 and 1864, totaling $2818.27. These were the largest contributions Prior Augustine received.

The King's almoner, Court Chaplain Mueller, believed that the royal aid for the Benedictine missions in America should be channeled through Abbot Wimmer, and Mueller disliked Prior Augustine's independent approach. He wrote the Abbot that Prior Augustine's frequent begging letters were likely to choke up the spring, and in 1859 he saw to it that there was no donation for the Prior.[113] When the King received Prior Augustine's letter asking for a second donation so that the Prior could meet his note and so save his newly-built priory, the King sought information from his chaplain. Mueller explained that the Prior was a worthy disciple of his Abbot, nay more, a rival, and that was the reason the Prior undertook too much and found himself in difficulties. But after Abbot Wimmer had given his approval, the Prior got his donation.[114]

109 Wirth an Ludwig I, Atchison, Dec. 16, 1859. (GHA 50/5 1)
110 Cashbook, May, 1860.
111 Wirth an Ludwig I, Atchison, May 7, 1860. (GHA 86/6 VI)
112 Ludwig I an Wirth, Munich, June 7, 1860.
113 Fellner, *loc. cit.*, 90.
114 Mathaeser, *Wimmer und Koenig Ludwig I*, 133, note 2.

Finally, Chaplain Mueller reprimanded Prior Augustine. As Mueller wrote to Abbot Wimmer on March 16, 1861, "I told him plainly what I thought, for that is beneath the dignity and decorum of a priest, and especially a Benedictine. . . If he does not understand from my letter how he has erred, I doubt his sincerity. Respect for him has been destroyed here. I will see how he answers. So it goes with youngsters, who always know better and can do better than experienced elders. Now he is stuck in debts, although he thinks he is about to pull off a particularly brainy coup. His apology is merely cheap."[115]

Prior Augustine sought to counter this criticism by explaining to the officials of the Ludwig-Missionsverein, who handled the King's largesse as well as the funds of the association, that as an independent prior it was his duty to seek support for his house and that he could expect nothing from Abbot Wimmer in the way of financial support. The Prior had first approached the Ludwig-Missionsverein by writing to Archbishop von Scherr of Munich, the ecclesiastical head of the society. He asked the Archbishop, who before his consecration had been Abbot of Metten, if he remembered Frater Franz, his novice of eight years ago, now Augustine, and then went on to describe his work in Kansas.[116] Two years later the Prior again wrote to the Archbishop, describing the progress made and the work accomplished with the King's donation. The Prior continued, mentioning that he received no financial aid from St. Vincent and complained that although he had twice asked aid of the Ludwig-Missionsverein, he had received nothing.[117] This was the letter about which Court Chaplain Mueller had complained so bitterly, and it did, indeed, create a small stir, because the Verein had sent 800 florins for St. Benedict's through Abbot Wimmer in 1858.[118]

The Ludwig-Missionsverein granted the Kansas Priory

[115] Fellner, loc. cit., 91.
[116] Wirth an von Scherr, Doniphan, Feb. 8, 1858. (LMV Leav II 1/2)
[117] Idem, Atchison, Feb. 7, 1860. (LMV Leav II 1/11)
[118] Zahlungsanweisung, June 16, 1858; Wimmer receipt, May 7, 1859. (LMV Leav II 1/4-6)

another 800 florins in 1860 and asked for explanations.[119] The Prior sent his thanks and said that Abbot Wimmer maintained there had been a misunderstanding but that he offered no explanation. The Prior added a few bitter words about people who deflected funds to sawmills and speculation.[120] Having been given an opportunity to complain, in a later letter the Prior added other causes of bitterness. He insisted that Abbot Wimmer had not given him travelling money for his trip to Kansas even though Bishop Miége said that he had sent money to Abbot Wimmer for that purpose. Furthermore, Father Fisch of Leavenworth had just returned from a visit to Munich and had congratulated the Prior on the successful mission of Father Henry Lemke, who was then in Germany collecting donations for the western missions, especially Kansas. The Prior stated coldly that he had never received anything from Father Henry.[121] That charge brought the inquiry around to Father Henry, who was asked by the officials of the Ludwig-Missionsverein to explain his mission and to give what testimony he could about the wandering donation of 1858.

The old missionary was pleased to help dispose of Prior Augustine, and Father Henry answered that, first, as the appropriation was approved in the summer of 1858 and St. Benedict's was not made an independent priory until autumn, Father Augustine had "as little right to dispose of it, as he had to get it without the foreknowledge and approval of the Abbot." Secondly, the Abbot had considered himself justified "because it was needed more in other places, and he had already advanced considerable sums from St. Vincent." And thirdly, Father Augustine need not have begged if he had followed Father Henry's plans.[122]

[119] Zahlungsanweisung, June 9, 1860. (LMV Leav II 1/12-13)
[120] Wirth an LMV, Atchison, Aug. 14, 1860. (LMV Leav II 1/14)
[121] Wirth an LMV, Atchison, Jan. 2, 1861 (LMV Leav II 1/17-18)
Lemke maintained he had collected $6000.—Lemke to Johnston, Vienna, Dec. 21, 1859. (ACHS)
[122] Lemke an LMV, Schwerin, Mar. 15, 1861. (LMV Leav II 1/16)

This exchange may have made the Ludwig-Missions-verein more receptive to voices other than Abbot Wimmer's, but obviously its most important result was bitterness between Abbot Wimmer and Prior Augustine. However, complete lack of sympathy between the two was well advanced on all fronts by this time. At any rate this dispute ended the attempt to have all funds channeled through Abbot Wimmer. The Ludwig-Missionsverein or the King generously made a grant to the Kansas Priory each year, except 1865, while Prior Augustine was in office. Between 1860 and 1868 the donations of the Ludwig-Missionsverein to St. Benedict's totaled about $2200.[123]

As long as Bishop Miége had hope that St. Benedict's College might develop a seminary, he backed it fully. Undoubtedly because of his influence the Lyons Society for the Propagation of the Faith made grants totaling about $1700 from 1860 to 1862, ordinarily through the Bishop, as the rules of the society provided. The Bishop himself was generous, not only paying conscientiously for the students he sent to Atchison but making donations totaling more than $800 from 1857 to 1863, every penny of it as precious as the widow's mite.[124]

In spite of this outside aid, income never quite caught up with expenses at St. Benedict's. Prior Augustine stated that his Priory and College building in Atchison had cost $16,000. The community's annual income failed to reach $5000 before 1863, and after that the records are so scanty that one can only suppose that the situation had not improved.

The Abbot and the Prior

The recriminations aired in the offices of the Ludwig-Missionsverein were simply one aspect of the normal air of distrust between Abbot Wimmer and Prior Augustine. Abbot Wimmer was convinced that the Prior was en-

---

[123] (LMV Leav II 1/14-41a, *passim.*)
[124] Cashbook, *passim.*

gaged in a conspiracy that would wreck the American Cassinese Congregation. Writing to Abbot Pescetelli, his Roman agent, the Abbot said that he had heard that the Prior had asked the Holy See for permission to establish his own novitiate and seminary. The Statutes of the Bavarian Congregation, which were to be followed by the American foundation in so far as was practical, provided for a common novitiate and seminary for the congregation. The Prior's excuse was that his monastery was poor and could not afford to pay twenty dollars to send a novice to Pennsylvania. Abbot Wimmer argued that paying travel expenses was cheaper than taking men from other work to be master of novices and seminary faculty. Furthermore, the Prior had not the men and facilities for a proper novitiate and seminary. Abbot Wimmer pleaded with eloquence that the only hope for unity and proper religious development in a new congregation was through insistence on training the monks in a common novitiate and common seminary. Therefore he asked, that Prior Augustine be confirmed in his office for another three-year term, with a formal mandate attached to the appointment, namely, that the independent priors must send their clerical candidates to the common novitiate and seminary at St. Vincent under pain of deposition from office.[125]

Abbot Wimmer attributed Prior Augustine's desire for a local novitiate to overweening ambition. Speaking of the opposition and defections from which he himself had suffered in 1860, he accused the Prior of trying to wreck the Abbot's reputation in St. Vincent.[126] Prior Augustine had intended, according to the Abbot, to have himself elected abbot of St. Vincent. Disappointed in that plan, the Prior asked to have his vows transferred to the Kansas foundation, which the Abbot permitted, probably with some relief. Now the Prior was straining every nerve to have enough chapter members so that he could be-

---

[125] Wimmer ad Pescetelli, St. Vincent, May 12, 1861. (SPexM)
[126] *Idem*, Feb. 12, 1861. (SPexM)

72

come an abbot in Kansas. For that reason he wanted his own novitiate. For the same reason, Abbot Wimmer insisted, the Prior was always asking for more priests, not because the need was so great but to satisfy his ambition. The Abbot told his Roman agent that the creation of another abbey would not displease him, but Prior Augustine was only thirty-two. Abbot Gregor von Scherr of Metten, now archbishop of Munich, had dismissed Wirth from the novitiate, and out of pity Abbot Wimmer had brought him to America in 1851. The Abbot admitted that Prior Augustine had done good work, but his excessive ambition and impatience made Wimmer doubt his fitness to be an abbot.[127] Abbot Wimmer was deeply troubled and in August, 1861, again wrote to Abbot Pescetelli, reminding him that independent priors must be kept subject to the Congregation. Prior Augustine, he again insisted, was ready to wreck the Congregation in order to become an abbot more quickly.[128]

Meanwhile Prior Augustine had, in fact, opened his own novitiate. Abbot Wimmer finally investigated the matter, apparently not on account of the Prior's known intentions but under the impulsion of prophecy. There was at St. Vincent at that time a cleric named Paul Keck, who, evidently inspired by recent events at Lourdes, had set himself up as a visionary. He seems to have been a fairly clever lad, and he played on Abbot Wimmer's fears and troubles like harp strings. He was later exposed, but in 1861 his influence was undimmed, and he had visions that the Prior in Kansas was up to no good.[129] As Abbot Wimmer wrote to Abbot Pescetelli: "Frater Paul, the prophet, often warned in visions, urged that I should send

[127] *Idem*, May 12, 1861. (SPexM)

[128] *Idem*, Aug. 3, 1861. (SPexM)

[129] The community at St. Vincent was divided on the issue, and those who had faith in Keck, among whom were Wendelin Mayer, the master of novices, and Othmar Wirtz, forced the case to Rome where the Holy Office pronounced against Keck's visions and revelations, Aug. 16, 1865.—Sheet numbered 503 in Pescetelli letter file. (SPexM)

Louis Mary Fink, later bishop of Leavenworth, and at that time prior in Chicago, was one of Keck's admirers and tried to have him ordained in Chicago.—Wimmer ad Pescetelli, St. Vincent, Dec. 21, 1862. (SPexM)

on visitation to Kansas, Father Wendelin [Mayer], the
master of novices, with Father Louis [Fink], whom I had
made the first prior in Chicago, to turn Father Augustine
from evil counsel. . . He had already instituted a novitiate
and admitted five novices to simple vows. Agreeing with
this advice, I sent the above-named Fathers to Kansas as
regular visitators, and they were so successful that Father
Prior Wirth surrendered completely, dissolved his novitiate, and ordered everything in the priory according to
the Rule and the Sacred Canons. . . There was hardly the
shadow of regular life in the house; no choir, no silence,
no clausura, and no spiritual exercises. Three of the
pseudo-professed promptly left the Order; one came to
St. Vincent to make his novitiate." The Abbot went on
to say that the Prior had retracted his calumnies and re-
pented. "You can easily understand what a relief this is
to me. It is a great triumph for our policies. I have
freely forgiven all. . . The opposition is now without a
head."[130]

Abbot Wimmer had reason to rejoice but not just yet.
Prior Augustine, after his humiliation in May, had asked
Father Edward Hipelius, then in England for further
study, to secure for him copies of Roman decrees that
might be useful, particularly on the matter of receiving
novices.[131] Apparently nothing useful to the Prior on the
matter of novitiates was found, but at the General Chapter held at St. Vincent, September 15-18, 1862, he introduced a letter from Father Hipelius maintaining that
according to a Papal Decree of May 7, 1859, not only
solemnly-professed members but also those in simple vows
had a right to vote in the election of an abbot. This led

[130] Wimmer ad Pescetelli, St. Vincent, May 30, 1862. (SPexM)
    On his return from Europe in 1880 Abbot Innocent stopped at St. Vincent,
gathered data from Abbot Wimmer and others concerning the early days at
St. Benedict's, and then evidently made this entry in his memorandum book
after Oct. 25, 1880: "John Meurs ordained in Quat. Temp. before Easter in
1862 with Fabre [Favre] . . these two were the first who wore singulum and
capuch. Novices were Wattron, Bernard, McCarthy, and Aloysius Donahue,
and John Meurs."
    Abbot Innocent was of the opinion that this novitiate question "was settled
against all rules."—Wolf to Edelbrock, Atchison, Apr. 4, 1884. (SJA)
    [131] Hipelius ad Pescetelli, Hereford, June 3, 1862. (SPexM)

74

Abbot
Boniface
Wimmer
at the
Vatican
Council
1870

Prior Augustine Wirth
in the 1860's

Father
Henry
Lemke
(probably
1880's)

Father Casimir Seitz

Front view of
St. Benedict's Church
in the 1870's

Rear view of
St. Benedict's Church
and the Priory
in the 1870's

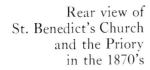

Announce-
ment of St.
Benedict's
College
in the
Atchison
City
Directory
1859

St. Joseph's Convent
Second and Division
home of the
Benedictine Sisters
in the 1870's

Letterhead of
St. Benedict's College
about 1864

Atchison about 1869

Looking west on Commercial Street with the corner of Third Street in the foreground. *Photo courtesy of the Kansas State Historical Society.*

Prior
Giles Christoph

Prior
Oswald
Moosmueller

Prior
Louis M. Fink
in 1868

Abbot Innocent Wolf

in the
first year
of his
administra-
tion

Father Emmanuel Hartig
in the 1860's

Father Thomas Bartl in 1881

Father Timothy Luber in the 1860's
shortly before his ordination (1863/1865)

Father Peter Kassens

Father Pirmin Koumly

Father Boniface Verheyen
in the 1870's (This photo
was taken during one of his
western trips in a U.P.R.R.
Photograph Car)

Brother Joseph
von Bragel

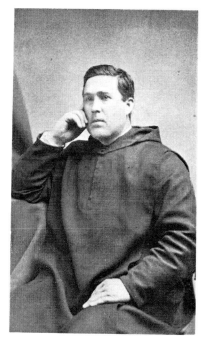

Father Eugene Bode
in 1869 (photo taken
when he was a cleric
at St. Vincent)

Father
Placidus
McKeever

Father Adolph Wesseling
in 1882

Father Winfried Schmidt

Father Adalbert Mueller

Father Ambrose
Huebner in 1879

Father John Stader

Brother Andrew Allermann

to a heated argument in the chapter, and Abbot Wimmer was forced to postpone the abbatial election for St. Vincent that he had intended to hold while most of his monks were present. The insurgents' position proved untenable, but they obviously felt that there was considerable opposition to the Abbot among the younger men. This time Abbot Wimmer was convinced that they were trying to elect Father Alphonse Heimler, who was angry, said the Abbot, because he had not been appointed rector of St. Vincent College and so had joined Prior Augustine in Kansas and asked to transfer his vows there.[132] Abbot Wimmer scored a technical victory when he had the General Chapter elect Father Wendelin Mayer the master of novices of the Congregation.[133]

Prior Augustine was subdued momentarily. He wrote to the Ludwig-Missionsverein: "When I wrote my last report, I believed that I could report to you this year from another place. My wish had been to wander farther west to preach the Word of God to the poor and abandoned Catholics." He had hoped that the General Chapter would allow him to go in peace, he said, but he had been sent back to Kansas as prior for another three years.[134] However, he was already planning a school for girls. He had many promises of help, and in January, 1863, he had

[132] Wimmer ad Pescetelli, St. Vincent, Oct. 1, 1862. (SPexM)
   Abbot Wimmer's account of Prior Augustine's intentions may be exaggerated. The Abbot tended to view most criticism as conspiracy.
   Wimmer was appointed abbot by the Holy See for a three-year term in 1855. He was elected abbot in 1858, but Rome disallowed the election, appointing him for another three-year term, later extended indefinitely. In 1866 he was finally appointed abbot and president of the Congregation for life. Abbot Wimmer always had the support of a good majority of his monks. The Holy See's refusal to confirm the election of 1858 no doubt indicated primarily that Rome was not fully convinced of the new foundation's permanence. Although not absent in 1858, more dangerous implications for the future of the Order in the United States had become a major factor by 1865. At that time several influences in Rome opposed the principle of abbots being elected for life. A notable portion of Abbot Wimmer's correspondence with Abbot Pescetelli is devoted to this question. See also Mathaeser, *Wimmer und Koenig Ludwig I*, 105 f., 155 note 5, 166, 172, 174.
[133] Records of General Chapters. (SVA)
   This chapter legislated also that all should use the name Mary, hence, Louis Mary Fink, O.S.B.
[134] Wirth an LMV, Atchison, Dec. 3, 1862. (LMV Leav II 1/26-27)

Father Smarius, S.J., who preached a mission in St. Benedict's Church in Atchison, pledge all the fathers of families to give ten or twenty dollars for the convent. Prior Augustine borrowed the rest of the needed funds, and work on the building, diagonally across the street from the church, was begun in the spring. Father Thomas Bartl was sent to St. Cloud, Minnesota, for the seven Sisters, who arrived on November 11, 1863. On December 1 they opened their school, and Mount St. Scholastica Academy was born.[135] The convent, dedicated to St. Joseph, was completed but was unfurnished, and for some time Mother Evangelista Kremmeter and her little community suffered from extreme poverty which Prior Augustine could do little to alleviate.[136]

In 1864 Abbot Wimmer visited Kansas for the first time since 1859. Living in the monastic community at Atchison were only Prior Augustine, Father Thomas Bartl, who was visiting the surrounding missions much of the time, two clerics, and three Brothers. The Prior, the clerics, and one lay teacher operated the school.[137] The Abbot visitator observed that the essentials were well observed, although since there were rarely four professed members at home, the Divine Office was not recited in common. He promised to send another priest if the Prior would have Office chanted in choir. The Abbot considered the temporalities of the Priory very satisfactory. St. Benedict's College had twenty boarders and thirty day students at the time, and the buildings were adequate for even a larger school. The frame church accommodated a parish of 124 families. Father Thomas Bartl's missions were poor and scattered, and his missionary work was consequently most difficult. The Priory's annual income from pastoral and missionary work was about $800. The community owned 640 very fertile acres, but these were fifteen miles away, and the Abbot advised the Prior

<hr>

135 *Idem*, Jan. 6, 1864. (LMV Leav II 1/29)
136 Sister M. Regina Baska, *The Benedictine Congregation of St. Scholastica* (Washington, 1935), 87.
137 Wimmer ad Pescetelli, Atchison, Apr. 30, 1864. (SPexM)

to sell them and secure land nearer the Priory. Outstanding debts at the time amounted to $3330, but since the Prior had $1400 on hand, the net debt was only $1930.[138] Abbot Wimmer had always been more concerned with keeping Augustine Wirth out of St. Vincent than with making a success of the Kansas venture. After this visitation the Abbot seems to have seriously considered for the first time the possibility of developing the Atchison priory into an abbey. He wrote King Ludwig that he hoped to do this within three years. The buildings were adequate, but the community was still too small.[139]

The Church and the Crisis

Prior Augustine's next move toward a mitre was to build an impressive church. He had added thirty feet to the old frame church in the autumn of 1860, but the congregation was growing large enough to erect a permanent church.[140] However, a parish church was not what the Prior had in mind. His intention was to have an abbey church ready when he became an abbot. That the plans of the church provided no space for a monastic choir merely testified to the Prior's limited notions of monasticism. The main goal was that the church should be as large and impressive as his optimistic hopes of financial aid dared to make it.[141]

The year 1865 had been the most prosperous in Atchison's history to that date. It was wartime prosperity, western style, that brought hundreds of wagon trains to move ten thousand tons of goods from Atchison's levees and warehouses to the military posts and to the exciting

---

[138] Record of Visitation, Apr. 29, 1864.
Father Timothy Luber considered this statement of conditions inaccurate. (infra)
[139] Wimmer an Ludwig I, Apr. 21, 1865, in Mathaeser, *Wimmer und Koenig Ludwig I,* 168.
[140] Wirth an LMV, Atchison, Jan. 2, 1861. (LMV Leav II 1/17-18)
A correspondent writing of confirmation at Atchison says it was held at Sts. Peter and Paul's Church, May 25, 1864.—*Wahrheitsfreund,* June 15, 1864.
[141] See the announcements that he submitted to the LMV. (LMV Leav II 1/36-37)

new gold diggings in the West. It was also frontier prosperity, speculative and impermanent. But frontier town boosters were always urging the construction of impressive landmarks to attract the tremendous immigration expected next spring and for the improvement of land values. Many influential men in town no doubt urged Prior Augustine to build big. And he was by no means the only clergyman who had built a little church, who was then forced to enlarge it almost immediately, and who finally decided to build on a relatively grand scale for the population growth that was bound to come next year, especially since money had become so plentiful. Bishop Miége went through the same experience in Leavenworth.

Before turning any ground Prior Augustine announced the inauguration of a Foundation Mass to be offered daily for one hundred years for the benefactors of St. Benedict's. Fathers Thomas Bartl and Pirmin Koumly were sent East to collect for the new church.[142] Prior Augustine next decided to hire workers and to manufacture his own brick. He bought a patent brick-making machine, but his brick turned out to be too soft for church building.[143] The failure of this experiment forced him to buy brick from local yards, but to salvage his investment he built houses on the lots he had bought at tax sales.[144]

Ready to begin construction, he closed the school a month early, sending the students home at the end of May, but excavation for the foundations did not start until July.[145] The cornerstone was laid August 26, 1866. Bishop Miége could not attend on account of illness, and so the stone was laid by the preacher for the occasion,

[142] Miége testimonial for Bartl, Leavenworth, Jan. 2, 1866, endorsed by Bishop Young, of Erie, Pa., Jan. 13, 1866. Koumly's traveling expenses are in "Expenses on the new church." A list of pledges called "Contributions towards the new church," 1866, totals more than $7500, but only a small fraction are marked paid.
[143] *Champion*, Apr. 19; May 4, 1866.
[144] Wirth to Bartl, St. Paul, July 29, 1868.
  According to Gerard Heinz, O.S.B., *St. Benedict's Parish* (1908), these houses were at 302 and 305 Division St., 601 South Fifth St., and a storebuilding at 826 North Second St.
[145] *Champion*, July 1, 1866.

the Rt. Rev. John Hennessey, bishop-elect of Dubuque, Iowa, and lately a pastor in St. Joseph, Missouri. Bishop-elect Hennessey's forthright sermon on the Church would not, said the Editor of the *Champion*, "be accepted as correct by any of his Protestant hearers," and Rev. W. K. Marshall announced that he would answer it in the M. E. Church.[146]

Almost a year elapsed before workmen began laying brick.[147] The delay could have been due to the difficulty of raising funds, or it might have been the result of changing the plans. The original design for the church was prepared by W. Angelo Powell (sometimes called Michael Angelo Powell), of St. Joseph, Missouri. The dimensions were about 150 by 50 feet. The photograph of the model reveals an ugly travesty of Gothic.[148] In 1867 the plans were changed. Mr. Powell received his last payment in July, and in August Mr. Francis Himpler was the new architect.[149] The new plans were for a church of moderately severe romanesque lines, reminiscent of Rhenish, and about ten feet larger in each ground dimension (162 by 60) than the first plan. According to tradition the change in plan resulted from a change in purpose, namely, from building a parish church to building an abbey church. But Prior Augustine might have belatedly recognized bad architecture when he saw it.

At the beginning of 1868 the walls were not yet complete, and the church had already cost a great deal not only in money but in other values. Trenches for the foundation had been dug round the old frame church in 1866, but as work progressed in 1867 the old church was torn down. The College dormitory was then used as a chapel for the parish, and so the College was closed for the year 1867-68.[150] By June, 1868, the building had already cost $35,000, and the Prior's hopes of paying for it by collections throughout the country had come to

[146] Aug. 28, 1866.
[147] *Champion*, July 6, 1867.
[148] *Ibid.*, June 4, 1867.
[149] "Expenses on the new church."
[150] Wirth an LMV, Atchison, Jan. 21, 1868. (LMV Leav II 1/39-40)

thorough disappointment. The closed College could produce no income. The small salaries of the missionaries defrayed the ordinary operating costs of the monastery, and when the salaries proved insufficient, $1200 was borrowed from the building fund.[151] Prior Augustine and St. Benedict's were caught in the post-war deflation.

Meanwhile, monastic affairs had been going from bad to worse. As Prior Augustine's problems increased, the weaker points in his character came to the fore. He had never had much to offer as a spiritual leader. As the monks then present told Abbot Innocent years later: "There was no sign of a community life, except perhaps the common table. [The Prior] did not wear the habit, but a cassock like secular priests, so that the Bishop. . . made remarks about it."[152] As his position became more hopeless, he wrangled increasingly with his confreres,[153] and he began seeking escape in the bottle. Abbot Wimmer visited Kansas and Nebraska in 1867, but no report of what he found survives, and he made no changes.[154]

Prior Augustine, accompanied by his outspoken critic, Father Timothy Luber, attended the General Chapter held at St. Vincent, August 17-19, 1867. Two portions of the chapter's legislation were intended to affect Prior Augustine directly. The chapter voted that the five clerics in Atchison should study their philosophy and theology in St. Vincent Abbey and that real-estate deeds should be registered in the names of the respective religious corporations.[155] St. Benedict's had never been incorporated, and Prior Augustine still held its property in his own name. This situation particularly worried Abbot Wimmer.[156] The Prior had forgotten to bring a financial statement on his Priory, but he sat down and easily drew

---

[151] Wirth to Bartl, St. Paul, July 29, 1868.
[152] Wolf to Abbot Primate, Atchison, Mar. 4, 1899. (SA)
[153] Wirth an Hartig, Atchison, Jan. 19, 1867; Br. Lucas an Bartl, Butler, Oct. 15, 1867.
[154] Wimmer an Lang, St. Vincent, Aug. 28, 1867. (AM)
[155] Records of General Chapters. (SVA)
    This chapter voted also that newly-professed members must promise to wear beards.
[156] Wimmer ad Pescetelli, St. Vincent, Mar. 9, 1860. (SPexM)

up an "Approximate account of St. Benedict's," which admitted debts totalling only $6710 on the Priory and $4000 on the new Sisters' convent.[157] The official records of the General Chapter give no hint of the vigorous discussion regarding the state of affairs in Atchison. Father Timothy complained later that the General Chapter had given no credence to his complaints,[158] but Abbot Wimmer said that the Prior had again promised amendment.[159]

And so conditions remained unchanged at St. Benedict's until the middle of May, 1868. As Abbot Innocent, who knew the story from the participants, explained later, the complaints of the younger men to Abbot Wimmer "were not heeded, were not believed. At last, at the suggestion of the Bishop, two of the Fathers [Luber and Koumly] left for Chicago, and from the Priory there wrote the R. Rev. President that they [had] left Atchison and that they would not return until something were done to prevent great scandal."[160] The chief complaints were regarding the Prior's chronic drunkenness, his mistreatment of his confreres, the complete absence of any organized spiritual life, and the grave mishandling of material affairs.[161] Abbot Innocent continues the story with information not now, if ever, in the documents: "They were scolded severely for appealing to the Bishop, and were commanded to return; [they were told that] they were fugitives and apostates. They answered that they did not appeal to the Bishop, but the Bishop had advised them to act, and if the appeal to the Rt. Rev. President would not be heeded, they would appeal directly to Rome. Then the President came out taking along the Rt. Rev. Abbot of St. John's Abbey and also the Prior of Chicago. They found matters in such a condition that Father Augustine was asked to resign."[162]

Abbot Wimmer had written to Prior Augustine on

157 Records of General Chapters. (SVA)
158 Luber and Koumly to Wimmer, [Chicago, May, 1868]. (SVA)
159 Wimmer ad Pescetelli, St. Vincent, Mar. 9, 1869. (SPexM)
160 Wolf to Abbot Primate, Atchison, Mar. 4, 1899. (SA)
161 Luber and Koumly to Wimmer, [Chicago, May, 1868]. (SVA)
162 Wolf to Abbot Primate, Atchison, Mar. 4, 1899. (SA)

May 21, 1868, and the Prior had answered that he was ready to resign and sign over the property. Nevertheless, he insisted that Fathers Pirmin Koumly and Timothy Luber were the "impeachers and managers" of a conspiracy, that they had given great scandal and had been guilty of grave disobedience, and so he insisted that they be taken away from Atchison. He maintained that he had "offered to leave on the 15th if they would come back. I sent a letter after them to the ferry." The Prior added that he wished to go to Rome.[163] In Chicago Abbot Wimmer met Abbot Rupert Seidenbusch, of St. John's Abbey, and they appointed Father Louis Mary Fink, then prior of St. Joseph's Church in that city, the new prior in Kansas. The three arrived in Atchison on June 10, called in a lawyer, and promptly set to work and formed a corporation: St. Benedict's College in Atchison, Kansas. The charter was received on June 15, the property was transferred from Prior Augustine's name to the corporation, and on June 18 all formalities were concluded.

The protocol listed as assets, other than the College property, $3500 which had been loaned to Michael Doyle, twelve lots and five houses worth $1650, a list of pledges amounting to $6000, and the Sisters' convent worth $8000 — a total of $19,150, but the pledges at least were a doubtful asset. The Sisters' convent and the debt upon it were soon transferred to the Sisters. The liabilities were stated to be $20,402. Regarding the church with its walls raised only to the height of the side aisles, the protocol states that the monks all agreed that the new church should be finished and that they accepted the offer of Brown and Bier, the contractors, to complete the church and to take a mortgage at twelve per cent.[164] Prior Fink later insisted that the decision to complete the church and to accept Brown and Bier's terms was Abbot Wimmer's alone.[165] However, there was apparently no thought of abandoning the Kansas venture. In spite of the troubles

---

[163] Wirth to Wimmer, Atchison, May 28, 1868. (SVA)
[164] "Protocollum de resignatione V. R. Augustinus Wirth," June 18, 1868.
[165] Fink to Wolf, Kansas City, Apr. 24, 1902.

at the Priory the missionary monks were caring for constantly increasing numbers of Catholic settlers. The school had been promising and could be made a success. Finally, the investment already made and particularly the debt could not be abandoned lightly.

Abbot Wimmer reported to his Roman agent, Abbot Pescetelli, that by a promise of leniency he had persuaded Prior Augustine to resign. He had feared that the Prior might apostatize and make off with any available funds. The Abbot hoped that the Roman authorities would be satisfied with Abbot Pescetelli's assurance that the removal had been necessary and that they would make no further inquiries.[166] Father Augustine was permitted to take an unspecified sum of money and accept a mission under a bishop in Minnesota.[167]

St. Benedict's was to struggle long in the shadow of those first years. Looking back, it becomes evident that Abbot Wimmer had not welcomed Bishop Miége's invitation to send monks to Kansas but had permitted Father Augustine to accept it. Kansas was not the Abbot's project, and his interest was in the possibilities of expansion to California, to Texas, to Canada, but especially to Minnesota, where he wisely concentrated his resources of men and money to ensure success. Those involved refer to the Abbot's outspoken unfriendly attitude to the Kansas foundation.

No less responsible, of course, was Prior Augustine. He was a reasonably able and hard working man. Bishop Miége at first praised his ability to get things done. To the people of Atchison he was an able businessman and a

[166] Wimmer ad Pescetelli, St. Vincent, Mar. 9, 1869. (SPexM)
[167] Wimmer an Wolf, St. Vincent, July 29, 1877.
Father Augustine remained technically a Benedictine for the rest of his life. He transferred his vows to St. Mary's Abbey, Newark, N.J., May 15, 1887, but he carefully avoided living in any abbey or making any but the slightest gestures towards his vow of obedience. He made a comfortable sum by translating classic sermons. Father Augustine died Dec. 20, 1901, in Springfield, Minn., and his relatives claimed his estate without success. The case was carried to the Supreme Court of the United States and is fundamental in establishing recognition of religious vows under the laws of the United States.

town booster.[168] There is no evidence that he had any of the spiritual qualities of a religious superior. He could be ridiculously vain; he wrote from Pennsylvania that his parishioners worried every time he threatened to return to the West.[169] He was jealous, and he was particularly bitter towards Prior Louis Fink.[170] Even under more favorable circumstances he could hardly have formed a sound religious community.

It must be admitted that the Prior worked under grave handicaps. A circumstance that has so far not been stressed, but which was long a determining factor in the slow growth of St. Benedict's, was the small percentage of Catholics in Kansas. The percentage has always been below the national average. In 1864 Father Defouri estimated, certainly with great optimism, that there were perhaps fifteen or twenty thousand Catholics in the State.[171] This number would have been ten or twelve per cent. More important was the attitude both of the other ninety per cent and of the press to the Catholics, who were usually immigrants. In the newspapers of the time practically all friendly references to Catholics were patronizing. An editor did not dare express approval of a new Catholic church without hastening to assure his readers that such approval implied no endorsement of the religion. The Editor of the *Free Press* prefaced his remarks on the new St. Benedict's Church with the following: "However wide our dissent from the peculiar ecclesiastical and theological views of our Catholic friends, or however much we may think these views fall short of finding a sympathetic response in the ears and consciences of the American people. . ."[172] Influential Sol Miller of the White Cloud *Kansas Chief* was a flatly outspoken Nativist. His atti-

[168] *Champion*, Jan. 3, 1863.
[169] Wirth to Edelbrock, Greensburg, Feb. 21, 1876. (SJA)
[170] Wirth to Bartl, Marystown, Apr. 11, 1870.
    "It took me by surprise to learn that F. Aug. Wirth was the author of the 'anti-Louis' . . "—Hipelius to Edelbrock, St. Mary's, Pa., May 20, 1870. (SJA)
[171] *Kansas Annual Register*, 1864, 92.
[172] June 1, 1868.

tude to the sacrifices made by Catholic immigrants to build churches was that of giving the devil his due: "Somehow, the Catholics, bad as they are, are more devoted to their cause than the Protestant denominations among us. The great trouble with the latter seems to be a stronger disposition to speculate and fill their purses, than to advance the cause they pretend to advocate."[173]

Another factor contributing to the crisis in Kansas was the anomalous condition of the independent priories. Abbot Wimmer's ideas on the subject had many practical advantages, but canon law made no provision for the exact arrangement he had in mind. The General Chapter of 1858 voted the priories independent so that the priors and priories could have their own administrations and chapters as well as accept novices and admit candidates to profession according to the Holy Rule and the statutes of the Congregation. According to the Bavarian statutes then in force, if that article of the statutes was considered practicable, novices were to be sent to St. Vincent. Priests sent to the priories could transfer their vows, but they need not do so.[174]

Abbot Wimmer later wrote that his reasons for having the priories made independent were distance for travel and communication as well as more efficient administration by a superior on the local scene. He had been disappointed in his hopes, however, because the priors lacked either sufficient authority or the ability to rule successfully. Consequently, the priors or their subjects frequently appealed to the Abbot.[175] This semi-independence of a priory, as favored by Abbot Wimmer, left the Abbot free to act in case of trouble, but it also severely weakened the prior's authority. Under those conditions, community spirit was practically impossible, and in those rare souls in which it did appear, it seems almost a miracle. It was utterly impractical to pretend that a weak, new

---

173 Dec. 2, 1858.
174 Records of General Chapters. (SVA)
175 Wimmer ad Pescetelli, [Sept. 14, 1875]. (SPexM)

community could be declared financially independent by fiat. Actually, this policy was applied strictly only to St. Benedict's during Prior Augustine's term of office. In the last analysis perhaps the worst result of this policy was that the denial of financial responsibility on the part of the motherhouse tended, in practice, to become a denial of any responsibility. Only when conditions had become almost hopelessly bad did Abbot Wimmer suddenly seem to realize that no matter what he had made the General Chapter say, the Church would hold him responsible for what his Benedictines did in Kansas.

Father Boniface Verheyen, who had lived through these difficulties, gave a good summary of what had been wrong in the Kansas priory. Father Leo Haid had written: "I don't see that St. V. is doing anything to prevent [Kansas] from getting on." Father Boniface answered: "I wish I could feel, or make myself believe, that St. V. *never* did anything to prevent Kansas from getting on. . . At the bottom of the present and past misfortunes of Kansas is this — that a man was sent to K. to establish and take charge of a branch house, who should have been kept at home, yet who was let go, and do as he pleased, because at home nothing could be done with him, and hence they were glad of his riddance. . . The course of such a person could have been foreseen without much claim to mental acumen." Father Boniface goes on to say that conditions in Kansas were kept out of the General Chapter by responsible authority; that the visitators never went to the bottom of things, but were even blindfolded; that the Kansas priory was not helped as it should have been; and concludes that the superior is accountable for the deeds of his authorized representatives.[176] Father Boniface's complaint was of the past. In the future aid in men and money from St. Vincent was to prove essential to the survival of St. Benedict's.

[176] Verheyen to Leo Haid, draft marked "Mailed June 6, 1875."

Battling Bankruptcy

Prior Louis Mary Fink

The problems of St. Benedict's Priory were solved only slowly. In the seven years following the crisis of 1868
the community had three priors, two of whom tussled with
the problem of the debt and then resigned in desperation.
The debt grew larger for six successive years. Men still
came and went. But slowly the community grew.

When Prior Louis Mary Fink[1] took over the administration of the Priory on June 18, 1868, four priests and
five clerics formed the community. At the old St. Benedict's Colony in Doniphan County, Father Thomas Bartl
had just become the first resident pastor since Father
Lemke's time. Father Pirmin Koumly had been sent,
temporarily, to assist Father Emmanuel Hartig at Nebraska City. Father Timothy Luber was made rector of
the College as soon as it was reopened in 1868. The
clerics — Peter Kassens, Boniface Verheyen, Placidus
McKeever, Eugene Bode, and Casimir (later Alban)
Rudroff — had returned from St. Vincent to help staff
the school. The first three were ordained in 1869, Rudroff in 1871, and Bode in 1873.[2]

Prior Louis' first task was to get the church under roof

---

[1] Right Reverend Louis Mary (Michael) Fink, O.S.B., was born in Trif-
tersberg, Bavaria, July 12, 1834, professed Jan. 6, 1854, was ordained May
28, 1857, consecrated as Bishop Miége's coadjutor (*Epis. Eucarpiensis*) June
11, 1871, was named the first bishop of the Diocese of Leavenworth May
22, 1877, and died Mar. 17, 1904.—*Necrologium*, No. 318.

[2] Registrum Monachorum. At this time St. Vincent had fifty-five priests
and eleven clerics, and St. John's had thirteen priests and two clerics.—Wimmer
ad Pescetelli, St. Vincent, Feb. 28, 1868. (SPexM)

and reopen the College. This was accomplished by the autumn of 1868. A rough plank floor was installed, doors and windows were provided with the same rough closure, and the church was dedicated on Trinity Sunday, May 23, 1869, by Bishop Miége. Father Bede O'Connor, a member of the Benedictine community at St. Meinrad's and vicar-general of the Diocese of Vincennes, preached the sermon.[3]

Once the decision had been made to complete the church and reopen the College, it was necessary to provide better facilities and more room for the students if the College was to grow. So the community increased the debt still further by spending $6500 to buy additional land. This new property enlarged the campus to a total of about thirty acres and extended it east to the Missouri River.[4] This campus proved adequate until the end of the century. On the other hand, to cut down expenses, Prior Louis undertook serious farming at Bendena. Before his time the community had neither the men nor the means to develop the farm, but now he had several Brother candidates and began the work.[5]

The Prior's main problem was, of course, the debt. When he took charge, the community had already borrowed $16,000, most of it at an interest rate of twelve per cent, the rest at ten per cent. Outstanding bills brought the total debt to $20,000. By the end of 1868 the addition to the College campus and the rough completion of the church had brought the total debt to $44,000.[6] Interest charges were more than $4000 a year, whereas in 1869, for example, the gross income of the College and the missions was only about $7500. This situation was typical for years to come and, unless some very generous donations were forthcoming, was obviously hopeless. Prior Augustine had begun his church in a period of wartime prosperity when building costs particularly were

[3] *Champion*, May 15, 1869; *Catholic Telegraph*, June 9, 1869.
[4] Contract of sale with Abell and Stringfellow, July 1, 1869.
[5] Fink an LMV, Atchison, Jan. 23, 1870. (LMV Leav II 1/46)
[6] Ledger, 591.

very high, but on the other hand wheat, for example, was worth almost two dollars a bushel even in Atchison. By the end of the decade, when St. Benedict's was trying to pay the bill, wheat was worth less than a dollar. The deflation following the Civil War in effect doubled the size of the community's debt.

Abbot Wimmer, of course, knew what was needed and, as he wrote to Abbot Pescetelli, even though it was at some material and personal cost, he was always "willing to help our new institutes according to the Statutes, so that *esprit de corps* may be nourished and strengthened."[7] Referred to the past this statement was ironic, but Abbot Wimmer was to make it true in the future. He said that he had given Prior Louis about $500 when he first assumed office in Atchison in 1868, and thereafter the Abbot helped to find loans at reasonable interest.[8] At the same time he asked the Ludwig-Missionsverein to aid Prior Louis with generous donations, omitting for the time being their usual donations to St. Vincent and St. John's "because he needs it most and uses it well. He is also a very zealous priest and missionary, and will, if I live, soon be an abbot."[9] The Verein responded generously with gifts totalling $3200 from 1869 to 1871.

For a few years donations to the Foundation Mass inaugurated by Prior Augustine Wirth were an important source of income, but the success of this program depended on publicity, and the idea was criticized in some circles. In any case, although donations totalled almost $10,000 between 1868 and 1870, they declined rapidly toward the vanishing point for a while. Another source of a few hundred dollars was Prior Augustine's houses and lots, most of which were sold in 1869.

St. Benedict's Priory nevertheless continued to slide towards bankruptcy. The end of 1870 brought another crisis. Prior Louis became ill, went to Chicago, and sent

[7] Wimmer ad Pescetelli, St. Vincent, Mar. 9, 1869. (SPexM)
[8] Wimmer an LMV, St. Vincent, Mar. 5, 1869. (LMV Leav II 1/44) Wimmer ad Pescetelli, St. Vincent, Mar. 9, 1869. (SPexM)
[9] Wimmer an LMV, St. Vincent, Mar. 5, 1869. (LMV Leav II 1/44)

his resignation to Abbot Wimmer. The community in Kansas asked the Abbot not to accept the resignation.[10] This peculiar situation was resolved when the Holy See on March 1, 1871, named Prior Louis Mary Fink to the titular See of Eucarpia and appointed him coadjutor to Bishop Miége.

Bishop Miége held Prior Louis in high regard. Before leaving to attend the Vatican Council in Rome, he appointed the Prior administrator of the Vicariate during his absence.[11] While in Rome Bishop Miége had asked to resign, but he received a coadjutor instead. On June 11, 1871, Bishop Fink was consecrated in St. Joseph's Church in Chicago, where he had been prior before coming to St. Benedict's. He was in such poor health at the time that Bishop Foley, his consecrator, remarked that the consecration was a waste of holy oil.[12] Bishop Miége wrote of Fink: "At last I have a coadjutor! He is a worthy man, fearing God and the devil, and serving the Good Master with all the generosity of a true son of St. Benedict. He is nearly six feet tall, with a beard a foot and a half long, but is as thin as a rail."[13]

Meanwhile, at a meeting of the directors of the St. Benedict's College corporation held in Chicago immediately after Bishop Fink's consecration, Father Timothy Luber was appointed temporary prior of St. Benedict's.[14] When the General Chapter met in October, the sad state of the Kansas Priory was naturally one of the topics considered. A report revealed that at the end of 1870 the material affairs of the Priory were in "a calamitous condition."[15] When Prior Louis had been appointed a bishop, Abbot Wimmer made a visitation of the Priory. The monks were still too few in number and too badly overworked to recite the Divine Office in common

10 Wolf Diary, Jan. 2–7, 1871.
11 Miége to Fink, Leavenworth, Sept. 8, 1869.
12 Anton Kuhls, *A Few Reminiscences of Forty Years in Wyandotte County, Kansas* (Lane Printing Co., 1904), 36.
13 Garin, *Miége*, 166.
14 Corporation Minutes, June 13, 1871.
15 Records of General Chapters. (SVA)

very often.[16] Prior Louis had been unable to meet the interest payments, and new loans were made to pay $3000 in interest that had been due January 1, 1871. Prior Boniface Krug, of Monte Cassino, formerly a member of St. Vincent Abbey, was collecting money in the United States for the restoration of the mother abbey. The troubled state of affairs in Italy prevented Monte Cassino from using the money at the time, and so Prior Krug was persuaded to lend $5000 to St. Benedict's at eight per cent. Abbot Wimmer commented that the conditions were rigorous but not evil, because the common interest rate in Kansas was ten per cent.[17] This loan, along with various sums from St. Vincent for urgent needs, made a total of $8975 for which St. Vincent Abbey was security, or, with interest, approximately $10,000.[18] As a further aid to St. Benedict's, Abbot Wimmer sent out Father Wendelin Meyer to give missions, with instructions that his financial receipts should be given to the Atchison Priory. At the time of the General Chapter about $1000 had been realized from this source. At the chapter St. Benedict's total debt was reported as $49,500. Of this total, $45,000 had been borrowed at an average interest of eleven and one-half per cent, and the balance of $4,500 had been borrowed without interest.[19] Abbot Wimmer hoped to borrow money at a cheaper rate of interest for Atchison, but he did not succeed.[20] The Chicago fire, which destroyed St. Joseph's Church, had presented Abbot Wimmer with another crisis that same year, but he decided that the problems of his Benedictines in Atchison had been the bigger headache.[21]

[16] Record of Visitation, May 26, 1871.
[17] Wimmer ad Pescetelli, St. Vincent, Aug. 7, 1871. (SPexM)
[18] Abbot Wimmer wrote that some complained of his generosity although he had not given but lent money to the Atchison Priory, but he goes on to say, "it is well understood that never, or hardly ever, can we recover it." —*Idem.* The $10,000 remained on the books until after Abbot Wimmer's death when an agreement was reached that the sum must be considered the usual grant or cost of making a new foundation.
[19] Records of General Chapters. (SVA)
[20] Wimmer an von Scherr, St. Vincent, Mar. 16, 1871. (AM)
[21] Wimmer ad Pescetelli, St. Vincent, Aug. 7, 1871. (SPexM)

Poverty-stricken St. Benedict's had been a stepping-stone to the episcopate for Prior Louis, but back in St. Vincent the Kansas Priory meant poverty, a hopeless debt, and possibly fever. Nevertheless, St. Benedict's needed a new prior, and, according to Abbot Wimmer, the monks in Kansas had asked that the Prior of St. Vincent, Very Reverend Giles Christoph, be appointed.[22] The diary of young Father Innocent Wolf, then a monk at St. Vincent, tells what happened:

July 11, [1871] Tuesd. . . After dinner the Prior came into the chapter room; the Abbot introduced him as Prior of Kansas. P. Prior protested, saying he had told the Abbot already, and he would reaffirm it, that he would not go to Kansas. The Abbot said: Well, if you do not want to go, I must command you under obedience. The Prior would not even go then, he said. Afterwards he gave the reason why he could refuse obedience in this case, viz., that he did not make the vow to be transferred from one place to another. The reasons why he did not like to go out were financial, personal, historical, and hygienical. We all . . . tried to persuade the Prior but he commenced to cry, and said we had easy talk. . .

July 18, Tuesd. . . P. Abbot had gone to the ridge, and told P. John to inform P. Prior to leave tomorrow for Kansas!!

July 22, Saturd. . . P. Prior has consented to go to Kansas, and will leave on the 15th of August with P. Urban [Bayer].

So Prior Giles Christoph came to Kansas. In view of St. Benedict's financial status, Abbot Wimmer felt that it would be wiser not to ask Rome to confirm the appointment so that Prior Giles would not be considered an independent prior.[23] Abbot Wimmer nevertheless thought that conditions in the Kansas Priory were showing signs

[22] Giles (Caspar) Christoph was born in Regensburg, Bavaria, Dec. 18, 1830, professed Jan. 6, 1853, ordained May 18, 1856, and died Mar. 6, 1887. —*Necrologium*, No. 138.
[23] Wimmer ad Pescetelli, St. Vincent, May 4, 1872. (SPexM) In the records of the General Chapter of 1871 references to Prior Giles as independent prior are deleted and the title, Administrator of the Priory in Atchison, was substituted.

of improvement, particularly because the college enrollment was growing.[24]

Furthermore, Prior Louis Fink's resignation had stimulated Abbot Wimmer to send more priests to St. Benedict's. When Prior Louis was in Chicago trying to resign, Bishop Miége had complained that only Father Pirmin Koumly was available to care for all the settlers north and northwest of Atchison. He pleaded with Abbot Wimmer; "For God's sake and for the sake of so many Catholics who are settled in that country, please send two fathers more at least. They are absolutely needed. . . I most earnestly beg of you to give me a helping hand at least for that portion which was always intended to be placed under the care of the fathers of St. Benedict."[25]

In the first months of 1871 Abbot Wimmer sent three priests to Kansas. Father Agatho Stuebinger served as assistant in the Atchison parish for a few months in 1871. Father Suitbert Demarteau was active as a missionary until 1875. Father Urban Bayer was sent to Kansas with the new Prior to teach in the College, particularly music, and exchanged places with Father Placidus Pilz.[26] Two years later Father Urban died at Seneca, Kansas, where he had gone to recuperate his health. His was the first death in the monastic community.[27] About this time also a secular priest, a Father Majerus, lived in the community, taught mathematics and took care of various missions, particularly St. Patrick's south of Atchison. He seems to have left in June, 1872.[28]

Prior Giles devoted most of his energies to the church. He completed the facade, bringing the towers to the level of the clerestory, and he himself climbed the scaffolding

[24] Wimmer an Lang, St. Mary's, Pa., Feb. 7, 1872. (AM)
[25] Miége to Wimmer, Leavenworth, Jan. 2, 1870 [1871]. (SVA)
[26] Wolf Diary, Jan. 7, 28, Feb. 1, June 21, 1871.
[27] *Champion*, Aug. 7, 1873. Urban (Edward) Bayer was born in Neuhausen, Wuerttemberg, Sept. 8, 1841, was professed Nov. 13, 1862, ordained May 26, 1866, and died Aug. 5, 1873 — *Necrologium*, No. 66.
[28] Cashbook, *passim*.

to help with the job.[29] The rose window was installed, and the interior was vaulted, plastered, and then decorated. Father Gerard Pilz, O.S.B., of St. Vincent, painted a Nativity scene above the altar. Furthermore, several large stained-glass windows were installed, and floors, seats, and altars were "visibly improved."[30] The improvements had cost a little over $7000 but had been accomplished, Abbot Wimmer noted with approval, without further increasing the debt. He even hoped that in the following year it might be possible to begin reducing the debt.[31]

On his arrival on August 20, 1871, Prior Giles had noted that the debt of St. Benedict's Priory, excluding current bills, was $49,214.98. Within the next year Abbot Wimmer obtained $16,000 at six per cent to substitute for a similar amount in loans at ten per cent, thus materially reducing the Priory's interest charges.[32] He hoped to continue the process. Father Wendelin Mayer's receipts from giving missions continued going to the Kansas Priory, and by the spring of 1872 this amount reached $2100.[33] Father Boniface Krug's continued success in his appeals for Monte Cassino enabled him to lend St. Benedict's another $5000 at eight per cent.[34]

The parishioners responded favorably to Prior Giles' policy of beautifying the church. They worked so successfully at the big fairs favored by the Prior that on one occasion, in 1873, they cleared more than $2500. Other features of his financial policies were considered less wise. To raise ready cash he sold the lots in front of the church and the herd stock off the farm.[35] He received no aid from the Ludwig-Missionsverein, apparently because he never asked for it.

[29] *Champion*, Dec. 7, 1872, from W. H. Rossington in *Topeka Commonwealth*.
[30] *Ibid.*, Oct. 19, 1873; Jan. 1, 1874; Jan. 1, 1875.
[31] Wimmer ad Pescetelli, St. Vincent, Mar. 23, 1874. (SPexM)
[32] *Idem*, Aug. 8, 1872. (SPexM)
[33] *Idem*, May 4, 1872. (SPexM)
[34] Krug an Christoph, Newark, June 19, 1873. The interest was reduced to six percent in 1881, and final payment was acknowledged in 1887.—Krug an Wolf, Monte Cassino, June 12, 1881; Apr. 12, 1887.
[35] Wolf an Wimmer, Atchison, Sept. 27, 1877. (SVA)

Abbot Wimmer's earlier hopes were not realized. The depression following the panic of 1873 brought a decline in income, particularly from the College. The effects of the depression were intensified by the grasshopper plague of 1874. Prior Giles, like his predecessor, overwhelmed by the task of trying to pay the interest, fled his hopeless burden and sent in his resignation in November, 1874. Abbot Wimmer persuaded him to return to his post but began looking for another who might, by some sort of magic, make the Atchison Priory financially solvent.[36] Prior Giles was not an aggressive man, but the young Father Boniface Verheyen, and presumably other members of the community, greatly admired the Prior's spirit of religious obedience and his humility.[37]

Prior Oswald Moosmueller

Abbot Wimmer next sent Oswald Moosmueller, the prior of St. Vincent and an able financial manager, to take over as administrator in Atchison. Father Moosmueller is one of the most interesting early Benedictines in America. One of the few to rate inclusion in the *Dictionary of American Biography*, he is there characterized by Dr. Richard Purcell as "a gifted man of decided ability as a missionary and as a preacher in several tongues; but he was a visionary and a dreamer, and somewhat impractical." That description is largely true, but Oswald Moosmueller represented a minority opinion among the Benedictines of the American Cassinese Congregation. He was an idealist, and idealists are essential to the well-being of religious communities.

Oswald William Moosmueller was born February 26, 1832, of a wealthy family at Aidling in the Bavarian Alps. He was educated at Metten and after completing his noviciate came to St. Vincent in 1852. He was ordained in 1856. In 1859 he was sent to Rio de Janeiro, where he

[36] Wimmer ad Pescetelli, St. Vincent, Nov. 18, 1874. (SPexM)
[37] Verheyen to Haid, Draft marked "Mailed June 6, 1875."

supervised the organization of agricultural and trade schools whose purpose was to continue Catholic education in spite of anti-clerical laws aimed at preventing the development of native clergy in Brazil. Here Father Oswald did not complete the full plan, but he did lay permanent foundations for later work. In the following years he was prior at Newark, N.J., procurator and director of Abbot Wimmer's house of studies in Rome, prior and treasurer of St. Vincent, prior of St. Benedict's in Atchison, superior of the Negro mission in Georgia, and was elected first abbot of Belmont Abbey in North Carolina but refused the election. Finally, in 1892 he became prior of the new community called Cluny, at Wetaug, Illinois. There he died on January 10, 1901. He believed that Benedictines should be scholars, and he almost always found time to write, except in Kansas.

Prior Oswald arrived in Atchison January 9, 1875. The next day he held a chapter, and before the month was out he had determined that the debt amounted to $52,588.95, not including current bills.[38] The outlook, as he summed up the conditions he found, was gloomy. "The affairs of this priory are in such a condition that there is no prospect for redeeming the debts. . ."[39] Expenses had for years regularly exceeded income, the debt increased steadily, and now the average interest of nine per cent ate up $4500 annually. Even in good years the interest took one-third of the gross income. Even after Prior Giles Christoph's work the church was still incomplete. The ornamental stonework round the doors and windows was not yet installed, the floor was of rough boards, and there were no proper pews, no pulpit, and no confessionals.[40] According to the Prior, the College had fewer students than in previous years. He had twenty-nine boarders, with two more at home with their parents at the moment, and twenty day students. But he felt that he could expect nothing from the parishes and mis-

---

[38] Moosmueller to Wimmer, Atchison, Jan. 28, 1875. (SVA)
[39] *Idem*, Jan. 10, 1874 [1875]. (SVA)
[40] *Idem*, Jan. 28, 1875. (SVA)

sions, and so he wrote, "The only hope after prayer must be in the College."[41]

Six months later Prior Oswald was still tempted to despair by the apparent hopelessness of his task. "I have not one single dollar bill," he wrote to the Abbot. And thousands of dollars worth of notes were due. He was convinced that the Priory could not be saved from bankruptcy by its own resources. "The best would be if we could sell the whole concern to the Franciscans who are coming from Germany, just for the debts, and commence a new place out West."[42] Prior Oswald's problems were aggravated by circumstances of the time. Abbot Innocent Wolf later ascribed the failure to pay the debt to the depression following the panic of 1873, aggravated by the drought and the grasshoppers of 1874 and the years following.[43] Real want was prevalent in those years. Prior Oswald reported that half the Atchison parishioners were so poor that they could afford only one square meal a day. Furthermore, some people depended on pork and corn distributed by government agencies.[44]

Even if there had been no depression and no famine caused by the grasshoppers, Prior Oswald could not have expected much financial help from the new parishes. The parishioners were for the most part young families who were just getting established. The community was then in charge of eighteen parishes and missions, and of these only two were not in debt.[45] In searching for work that would help pay the debt, the monks found parish work not very promising. On the other hand, caring for souls was the most urgent apostolic work on the frontier, and the community could not possibly refuse it. Prior Oswald placed his hope in the College. In the long view the College was essential to the life and growth of the monastery and was to become the Abbey's chief contribution to the

41 *Idem,* Jan. 10, 1874 [1875]. (SVA)
42 *Idem,* St. Benedict's Farm, Doniphan Co., July 22, 1875. (SVA)
43 *Berichte der Leopoldinen Stiftung,* XLVIII (1878), 15.
44 Moosmueller to Wimmer, Atchison, Jan. 10; 28, 1875. (SVA)
45 *Idem,* July 9, 1875. (SVA)

life of the Church in this area. In 1875, however, able-bodied boys of college age often simply could not be spared from helping develop the farm, and college education was in little demand except by priesthood students and by some boys looking for elementary commercial courses.

These facts presented Prior Oswald with a complex problem. He was called upon to expand the missionary work, although it could offer little help in paying the debt. He worked to improve the College, but at the same time he weakened it both by sending men to establish claims to government land and by detailing two of his tiny community to preach missions. These latter activities offered hope of solving his financial problems, but each involved conflicts with other aims of the community.

As was noted above, Prior Oswald's first reaction to the problems he inherited in Atchison was an inclination to dispose of the whole lot and make a fresh start farther west. He first thought of founding a mission house in the western territories of the Vicariate of Nebraska.[46] Bishop Fink, however, proposed to establish two "Christian Forts" in the form of religious communities in the western part of Kansas. These forts would care for the immigrants who kept coming "in spite of all the grasshoppers and years of misery." The Bishop intended to place the Franciscans in the southwest and asked Abbot Wimmer to send "a few soldiers and a captain to raise a Fort OSB in the N. West."[47]

Prior Oswald naturally found this idea congenial, and in August, 1875, he sent Father Boniface Verheyen to accompany Father Felix Swembergh to western Kansas to visit the scattered settlers. Father Swembergh was a diocesan priest whose mission territory was the entire area along the new Santa Fe Railroad west of Hutchinson, Kansas. Settled eighteen miles northwest of Great Bend were fourteen Catholic families just arrived from Moravia. Father Boniface found not only these new families but also five more at Ellinwood and eight at Kinsley. He ob-

---

[46] Moosmueller an Bartl, Atchison, June 11, 1875.
[47] Fink to Wimmer, Leavenworth, Aug. 14, 1875. (SVA)

served that Dodge City, then at the height of its fame, was quiet and practically respectable during the daylight hours. From Fort Dodge he and Father Swembergh traveled south to Camp Supply in Indian Territory. From Camp Supply they traveled with the mail to Cantonment (elsewhere called Fort Elliott), a new post in the Texas Panhandle. Here Father Boniface was welcomed by the commanding officer, Major Wendelbrock, and his family. On the road to Texas Father Boniface met a band of 1500 Arapaho Indians. Most of the Catholics among them were away on a buffalo hunt, and one of them, Father Boniface learned, was a St. Benedict's alumnus, presumably Andrew Jackson Fitzpatrick, who had not been one of the school's best students.[48]

When Prior Oswald went to Pennsylvania for the General Chapter in August, 1875, Abbot Wimmer gave him three Brothers — Raymund Huber, Clement Wirtz, and Fridolin Rosenfelder — who were to take up land in the West and establish Bishop Fink's Christian Fort.[49] A month later the Prior, accompanied by Brother Fridolin, in a light canvas-topped wagon with two ponies, inspected both forks of the Solomon River in Osborne, Smith, Phillips, and Rooks Counties. He found only scattered Catholic families. He reported to the Priory chapter that he was not pleased with that part of the country and did not plan to locate there.[50] At the beginning of the new year, 1876, the Prior was evidently thinking of the Great Bend area, where Father Boniface had found the new Catholic families. In any case, Prior Oswald needed another priest to replace whoever would go west with the Brothers. The Prior wrote to Abbot

[48] Moosmueller an von Scherr, Atchison, Dec. 19, 1875. (LMV Leav II 1/47) Moosmueller to Wimmer, Atchison, Dec. 6, 1875. (SVA) Verheyen Reminiscences, [1884?] and 1922.

[49] Chapter Minutes, 48-49. Prior Oswald was the first to keep records of the local chapter. Besides the chapter minutes he also entered a record of events. References to the latter, since they are not exactly dated, are by page number.

[50] *Ibid.* However, he wanted to move in quickly if a talked-of railroad up the Solomon became a reality.—Moosmueller to Wimmer, Atchison, Dec. 20, 1875.

Wimmer, "If I only had a priest to spare I could get 640 or even 1280 acres in one piece next week without running into debts. What is needed for the enterprise I have ready on hand; a new wagon, three horses, provisions for six months, four Brothers, etc., etc. The locality is already selected, and twelve Catholic families are already settled in the neighborhood and a hundred Catholic families would move out there next spring."[51]

The golden jubilee of the episcopal consecration of Pope Pius IX was extended to 1876, and Prior Oswald was invited to preach the jubilee to the Catholic officers and soldiers in the Southwest military posts. He visited Camp Supply in February and went on to Fort Cantonment in the Texas Panhandle.[52] The Prior returned to Atchison, convinced that the country along Bear Creek in Clark County, Kansas, was the spot for the foundation of that Christian Fort in the West. The choice of this particular site, however, was dictated more by its financial possibilities than by anything else. Settlement was expected to increase, and spiritual ministration at the military posts would provide support for a priest. The chief attraction, however, was that the land would provide collateral for cheaper loans and thus improve the Priory's financial status. Furthermore, since the site was located on the Western Cattle Trail where drovers were happy to sell young calves for fifty cents a head and less, the Brothers could soon build up a large herd of cattle. The sale of these cattle would be a wonderful source of income for the Priory.[53]

The foundation of the Christian Fort, which the Prior grandly called Monte Cassino, got under way in May, 1876. Brother Andrew Allermann and Brother Fridolin Rosenfelder drove a team and wagon to Clark County. Old Brother Clement Wirtz started with them but turned back at Emporia. Father Boniface Verheyen took the

51 Moosmueller to Wimmer, Atchison, Jan. 3, 1876. (SVA)
52 *Idem*, Feb. 19, 1876; Camp Supply, Indian T., Feb. 29, 1876. (SVA)
53 Chapter Minutes, 46-50.

train to Dodge City and then joined the Brothers. They built a dugout or sodhouse, turned some sod, and put up a quantity of prairie hay.[54] According to an account written nearly ten years later, the little foundation was the victim of the cattle trade, for herds being driven north to the railroad trampled the fields sown by the Brothers.[55] Furthermore, some of the monks, Father Timothy Luber in particular, opposed the idea of a new foundation while the community in Atchison was chronically shorthanded.[56] The place was too far beyond the line of heavy settlement to accomplish what Bishop Fink had intended, and he scornfully branded the place *"Bueffel Au,"* or Buffalo Valley. Innocent Wolf, who was elected abbot on September 29 of that year, no doubt also disapproved of the project. Father Boniface, who had returned to Atchison for the election, was sent back to Clark County to liquidate the project.

Prior Oswald sadly gave a final report on the project to Abbot Wimmer:

> The Brothers, who had been with Father Boniface Verheyen OSB out West think that he will not come home before Christmas. He is fond of hunting buffaloes and antelopes and there is a first rate place out there for that. . . The only thing that grieves me is that the new place out West, from which I had such great expectations. . . was not appreciated by the Kansas fathers. The Brothers sold their hay, etc., for seventy-two dollars cash; their building was occupied by other people the same day they left.[57]

Father Boniface came home to the prosaic business of teaching school in November and so ended one of Prior Oswald's attempts to solve the problem of the debt. Though the venture was a failure, it made Prior Oswald and Father Boniface, along with Father Swembergh, the first missionaries to the Texas Panhandle since Spanish

[54] Verheyen Reminiscences, 1922. The dray ticket for freight is dated 5/16/76.
[55] *Berichte der Leopoldinen Stiftung,* LV (1885), 27-30.
[56] Luber to Bartl, Atchison, Sept. 16, 1875.
[57] Moosmueller to Wimmer, Atchison, Nov. 10, 1876. (SVA)

times.[58] Visits to the southwestern posts were continued at irregular intervals until about 1880.

Prior Oswald tried another means to help pay the debt. He decided to have his monks give missions. His difficulty in arranging a mission during the jubilee year for the parish in Atchison might have given him this idea. He wrote to Abbot Wimmer that since there was a great shortage of mission preachers, he wanted Fathers Timothy Luber and Peter Kassens trained to give missions because they spoke English well.[59] The Prior urged that two good missionaries could save many souls and perhaps earn thousands of dollars.[60] In the latter hope he was much too sanguine. After three months of preparation and with twenty sermons in their repertoire, Fathers Timothy and Peter began to give missions, at first in Benedictine parishes for practice, and then generally throughout the neighboring states.[61] From September, 1875, when they began, until June, 1876, when they completed their series of missions, the two contributed almost $1300 to the Priory treasury.[62] The missions were successful enough spiritually, but as a means of reducing the Priory debt they were no great success.

"The only hope after prayer must be in the College," Prior Oswald had written in his first assessment of his problems. That solution was for the future, but the facts confronting him were that the number of students was so small and the fees so low that the College failed to make expenses.[63] Most of the students were non-resident, and they paid various sums from a dollar and a half to three dollars a month, if they paid at all.[64] Payment was not

[58] When the Prior wrote to the chancery office in Galveston asking approval for one of his priests to administer the Sacraments at Fort Elliott, the reply was that since the Fort was not on their map it must be in the Diocese of San Antonio. The reply from the San Antonio chancery was that the Fort might be in the Diocese of Galveston.—L. Chaland to Moosmueller, Galveston, July 12, 1876; F. J. Johnston to Moosmueller, San Antonio, Aug. 5, 1876.
[59] Moosmueller to Wimmer, Atchison, July 9, 1875. (SVA)
[60] *Idem*, July 10, 1875. (SVA)
[61] *Idem*, Sept. 6, 1875. (SVA)
[62] Ledger, 534
[63] Moosmueller to Wimmer, Atchison, May 5, 1875. (SVA)
[64] *Idem*, Apr. 17, 1875. (SVA)

very regular, and at the end of 1875 the College had $2000 in accounts receivable but not very much hope of collecting.[65]

Another problem arose when Bishop Fink expressed dissatisfaction with the religious training his priesthood students had been receiving.[66] Furthermore, the College had a poor reputation in the neighboring cities from which students might be drawn. Prior Oswald accepted invitations to preach in neighboring towns in order to improve the reputation of the College.[67] The Prior wrote to Abbot Wimmer, "I will use my utmost exertions to raise this College to a higher standard."[68] However, his other projects frequently conflicted with the interests of the College. The missions of Fathers Timothy Luber and Peter Kassens demanded a great sacrifice in the College. Father Timothy had been director of the school a long time, but the Prior was anxious to relieve him. Father Peter was the only faculty member trained to teach commercial courses.

But the Prior proposed suspending the commercial course for a year, with the idea that only three priests would be needed for teaching the classical students. He expected the College income to continue as usual and the expenses to be reduced.[69] This proposal would have been a strange solution to St. Benedict's difficulties because in 1875 twenty-nine of the sixty students were taking commercial courses. Only nineteen were taking the classical course; the other twelve were in elementary school.[70] Fortunately the commercial courses were not discontinued, for Father Placidus Pilz was sent out from St. Vincent to teach them. Similarly in the spring of 1876 the Prior wanted to send Father Boniface back to St. Vincent for six months of preparation to teach "Natural Philosophy," but instead he sent him to Clark County to found the abor-

[65] *Idem*, Dec. 6, 1875. (SVA)
[66] Chapter Minutes, Feb. 18, 1875.
[67] Moosmueller to Wimmer, Atchison, May 5, 1875. (SVA)
[68] *Idem*, Apr. 17, 1875. (SVA)
[69] Chapter Minutes, May 19, 1875.
[70] Record of Students, 1869-1881.

tive community of Monte Cassino.[71] Abbot Wimmer
complained that the Prior's revolutionary changes threatened to dissolve the College by stripping it of teachers.[72]
The Prior's actions even occasioned a rumor that the
College was closing.[73] Instability had long been one of
the most discouraging features of St. Benedict's, and the
Prior's policies did nothing to improve matters.

While the Prior was assigning men to projects in a
desperate attempt to begin reducing the debt, (and perhaps to shake some deadwood out of the College), he depended on Abbot Wimmer to give him priests whose teaching would improve the reputation of the College. The
Prior expected to procure these monks when he returned
to St. Vincent for the General Chapter in August, 1875.
Abbot Wimmer, however, gave him Brothers to take up
land out West but no teachers. In his disappointment
Prior Oswald penned his most emotional letter to the
Abbot, describing his arrival in Atchison with only
Brothers, whereas he had promised to return with college
professors. He was the laughing-stock of the town, and
those who had spread the rumor that the College was closing were triumphant. On the opening day of school there
was none but himself to fill all the offices of the College:
"Director, Rector, Prefect, and Professor of each and
every class." The Prior protested that all his policies had
been undertaken with the advice and consent of the
Abbot and had been approved by the recent General
Chapter. Abbot Wimmer underlined these statements
and flanked them with large question marks in the mar-
gins of the letter.[74]

Nevertheless, things improved slowly. To bolster the
College Abbot Wimmer sent Fathers Albert Robrecht,
Raymond Daniel, and Paul Mueller.[75] Father Raymond

[71] Moosmueller to Wimmer, Atchison, Mar. 17, 1876. (SVA)
[72] Wimmer to Phelan, St. Vincent, Sept. 30, 1875.
[73] Phelan to Moosmueller, Creston, Aug. 2, 1875.
[74] Moosmueller to Wimmer, Atchison, Sept. 6, 1875. (SVA)
[75] When Prior Oswald arrived at the beginning of 1875, his predecessor,
Father Giles Christoph, remained to help in the missions but was recalled a
few months later to take charge of St. Joseph's Church in Chicago.—Wimmer
to Phelan, St. Vincent, Apr. 9, 1875. Father Denis Stolz was sent down

taught in the College until 1878, and Father Albert, who was a bear for work and a good band director, taught until 1881. Father Theodosius Goth, who had come to Kansas in 1873 and whom the Prior considered his right-hand man, was appointed vice-president of the College. But at the end of 1875 Father Theodosius came down with a touch of fever and returned to St. Vincent in the summer of 1876.

The College enrollment grew slowly, but most important for the future was the fact that Prior Oswald organized a scholasticate, that is, he provided special training for a group of young men who wished to become members of the community. His first group of seven scholastics included the young Dennis Murphy and Ferdinand (later Father Charles) Stoeckl.[76] With this provision for growth in the membership of the community, the future was assured if the problem of the debt could be solved.

Prior Oswald's greatest service to St. Benedict's was refinancing the debt. Before coming to Kansas he had offered as much as nine per cent to Benziger Brothers and others in order to redeem the twelve per cent mortgage on St. Benedict's but without success.[77] Buying cheap western lands and giving missions had alike been financially disappointing. His predecessor had added as much as $2500 to the annual income by means of elaborate fairs. Prior Oswald horrified Abbot Wimmer by discontinuing these "on account of the hard times and especially because I believe that a Congregation loses at least ten percent of piety and Christian virtues by such fairs. . . On the 4th of July we had a small Picnic that brought $142.50."[78] The ex-

from Nebraska City, where he had been assistant for a short time, to replace Father Giles as pastor of St. Benedict's Church in Atchison.—Stolz to Edelbrock, Atchison, Oct. 8, 1875. (SJA) Father Denis remained until 1876. Father Suitbert Demarteau returned to the East in May, 1875, and Father Richard Wolpert was sent out to Kansas, but he seems to have lasted only a few months. Father Maurus Lynch also returned to St. Vincent in July, 1875, after a very brief stay in Kansas.

[76] Moosmueller an von Scherr, Atchison, Dec. 19, 1875. (LMV Leav II 1/47)
[77] Moosmueller to Wimmer, Atchison, May 5, 1875. (SVA)
[78] *Idem*, Jan. 1, 1876. (SVA)

clamation points that Abbot Wimmer put in the margin of this letter would seem to indicate that he thought the Prior's conscience rather too tender. On the other hand, Prior Oswald again sought the aid of the Ludwig-Missionsverein and received three or four hundred dollars from the society in 1875 and 1876.[79]

The greatest improvement of the financial situation was brought about by Prior Oswald's success in securing loans at seven per cent to replace those at ten and twelve per cent. He borrowed $10,000 from his sister in Bavaria. This loan was in gold, and in 1875 the premium in exchange added fifteen or sixteen hundred dollars. No security had been asked, but he later sent a mortgage on the College farm near Bendena, though this was totally inadequate as security. He promptly used the money to pay off Brown and Bier, the contractors, who held a mortgage for $10,000 at twelve per cent on the church and the Priory. Then Prior Oswald persuaded the Abbot of Metten, to whom he seems to have been favorably known, to lend the community $20,000 at six per cent on the property so recently redeemed from Brown and Bier.[80] The Prior then paid off thirteen other creditors in 1875, most of whom had held notes bearing interest at ten per cent.

The benefit of Prior Oswald's refinancing appeared only after a year had passed. Although the gross income of the Priory was less than $10,000 in 1875, he paid out slightly more than $6000 in interest, some of it overdue, of course. He could console himself that in the following year his interest costs would be only half that amount. He rejoiced that it was "almost a moral certainty that in 1876 the amount of debts on this house will for the first time begin to decrease, however small that amount may be. . . *Deo Gratias.*"[81] One year later he submitted his final report to Abbot Wimmer. For the first time in many years there was no increase in the Priory's liabilities.

[79] 1200 fl. in 1875. *Annalen der Verbreitung des Glaubens*, XLIV (1876), 390. 1500 M. in 1876. *Ibid.*, XLV (1877), 392.
[80] Moosmueller to Wolf, Skidaway Island, June 16, 1879.
[81] Moosmueller to Wimmer, Atchison, Jan. 1, 1876. (SVA)

The debt had been reduced only a hundred dollars. "Still," Prior Oswald wrote, "it is a victory over which we may rejoice, especially under the present circumstances and scarcity of money." St. Benedict's debt in December, 1876, totalled $52,376.12. The Priory owed $10,000 to St. Vincent Abbey, $20,000 in gold to the Abbey of Metten, $10,000 in gold to Prior Oswald's sister in Bavaria, $6,000 in paper to Monte Cassino, and the remainder in small sums to various creditors.[82] As the Prior pointed out, refinancing St. Benedict's debt meant that, all other things being equal, the debt would gradually diminish and the Priory would be financially sound. This accomplishment marked the turning point in the history of the community.

Prior Oswald also energetically improved the spiritual life in the Priory. St. Benedict's troubled history of debt and rapid turnover of personnel was not conducive to regular observance. The Prior found himself in perfect agreement with St. Theresa's observation that when the temporalities of a religious house get into confusion, the spiritualities are sure to go wrong.[83] He did not spare himself in his attempts to remedy the situation. Shortly after his arrival he reported that he preached every Sunday, gave weekly spiritual conferences to the Brothers and to the priests, and heard confessions in the parish and at the convent.[84] Furthermore, he had annual retreats for the community,[85] and after his arrival the public recitation of the Divine Office was never missed, though at times only two or three priests constituted the choir.[86] Occasionally he must have been tempted to use drastic measures to enforce his rules, for he wrote with obvious

[82] Moosmueller to Wimmer, Atchison, Dec. 19, 1876. (SVA) The date of this final report is explained by the fact that telegraphic confirmation of Abbot Innocent Wolf's election had been received the preceding day.
    Prior Oswald had paid $4000 of the $10,000 borrowed from Monte Cassino. This part of the loan was simply transferred to St. John's Abbey.—Moosmueller to Wimmer, Atchison, Dec. 6, 1875. (SVA)
[83] *Idem*, July 9, 1875. (SVA)
[84] *Idem*, Jan. 29, 1875. (SVA)
[85] *Idem*, July 9, 1875. (SVA)
[86] *Idem*, Apr. 17, 1375. (SVA)

interest to Abbot Wimmer, "The Rt. Rev. Abbot of Minnesota told me he introduced the rule that a Priest who does not visit the Choir in the morning will get no beer on that day, and he who does not celebrate Mass gets no breakfast. . . There are some who scarcely ever get up at four o'clock, but some get up every day. I cannot do much in this respect."[87]

Prior Oswald improved relations and provided contact with the diocesan clergy by inviting them to help the community celebrate St. Benedict's Day each year. Bishop Fink pontificated for the occasion. As the Prior explained to Abbot Wimmer, he had celebrated St. Benedict's Day in 1875 "in as grand a style as possible," first, to honor St. Benedict and to gain his protection, "which we need more than any of his houses," and secondly, to convince the diocesan clergy that they were safe in encouraging boys to attend St. Benedict's College.[88]

The Prior kept himself informed about Benedictine development throughout the world and believed that closer bonds among all branches of the Order should be fostered. In this spirit he offered to unite the Atchison Priory in a union of prayer with the Abbey of St. Boniface in Munich and with the Abbey of Raigern. In writing to Raigern the Prior also asked for a donation of books, and a friend of his in that community, Father Bede Dudek, sent 485 titles totalling 857 volumes.[89] This collection included valuable theological classics and even incunabula. These books became the nucleus of the Abbey Library.

Prior Oswald was also an early advocate of the free parochial school. In those depression years he observed that many parishioners could not afford a dollar or even fifty cents a month to send a child to the parochial school, and so on April 23, 1876, he organized the St. Bede School Society to pay the Sisters' salary and the operating ex-

[87] *Idem*, Mar. 20, 1876. (SVA)
[88] *Idem*, Apr. 6, 1875. (SVA)
[89] Abbot Zenetti an Moosmueller, Munich, Sept. 20, 1876.

penses of the school. He began with eighty members who paid monthly dues of twenty-five cents.[90] The German members of the parish withdrew to form a separate division of the society on August 27 and agreed to raise half the $600 annual budget. The project was also aided by special collections and social events. A less enthusiastic pastor abandoned this plan in 1880.[91]

St. Benedict's Abbey

Convinced that Prior Oswald's plans for preventing the bankruptcy of St. Benedict's Priory probably would be successful, Abbot Wimmer was eager to have the Priory made an abbey. Shortly after the Prior first arrived in Kansas the Abbot expressed the hope that the Priory could become an abbey before the summer was out.[92] Bishop Fink, too, thought the time ripe for such a move. In a letter to Abbot Wimmer, asking that such a petition be sent to the Holy See, he argued that the status of an abbey would give stability to the community. He was aware of the difficulties, but he felt that an abbot wielding the crozier according to the Rule would give unity of spirit and purpose. The Bishop maintained also that certain evils would have been avoided if the monks had known who their superior was.[93] Prior Oswald, however, thought such action would be premature. He pointed out to Abbot Wimmer that order and harmony in the administration of the Priory's affairs had been achieved very recently and that all administrative offices were in the hands of monks on loan from St. Vincent. If the Priory was now made an abbey, the Kansas monks naturally

---

[90] Moosmueller to Wimmer, Atchison, July 21, 1876. (SVA)
[91] Minutes of St. Bede's School Society. The last minutes are dated Oct. 31, 1880. The constitutional provision that feminine members were to be represented and vote by male proxy was typical of Prior Oswald. He was afraid of women.
[92] Wimmer to Phelan, St. Vincent, Mar. 13, 1875.
[93] Fink to Wimmer, Leavenworth, Aug. 14, 1875. (SVA)

109

would wish to administer their own affairs, and the order achieved by the Prior would be undone.[94]

At this time twelve priests were attached to the Priory at Atchison. Six priests, besides the Prior, taught in the College, and four of these instructors took care of sixteen missions on weekends. Of the other five, two were giving missions, one was pastor in Atchison, and the other two, one residing at St. Benedict's Colony near Bendena and the other at Seneca, took care of eight churches. Ten Brothers were also attached to the Priory.[95] Father Timothy Luber commented that three of the Brothers on loan from St. Vincent were very old: Brothers Raymund, Fridolin, and Clement.[96] Two or three of the Brothers were on the farm at St. Benedict's Colony, and one was ordinarily stationed with each resident pastor as cook and handyman. After Fathers Peter Kassens and Timothy Luber had finished their round of preaching missions, Abbot Wimmer recalled Fathers Denis Stolz and Theodosius Goth. The only new man sent on loan in 1876 was Father Pirmin Leverman, whose habit of quarreling with the Brothers caused frequent comment. He remained until 1877. The only priests on loan from St. Vincent at the end of Prior Oswald's administration were Fathers Raymond Daniel, Albert Robrecht, and Pirmin Leverman.

In any case, Prior Oswald's argument for delay came too late, for the General Chapter of 1875 had already recommended that St. Benedict's Priory be made an Abbey, and the petition, endorsed by Bishop Fink, was sent to the Holy See in January, 1876.[97] St. Benedict's

[94] Moosmueller to Wimmer, Atchison, Dec. 20, 1875.

[95] Moosmueller an von Scherr, Atchison, Dec. 19, 1875. (LMV Leav II 1/47) This list omits Nebraska City. At the time Prior Oswald considered that mission dependent directly on St. Vincent.

Besides the priests previously mentioned, another monk in Kansas on loan at this time was Father Boniface Moll. He had been sent by the Abbot of St. John's as an assistant to Father Augustine Burns in Creston, Iowa, which was a foundation from, if not by, St. John's. Since Father Boniface was very deficient in English, he was traded to Atchison for Father Placidus McKeever. The Abbot of St. John's recalled Father Boniface towards the end of 1876. Bishop Fink considered him rather less than competent.—Fink to Moosmueller, Leavenworth, June 19, 1876.

[96] Luber to Bartl, Atchison, Sept. 16, 1875.

[97] Wimmer ad Pescetelli, St. Vincent, May 24, 1876. (SPexM)

was raised to the dignity of an abbey by the Apostolic Brief of Pope Pius IX on April 7, 1876. Transmittal of the brief was delayed, and the news arrived in Atchison only on June 3.[98]

Abbot Wimmer was confident that Oswald Moosmueller would be the first abbot of St. Benedict's, but a number of perplexing features complicated the situation. The question arose regarding the number of capitulars necessary for the election of an abbot. Even including Father Augustine Wirth, only seven priests belonged to the community by vow. Four St. Benedict's clerics were studying at St. Vincent, but they were not yet eligible to vote. The Abbot thought that perhaps all the Benedictines in Kansas, including those who were on loan from St. Vincent, could properly take part in the election. On the other hand, the Prior might possibly refuse the election, so the Abbot even toyed with the idea of having Prior Oswald appointed abbot by Rome. The Abbot finally decided, however, that such a move would be too dangerous, because Rome might later do uninvited what it once had been invited to do.[99]

Meanwhile Prior Oswald had begun a quiet and dignified campaign for the election of the Prior of St. Vincent, Father Innocent Wolf, who had been one of his charges when Prior Oswald was director of Abbot Wimmer's house of studies in Rome. To Father Thomas Bartl he wrote that Father Innocent would make the best candidate and that if the community made the election unanimous, Abbot Wimmer would have no choice but to approve.[100] A year earlier Abbot Rupert Seidenbusch, of St. John's Abbey in Minnesota, had been made a bishop. At the election of his successor Abbot Wimmer had announced that he would not approve the election of Oswald Moosmueller, who was indispensable in Kansas, or of Innocent Wolf, whom he needed as prior at St. Vincent. St. John's chapter nevertheless tried to elect Father In-

[98] The Brief arrived June 17.—Chapter Minutes, 38-39.
[99] Wimmer ad Pescetelli, St. Vincent, Jan. 24, 1876. (SPexM)
[100] Moosmueller an Bartl, Atchison, June 19, 1876.

111

nocent, but Abbot Wimmer refused his consent.[101] Abbot Wimmer hoped that Father Innocent would be his successor at St. Vincent.[102]

Father Innocent had developed a stubborn throat infection that was to trouble him most of his life, and so he was in Chicago vacationing to regain his health. Prior Oswald rather slyly wrote to the Abbot, asking him to permit Father Innocent to recuperate in Kansas.[103] Consequently, Father Innocent visited St. Benedict's late in July, 1876, was not well impressed with the spiritual tone of the community, and then went on to Colorado.[104] Abbot Wimmer hoped that Father Innocent's condition would improve, but he expected no complete recovery.[105]

September 29 was the date set for the election. Three of the four Kansas clerics at St. Vincent had made solemn vows and were ordained subdeacons so that they could vote by proxy.[106] Father Thomas Bartl, who in the previous ten years had become closely associated with the Kansas community, was expected to transfer his vows to St. Benedict's and bring the number to twelve, but he declined to do so at the time.[107] The idea of permitting St. Vincent Abbey monks who were working in Kansas to vote in the election was abandoned owing to Bishop Fink's opposition.[108] When the plan had been proposed in the local chapter, Father Timothy Luber had also protested with great vigor and a bit of heat.[109]

Seven electors were present, namely, Fathers Emmanuel Hartig, Timothy Luber, Pirmin Koumly, Peter Kassens, Boniface Verheyen, Placidus McKeever, and Eugene Bode. Father Augustine Wirth, and the three clerics — Adolph Wesseling, Winfried Schmidt, and John

---

[101] Wimmer ad Pescetelli, St. Vincent, July 30, 1875. (SPexM)
[102] *Idem*, [Sept. 14, 1875]. (SPexM)
[103] Moosmueller to Wimmer, Atchison, July 16, 1876. (SVA)
[104] Wolf to Wimmer, Atchison, Aug. 4, 1876; Manitou, Aug. 22, 1876. (SVA)
[105] Wimmer an Lang, Creston, Sept. 24, 1876. (AM)
[106] Wimmer ad Pescetelli, St. Vincent, Sept. 18, 1876. (SPexM)
[107] Moosmueller an Bartl, Atchison, June 19, 1876.
[108] Fink to Wimmer, Leavenworth, June 5, 1876. (SVA)
[109] Moosmueller to Wimmer, Atchison, July 11, 1876. (SVA)

Stader — voted by proxy. Father Casimir (later Alban) Rudroff was absent and did not vote. Abbot Wimmer, president of the Congregation, told the electors that they were free to elect any of the St. Vincent priors except, as was expected, Innocent Wolf, and, apparently at his own insistence, Oswald Moosmueller. In those days the pastor of almost any parish large enough to need an assistant was dignified with the title of prior. Father Innocent Wolf received eight of the eleven votes on the first ballot, and Abbot Wimmer declared him elected. Prior Oswald received two votes, and Father Augustine Wirth had insisted that his proxy vote for Father Benno Hegele.

Father Innocent, who was in Topeka, Kansas, visiting a former student, Father Bernard Hayden, and evidently waiting to accompany Abbot Wimmer back to Pennsylvania, was notified by telegram. He thanked the chapter for the honor but declined the election. Another telegram urged him to come to talk over the matter. He arrived the next day and, strongly urged by Abbot Wimmer and Abbot Alexius Edelbrock, of St. John's, accepted the office.[110] As the *Champion* reported the event, the newly-elected Abbot had been "met at the depot by all the Fathers of the college, who welcomed him to this, his new field of labor. Last evening his arrival was honored with the booming of cannon, and the music of Prof. Phillips' band added an enthusiasm to the occasion that will be long remembered."[111]

Abbot Wimmer professed to be well satisfied with the results of the election, particularly for the sake of St. Benedict's. He did not surrender Father Innocent gladly but felt that his choice a second time was too much to oppose and that it was God's will. He had faith that Divine Providence was at work for the good of the new abbey and of the whole Congregation.[112]

[110] Protocollum super acta Capituli Electoralis in Abbatia S. Benedicti habiti in Atchison, die 29 Sept. 1876.
[111] Oct. 1, 1876.
[112] Wimmer ad Pescetelli, Atchison, Oct. 3, 1876. (SPexM)

If Abbot Wimmer was disappointed that Prior Oswald had not been elected abbot of St. Benedict's, the Abbot was philosophic in his disappointment. He explained that the Prior was not loved by the community though he was respected. He had certain peculiarities that were feared in case he should become abbot.[113] Abbot Wimmer continued to have high regard for Father Oswald, and when, some years later, he refused the election as the first abbot of Belmont Abbey in North Carolina, Abbot Wimmer was indignant.[114] Prior Oswald had no desire to become an abbot, partially because he bore responsibility as a heavy burden and lacked a sense of humor. Halfway through his term of service in Kansas the Prior wrote to Abbot Wimmer that he was consoled by the fact that he was only a temporary superior. He would never accept such responsibility for life. He complained that he was getting gray and bald and had lost twenty pounds as a result of worrying about the Kansas Priory.[115] Perhaps he was exaggerating, but any weight he might have lost was not sacrificed in vain.

Father Fidelis Busam gives us this picture of Prior Oswald: He was a "total stranger to useless conversation, to raillery, to joking and to loud laughter; on the other hand he proved to be most affable and sweet-tempered. . . Nobody ever heard him complain." He goes on to note that Father Oswald was distinctly ascetic in his life.[116] He was clearly a difficult superior, but he held ideals of the monastic life that were high and true, and he successfully demonstrated those ideals in his own life. He inspired little love, but he was respected, and through his example alone he undoubtedly raised the standards of monastic life in many hearts. He possessed a passionate

113 Wimmer an Lang, Atchison, Oct. 2, 1876. (AM)
114 Wimmer an Wolf, St. Vincent, Feb. 17, 1885.
Abbot Innocent, judging by his four years under Father Oswald in Rome, considered him too impractical, opinionated, and stubborn ever to be a successful superior.—Wolf to Edelbrock, Atchison, May 16, 1888. (SJA)
115 Moosmueller to Wimmer, Atchison, Jan. 3, 1876. (SVA)
116 Quoted by Felix Fellner, O.S.B., "Oswald Moosmueller," *Records of the American Catholic Historical Society*, XXXIV (Mar., 1923), 1–16.

devotion to the Order and to the ideal of truly monastic life. Through all his years as a monk and through his numerous difficulties and many jobs — all of them rather thankless tasks — he kept his vision clear: to serve God and man under the guidance and in the true spirit of St. Benedict's Rule.

St. Benedict's Abbey owes much to Oswald Moos-mueller. He was in Kansas only two years, but during his administration the finances were finally brought back into the realm of the possible, a program for the development of future members and for the growth of the community was inaugurated, and a new stress on the spiritual aspects of the religious life was added. Prior Oswald made it possible for the Priory to become an Abbey.

C H A P T E R   IV

The Mission to the
Settlers, 1857-1876

The story of the Kansas Priory's problems — financial, personal, and spiritual — might lead one to believe that little excuse could be found for the existence of so luckless a monastery. As a matter of fact one task called urgently for the services of the community, and that task was the mission to the settlers. Missionary work was the real reason for the community's existence in the early years and was a job that called for extraordinary sacrifice and devotion. The monks of St. Benedict's had an honorable part in this historic task. If the community had had more men, it could have done more, but it did reasonably well with what men it had, and some of them were truly fine missionaries.

Both Bishop Miége and Prior Augustine Wirth began to notice an increased immigration of Catholics into Kansas after 1857.[1] The panic of 1857 forced many to seek new opportunities, and it deflated the fancy prices that speculators had pinned on Kansas lands. But at the same time the panic moved a great deal of the land into the hands of speculating mortgage holders. Sol Miller wrote that the hard times were not felt much in Kansas until the spring of 1858. He attributed these hard times to the prevalent fever of speculation and its consequence, the failure to cultivate land held for a speculative rise, and also to the common complaint of the frontier, "the scarcity of mechanical branches" or industry. He made an exception of Nemaha and Mar-

1 Wirth an LMV, Doniphan, Feb. 8, 1858. (LMV Leav II 1/1)

116

shall Counties, through which passed the military road to Fort Kearney and the West, noting that those counties had raised large crops of corn for sale to government and immigrant trains at a dollar a bushel.[2]

Whatever the cause, noticeable numbers of Catholics began to move into Kansas by 1858. During that year Prior Augustine directed the building of churches at Atchison and at St. Patrick's, a few miles south of Atchison. St. Patrick's in 1858 was an Irish settlement of about thirty families, but they were expecting more of their friends from Philadelphia and Baltimore to join them soon.[3] Their first church was destroyed by a cyclone in the summer of 1860 but was promptly replaced by another frame or log church.[4] The present stone church was built in 1866 and is consequently the oldest Catholic church still in use in Kansas.[5]

The general pattern of missionary circuits that had been developed shortly after Prior Augustine's arrival — the missions near the Priory, those along the Missouri River, and those along the Fort Kearney road — was continued for a number of years. By 1860 the Atchison Priory was caring for twenty-three mission stations, and at least up to that time one of the priests usually visited St. Joseph, Missouri, once a month to take care of the German Catholics there.[6]

The mission stations attended on week-ends by professors from the College included St. Patrick's, Monrovia, and Mooney Creek — all south and west of Atchison— and St. Benedict's Colony and Wolf River (Fanning) to the north.[7] After the Priory was moved to Atchison, Doniphan became simply another mission to be visited once a month. Father Henry Lemke's chapel and house burned to the ground on the night of October 28, 1863,

[2] White Cloud *Kansas Chief*, Apr. 1, 1858.
[3] *Wahrheitsfreund*, Sept. 2, 1858, from *Herold des Glaubens*.
[4] Wirth an LMV, Atchison, Jan. 2, 1861. (LMV Leav II 1/17-18)
[5] *Champion*, June 26, 1867.
[6] Wirth an LMV, Atchison, Jan. 2, 1861; *Wahrheitsfreund*, Aug. 18, 1859, "Augustinus Kansatensis," from *Kath. Kirchen-Zeitung*.
[7] Mooney Creek first appears in the records Apr. 7, 1859, and Monrovia in June, 1859.—Cashbook.

and no attempt was made to replace it until after the Civil War.[8] When the new brick church was built in 1867, it was located not at the old site but on land donated by a parishioner in the "western suburbs" of the town.[9]

The group of stations on or near the road to Fort Kearney and the West included St. Augustine's Settlement (Capioma, now Fidelity), St. Mary's on Wildcat Creek, a few miles north of Seneca, St. Bridget's near the Nebraska line, the short-lived town of Eureka, and a group of Catholic families on the Black Vermillion, a tributary of the Blue River. The third group were the river towns, many of them soon to disappear from the maps. From south to north they were Geary City, Palermo, Elwood, and Iowa Point in Kansas; Rulo, Brownsville, and Peru in Nebraska; Sonora in Missouri; and Turkey Creek, Yankee Creek, and Nebraska City in Nebraska. After 1861 the Nebraska stations were visited from the mission center established at Nebraska City.

The second group of mission stations, the Catholic settlements near the great road to the West, was in many ways the most promising. Father Philip Vogg found more Catholics inland than along the river, as might be expected when one remembers the way in which the local

[8] *Wahrheitsfreund*, Nov. 11, 1863.
Father Alphonse Filian made the following notes of the oral tradition at Doniphan sometime after 1900: After the Benedictines moved from Doniphan a Mrs. Burke lived in the rooms adjoining the church and kept it clean. The explanation for the fire was that a Mrs. Leary put long sticks of wood in the stove with their ends extending out onto the floor, and so set fire to the building.—Filian Notebook.
St. John the Baptist's Church in Doniphan, the Benedictines' first parish in Kansas, is now the only mission served from the Abbey.
[9] *Historical Plat Book of Doniphan County* (Chicago, 1882), 26-7.
The old plat of Doniphan was destroyed in a fire at the courthouse in Troy. The plat now on file is notarized to be an exact copy of the original, but Father Lemke's block is labeled "Public Square." Whether payment on the lots was completed or not (the record is confused), ownership of the lots was never recorded in the county records. The absence of official record and the decision to build the new church on Brenner's land are probably explained by a notice in the *Champion* on July 12, 1865, that the question of the long-contested townsite of Doniphan was settled by the Commissioner of Indian Affairs in favor of Lyman Allen, attorney for "Peacock," a Wyandotte. The town company had thirty days to appeal to the Secretary of the Interior.

hopefuls had laid claim to all land along the river as soon as the territory was opened.[10] Father Philip's visits to the Catholics in Nemaha County in 1860 can hardly have been the first, for on January 3, 1859, Peter Bloomer donated twenty acres and a log house to the Catholic Church of St. Mary's (Wildcat) on condition that the congregation maintain the log house as a place of worship and construct a church within twelve months.[11] Prior Augustine also visited these settlements in 1860, blessing the cemetery at Wildcat and laying the cornerstone for the church at St. Bridget's, which was the largest settlement of the group. The people at Wildcat had begun building a *Blockhaus* in anticipation of having a resident pastor the following spring.[12]

In June of the following year Father Emmanuel Hartig, lately arrived in Kansas, visited these stations. He was impressed and related his experience to convince his young friend Father Thomas Bartl back in Pennsylvania that Kansas offered wonderful opportunities for truly apostolic labor:

Two weeks ago I spent about two weeks on a mission seventy-five miles from Atchison and found there large Catholic congregations, also a church and a nice new house for a priest. The people did not want to let me depart. I also found three other congregations who had already gathered materials for building churches, and they also wanted to detain me for a time to direct the building. I could not accede to their wishes but consoled them by telling them that I would use my influence to get them a priest as soon as possible. The good people were by no means satisfied with this, however, and they determined to send some men to Atchison without delay to ask Father Prior for a priest to take over the supervision of their building and to remain permanently with them. Accordingly, four men from the various congregations came with me to Atchison and were successful in obtaining a resident priest. I would have been happy to return with these good people, but the lot fell to Father Severin [Rotter]. They will come to get him in a few days, and he now has a large field of action which

---

[10] Clipping of letter dated Dec. 5, 1860. (LMV Leav II 1/20)
[11] Deed, Peter Bloomer and wife (of Wisconsin) to St. Benedict's College.
[12] Clipping of Vogg letter, Dec. 5, 1860. (LMV Leav II 1/20)

extends over three counties and is more than a hundred miles in circumference. For the time being he has four congregations to attend. One, about sixty miles from Atchison, already has a church and a rectory. The other congregations intend to build churches within the year.[13]

Father Severin Rotter took up residence at Wildcat on schedule and from there visited St. Bridget's, St. Augustine's (Fidelity), and Marysville, where the road to the West crossed the Blue River. He taught catechism to the children on the weekdays when he was at home.[14] Father Severin built churches at Wildcat and at St. Bridget's but remained only one year. His successor, Father John Meurs, a diocesan priest then, remained in the area from 1862 to 1864,[15] and after his departure the settlements were visited from Atchison by Father Thomas Bartl. The Catholics of Nemaha County had to wait until the end of the sixties before they again had a resident pastor. The effects of the drought and the war were no doubt largely responsible for the failure of this first attempt to establish a mission center in the area. During Father Severin's year at Wildcat, for example, the settlers could give him only $35.35 for his salary.[16]

However, there was some growth in the Catholic settlements, even during the war. Father Thomas Bartl gave the following account of the missions cared for from Atchison in 1864: St. Patrick's had a wood chapel, forty families, mostly Irish, and had Mass one Sunday each month. Mooney Creek had fifteen German families, no chapel, and Mass once a month. Monrovia had fifteen families — German, Irish, and French — no chapel, and Mass four times a year. St. Benedict's Colony had thirty Irish and five German families, an unfinished church, and Mass once a month. St. Thomas (St. Mary's, Purcell) had sixteen German and nine Irish families and a frame church. Doniphan had twenty families

13 Hartig an Bartl, Atchison, June 6, 1861.
14 Woechentliche Verkuendigung, June 16, 1861, ff.
15 Baptismal record, Sts. Peter and Paul Church, Seneca.
16 Gilbert Wolters, O.S.B., *A Socio-Economic Analysis of Four Rural Parishes in Nemaha County, Kansas* (Washington, 1938), 14, note 3.

and no chapel. Palermo had thirty-four families and no chapel. Bellemont had forty German and Irish families and no chapel. Ellwood had twelve Irish families, Iowa Point had five families, White Cloud four families, Forest City, Missouri, and Wolf River (Fanning) had twelve families. The Nebraska stations were visited from Nebraska City.[17]

When construction on the Atchison and Pike's Peak Railroad (Central Branch) was begun in 1865, regular visits were made to the Catholic laborers along the line. Catholic settlers in the counties west of Atchison through which the new railroad passed were already being cared for from mission centers along the Kansas River. Father Thomas' records for 1864-67 include all the regular stations north and west of Atchison and also some places, identified only by a family name, which were evidently visited as occasion offered. He missed only three or four Sundays a year, when he marked his record "sick" or "snow." Once he experienced the frustration of making a long trip only to find himself unable to offer Mass—*Weinbottle gebrochen*. The income for the Priory from his considerable labors was in the best years about $800.[18] Father Thomas was not the only missionary in the community at Atchison, but unlike most of the monks, he devoted full time to the missions for many years, and he left some records of his work.

As the number of settlers increased, the practice of having one priest take care of three or four counties was no longer practical. Father Lemke's old claims, where Prior Augustine had once thought to build his monastery, had now become the College farm and was reasonably well situated for a mission center for the northeastern corner of Kansas. In 1862, in spite of the effects of the war, a church had been built at St. Mary's Colony (sometimes referred to as St. Thomas, now Purcell), a few miles

---

[17] Record of Visitation, Apr. 29, 1864.
[18] Bartl records, 1864-67.

from the farm. The cornerstone of a stone church at St. Benedict's Colony had been laid January 1, 1861, but poverty and the war delayed completion of the church.[19] Father Thomas now encouraged the work and celebrated the first Mass in the church on the second Sunday in November, 1865, before the roof was completed. He built a house in 1867, and he and Brother Luke began to live there on January 20, 1868. The new Prior, Father Louis Fink, called them back to Atchison temporarily, but they returned to St. Benedict's Colony before the end of the year, and Father Thomas worked a steady round of missions from that center. The missions that were regularly visited on a fixed schedule were Purcell, Fanning, All Saints (Bohemian Settlement, Marak, now Everest), and Wathena (successor to Bellemont and Ellwood), but other stations were frequently attached to the new center in Doniphan County.[20]

It was even more important that a mission center be established in Nemaha County. For a number of years the unsatisfactory arrangement of infrequent visits by priests from Atchison was continued, but the number of Catholics in the area grew larger, and the coming of the railroad made Seneca a more useful center than Wildcat. Finally the Catholics of Seneca, led by Mr. Matthias Stein, seized a handy opportunity. When the town outgrew its first public school and built a new one, the Catholics bought the old school and the two acres of ground on which it stood.[21] The old schoolhouse was converted into a church, and in 1870 Father Pirmin Koumly took up residence in Seneca He was joined by Father Suitbert Demarteau, who took care of the missions of Nemaha and Marshall Counties, particularly St. Bridget's, Hanover, and Parsons Creek. At the same time Prior Louis Fink used the columns of the German Catholic press to publicize the new mission center and its opportunities for

[19] Wirth an LMV, Atchison, Jan. 2, 1861. (LMV Leav II 1/17-18)
[20] Bartl records; Annual reports.
[21] *Champion*, May 9, 1869.

St. John
the Baptist Church
Doniphan

Father Suitbert
Demarteau

St. Patrick's Church

Father Thomas Burk

Father John
and a country
church choir

The rock church
Bendena, 1894

Father
Charles Stoeckle

An Altar Society
of some years ago

The
old church
at Wildcat

St. Benedict's College in 1879

The hill on which the Administration
Building now stands, about 1884

St. Benedict's College in 1884

Interior of St. Benedict's
Church in the 1870's

The Faculty of 1886

Top Row: Aloysius Bradley, Joseph Sittenauer, Alphonse Filian, Placidus Baker, Stanislaus Altmann, Edwin Kassens, Andrew Green. Middle Row: Coloman Zwinger, Leo Aaron, Denis Murphy, Louis Flick, Herman Mengwasser, Gerard Heinz, Thomas Burk, Bernard Ulbrich. Bottom Row: Matthew Bradley, Boniface Verheyen, Pirmin Koumly, Peter Kassens, Abbot Innocent Wolf, Adalbert Mueller (SV), Alban Rudroff, Alexius Grass (SV), Charles Stoeckle.

The Students of 1886.　More than one-third of these boys became priests.

Catholic settlers. The result, according to Father Suitbert's notes, was that whereas the Seneca parish had only ten families at the beginning of 1869, two seasons later, at the end of 1870, the parish numbered eighty families. All but about a dozen of these families were of German origin. At that time St. Mary's Church on Wildcat Creek had about thirty-six families, also predominantly German. In 1872 when the parish at Seneca was planning to build a proper church and Father Timothy Luber had replaced Father Pirmin as pastor, Father Suitbert was taking care of a number of missions in the surrounding area and as far west as Concordia. Under his direction the congregations on "Lower and Upper Parsons Creek," at Hanover, Capioma (Fidelity), and St. Bridget's built churches. He attended also the Catholics at Marysville, Guittard's Station (an overland stage stop), and on Mill Creek, as well as those on Mission Creek and Plum Creek in Nebraska.[22]

The mission center at Nebraska City had been the first to be established outside Atchison. The first reinforcements that Abbot Wimmer sent to Prior Augustine were intended specifically to expand missionary activity in Nebraska. When the newly-ordained Father Francis Cannon arrived in the summer of 1858, he was sent directly to Omaha. Bishop Miége had visited Nebraska shortly after the territory was created and again in 1855, securing sites for churches in all the promising towns. Omaha was at first the only place with a sufficient Catholic population to support a resident priest, but the Bishop found it difficult to secure a suitable priest for the place. In 1858, when Omaha was again without a pastor, Prior Augustine made a missionary tour up the river and in Omaha found a marriage to be witnessed and a backlog of baptisms to be administered.[23] In June he returned to Omaha in the company of Bishop Miége.[24] Not long

[22] Demarteau memoranda in baptismal record, Sts. Peter and Paul Church, Seneca.
[23] Cashbook, Mar., 1858.
[24] *Wahrheitsfreund*, June 24, 1858.

thereafter Father Cannon took over as pastor of St. Philomena's Church in Omaha, but when Bishop James O'Gorman arrived in 1859, St. Philomena's became a cathedral, and Father Cannon moved down the river to Nebraska City. He was evidently recalled to St. Vincent at the end of the year to help staff a college in Canada.[25]

Nebraska City was visited from Atchison until 1861, when Father Emmanuel Hartig was sent there as resident pastor. Father Emmanuel completed the church, which had been begun in the previous year.[26] From that time on Nebraska City was a mission center, caring for Catholic settlers in the southeastern corner of Nebraska. Although Nebraska City was attached to Atchison for administration, and although Father Emmanuel, who was stationed there from 1861 to 1875 and from 1881 to 1908, belonged to the Atchison community, he permitted a minimum of interference from his religious superiors. If the frontier was rough, so was Father Emmanuel, but he was an indefatigable worker and an effective missionary. He was the crotchety apostle of southeastern Nebraska.

When Father Emmanuel went to Nebraska City in 1861, the town was in the midst of its only boom in history. The government freighting business of Russell, Majors and Waddell had grown too large to be accommodated at Fort Leavenworth, and they had chosen Nebraska City as the other eastern terminus for their numerous wagon trains. Father Emmanuel not only completed the church, but he opened a school.[27] When five Benedictine Sisters from St. Mary's in Pennsylvania arrived in 1865 to teach in the school, they were given the pastor's residence, and he bought another house for his own use.[28] While the boom was on Father Emmanuel bought up as many lots as possible around the church until he had something more than a block. Two lots for

[25] Wimmer ad Pescetelli, St. Vincent, Dec. 21, 1862. (SPexM)
[26] Hartig report, July 11, 1862.
[27] F. C. Morrison to Hartig, Nebraska City, Feb. 5, 1863.
[28] Wirth an LMV, Atchison, Jan. 26, 1866. (LMV Leav II 1/32)

which Father Emmanuel had paid $600 were finally sold for $200 in 1881.[29]

Encouraged by Bishop O'Gorman, Father Emmanuel was founding another independent Benedictine priory. When Prior Louis Fink expected Father Emmanuel to send part of his salary to the Priory, the Bishop complained bitterly and added, "I wish to establish a house of Benedictines in Nebraska, but I am sure that Atchison and Nebraska will never be united nor satisfied with one another."[30] Father Emmanuel never spoiled any of his religious superiors by sending much of his salary back to the community.

Meanwhile Father Emmanuel had been given an assistant, and the two were busily carrying on their missionary labors. The missions varied from year to year, but the list of 1864 is typical: Besides Nebraska City there was Sidney in Iowa, Sonora in Missouri, and Yankee Creek, Turkey Creek, Brownsville, Aspinwall, and temporarily Rulo and Arago in Nebraska.[31] After the resignation of Prior Augustine Wirth in 1868, Abbot Wimmer took a more direct hand in supplying missionaries for Nebraska, and Father Michael Hofmayr was sent to become the first resident priest in Lincoln and to care for the missions in that area. But within a year there was a disagreement between Bishop O'Gorman and Abbot Wimmer, and the Abbot recalled his men, leaving Father Emmanuel alone with his dreams in Nebraska City.[32]

When Prior Oswald Moosmueller came West to straighten out the tangled financial situation of the Benedictines in Atchison, he found a smaller version of the same trouble in Nebraska City. Aside from the debt on the church, Father Emmanuel owed $2290 for the lots for his foundation, and he wished to retain them in his own name.[33] As Abbot Wimmer put it, Father Emmanuel

[29] Wolf an Bartl, Atchison, Oct. 29, 1881.
[30] O'Gorman to Fink, Omaha, May 3, 1869.
[31] Record of Visitation, Apr. 29, 1864.
[32] Wimmer ad Pescetelli, St. Vincent, Aug. 7, 1871. (SPexM)
[33] Hartig report, Feb. 25, 1875.

thought that no one but himself knew how to pay a debt.[34] Father Emmanuel was finally persuaded to transfer title to his lots, now sadly deflated in value, to his community, and was moved to Seneca for a few years.[35]   Prior Oswald, disgusted and eager to give up the parish in Nebraska City, even offered to assume the debt and give the property to Abbot Alexius Edelbrock, of St. John's Abbey, if that community would assume charge of the parish.[36] Nothing came of this offer, and Father Thomas Bartl was pastor of the parish until 1881, when Father Emmanuel returned to his first love and remained until shortly before his death.

In January, 1876, Prior Oswald made up a list of the mission stations attended from Atchison, excluding Nebraska City and its missions, and the mission centers at St. Benedict's in Doniphan County and Seneca, both of which were by that time staffed by two priests. Two missions which were "attended twice a month from Seneca on horseback" are listed: St. Bridget's, with a stone church built in 1871-72 under the direction of Father Suitbert, numbered sixty families, and St. Augustine's, Capioma (Fidelity), where Father Suitbert had also built a church in 1873, had twenty Irish and fourteen German families. The missions attended from Atchison were Doniphan with "maybe" twenty-five English-speaking and ten German families; Grasshopper Falls (Valley Falls), where a brick church had been built in 1870 by Father Defouri of Topeka; Mooney Creek with nineteen German and three English-speaking families; St. Patrick's with eighty-nine families; Holton with nineteen families; Effingham with nineteen families; Netawaka with fifteen families; Slattery's or Independence (Good Intent), where there had been ninety communions at the Jubilee services; and Wolf River (Fanning), where there had been seventy-five communions.[37] This list is clearly incomplete, but it

[34] Wimmer an Bartl, St. Vincent, Mar. 10, 1875.
[35] Moosmueller to Wimmer, Nebraska City, Feb. 25, 1875. (SVA)
[36] Moosmueller to Edelbrock, Atchison, Apr. 7, 1876. (SJA)
[37] Chapter Minutes, last pages of the first volume.

indicates that while such congregations as that at St. Patrick's had doubled in numbers since 1864, some of the old riverside towns had disappeared. Meanwhile new rural stations — Netawaka, Slattery's, and Effingham, as well as Valley Falls, which had previously been visited from Topeka — were added to the Priory's mission circuits.

The problems of the missionary in Kansas were made more difficult by the fact that the Catholics were a comparatively small proportion of the immigration, they scattered quite widely, and too often could be organized only in groups too small to build a church easily or support a pastor. Further complications grew out of the fact that even in a very small mission a number of nationalities would often be represented. Too few priests were available for the number of square miles to be covered, and a rather high rate of turnover among the missionaries was not helpful.

The comparatively slow growth of Catholic institutions in Kansas cannot be understood unless one remembers Kansas' early misfortunes and the fact that Catholics were always a small minority of the immigration. During its early years Kansas was almost a synonym for hard luck. The fight over slavery produced more fireworks than solid development. The first wave of settlement after the slavery question was settled was hard hit by the severe drought of 1860.

The drought began in October, 1859, and the winter and spring of 1860 brought far too little moisture. Atchison's *Champion* twice noted rain in poetic terms but otherwise breathed no word of drought until it published a letter concerning the need of relief for the drought-stricken in October.[38] The crop was a complete failure. Prior Augustine reported that there was no hay, no corn, nor anything else.[39] There were no reserves from the pre-

[38] Oct. 27, 1860.
[39] Wirth an LMV, Atchison, Jan. 2, 1861. (LMV Leav II 1/17-18)

vious year's crop because the new mining areas of the West had provided such a good market for corn to men who needed the money badly.[40] Those who could, left Kansas, but some were too poor to move.[41] Those who stayed, particularly the recent settlers, were soon in desperate straits. Thaddeus Hyatt and S. C. Pomeroy headed a state committee for relief of the destitute and maintained that 50,000 people were in danger of starvation. Most estimates, however, put the number at about half that figure. The committee solicited aid from the people of the United States and distributed it through county committees.

Father Philip Vogg, who had been attending the missions west into Nemaha and Marshall Counties during 1860, was sent East at the end of the year to beg for the needy Catholic settlers.[42] He wrote that many of his parishioners had had only cornmeal to eat all summer and that they were now badly in need of clothing. He pointed out also that the lack of water and fodder for the stock had made the draft animals so weak that the settlers had difficulty even getting firewood. The severity of the winter increased the suffering of the needy. Prior Augustine reported that a steady procession of people came to the Priory to ask for food and especially clothing, but the Priory's small supply of clothing was soon exhausted.[43]

Father Philip continued to beg for the drought-stricken Catholics of Kansas through the early months of 1861. In February he reported that the collection had thus far surpassed his expectations. Clinton County, Illinois, for example, had donated fifteen hundred dollars worth of food, a hundred dollars worth of clothing, and some three hundred dollars in cash.[44] Lists of donations from individuals and churches throughout the Middle West

[40] E. N. Morrill, *History of Brown County, Kansas* (Hiawatha, 1876), 39-40
[41] Garin, *Miége*, 129; *Wahrheitsfreund*, Dec. 20, 1860.
[42] Clipping of Vogg letter, Dec. 5, 1860. (LMV Leav II 1/20)
[43] *Wahrheitsfreund*, Mar. 14, 1861.
[44] *Ibid.*, Feb. 28, 1861; Mar. 7, 1861 from *Herold des Glaubens*.

continued to appear in the *Wahrheitsfreund* through the month of March.

The Priory, of course, shared to a certain extent the fortunes of the people it served. The Prior asked the Ludwig-Missionsverein for extra aid because the crop on the College farm had been a complete failure and whereas "in the past the priests usually brought a few dollars home from the stations, this year they rarely get anything. I have never seen such times."[45] On the other hand, he did not hesitate to build a considerable addition to the College in 1861. According to an account written years later, the purpose of building at that time was to provide work for the unemployed.[46] That account might be true, but it should be noted that although the drought brought business in Kansas practically to a standstill, river towns like Atchison were not too severely affected. Atchison at that time depended very little upon agriculture, for the town's whole energies were engaged in forwarding and freighting over the plains. The year 1860 was a good one for Atchison, and the decline in business noticeable in 1861 is attributable to the war rather than the drought.

Prior Augustine reported in the spring of 1861 that the need of the drought-stricken settlers would continue until harvest but that the prospects for that were good. He warned prospective settlers that the speculators were crying that there was no need in Kansas because they wanted to unload their claims and lots. They maintained that the immigrant wagons were again moving into Kansas, but the Prior reported that those he had seen and interviewed were people who had left in the previous autumn to stay with relatives in Missouri or Iowa and were now returning for another try. He advised immigrants not to come to Kansas unless that year's harvest was good. And he thanked all for helping the sufferers in Kansas.[47]

[45] Wirth an LMV, Atchison, Jan. 2, 1861. (LMV Leav II 1/17-18)
[46] Mengwasser an Leopoldinen Stiftung, Jan. 28, 1882 draft.
[47] *Wahrheitsfreund*, May 9, 1861.

The harvest of 1861 was good. Prior Augustine reported a bumper wheat harvest and a promising corn crop.[48] But the Civil War had begun and the fight for the control of Missouri remained in doubt through much of 1861. Guerrilla action crippled both river and railroad traffic, and Kansas farmers had no eastern market. The settlers could not sell their crops, little money was available, and trade was mostly on a barter basis. Under the circumstances the missionaries still found it practically impossible to make a living from the missions.[49]

Throughout the war Atchison, like other Kansas towns, was periodically alarmed by the possibility of invasion by guerrilla forces from Missouri. On September 7, 1861, for example, the *Champion*, under the headline "LOOK OUT FOR DANGER," announced that "On Thursday last we received positive information that the traitors at Rushville, DeKalb, Iatan and Platte City had large camps in the vicinity, and were marching on our city." Mayor Fairchild, a Union Democrat, and Editor John A. Martin, leader of the new Republicans and colonel and aide-de-camp to the Governor, vied with each other in calling for the home guards from surrounding counties as well as for those of Atchison County. The ferry was firmly tied to the Kansas bank of the Missouri River, and a guard was placed aboard it. Even skiffs were forbidden to cross the river without permits. Within a week defensive forces totalling 650 men had been mobilized.[50] The invasion failed to materialize, but such alarms occurred regularly throughout the war.

J. W. Reilly, '62-'65, recalled that a large bell was mounted on a tower in the back yard of the College. "Besides being used for church services and the Angelus, it was used for an alarm bell. During the war, I remember, there was great fear that the bushwhackers would make a raid on the College. And, as there was

    [48] *Ibid.*, Aug. 1, 1861.
    [49] Wirth an Ludwig I, Atchison, Dec. 18, 1861. (GHA 50/5 I); Wirth an Lebling, Atchison, Nov. 10, 1861. (LMV Leav II 1/22)
    [50] Sept. 7 and 14, 1861.

no way of notifying the authorities and the populace, this bell was to be used for that purpose. I believe, too, that during those troublesome times the Brothers stood 'guard duty' at night."[51]

After the first year of the war communications with the eastern states were restored almost to normal, and, what was more important, the overland trade with the military posts and the new mining camps grew steadily and brought a degree of prosperity. However, during the first year or two of the war many had left their farms to follow the flag or other opportunities. Looking back at the effect of those turbulent years on the new State, the Editor of the *Champion* wrote:

> Politics and [the Kansas] civil war left no opportunity for the development of the resources of the country. And when tranquility was restored, the people were without occupation, without capital, and without inducements to labor. Debauched by excitement, they had lost all habits of industry, and the public places were infested with a hungry horde of wretched parasites who ate out the substance of the people. Debts were unpaid. Farms disappeared under the incubus of an intolerable usury. Capital withdrew, and when the drought of 1860 added famine to the other evils of those wretched years. . . Kansas was a beggar. . . During this epoch of desolation and doubt the war began. To many it was a refuge. . .[52]

After the Civil War Kansas became relatively normal, suffering only such comparatively minor disturbances as grasshoppers and Carrie Nation.

After a year of experience Prior Augustine wrote that the missionary's life in Kansas was hard. Essentially he shared the poverty and deprivations of his flock, but to these were added in his case the hardships of constant travel and the discomfort of near homelessness. Practically all of the missionaries travelled on horseback during the early years. Buggies were expensive, and in many

---

[51] Reminiscences [c. 1911]. This could have been only during the last year of the war, for the bell was purchased in 1864.—Cashbook, Feb. 1864.
[52] Apr. 10, 1870.

places the roads were hardly adequate for buggies. As the Prior described the life to King Ludwig I:

With an entire chapel in a traveling bag, which is tossed on the horse's back, the priest wanders from one station to another, the family table serving as an altar. Often there were no candlesticks; I wanted to say Mass, so there was nothing to do but to put the candles in bottles. The most difficult thing in this new land is to find a stopping place for the night. The houses in which the people live do not deserve the name; they are ordinarily of one room, sixteen feet square, that also serves as the kitchen. In this room there are one or two beds, a table and a stove, so the room is already full, and here in the midst of a crowd the priest must also sleep, which is very unpleasant. The houses are so badly built that the wind whistles in from all sides, so that it is a wonder that the people do not get sick and die. But they bear all their hardships in the hope that in a few years they will have a good home.[53]

Once a circuit had been established, the missionary designated certain homes as stations and tried to inform these people of the date of his next visit by letter so that all the neighbors could be informed.[54] Small boys afoot or on ponies, however, were probably the more usual method of spreading the news. These circuits always involved a good bit of riding, and Father Emmanuel maintained that he often rode forty or fifty miles a day.[55] A fragment of a letter in which Father Emmanuel gives instructions for visiting certain missions in Nebraska to the newly-arrived Father Thomas Bartl preserves details that are ordinarily lost and gives a rather vivid picture of the life:

Go from here to ROCKBLUFF about eighteen miles from Nebraska City and ask after Mr. Haskins the owner of the flouring mill. If you find him he will invite you to say Mass on Saturday. From ROCKBLUFF go to PLATTSMOUTH and ask after Mr. Gottfried Fickler a German butcher, he will tell you what you have to do. You can say Mass and preach there on Sunday. On Monday you can ride to OMAHA and see the Bishop. Ask him about the German settlement HELENA whether you should go there or not and how far it is. On

53 Wirth an Ludwig I, Doniphan, Dec. 18, 1858. (GHA 86/6 V)
54 *Wahrheitsfreund*, Mar. 14, 1861.
55 Hartig an Bartl, Atchison, June 6, 1861.

Tuesday you may start for WEST POINT. Ride as far as ELKHORN CITY and take your dinner there, it is about twenty miles from Omaha. There you have to take another road to FONTANELLE it is about twenty miles from ELKHORN CITY.

In Fontanelle you may stop at Mr. Hancock — Hotel or go to the Fitzsimmons. . . In Fontanelle inquire after the road to West Point, you have always a good road along the Elkhorn River. On the road you will come to a saw mill, there you have to cross at a large creek and when you see once on the other side of the Elkhorn River some houses and a road to the river you will find the German Settlement. You may inquire where Mr. Grovian is living or Mr. Kappins. West Point is about thirty-five miles from Fontanelle. In West Point you may stay as long as you please, from there you can probably ride to Helena and back to Omaha. Be here 23 August, you must go to Missouri on the 4th Sunday. . .[56]

During those early years the missionaries sometimes felt that they were caught in a vicious circle. They needed churches to give adequate service to the growing population, but the settlers were poor and needed every penny they had to get settled and to hold on until they had raised a few successful crops. They had no surplus with which to build churches.[57] Once established, however, the settlers raised money in the time-honored ways, with some changes dictated by the facts of life on the frontier. For example, at a two-day fair held at St. Benedict's Colony in Doniphan County when Father Thomas Bartl was finishing the church and about to build a house, some of those who came from a distance simply slept in the new church.[58]

The missionaries were often called upon to give impartial advice to prospective settlers. In the early days Prior Augustine gave good sane advice through letters to the Catholic press. He particularly stressed the often-overlooked fact that the cost of the land was a compara-

[56] Hartig to Bartl, Nebraska City, Aug. 1, 1862.
This was not one of the regular monthly circuits but one of the special visits made annually to give German-speaking Catholics in other missions an opportunity to receive the Sacraments.
[57] Wirth an LMV, Doniphan, Feb. 8, 1858. (LMV Leav II 1/1)
[58] Gray, *Doniphan County History*, 71.

tively small part of the cost of making a farm out of virgin
prairie. As he explained the process to his benefactor,
King Ludwig I:

The people here are still poor. The Catholics who have
come in the last three years to make homes for themselves
brought some money it is true, for only those come for the most
part, who saved a few hundred dollars in the cities but owned
no home. They come to make a home for themselves and to
better their condition. When they arrive they find what they
are looking for, namely, land, but it has lain fallow since the
Deluge and is consequently very difficult to break. Everyone,
immigrant as well as native, who has reached the age of twenty-
one has the privilege of claiming 160 acres of land, for which
he must pay a dollar and a quarter an acre to the government
of the United States, so that 160 acres costs $200 or in German
money 500 fl. The land is all surveyed and every 160 acres
is marked with boundary stones. When the settler has chosen
a piece of land, he must build a house on it, break a part of it,
put in a crop, and he must buy all his provisions for at least a
half-year, and besides, he cannot plant much the first year.
There is little woodland here, it is mostly meadowland or
prairie, but, as I said, plowing the land for the first time is
hard and expensive work. Special big plows are used, to which
from five to eight yoke of oxen must be hitched to break up
the extremely solid ground, and that is why the first plowing
costs so much. The usual price for breaking an acre of land
is five dollars. The settler, therefore, needs all the money that
he brings with him, and with the best will in the world can do
little or nothing for church and school. It is three or four
years before he can spare something, and for that reason an
alms for these poor missions is so great a benefaction.[59]

The missionaries received many letters seeking advice about land and opportunities. Sometimes the missionary offered the only ray of hope to nearly desperate
men. Joseph Neukirchen had somehow got himself
settled in Tennessee, seventy-five miles from the nearest
Catholic church, and he wanted out. As he wrote to
Prior Oswald, "A man with plenty of means would travel
through the country, and select his new home; if I would
do that, it would exhaust my means to the bottom. I
need a friendly kind hand, to direct my path, to give

[59] Wirth an Ludwig I, Doniphan, Dec. 18, 1858. (GHA 86/6 V)

me some advice..."[60] Not only farmers sought such help, but even a Swiss baker in Chicago, badly pressed by the depression and the growth of "steam bakeries," hoped to locate in Atchison or Topeka.[61] A German school teacher and a group of Irish immigrants in New York with farmers, machinists, railroad blacksmiths, carpenters and storekeepers among them, all sought the aid of the missionaries.[62]

Father Emmanuel was right when he wrote to Father Thomas Bartl that Kansas offered a wonderful opportunity for truly apostolic labor. This was the Priory's most important work. Viewed in retrospect it was a thrilling challenge, but on the spot it was an endless round of very hard work with many deprivations. The task would have been strenuous at best, but it was made even harder by the effects of drought and war which aggravated the settlers' poverty. The work was hampered also by the troubled state of affairs at the Priory. Not until the end of the sixties was it able to establish the badly-needed new mission centers at Seneca and at St. Benedict's in Doniphan County. But no matter how discouraging conditions at the Priory might be, this job had to be done. Some of the missionaries, like Casimir Seitz, undoubtedly had their lives shortened by fever and the hardships of the life. Some found the demands too great, but others, those who formed the first stable community at St. Benedict's, were blessed with the grace and the strength to carry on as true apostles.

[60] Neukirchen to Father Prior, Chattanooga, Sept. 27, 1875.
[61] Joseph Widmer an Luber, Chicago, Feb. 16, 1876.
[62] Henry Schmidt an Prior, Macon City, May 4, 1874. Joseph M'Laughlin to Bartl, New York, Jan. 17, 1876.

CHAPTER V

Abbot Innocent and the Pioneer Community, 1877-1887

Abbot Innocent Wolf was blessed by Bishop Fink in St. Benedict's Church, Atchison, March 21, 1877.[1] The Abbot was the son of Johann Peter Wolf and his wife, Anna Gertrud Molitor, and was born April 13, 1843, at Schmidheim, in the Archdiocese of Cologne. On the following day he was baptized Thomas Friedrich Wilhelm but in later years answered to the name of Wilhelm. He was the youngest of nine children. The Wolfs emigrated to Wisconsin in 1851, and three years later Wilhelm was enrolled in St. Vincent College in Pennsylvania. There he joined the community, making his profession on July 11, 1861. He became a citizen of the United States on October 4, 1866. After his ordination on May 26, 1866, he was sent to Rome to complete his studies.

One mark of greatness in Archabbot Wimmer[2] was his realization that the Benedictines of the world needed a greater sense of community, and he took a number of practical steps to help further this end. He favored meetings of the abbots, he undertook the publication of a directory of Benedictines throughout the world, but most important was his proposal for an international Benedictine college in Rome. The college was twenty years in the future and would require a push from the Pope. Meanwhile the Archabbot did what he could on his own initiative. He chose three of his most promising

---

[1] The following data are from Abbot Innocent's personal papers.

[2] On Dec. 29, 1883, Pope Leo XIII conferred on Abbot Wimmer the Cappa Magna and the title of Archabbot. To avoid confusion that title will be used hereafter in this book.

young men — Adalbert Mueller, Hilary Pfraengle, and Innocent Wolf — entrusted them to that ardent, though un-
trained champion of scholarship, Father Oswald Moosmueller, and sent them to Rome to set up a little Benedictine house of studies. Innocent Wolf, like the others, was
a very conscientious student. He received his doctorate
in theology from the Universita Romana on July 25, 1870,
just beating the fall of Rome to the forces of Victor Emmanuel by a month or two.

Back at St. Vincent he taught moral and dogmatic
theology, was prefect in the seminary, master of novices,
procurator, and finally prior before he lost his voice because of a painfully infected throat in the winter of 1875-
76. He was elected abbot of St. Benedict's when he was
thirty-three years old. He wore a rather straggly beard
because he believed it a part of a monk's proper equipment. His passport of 1880 describes him as only five
feet six inches tall, with hazel eyes and a "conspicuous"
nose. He loved Archabbot Wimmer, and he loved St.
Vincent Archabbey. He had come there at the age of
eleven, and it was his home. When in 1877 he left for
Kansas to take up his burden as abbot, he broke down
and cried.[3] Archabbot Wimmer, of course, disliked losing a loving son, a good theologian, and an outstanding
religious. But the Archabbot wrote that he was happy
that the Atchison community was finally organized, because it was bound to be an important Benedictine out-
post looking to the south and west.[4]

The Pioneer Community

Abbot Innocent's first concern in Kansas was not the
debt, the College, nor the missions, but the community.
When he had passed through Atchison in the summer of
1876, he had noted with some concern that "there seems
to be a bad spirit among all here. What struck me most

---

[3] Wolf an Wimmer, Atchison, Jan. 10, 1877. (SVA)
[4] Wimmer an Lang, St. Vincent, [Feb., 1877]. (AM)

137

is that the office is not always said in choir. One day only three were here, while four are required for choir. The excuse is that there are not enough people. I think that will not bring any blessing on the house."[5] The development of a real feeling of community is notable after Abbot Innocent's coming. Bishop Fink had been correct in his prediction that having an abbot would give the house a sense of unity it had never yet known. Fathers Timothy Luber, Pirmin Koumly, and Boniface Verheyen, who had by some miracle kept a spirit of community alive through so many discouraging years, now had a real home in which to rest their loyalty.

The community that had chosen Innocent Wolf to be its father and leader in doing the work of God in Kansas was pitifully small. Only ten chapter members were actually engaged in monastic work or studying for ordination. None of them was a perfect instrument in the hands of his superior, and so the Abbot had only fractional monks with whom to do the work at hand. Only the great saints really deliver to God all that they promised and intended on the day they made their vows. The typical monk has his limitations, his areas of holding back, and his crotchets, for which abbots must resignedly make allowance.

Seven active priests were members of St. Benedict's Abbey. Father Emmanuel Hartig, the hard-working but very independent missionary, was at this time 'exiled' to Seneca, but in 1881 he was to return to Nebraska City, where he remained until shortly before his death. His confreres complained of his scornful, contemptuous, and arbitrary ways.[6] The Bishop complained of his harshness to the Sisters.[7] But he was a hardworking missionary, was honored by being made administrator of the Diocese of Lincoln during Bishop Bonacum's absence in 1892, and was made vicar general of the Diocese in 1893.[8]

[5] Wolf to Wimmer, Atchison, Aug. 4, 1876. (SVA)
[6] Luber to Wolf, Seneca, Jan. 23, 1878.
[7] O'Connor to Wolf, Omaha, Sept. 17, 1884.
[8] Bonacum to Hartig, Lincoln, Oct. 17, 1892; Aug. 3, 1893.

A picture of Father Timothy Luber, taken in the sixties, shows a lively young priest rather snappily dressed from top hat to boots. He believed in speaking his mind to all and sundry and helped to make chapter meetings lively. He was a very able missionary, but Abbot Innocent complained that he himself was permitted no voice in whatever assignment he gave to Father Timothy,[9] and "he cannot save anything for the monastery, no matter how good a parish he has."[10] But as Father Timothy grew older he became more reliable, more typical — careful that his assistant did not fritter away too much time with the violin — and much less interesting.

There was nothing flamboyant about Father Pirmin Koumly. He was the quiet type that enjoys the confidence of his confreres. In the days when there was an official known as the Monitor, whose duty it was to keep the abbot informed of problems and possible abuses in the community, it was Father Pirmin who was elected to the office.[11] His lifetime hobby was birdwatching. Most of his life was spent on the missions, but in 1895 he was appointed master of novices and director of the clericate. Abbot Innocent held him in high regard because he was an excellent religious.[12]

The character of solid, dependable Father Peter Kassens also helps to explain the survival of St. Benedict's.[13] He was sent to St. Louis to get a business-college diploma so that St. Benedict's could offer those popular courses without hiring a lay teacher. Under Prior Oswald Moosmueller he was a self-trained missionary. In 1878 he was back teaching forty hours a week.[14] He was director of the College, then prior, and then director again. Abbot Innocent was delighted to discover, after he had appointed Father Peter to the office, that a prior with courage could

[9] Wolf to Edelbrock, Atchison, Aug. 31, 1889. (SJA)
[10] Wolf Diary, May 30, 1888.
[11] Chapter Minutes, Feb. 7, 1877.
[12] Wolf to Engel, Atchison, Mar. 30, 1899. (SJA)
[13] Peter (John) Kassens was born in Esterwege, Hanover, May 28, 1841, professed Aug. 15, 1866, ordained Aug. 26, 1869, and died Jan. 17, 1916.—*Necrologium*, No. 463.
[14] Wolf an Wimmer, Atchison, Nov. 21, 1878. (SVA)

do much to ease an abbot's burdens. Father Peter was just, calm, and definite — fine virtues on which to build a sound community.[15]

Equally important in the formation of the early community was the warm enthusiasm of Father Boniface Verheyen.[16] He was Abbot Innocent's first prior and held the office off and on, although the Abbot considered him rather too easy-going for the position. His parish experience was brief because he had no talent for raising money, but he observed as scientifically as possible the cyclone that wrecked his church in Seneca. He was secretary of the monastic chapter for many years and injected life and color into those ordinarily drab minutes. For example, in recording the introduction of a picayune point, he once wrote, "This occasioned much useless discussion, the Secretary particularly was very windy in the matter. . . Time of discus. 60 min."[17] His greatest contributions to St. Benedict's were as a monk and teacher. One of the best tributes to him was at the time of his death when the *Rambler* reported that he had been a student and a teacher until the day he died. Abbot Innocent considered him "our main professor."[18] He taught history and literature for the most part, but he was insatiably curious about the wonders of God's creation. He studied geography, geology, astronomy, flowers and trees. Furthermore, he was constantly busy in beautifying the campus. He purchased a magic lantern and entertained early generations of St. Benedict's students with his illustrated science lectures. Trained as a carpenter's apprentice, he was able to do the estimating for the new buildings. He turned out a homely and practical translation of the Rule of St. Benedict and of some other small works, such as the quaint *General Principles of the Religious Life* of happy memory.

---

[15] *Idem*, Feb. 20, 1883. (SVA)
[16] Boniface (Frederick) Verheyen was born in Qualburg, Rhenish Prussia, May 22, 1844, professed Aug. 15, 1866, ordained Aug. 26, 1869, and died Dec. 23, 1923.—*Necrologium*, No. 590.
[17] Chapter Minutes, June 25, 1879.
[18] Wolf an Wimmer, Atchison, Jan. 28, 1884. (SVA)

One of Father Boniface's outstanding characteristics was his great-hearted loyalty. On one occasion when a young monk complained of what he termed the tyrannical ways of a confrere, Father Boniface answered, "As to your 'tyrants' — would to God our Order had a goodly number with their characters! That the world has praise for the Order and its work is entirely due to such as would answer your idea of tyrants. They have made mistakes; posterity has sat in judgment on those tyrants and condoned their mistakes, because theirs were mistakes of policy and judgment. But your mistakes and those of your kind are mistakes of heart and will; for these there is neither palliation nor excuse."[19] Prior Oswald, who was a good but rather severe judge of men, said the last word on Father Boniface: "He can fill any post with honor to himself and to the house."[20]

Good, blunt Abbot Innocent characterized the young Father Placidus McKeever as not merely lazy but "stinking lazy." The Abbot complained that he would in any case have been worth but half a man because he could not preach in German. But the Abbot did not completely blame Father Placidus, remarking that the poor man was a product of Prior Augustine Wirth, with only three years of Latin and the barest elements of theology. The Abbot forgot that Fathers Peter and Boniface also were products of the same school.[21] Nevertheless, Father Placidus became a useful member of the community and was a good pastor in many missions. He transferred his vows to the Creston Priory, but when that monastery failed to develop, he returned to the Atchison community.[22]

Father Eugene Bode was Abbot Innocent's chief

[19] Verheyen to Ambrose Rank, Atchison, Oct. 17, 1899.
Father Ambrose's notation on this, and understandably since the person in question was Father Thomas Burk, was, "Monumental gush! God deliver us from such missionaries as apotheosized above."
[20] Moosmueller to Wimmer, Atchison, Apr. 21, 1876. (SVA)
[21] Wolf an Wimmer, Atchison, Dec. 23, 1877. (SVA)
[22] Chapter Minutes, Mar. 7, 1887.
Placidus (Neel) McKeever was born in Derry, Ireland, Apr. 19, 1840, professed Aug. 15, 1866, ordained Aug. 26, 1869, and died Sept. 22, 1896.—*Necrologium*, No. 246.

problem child. His extreme individualism, weakness for drink, and pathologically bitter tongue kept him at odds with his religious superiors most of his life. He spent much time in penance, and he always kept the faith. The community would have been incomplete without him, because every family has its problem child. In extreme old age Father Eugene mellowed to a mildly profane crustiness that was the delight of his youngest confreres. In him they had a whiff of the dusty frontier, still fresh in the days of the great depression.[23]

Father Thomas Bartl had been sent to Kansas because the community was badly in need of a "lover of order, a God fearing religious," and he was that and more. Prior Oswald noted that he was one of the best-liked priests in Kansas.[24] When St. Benedict's was made an abbey, the assumption was that Father Thomas would transfer his vows there, since he had identified himself so completely with the mission in Kansas. But he preferred to wait until after the abbatial election, and when Abbot Innocent shortly asked if he wished to transfer his vows, Father Thomas explained his position:

I would like to have my stability at Atchison and it would have been transferred long ago if the Lord Abbot [Wimmer] had ever indicated his willingness to have me transfer my vows. I did not want to ask him because it seemed to me to be a temptation to add an amendment to my profession, something about which I might later reproach myself. Of course, I know I cannot escape reproaches, no matter what I do. If I do not transfer my vows, I will probably regret it. If I do transfer them the same may happen. Then I would have to say to myself: You have placed your will in the hands of your superior by solemn vow and now you have taken it back again. You should not have amended your profession. That is the *sole reason* for my decision. I do not know whether it is conscientiousness or cowardice. It think it is the latter.[25]

That explanation agrees with Father Boniface's memory of St. Benedict's outstanding missionary: "Father

---

[23] Eugene (Charles) Bode was born in St. Louis, Mo., Nov. 19, 1848, professed Aug. 15, 1866, ordained Apr. 24, 1873, and died Nov. 8, 1933.—*Necrologium*, No. 733.
[24] Moosmueller to Wimmer, Atchison, Jan. 28, 1875. (SVA)
[25] Bartl an Wolf, Nebraska City, Feb. 21, 1877.

Thomas was a lovable character, of a serious turn of mind, not much given to pleasantries, very zealous and devoted to his work, happy when he could be of service to others. He was very unselfish, his own appearance, convenience, and personal comfort being the least of his troubles."[26] If Father Thomas was so reserved, his popularity can be accounted for only by the sanctity that showed through. He finally transferred his vows to St. Benedict's in 1883, and two years later, after two decades of hard labor in the care of souls, he was felled by a bad heart. Abbot Innocent could write truly, "We have the assurance that he died in the Lord."[27]

Although both Father Pirmin and Father Thomas were rather serious, the warm fraternal charity that existed between them broke out in typical brotherly nonsense. Father Pirmin wrote a second nocturn for Father Thomas, hailing him as the apostle of northeastern Kansas.[28] The intended joke turned out to be the simple truth. Father Pirmin also sent a formal announcement of his coming visit to Father Thomas' "palace," using burlesque chancery-style German to convey the information that the sender would arrive by freight train.

The remaining members of the chapter in 1877 were the three clerics, Adolph Wesseling, Winfried Schmidt, and John Stader. Father Adolph was ordained in 1878, served on the missions, collected money in eastern dioceses for St. Benedict's from 1883 to 1886, was appointed the first pastor of St. Peter's Church in Council Bluffs, Iowa, and died there of typhoid fever in 1891.[29] Father Winfried was ordained also in 1878. At first he taught in the College — everything from dogma to telegraphy. He was not a particularly successful teacher and was appointed pastor of St. Mary's Church in Des Moines, Iowa, in

---

[26] Verheyen Reminiscences, 1922.
[27] Wolf an Wimmer, Atchison, Jan. 1, 1886. (SVA)
[28] The lessons of the second nocturn in matins for the feast of a saint are biographical.
[29] Adolph (Herman) Wesseling was born in Gross-Fullen, Hanover, Jan. 10, 1846, professed July 16, 1873, ordained July 5, 1878, and died Sept. 24, 1891.—*Necrologium*, No. 189.

1883.[30] Father John was ordained in 1879. Abbot Innocent commented that although Father John had been a poor student, he was nevertheless well satisfied with himself.[31] He talked too much, invariably built up formidable opposition to himself, and consequently had to be moved pretty regularly but otherwise made a decent country pastor.[32]

Besides these members of the community a number of priests were on loan from St. Vincent during Archabbot Wimmer's lifetime. Some of them were problems,[33] but most of them were remembered with gratitude and affection. When Father Ambrose Huebner was sent to Kansas in 1877, he was at first rather unhappy and kept himself aloof from the community. While stationed at Bendena he jumped from a wagon in a runaway and broke his leg. The local doctor did a clumsy job, and for a long time Father Ambrose had an infected leg.[34] Since he could no longer ride the missionary circuit, Father Ambrose was made procurator of the Abbey and turned out to be invaluable. When the need of caring for his widowed mother dictated his return to the East in 1884, Abbot Innocent wrote sadly, "He is a good administrator and I will not get such a one again."[35] When Father Ambrose came to Kansas he was rated *"etwas legér"* and eccentric.[36] The light-mindedness turned out to have been light-heartedness and was a distinct asset in Kansas. Father Ambrose lived life with enthusiasm and apparently could bear almost any burden so long as he need not suffer in silence. Beneath the grumbling was an affectionate

[30] Winfried (Friedrich) Schmidt was born in Siedlinghausen, Westphalia, Mar. 31, 1851, professed July 16, 1873, ordained Apr. 23, 1878, and died July 16, 1911.—*Necrologium*, No. 401.
[31] Wolf an Wimmer, Atchison, Nov. 10, 1877. (SVA)
[32] Wolf to Luber, Atchison, Oct. 4, 1891.
John B. Stader was born in Youngstown, Pa., Apr. 12, 1850, professed Aug. 18, 1873, ordained July 5, 1879, and died May 20, 1919.—*Necrologium*, No. 525.
[33] Wolf an Wimmer, Atchison, June 8, 1881; June 13, 1887. (SVA)
[34] *Idem*, Nov. 6; 21, 1878. (SVA)
Ambrose (George) Huebner, born in Brooklyn, N.Y., Dec. 9, 1848, professed Sept. 17, 1869, ordained Dec. 21, 1872, and died Feb. 5, 1941.—*Necrologium*, No. 878.
[35] Wolf an Wimmer, Atchison, July 31, 1884. (SVA)
[36] *Idem*, June 18, 1877. (SVA) Wimmer an Wolf, St. Vincent, Apr. 12, 1878.

144

heart. While Abbot Innocent was on his trip to Europe in 1880, Father Ambrose wrote, "I am the same old pestered poor christian. . . I like this place yet, but I am the same old growler. Deserving a good scolding I am preparing for it and you will find me well steeled when you — brush me up. Come soon everybody wants you— needs you."[37]

Archabbot Wimmer sent also some able professors on loan, such as Fathers Albert Robrecht, Casimir Elsesser, and Alexius Grass, who have been mentioned earlier. The prize of the lot was Abbot Innocent's old Roman classmate, Father Adalbert Mueller. St. Vincent could hardly have been expected to waste a Roman doctor on Kansas, but nevertheless he was at St. Benedict's from 1883 to 1887 and taught both philosophy and theology. Furthermore, he was an outstandingly good religious and added much to the development of the community.[38]

The other members of the community in 1877 were Brothers Luke Zaeune, Lambert Bliemel, Joseph von Bragel, Placidus Feser, Andrew Allermann, Lawrence Egan, Adam Gansen, and Bernard Ball.[39] These were the men who did the farming, the cooking, the building, and the repairing. Some were treasured for their solid piety, and some were characters. Brother Luke had come out to Kansas with Father Emmanuel as a cook. He and Father Thomas had set up the first parochial residence

[37] Huebner to Wolf, Atchison, Nov. 4, 1880.
[38] Wolf an Wimmer, Atchison, Dec. 20, 1883; June 13, 1887. (SVA)
Adalbert (Karl) Mueller was born in Huefingen, Baden, Mar. 17, 1842, professed Dec. 19, 1859, ordained Feb. 17, 1865, died Jan. 25, 1906 in Rome. —Necrologium, No. 337.
[39] Lambert (Andrew) Bliemel was born in Regensburg, Bavaria, May 29, 1835, professed Jan. 20, 1856, and died Feb. 17, 1896 at St. Mary's, Pa.—Necrologium, No. 239.
Placidus (Michael) Feser was born in Binsfeld, Bavaria, Feb. 14, 1837, professed Aug. 15, 1869, and died Aug. 17, 1886.—Ibid., No. 136.
Andrew (Wilhelm) Allermann was born in Bottrop, Westphalia, Sept. 12, 1841, professed Feb. 10, 1871, and died Dec. 1, 1914.—Ibid., No. 447.
Lawrence (Thomas) Egan was born in Limerick, Ireland, June 18, 1843, professed Dec. 8, 1871, and died Nov. 27, 1919.—Ibid., No. 532.
Adam (John) Gansen was born in Boettingen, Rhenish Prussia, Aug. 16, 1836, professed Dec. 8, 1873, and died Apr. 11, 1919.—Ibid., No. 524.
Bernard (Albert) Ball was born in Catowa, Ill., Dec. 14, 1855, professed Apr. 13, 1876, and died Apr. 25, 1882.—Ibid., No. 95.

at St. Benedict's in Doniphan County. But Father Thomas finally sent Brother Luke back to the Abbey for insubordination at Seneca. Among other things he *would* play dominoes with his cronies until nine-thirty even on a Sunday night.[40]

Brother Lambert came out to Kansas in 1868 but returned to St. Vincent in 1886. He was a joy and a trial to Abbot Innocent. Brother Lambert was a good gardener, vintner, and a wonderful all-round workman. He could do anything. But he was tough, temperamental, reacted violently when things went wrong, and had a fabulous command of ill-tempered language. Brother candidates were shocked and left the community, and the older Brothers were kept in constant turmoil.[41] Brother Lambert was not a peaceful man, but he was missed when he returned to Pennsylvania.[42]

Brother Andrew Allerman was an altogether different person. Whether he was an adequate farm boss was a matter of debate, but no one doubted the excellence of his spiritual qualities.[43] He had been appointed dean of the Brothers by Prior Louis Fink, and the appointment was renewed by Abbot Innocent.[44] He had been just as popular as a journeyman cabinetmaker in Germany. He had been superintendent of a boys' industrial school in Stockholm until 1869 when he emigrated to Baltimore. There he read a letter from Prior Louis Fink in the *Katholische Volkszeitung* about the work in Kansas and applied for admission to the community. The record of the contribution of the Brothers is found not in the archives but in the buildings and the campus of the living St. Benedict's.

These were the men — priests, clerics, and Brothers— who gave form to the new community. Their personalities and the circumstances that conditioned their work

40 Bartl an Wolf, Seneca, Mar. 19, 1884.
41 Wolf an Wimmer, Atchison, Dec. 23, 1877. (SVA)
42 *Idem*, May 9, 1886 copy.
43 Record of Visitation, Sept. 13, 1888.
44 Wolf an Wimmer, Atchison, Dec. 23, 1877. (SVA)

gave the community its character. Time and changing circumstances, of course, have altered it a bit, but the life of a religious community is such that family characteristics, once formed, tend to persist. It was a small, strictly average, frontier community. The frontier had presented the monks with certain conditions and limitations, and they sensibly tended to take care of the necessities and leave the nicetiesto the future. All of them seem to have felt that there were distinct and fairly narrow limits to the area where uniformity was necessary in monastic life, and the more formal external evidences of monastic decorum seem to have won little favor. Their individual differences made it difficult for the Abbot to organize them into a smoothly functioning machine.

None had received more than a skimpy education, but the best of them were so successful at educating themselves for the rest of their lives that they were fine teachers. Some of them had character and personality of such high quality that they left an impress on decades of students or parishioners, and through family tradition their influence is still felt by the present generation. Practically all of them were amazingly hard workers. The load of work they carried without undue complaint makes a modern monk shudder. Short on education, without extraordinary ability, they had only their own willingness to work unbelievably hard, confident that they were doing God's work and that they were doing it with God's help — and it was with this that they built St. Benedict's.

The First Abbot

The men who made up the community were, of course, only a part of the force that gave the community its character. The other part was the man they had elected to be their religious superior and father of the family, the Abbot. Those who knew Abbot Innocent agreed that his outstanding quality was his fatherliness. This quality is apparent in all his relations with his monks but it is most easily illustrated from the many chatty letters he wrote to the novices, to those who were away at school, and to those who were away recruiting their health. Constantly ill himself, he was forever reminding his monks to dress warmly, to wear their rubbers, to chew their food well, and not to eat pork. Constantly living under the shadow of St. Benedict's famous debt, he reminded them of their monastic poverty and once asked Father Andrew Green, "Why did you send four sheets to write three and a half pages?"[45] He encouraged the clerics in their studies, reminding them that they could learn any nonsense by heart for a minstrel show, "so it must not be considered so hard to remember the Hebrew."[46] He always included a few words of spiritual encouragement or warning, reminding his clerics that loss of vocation was not the result of a sudden crisis but the consequence of long neglect of prayer and spiritual exercises. Another favorite counsel was that the monk who forgot to dedicate each task to God would find himself working for someone else.[47]

His letters always contained a steady stream of little items about life at home: a campaign against bedbugs, whitewashing, who went to whose First Mass, what the Brothers were doing, the construction of a tennis court, and how the band was improving. He kept the family in their hearts by detailing the minutiae of life in the community. Thus he portrayed a hot, quiet day in summer, "P. Eugene shoots off a firecracker once a day — that makes the birds stop their singing for half a minute, makes P. Ferdinand scold, fearing that the birds will not come here again next year — then all is as usual again for twenty-four hours."[48] As he laughingly told Abbot Alexius Edelbrock, "When the *cacoethes scribendi* has taken hold of me, there is no end to making a short story long."[49] But he had a serious purpose in mind. As he wrote to

---

[45] Wolf to Green, Atchison, Aug. 9, 1890.
[46] Wolf to Pius Pretz, Atchison, Sept. 22, 1911.
[47] Wolf to Clement Nordhus, Atchison, Apr. 24, 1911.
[48] Wolf to Green, Atchison, July 13, 1889.
[49] Wolf to Edelbrock, Atchison, Mar. 4, 1880. (SJA)

Father Gerard Heinz, then in Colorado to cure threatened consumption, "Now I told you all I can think of. . . so that you don't forget home."[50]

When Abbot Innocent first took over the duties of his office at St. Benedict's, he wrote to Archabbot Wimmer that he planned to leave conditions as they were except in the case of abuses and that he intended to make changes only after discussing matters with the community. From Archabbot Wimmer he inherited a principle of action, namely, seek advice before making changes and avoid regrets. The community, Abbot Innocent was happy to report, was in good spirits.[51] The monastic schedule naturally followed the pattern that all had known at St. Vincent. The community arose at three-forty in the morning for matins, lauds, Mass, and a period of mental prayer. Breakfast was at six o'clock, and classes began at seven. The other canonical hours were usually scheduled before or after the daily meals. Nine o'clock was the official hour for retiring. Since at first only four or five choir members besides the Abbot lived in the monastery, each realized that he was essential to the fulfillment of the community's choir obligation. Consequently, at this time choir attendance was no problem, even though each monk's heavy load of teaching made this early morning prayer a particular sacrifice.[52] The Abbot was careful to set a good example for his monks although his throat caused him great pain. Besides the official liturgical prayers the Abbot discretely encouraged his monks conscientiously to practice mental prayer. The clerics and Brothers meditated in common but the priests, privately. In the realm of penitential exercises the community observed Saturday as a day of abstinence until 1890 when the chapter voted to follow the practice of the rest of the Congregation by dropping Saturday but retaining Wednesday as an added day of abstinence.[53] The community

50 Wolf to Heinz, Atchison, Feb. 24, 1891.
51 Wolf an Wimmer, Atchison, Jan. 10, 1877. (SVA)
52 *Idem*, Nov. 21, 1878. (SVA)
53 Chapter Minutes, Aug. 5; Nov. 11, 1890.

could not be persuaded to abandon tobacco, but the Abbot regularly cautioned the monks to use it sparingly.

The smallness of the community put added burdens on all, but none could complain that the Abbot demanded more of his monks than he was willing to do himself. His first Christmas at St. Benedict's was a good example of this personal sacrifice. Since every possible man had to be sent to the surrounding missions, the Abbot, with the pastor and clerics, arranged that Christmas was properly celebrated in the Abbey Church. Matins were recited at four o'clock in the morning, followed by a Pontifical Mass and the recitation of lauds. The Abbot then heard confessions until eight o'clock, when prime, tierce, sext, and none were recited. Then he heard more confessions until his second Mass at nine-thirty. His third Mass, another Pontifical, was sung at ten o'clock. After the singing of Vespers at three o'clock his day's liturgical work was done, and he wrote to Archabbot Wimmer, "Now I have to be quiet for a couple of days to recover."[54]

The Abbot usually said Mass in the Sisters' convent on Sundays, preached to the students, and then gave the nuns a spiritual conference.[55] Weekly spiritual conferences and annual retreats were provided for the priests, clerics, and Brothers. The first chapters held by Abbot Innocent helped to adjust matters of monastic discipline and to provide an ordered system of spiritual exercises. The community was reminded of the necessity of monastic silence and of the need for regular examinations of conscience.[56]

Abbot Innocent's spiritual conferences were practical and concrete. His notes, all made on bits of old envelopes and similar scraps of paper, give no evidence of concern with the abstract principles of the interior life. His theme is almost always the specific application of Christian charity. Current ecclesiastical journals and the habits of his monks seem to have supplied most of his material.

[54] Wolf an Wimmer, Atchison, Dec. 23-25, 1877. (SVA)
[55] *Idem*, June 13, 1887. (SVA)
[56] Chapter Minutes, Feb. 7–June 28, 1877, *passim*.

His conferences covered all aspects of monastic life: manners, vows, virtues, and prayer. Sometimes he talked about elementary manners and religious modesty, exhorting the younger monks to stop wrestling, to avoid breathing so hard at table or at prayer that others were distracted, and to avoid prefixing 'N' to the first word of prayers, such as n'Deus, n'Dominus.[57]

The poverty of the community did not necessarily develop the virtue of monastic poverty, but it no doubt helped. Abbot Innocent stressed the spiritual value of this virtue and insisted upon it strongly. He made the assistants on parishes subject to their pastors in this matter. When one young priest balked at this, the Abbot laid down the law, remarking, "I would rather take care of the missions myself than let him ruin himself." The Abbot was happy to observe that conformity made the young priest more spiritual and more content with his work.[58] The different conditions of those who lived inside and of those who lived outside the monastery sometimes caused trouble. In one spiritual conference, devoted to the essential interdependence between the vows of obedience and poverty, the Abbot commented first on the natural tendency to prefer a certain kind of work, pointing out that the monk was certain to be disappointed so long as he thought only of his own will. The Abbot next stressed his favorite principle that the monk acts safely only under obedience. He then quickly sketched the neglect of spiritual life following from disobedience, pointing out that the monk next violates his vow of poverty in small things because he "wants all that outside Fathers have, and on that plea keeps money, and thus violates the vow without remorse of conscience."[59]

In later years Abbot Innocent expressed the fear that the Abbey's early poverty might have cramped the monastic view of charity to the poor. Discussing the matter of alms with Abbot Peter Engel, he wrote:

[57] Wolf Diary, Dec. 13, 1892.
[58] Wolf an Wimmer, Atchison, Feb. 20, 1883. (SVA)
[59] Wolf conference notes, n.d. See also Chapter Minutes, Sept. 16, 1897.

The goods of the Church were always divided into three parts, for the support of the Church, for the support of the members, and for the poor. So the poor are not considered an accidental expense but an ordinary one. . . . Here we began poor and got into a way of acting which omitted much consideration for the poor because we considered ourselves poor, and therefore 'charity begins at home.' I am afraid that the axiom is stretched too much even by those who are poor. . . Sometimes I am tempted. . . to see how much alms is given out already; then I don't, thinking I might do wrong in refusing alms when God sends a poor person again. Almsgiving is, I think, a special obligation of the Abbot, and not of the Procurator, nor of anyone else. Tramps may be helped by food and old clothes given by the Porter, but alms in money for poor families, etc., should be given by the Abbot, and, I think, as often as God sends them in one way or another. . . You asked me confidentially, and so I wrote candidly.[60]

One of Abbot Innocent's outstanding virtues was simplicity, and he once gave a conference on it, using his own translation of the Bible as his text: "With the simple God likes to converse." He stated that without simplicity monasteries would be only hiding places for sneaks and assemblies of hypocrites. He cautioned his monks to avoid satire and double-meaning subtleties in their conversation, as well as suspicion, flattery, and all pretense. He urged them above all to have confidence in their confessors.[61]

The Abbot naturally received periodic complaints that the Rule was kept too laxly. His answer was that "if it were made stricter. . . they would not want it themselves. As it is, each one can keep the Holy Rule strictly and cannot complain of the want of occasion and help to keep the Rule."[62] On this subject he could never resist falling back on the *argumentum ad hominem*, that those who complained talked better than they lived. When it suited his purpose, he could argue the other side — bad example — just as convincingly. The question of how much uniformity is a genuine spiritual aid remained, as always, a

60 Wolf to Engel, Atchison, Aug. 24, 1909. (SJA)
61 Wolf conference notes, n.d.
62 Wolf to Edelbrock, Atchison, Jan. 5, 1879. (SJA)

knotty problem. Abbot Innocent put great stress on the daily periods of recreation in common and insisted that monks should not excuse themselves from it. To him it was an indispensible source of good community spirit and a safeguard against murmuring and factions.[63]

One blessing of a small community is that it can get along with fewer rules and regulations than a larger community. Abbot Innocent wisely believed that such rules as were necessary should be definite and that each rule should have a definite sanction so that each monk knew his duty and none might be tempted to self-indulgence. In his first letter to Archabbot Wimmer he had expressed particular fear of one fault in himself — a tendency to be too quick to correct the faults of others — but he soon learned to tolerate minor lapses and to correct serious infractions of the monastic rule privately. As he said, he had once punished students publicly in order to impress their fellows but had learned that the culprit only became stubborn and won pity from others.[64] In later years the difficulty of resisting his kindly, fatherly, and private corrections became almost legendary.

Mention has been made that the early community was made up of men who had a rather scanty education. Abbot Innocent, of course, and by the end of the century one or two others, were educated in Rome, but that was largely a technical education. The Abbot rather wondered at himself when, while resting and dosing at Carlsbad in 1897, he read a novel, *Ben Hur*.[65] Nevertheless, he and his community were interested in educating their taste, at least in music, and the Abbot sometimes joined his monks in the community band or orchestra. Within the area of his professional training Abbot Innocent was a conscientious worker. While President of the American Cassinese Congregation he studied the legislation on abbatial elections so intently that one of his correspondents expected him to publish a treatise, but Abbot Innocent

---

[63] Wolf an Wimmer, Atchison, Feb. 20, 1883. (SVA)
[64] *Idem.*
[65] Wolf an Braunmueller, Carlsbad, May 29, 1897. (AM)

merely wanted to know the law.[66] As Father Alexius Hoffman, of St. John's Abbey, noted, "Abbot Innocent Wolf was the ablest (and only) canonist among the Abbots up to the year 1900."[67]

If the Abbot was fatherly, he was also naturally paternalistic. At first circumstances made this trait a practical necessity. In so small a community he was procurator, rector and director of the College, and even prefect of the students while the other priests were busy teaching.[68] From time to time some emergency would force him to assign himself to a Sunday mission.[69] In an attempt to organize his time better he once kept track of his activities from breakfast (6:15) to noon. In that period he made decisions as abbot, kept books and passed out socks as procurator, dosed students and monks as infirmarian, taught backward pupils their arithmetic, agreed that hay under the carpet would make the floor of the sanctuary warmer, answered a mother's querulous letter about her boy's complaints, and persuaded a student to move his horse from the fragile picket fence and tie it to a hitching post.[70]

But the monks complained because he did not appoint the usual officials.[71] The Abbot finally complied in 1883, but he always considered priors a problem. He had appointed Father Boniface in 1877, but he had resigned "a long time ago," and the Abbot had not bothered to appoint another until the visitators insisted.[72] Prior Peter Kassens, who was then appointed, became too busy with parish work, and when the Abbot consulted the community, he found their advice "as revealing as a *manifestatio*." The young men wanted more push, but the Abbot feared that the man they preferred might "have too much push

[66] Doerfler to Wolf, Rome, Mar. 5, 1899.
[67] Note on Wolf to Edelbrock, Atchison, Jan. 22, 1878. (SJA)
[68] Wolf an Wimmer, Atchison, Sept. 27, 1877. (SVA)
[69] Wolf Diary, Apr. 2, 1879.
[70] Wolf to Edelbrock, Atchison, Dec. 22, 1879, enclosing fragment dated Dec. 17, 1879. (SJA)
[71] Record of Visitation, 1879; 1883.
[72] Wolf an Wimmer, Atchison, Jan. 27, 1883. (SVA)

for our straightened circumstances," and so he appointed Father Boniface again.[73]

Procurators or business managers were an even greater problem. At first the Abbot was his own procurator. Father Ambrose Huebner, of St. Vincent, took the office quite capably in 1880, but after he left in 1884 the Abbot took the burden again and then began to experiment fitfully with the possibilities in his own community. Father Thomas Burk was bull-headed and wanted to put a chicken house in the front yard. Father Herman Mengwasser was outrageously overbearing.[74] The Abbot later found suitable officials, but he was always hyperconscious of his own responsibility and disliked delegating authority in school or abbey. Not until his final illness in 1920 did he have the prior keep the records of Mass intentions and make appointments for Sunday work on the parishes.[75]

The Abbot's paternalism was, of course, carried over into his relations with his chapter. His ordinary attitude towards the chapter was that it had "no business but to give advice."[76] For many years the members of the community had no idea whether their debt was decreasing or increasing. The Abbot refused to present a financial statement, and when the chapter complained, "he appealed to the Statutes, which do not prescribe such a course for Superiors."[77] He was angry because he thought his monks had so little trust in him and seemed to consider him an enemy of the community.[78] In the 1890's the chapter was still asking to see an annual financial statement and added the complaint that the Abbot "tried to influence the chapter too much when there was question of admitting Scholastics to the Novitiate."[79]

[73] Wolf to Edelbrock, Atchison, May 26, 1888. (SJA)
[74] Wolf Diary, Feb. 13, 1891; Jan. 8, 1892.
[75] Wolf to Engel, Atchison, Aug. 5, 1920. (SJA)
[76] Wolf an Braunmueller, Atchison, Sept. 14, 1892. (AM)
[77] Chapter Minutes, Sept. 21, 1885.
[78] Wolf to Edelbrock, Atchison, Dec. 20, 1888. (SJA)
[79] Wolf Diary, Sept. 5, 1892.

The Abbot's attitude toward the chapter naturally tended to make the chapter more sensitive about its prerogatives. The Abbot reported one ludicrous instance to his old friend Father Adalbert. In a meeting for the purpose of electing a delegate to the General Chapter in 1890, the Abbot left the chapter to its task without a chairman. "Many wanted P. Prior [Boniface], but others said that the prior is one person with the Abbot!! — hence he will not represent the monastery!!! Therefore, I must conclude the Abbot and Prior do not represent the monastery! Take care of an Abbot, he may ruin a monastery, that was done in old times! — Why should I remain Abbot if I am so dangerous!" The chapter deadlocked on three men and asked the Abbot to appoint a chairman. "I said, I will preside myself. Then I heard more about the Abbot and Prior, etc. At last I commanded silence, and insisting strictly on that prevented the fun, and then they elected at last P. Suitbert. — I must shut up."[80]

Abbot Innocent was not often really high-handed, but he was always very direct. In a letter to the Abbot one monk made the mistake of stating that he, "like many others," had no confidence in the Abbot. The Abbot called a chapter and demanded that he verify or retract the charge and left the room. A considerable uproar followed, and after the dust had settled the Abbot was given a vote of confidence, nineteen to one.[81] He handled intramural feuds in the same direct manner, at one chapter informing two members that since their differences were a "public secret," they might as well explain them in public.[82] This technique seems to have been effective.

St. Benedict in his Rule uses his strongest language to condemn the vice of murmuring — secret opposition — as being most destructive to monastic life. Every abbot in history, apparently, has learned personally just what St. Benedict meant. On one occasion Abbot Innocent wrote:

80 Wolf to Mueller, Atchison, June 29-30, 1890. (SVA)
81 Chapter Minutes, Dec. 3, 1889.
82 Wolf Diary, Feb. 2, 1891.

I will drag them to the light, show their sneaking mean ways, so that all will be ashamed to associate with them. I suppose we must suffer all kinds of persecution. Still I think we are allowed to defend our position whenever it is necessary for the good of the community. If the Superior is defamed in his own house, he loses all control. That is why I will show up these malicious persons.

It is singular that people are so ready to believe anything said about a superior. I wrote this lately to one of our big-mouthed Fathers, who has 'nothing against the Abbot, but does not like to see him take the advice of the Sisters,' etc. etc. Thousands of such thrusts with little pins will make a man so weak that he must break down. I fight them and am at it in dead earnest. If I don't gain anything, I'll not lose anything, and will make it easier for my successor.[83]

He seems always to have kept his motives pure in regard to this problem. As he explained to Prior Andrew Green:

I have many faults, but that can excuse no one from murmuring. . . For murmuring is hideous — not because against this or that superior — but because it is against the authority, against God. Let us all pray that God may protect our house from such an evil, . . to help us all, so that no one is lost.[84]

So long as the criticism or complaint was direct and open, Abbot Innocent heard it out and usually returned a soft answer. He was a genuinely humble man. In the winter of 1896, when he was in Rome trying to recover his health, he sent his community Christmas greetings in which he reviewed the past and concluded that if he were beginning again, he would do many things differently. He continued, "I know I have offended many of you, and that often, by my quick temper, rough and uncharitable answers, by my impolite and rude orders and directions; I beg forgiveness also for all that."[85]

St. Benedict's was apparently never racked by factionalism based on national differences, such as often divided Germans of diverse origins. The troubled history of the community and the sheer necessity for unity possibly account in part for this blessing, but Abbot Innocent's

[83] Wolf to Edelbrock, Atchison, Aug. 31, 1889. (SJA)
[84] Wolf to Green, Rome, Mar. 1, 1897.
[85] *Idem*, Dec. 10, 1896.

quick dismissal of any candidate deemed guilty of fomenting nationalism assured continued freedom from that particular evil.

An important influence in Abbot Innocent's life and in the history of St. Benedict's was his chronic poor health. He had had trouble with his throat since childhood,[86] and when it was so severely infected in 1876, the monks of St. Vincent, he said, thought he was going out to Colorado to die.[87] He recovered but had to be careful in choir, and teaching was too much for him.[88] In 1882 and 1883 his eyes gave him serious trouble, and he was threatened with the loss of sight in his left eye.[89] Rheumatism was added to his other ailments in 1885.[90] In 1886 his eyes were so bad that he had to spend many hours resting them.[91] He was further troubled with a swelling of the legs and feet that often prevented sleep.[92] What would have been an ordinary cold to another man nearly incapacitated Abbot Innocent since it aggravated his collection of ills and stayed with him for months.[93]

He was always subject to extreme nervousness, and this reached something of a climax in 1896 when his ailments were aggravated by trouble in the community.[94] Mental work was practically impossible, he had violent headaches and sleepless nights, and his stomach was a wreck.[95] It took a year in Europe, wintering in Rome, taking the water cures at Woerishofen, Jordanbad, and Carlsbad before he was cured. At the end of the year, visiting at the Abbey of Metten, he gave his stomach the acid test — a glass of beer — with no ill effects. The Abbot of Metten cheered: *Dann ist's gewonnen*, and Abbot

[86] Wolf to Aaron, Kansas City, Jan. 5, 1909.
[87] Wolf to Locnikar, Atchison, Sept. 10, 1891. (SJA)
[88] Wolf an Wimmer, Atchison, Nov. 10, 1877. (SVA)
[89] *Idem*, Nov. 24, 1882 copy.
[90] *Idem*, Jan. 11, 1885. (SVA)
[91] *Idem*, Jan. 1; June 6, 1886. (SVA)
[92] Wolf to Edelbrock, Atchison, Nov. 20, 1886; Mar. 9, 1887. (SJA)
[93] Wolf to Mueller, Atchison, Mar. 30, 1893. (SVA)
[94] Wolf to Pfraengle, Rome, Jan. 29, 1896. (SMA)
[95] Wolf Diary, Aug. 12, 1896.

Innocent was ready to return home and resume work.[96] The victory was only temporary, of course, and in subsequent years he was troubled by the same old ailments. Several months in 1903 were spent in Colorado and in taking the Kneipp cure at Rome City, Indiana.[97] In 1907 he had erysipelas and was so ill that he received the Last Sacraments.[98] At this time he considered resigning. The remaining years of his life were a steady procession of bodily infirmities. By 1909 he knew he had a bad heart.[99] His nervousness, of course, became worse, and he turned the chair over to the Prior and left chapter if a discussion threatened to become exciting.[100] He even absented himself from concerts by the college orchestra, of which he was fond, because they made him too nervous.

Always specifically welcoming the will of God, the Abbot bore his infirmities with patience. They were a tool which he used well for his own sanctification. On the other hand, when he was particularly ill, he had not the energy, as he confessed, to make troublesome but necessary changes in personnel.[101] Some portions of St. Benedict's history would certainly be different if Abbot Innocent had been a healthier man.

Sometimes, particularly during the earlier years, Abbot Innocent became extremely depressed under his burdens. Before he had been in office two years he wrote:

I often feel as though I could not stand it any longer; here a priest who visits saloons, . . . there a Pater who sets himself above church law, bishop, and abbot, and acts accordingly. Then the quarreling Brothers, the long faces, the complaining students, the regulation of the house, the accounts, the parishioners, etc., et. . . More than once I have been tempted to run away from it all. God help me.[102]

He soon became convinced that an abbot's life was full of crosses, and from Archabbot Wimmer he inherited the

[96] Wolf to Green, Metten, June 27, 1897.
[97] Wolf to Engel, Rome City, Nov. 30, 1903. (SJA)
[98] Wolf to Abbot Primate, Atchison, Dec. 11, 1907. (SA)
[99] Wolf to Engel, Atchison, Sept. 13, 1909. (SJA)
[100] Idem. Mar. 10, 1913. (SJA)
[101] Wolf to Pfraengle, Rome, Jan. 29, 1896. (SMA)
[102] Wolf an Wimmer, Atchison, Nov. 6, 1878. (SVA)

grisly belief that each great holiday brought a special cross.[103]

At other times Abbot Innocent could see the humor of his situation. After all, if even God cannot please all men, an abbot certainly should not expect to.[104] On one occasion Father Pirmin Koumly, the pastor at Seneca, was ill, and no other priest being readily available, Abbot Innocent substituted for him. The Abbot decided that he liked the work better than his own. In a note to the Prior he wrote:

> I was told the Abbot should be on a parish for a while, then he would learn what a parish priest has to do. Also that at home people sit around doing nothing. . . Moves and seconds that a new Abbot be elected. Moves and seconds amendment that the new Abbot shall not go against the will of anyone, but allow each one so much wine or beer as he wants — all are sensible enough and old enough that they won't abuse it. He must not have old-fogy notions, but must be progressive. He must send every priest the help he asks for, for the priest must know best what he needs. . . Won't we have nice times then! Hurrah! . . . Father Pirmin can take my place — I am satisfied to stay here.[105]

His usual attitude to trouble was that it was the will of God and that God would make good come of it somehow. When Abbot Innocent deferred to the will of God, it was not as a pious afterthought. The desire to do God's will was really an intimate part of his daily life. He once wrote, "You know, I believe, that I am pretty outspoken and say all that I can; if after that I am told that I am surely wrong, or that I should act anyhow, I. . . . submit without fear, for then I know that I do the will of God. . . and am not afraid of any consequences."[106]

Dedication to the will of God appeared, too, in his choice of a coat of arms. He chose the Sacred Hearts because his father had used that symbol, and for a motto he chose *Nisi Dominus Frustra* (Without the Lord we labor in vain) from the selection listed in *Webster's Dic-*

103 Wolf to Locnikar, Atchison, Dec. 21, 1890. (SJA)
104 Wolf to Schnerr, Atchison, Aug. 2, 1893. (SVA)
105 Wolf to Green, Seneca, Mar. 16, 1894.
106 Wolf to Edelbrock, Atchison, Apr. 3, 1889. (SJA)

tionary.[107]   The Abbey got along without a coat of arms for almost twenty years, but when the question of a motto was raised, there was really very little choice. It was bound to be *Dominus Providebit* (The Lord will provide) or nothing. As Abbot Innocent put it, "Under that we worked without fear and hesitation, although, humanly speaking, there was no hope. . . of getting enough men and money."[108]   The arms used during Abbot Innocent's administration incorporated the Benedictine cross and elements from the seal of the State of Kansas. It was designed by Father Laurent Janssen, the rector of Sant' Anselmo and a monk of the Abbey of Maredsous.

Facing the Problems

Abbot Innocent took up his duties at St. Benedict's Abbey on January 10, 1877. He found less than sixty dollars in the treasury. He complained that Prior Oswald had not only relaxed his control for the past six months and left all problems for the new abbot's attention but also intended to leave immediately.[109]   But a year later the Abbot could understand that Father Oswald had "had so much of it after two years that he did not want to stay a day longer than necessary" and admitted that he did not dare let himself think about his Abbey's problems too much, or he, too, would be tempted to run away.[110]

In that first year the gross income of the community was $14,759, while expenses were $15,254, and the debt increased slightly to $53,777. But the number of boarders in the College increased from thirty-eight in June, 1877, to fifty-one in the next school year, and the gross

[107]   *Idem*, Mar. 3, 1879. (SJA)
[108]   Wolf Diary, Mar. 14, 1895.
    Until 1894 even most of the insurance was in God's hands. At that time the College and the new monastery were insured for only $5000.   In case of a destructive fire it would be just enough, the Abbot wrote, "to give each one something to get away.   Still I don't feel like doing more as we cannot afford it."—Wolf to Locnikar, Atchison, Feb. 20, 1894. (SJA)
[109]   Wolf an Wimmer, Atchison, Jan. 23, 1877. (SVA)
[110]   *Idem*, Dec. 5, 1877. (SVA)

income of the College for the same year was $5730, an increase of $2500 over the preceding year. Income from the missions for that year, however, declined from $2000 to $1600. By the time Abbot Innocent, with the help of Archabbot Wimmer and the Ludwig-Missionsverein, had paid some $3000 in interest and a little on all the Abbey bills, he was convinced that only large donations could save the place.[111]

Meanwhile everything possible was done to cut down the expenses of the community. To reduce expenses the chapter first agreed to a half ration of beer.[112] Then the Abbot presented the monks with a kind of Hobson's choice by suggesting that they vote to abstain from beer and tobacco. The chapter probably did what the Abbot expected when by a vote of six to two it decided to discontinue beer and to limit smoking tobacco to a half pound a month for each smoker.[113] To appreciate the magnitude of the sacrifice, it must be remembered that those old Germans believed beer to be an absolutely essential part of the day's food. To Herr Ludwig Ignatz Lebling, of the Ludwig-Missionsverein, who could readily appreciate the enormity of the sacrifice, the Abbot explained that the community had given up beer so that they could afford to educate twelve poor German students for the priesthood gratis. And, as the Abbot added, his monks really needed the beer because each taught six or seven hours a day and "so much talking makes a man very dry."[114] A few years later, when the community began making its own Mass wine, the second pressing, called Milligan, was used as table wine on feast days and oftener if available.[115]

These sacrifices were more easily borne because the monks, grateful for an end to the instability of the priory days, were willing to do whatever was necessary for the good of the community. The visitators of 1879 compli-

[111] Wimmer an Wolf, St. Vincent, Aug. 21, 1877. Wolf an Wimmer, Atchison, Dec. 5; 23, 1877. (SVA)
[112] Chapter Minutes, June 28, 1877.
[113] *Ibid.*, Nov. 15, 1878.
[114] Wolf an Lebling, Atchison, Jan. 13, 1879. (LMV Leav II 1/54)
[115] Wolf an LMV, Atchison, Mar. 5, 1883. (LMV Leav II 1/59-60)

mented the community on its good spirit in religious life, in study, and in the external work of the priests, who, though few in number, taught a complete curriculum in the school. The visitators noted also that because the community was so small the members were seriously overworked. The poverty in food and especially in drink was complimented, and choir attendance was considered satisfactory. The visitators also praised the Abbot's good example, particularly since he was in poor health.[116]

Until some benefactor came along to pay the Abbey's debt, the Abbot's only hope was to expand the College. But expansion meant building, and this would increase the debt. Before he had completed a year in Atchison he was writing Archabbot Wimmer, telling how much he longed to build a forty-foot addition to the College but that the cost would be $3000.[117] The prospect of expanding the College and so increasing income to reduce the debt appealed to the Archabbot, and he sent plans made by Brother Cosmas and the necessary $3000.[118] The chapter, however, considered these plans inadequate, decided to build a somewhat wider building than the Archabbot had in mind, and in the end it cost almost $10,000 instead of $3000. The Archabbot was displeased and refused to help Abbot Innocent increase the debt any further by more loans.[119] Ground for the new building — the south section of the present refectory building, Bishop Fink Hall — was broken on June 5, 1878, and the new classrooms were first used in November of that year.[120] There was little change in the number of boarding students that year, but in the following year their number increased from fifty-two to eighty-two. Income from the College rose from less than $5000 to almost $7000.

About this same time new arrangements concerning

[116] Record of Visitation, 1879.
[117] Wolf an Wimmer, Atchison, Nov. 10, 1877. (SVA)
[118] Chapter Minutes, Apr. 12, 1878; Wimmer an Wolf, St. Vincent, Apr. 30; June 13, 1878.
[119] Wimmer an Lang, St. Vincent, Nov. 20, 1879. (AM) Wimmer an Wolf, St. Vincent, June 13, 1878.
[120] Wolf Diary.

the Abbey Church also had a bearing on the debt. As Father Gerard Heinz told the story in the jubilee history of the church in 1908, the Abbey gave the church to the congregation in 1879 for the nominal sum of $6000. Nothing in the records substantiates this account, and Father Gerard's papers indicate that he got the story largely from the memory of Mr. William Dolan, who had long been a church committeeman.

Abbot Innocent had no illusions about the church. He realized that it would never be a proper Abbey Church, for it had no provisions for a monastic choir and no practical possibility of adding one. He called it "a perpetual monument to the stubbornness and bad taste of a former prior."[121] But the Abbot did want to see the church put in decent shape. A proposal was made to put stone arches round the side doors, place steps in front of the church, and install better floors and pews. The parishioners were complaining about the cost of the church as if they had paid for it.[122] They failed to subscribe sufficient funds to finance the proposed improvements, and the community preferred not to increase its debt for this purpose.[123]

To secure the cooperation of the parishioners they were given a greater share in the administration of the church, and so a church committee was appointed for the first time. Abbot Innocent was its chairman until he left for Rome in 1880. Similarly he continued to keep the parish accounts through the year 1879. In preparation for his departure the Abbot distributed his various responsibilities. Beginning with the year 1880 the parish accounts were entirely separated from the Abbey accounts, the pastor began to draw the usual salary, and $6000 of the community's $60,000 debt was transferred to the parish books. At this time the construction of the church had cost in excess of $75,000. There was, of course, no trans-

[121] Wolf to Edelbrock, Atchison, Mar. 4, 1880. (SJA)
[122] Wimmer an Wolf, St. Vincent, June 13, 1878, referring to Wolf letter no longer extant.
[123] Chapter Minutes, Aug. 22, 1879.

fer of title to either building or land. In any case, the church, whether priory church or abbey church, had also been a parish church from the very beginning and has continued so to the present time.

While taking all possible steps locally to improve the financial condition of his community, Abbot Innocent could not put out of his mind the wonderful possibility of somehow getting enough donations to retire a large part of the debt and so give the Abbey a fresh start. The fourteenth centenary of St. Benedict's birth was to be celebrated with a great gathering of Benedictine abbots in Rome and at Monte Cassino in 1880. Abbot Innocent felt certain that generous and wealthy Catholics in Europe would make his dream come true. As he told Abbot Alexius Edelbrock, he had decided to go to Monte Cassino in 1880, in spite of his poverty, so that he could collect for his Abbey. "As we are now, we can just make enough to pay the interest, if the benefactors, St. Vincent's and St. Louis Abbey [now St. John's], and the Ludwig-Missionsverein, continue their contributions, and that all to pay yearly $3000 interest to strangers. It's discouraging in the extreme. I shall try my best to collect enough to pay off part of the debt, and am resolved not to return sooner, come what may, because now the whole discipline suffers from this incessant feeling of saving. . . We cannot go on as we have."[124]

Archabbot Wimmer stated frankly that trying to collect money in Europe from other than the established missionary foundations was a waste of time and added that a good solicitor could do much better in America than in Europe.[125] Nevertheless, he gave Abbot Innocent a good letter of recommendation, which was endorsed by the Abbot of Monte Cassino, and he gave Abbot Innocent much advice regarding places to go and whom to see.[126]

[124] Wolf to Edelbrock, Atchison, Mar. 4, 1880. (SJA)
[125] Wimmer an Wolf, Munich, July 3, 1880.
[126] Wimmer, Monte Cassino, May 21, 1880, Nicolaus d'Orgemont, May 22, 1880. Wimmer an Wolf, Metten, June 27, 1880; Munich, July 17; 27; 1880.

In preparation for his trip Abbot Innocent first distributed his numerous jobs to various members of the community: "Made Father Peter Director, and Father Ambrose [Huebner] Procurator, let the Pastor and the above-named officers keep separate accounts, and thus I got rid of the College, but entirely only after I had given P. Winfried the medicines."[127] Just before he left, the triduum in honor of St. Benedict was held in the local parishes. In Atchison the occasion was celebrated with pontifical Masses and solemn vespers, the Abbey and College were illuminated, and there were transparencies and Bengal fire. The Sisters' convent was illuminated on the final evening.[128]

Abbot Innocent traveled in the company of Abbots Wimmer and Edelbrock. He wrote to his Prior that they "discouraged me a great deal by prophecying no success at all, but I put my hope in the prayers of all at home. . . I make the pilgrimage to Monte Cassino especially also to obtain the intercession of St. Benedict for our house. . . If we do our duty, I am confident that God will help, even if I should not succeed now. But I will try my best, and leave the rest to God."[129]

Abbot Innocent's beautiful dream ended in heartbreak. Before leaving home he had drawn up a long list of European abbeys whose abbots he trusted would direct him to kind benefactors. After the meetings in Rome and Monte Cassino he doggedly went from one abbey to another: Salzburg, Lambach, Kremsmuenster, Linz (where the Bishop was very cold), Melk, Goettweig, Vienna (where the Abbot was very cold), and Raigern (where the Abbot was friendly).[130] He was homesick. Abbot Edelbrock and Bishop Seidenbusch had preceded him to Vienna, had seen the Emperor and done well. All Abbot Innocent did in Vienna was lose a week. He tried to have the Catholic press print items about the Foundation Mass.

[127] Wolf to Edelbrock, Atchison, Mar. 4, 1880. (SJA)
[128] Wolf Diary, Apr. 4-6, 1880.
[129] Wolf to Verheyen, On board the SS. *Arizona*, Apr. 26, 1880.
[130] *Idem*, Vienna, July 18, 1880.

He had collected little and was twice mistaken for a rabbi.[131] In Scotland the American Benedictines were considered materialists and not very spiritual. But he had made up the itinerary of his own little way of the cross and insisted on following it to the bitter end — "so that I can be satisfied. . . that I did everything I could."[132]

Abbot Innocent had dreamed of wiping out his Abbey's entire debt or at least a large part of it. In reality, when he returned to his Abbey after seven months, he had experienced many a chilly reception and had received just $817.29 beyond his expenses. The belated largesse of the Emperor of Austria was forwarded later — forty dollars. But the trip was not without its benefits. Archabbot Wimmer wrote that although Abbot Innocent had fished much and caught little, he was very healthy.[133]

While away he had been homesick, and letters from Atchison seemed never to catch up with him. His Prior was sympathetic: "No wonder you feel lost — almost a stranger among those who should greet you as a brother, meeting with cold receptions, everywhere poor prospects ahead, and no news from home. God forgive all of us. We'll make up for it at home."[134] Perhaps it was better that the letters failed to reach him. The Abbot would no doubt have rejoiced to know that the enrollment was up and that the wine harvest was good, but the Prior also wrote: "Your worry will begin anew when you come back and look over my accounts, such a medley! . . . Father Ambrose and I have often, when we [were] trying to clear up, said to each other, 'What will Father Abbot say when he sees this?' "[135]

Prior Boniface was at least sympathetic and loyal. The worst of Abbot Innocent's disillusioning experience

---

131 *Idem*, Scheyern, Aug. 8, 1880.
132 *Idem*, Fort Augustus, Sept. 1, 1880.
133 Wimmer an Lang, St. Vincent, Nov. 11, 1880. (AM)
134 Verheyen to Wolf, Atchison, Sept. 18, 1880.
135 *Idem*, Nov. 3, 1880.
    Some years later the Abbot complained that during his seven-month absence in 1880 "things went back very much" under Prior Boniface's direction. —Wolf to Edelbrock, Atchison, Mar. 18, 1889. (SJA)

in 1880 was that he seems to have been unfairly criticized by some members of the community. At any rate, he was more discouraged, depressed, and closer to resigning his office after his return than at any other time in his life. Furthermore, that Christmas was a nightmare for him. The community at St. Benedict's was so small that the incapacitation of even one man put a severe strain on the remaining members. When Abbot Innocent returned to Atchison on December 7, 1880, he found Father Pirmin Koumly, the resident pastor of St. Benedict's Church in Doniphan County, sick with fever in Atchison.[136] Father Winfried Schmidt was sent to take care of the Christmas services, but he fell off the porch in the dark and broke a shoulder blade, and so the Prior substituted. Frater Herman Mengwasser, whom the Abbot termed his best and most useful cleric, was very ill with pneumonia. Christmas services at the Abbey were somewhat simplified that year. Afterwards the Abbot wrote, "I am afraid I lost all the merit because I get so depressed and impatient. May God help me. I get low immediately."[137]

Having recited these misfortunes to the Archabbot, Abbot Innocent continued cryptically, "I beg you particularly for your prayers for myself because God is now visiting me with an affliction that I can hardly bear and which I cannot share with anyone for consolation and help."[138] Six months later when, if the crisis were not past, the Abbot had at any rate determined upon his own course, he again referred to the incident. He said that when he returned from Europe, he had heard that some members of the community would have been happy to hear that he had resigned. Lately one of his monks had written that electing him abbot had been a mistake. According to Abbot Innocent only three priests at the Abbey "support me in word and deed and work hard with me. . . I have already thought of resigning, but my

[136] Wolf Diary.
[137] Wolf an Wimmer, [Bendena], Jan. 12, 1881. (SVA)
[138] *Ibid.*

confessor advised me against it."[139]   This black crisis in his life passed, but it left permanent effects.

Since no European benefactor would erase St. Benedict's debt, the Abbot worked with the modest but steady aid of the Ludwig-Missionsverein and the resources at home.   The stubby building of 1878 had been occupied only three years when more room was needed.   The building had been erected to increase the capacity of the College and so improve the condition of the community. College enrollment and income had increased, and in 1882 the number of boarders passed the one-hundred mark for the first time.   By 1881 the problem of space had become acute.   Four clerics slept in a room intended for only one, and no accommodations were available for guests.[140]   The Abbot was less fearful of increasing the debt because he had finally managed to pay off about a thousand dollars in the preceding year.   Furthermore, he had decided to send Father Adolph Wesseling to the eastern states to collect money for the building.[141]

Ground was broken on April 19, 1883, and part of the building was occupied after the Christmas vacation.[142] To save as much as possible on the cost of the building, Father Boniface did the estimates, the Brothers did all the woodwork, the scholastics — sometimes aided by clerics and priests — carried materials, and everybody helped to put on the shingles.[143]   Archabbot Wimmer sent his carpenter, Mr. Hoffman, and seventy-year old Brother Thomas Lechner to help with the work.[144]   Steam heating was installed not only in the new building but in the older buildings as well, particularly to reduce the fire hazard.[145]   The new addition cost almost $20,000, bring-

139 *Idem*, Atchison, June 8, 1881. (SVA)
140 *Idem*, Nov. 11, 1881. (SVA)
141 *Idem*, Feb. 7, 1883. (SVA)
142 Wolf Diary.
143 Wolf an Wimmer, Atchison, May 31, 1883. (SVA) Report to Leopoldinen Stiftung, Feb. 15, 1884 draft.
144 Wimmer to Huebner, St. Vincent, Oct. 2, 1883.
   Abbot Innocent sent old Brother Thomas back to Pennsylvania after little more than a month.—Wolf an Wimmer, Atchison, Nov. 21, 1883. (SVA)
145 Chapter Minutes, May 15, 1883.

ing the cost of Bishop Fink Hall to $29,000. Installing steam heat added another $4000.

In the hope of completing the new building without increasing the debt, Father Adolph Wesseling was sent out to preach and to solicit donations. In a short sermon at the Sunday Masses Father Adolph announced the Foundation Mass, explaining that until 1966 a daily Mass would be offered for all who donated a hundred dollars to St. Benedict's. He invited interested persons to come to the rectory and have their names entered. He received no collection nor did he make a house to house canvass.[146] Father Adolph was on the road from the spring of 1883 to the spring of 1886, and the donations he secured were a very considerable aid. Subscriptions to the Foundation Mass had risen to more than a thousand dollars a year since 1880, no doubt as the result of Abbot Innocent's efforts, but in the four years of 1883 to 1886 the total was almost $20,000. Then such donations fell to the normal few hundred dollars a year again.

Another improvement at this time was accomplished by exchanging farms. The college farm was an important factor in the economics of the community. Prior Louis Fink had begun raising the community's food on the farm, but Prior Giles Christoph had sold the small herd to meet debts. Prior Oswald had resumed cattle raising, and when Abbot Innocent arrived, five beeves were ready for slaughtering. Each year the College and Abbey looked to the farm for beef, pork, potatoes, kraut, and other vegetables.[147] When these supplies failed on account of a bad crop year, less money was available to reduce the debt[148]. When potatoes went to two dollars a bushel and more, Abbot Innocent made ends meet with "canned corn, tomatoes, and fastday food."[149]

The farm on the old claims near Bendena was too far from the Abbey, however, and in the spring of 1883 the

146 Wimmer to Bishop Tuigg, St. Vincent, Feb. 9, 1886.
147 Wolf an Wimmer, Atchison, Sept. 27; Nov. 10, 1877.
148 Wolf an LMV, Atchison, Feb. 16, 1882. (LMV Leav II 1/58)
149 Wolf an Wimmer, Atchison, July 20, 1882. (SVA)

Father Matthew Bradley

Father Andrew Green

Father Leo Aaron

Father Philip Williams

Father Damian Lavery

Father Aloysius Bradley

Father Stanislaus Altmann

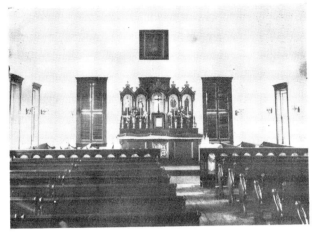

The Students' Chapel in 1886 (Lemke Hall)

The Student Refectory in 1893

A Study Hall about 1900

The Physics Lab with every piece of equipment posed 1893

The College Band 1887 (Father Alexius Grass second from right, middle row

Derbies were the latest

A May Day chow line

Society Hall 1893

Handball and tennis courts

The Scholastic
Baseball Team
1910

The Abbey Student Staff 1891

Champions
"Kansas vs. The World"
1908

A Picnic Hike 1909

Typical Graduates of the 1880's
Masters of Accounts 1889
Top Row
John Mesel, Joseph Schmandt,
G. Ryan, Dennis Hogan
Bottom Row
Joseph Ayres, John Tracey,
J. Hughes, M. Fitzpatrick,
David Degan

"Julius Caesar" 1916

Minims' Baseball Team
"The Little Giants" 1899

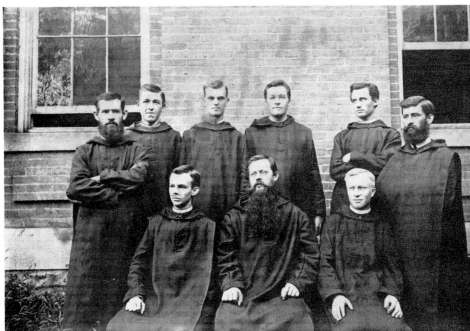

Prefects 1888 Top Row: Denis Murphy, Luke Blahnik, Gerard Heinz, Augustine Baker, Aloy.·
Bradley, Edwin Kassens. Bottom Row: Stanislaus Altmann, Matthew Brad|
Joseph Sittenauer.

A Picnic Hike 1909

chapter agreed to sell it and to buy the Jones' farm south of Atchison.[150] Soon a Brother was making a daily early morning trip to the new farm, and it was supplying the College with more perishable produce, such as butter and eggs, as well as the staple meat and kraut.[151]

Over the Hump

In 1884 the College was twenty-five years old, and optimism was in the air at St. Benedict's. In part, no doubt, the optimism was a reflection of the boom then exciting the West. Furthermore, the College now had a good large building, and the enrollment had grown to 139 in the year 1883-84. It was soon to drop again, but that development was round the corner. Since 1882, if the cost of the new building was excepted, the community's income was noticeably, if modestly, larger than its expenses — about $5000. The monks felt that the crisis had been passed and that the worst was over. That year an extra flourish was given to the celebration of the Abbot's patronal feast. Abbot Innocent seems to have been the only one who did not share in the general optimism. Thanking Archabbot Wimmer for greetings on his name day, the Abbot described the festivities and his feelings:

For the feast this year the Scholastics decorated almost the entire house. Father Prior set up a splendid meal. That hurt me because we did not have that much on Easter. I almost lost my appetite and had to force myself to look pleased. I also had trouble swallowing the congratulations — all praised what I had done. I am convinced that I did the least of all. The men of the house do the most. That is why I consider such congratulations to be flattery and the people who express them as not being entirely honest. I kept order, that is true. Father Ambrose took care of the business splendidly, so I did not have to worry about anything.

Many people think we are now in good shape. I reality everything is in bad shape. We are short of means and men,

[150] Chapter Minutes, Mar. 29; Apr. 7, 1883. It decided also to buy the McClintock tract south of the Jones' farm.—*Ibid.*, July 26, 1883.
[151] Wolf an Wimmer, Atchison, June 6, 1886. (SVA)

so that I often think all our labor is in vain. The College cannot support us. The parishes or missions contribute little and when they do they will certainly be taken from us. The farm alone cannot produce enough. If we can get out of debt we will be in a position so that no bishop can hurt us. Now they have the power to chase us out of good places and force us to keep the poor ones. If only Father Adolph holds out we can soon start to pay off the debt, and then a spark of life will be present.[152]

Part of the Abbot's pessimism is undoubtedly explained by the fact that any celebration or entertainment made him nervous and ill. Furthermore, he was taking a short view regarding the College. The missions did present him with something of a dilemma, which will be considered later. But the notable point is that in both cases his thought about his problems was dominated by the debt. Abbot Innocent had noted the ill effects on the community of the constant pressure of the need to save, but that black incubus also restricted his freedom. It elbowed all other considerations, including sometimes the finer Christian motives, into second place.

Men and means were the chronic shortage, and of the two, Abbot Innocent usually considered man power the greater problem. Sometimes he insisted that it was the only real problem.[153] Bishop Fink habitually mentioned St. Benedict's in half-pitying tones, as "doing fairly well; only it has too much debt and too few men, and many of them are sick."[154] The Bishop wanted the Abbot to give more of the growing missions resident pastors, but the Abbot had not the men. "We lose all the good places; we cannot take the big places," he complained.[155]

The last illness of Archabbot Wimmer and the thought of losing his sturdy support occasioned a discussion of St. Benedict's slow growth. Abbot Innocent ascribed it to four causes: the poverty of the house, the fact that the settlers needed their growing boys on the farm, the

---

[152] *Idem*, July 31, 1884. (SVA)
[153] *Idem*, May 31, 1883. (SVA)
[154] Fink an Wimmer, Leavenworth, Nov. 10, 1885. (SVA)
[155] Wolf an Wimmer, Atchison, June 13, 1887. (SVA)

tendency of Catholics scattered thinly in a predominantly non-Catholic milieu to lose the real religious spirit, and
premature independence of the Priory.[156] Archabbot Wimmer thought that independence had not been the cause
of slow growth. He pointed out that little growth could
be expected until the land had been fully settled and that
in any case a monastery needed time for development and
security. Unlike the European abbeys, built and endowed
by lay benefactors, American abbeys had to be satisfied
with small beginnings and to grow largely on their own
resources.[157] Both men agreed that the scholasticate, a
program for recruiting and training candidates, was the
only sound answer for the future.

Abbot Innocent pointed out that neither Prior Louis
nor Prior Giles had set up a scholasticate, and thus the
growth of the community had been set back eight to ten
years.[158] The Abbot encouraged vocations wherever he
found them but complained that the area served by the
community provided too few. Ten years after the creation of the Abbey there were only eight members, all
clerics, from the area west of the Mississippi. The Abbot was confident, however, that the situation would improve in the future.[159] Others were from the eastern
states, and worthy young men of poor families in Europe
were also welcomed. When the Abbot was in Europe in
1880, he arranged for a considerable number of young
men from Bohemia to go to Atchison. A few wished to
study for the priesthood, and the others were candidates
for the Brotherhood.[160] The Abbot of Metten also recommended an occasional candidate for St. Benedict's.[161]

The results of the vocation program were sometimes
disappointing. The scholasticate was necessary if the
house was to grow, but it was also expensive since many
of the candidates were not only too poor to pay the costs

---

[156] *Idem*, June 2, 1887. (SVA)
[157] Wimmer an Wolf, St. Vincent, June 17, 1887.
[158] Wolf an Wimmer, Atchison, May 31, 1883. (SVA)
[159] *Idem*, July 15, 1887. (SVA)
[160] Verheyen to Wolf, Atchison, Sept. 18, 1880.
[161] Wolf an Braunmueller, Atchison, Apr. 11, 1888; June 11, 1889. (AM)

of their schooling but had to have even their clothing furnished by the community.[162] Furthermore, as is the universal experience, only a small percentage turned out to have vocations. By 1887 Abbot Innocent had received nineteen candidates from Bohemia. Two of them were then in the clericate, but the others were gone. Some of them, however, had vocations to the diocesan priesthood and were a part of the community's contribution to the Church.[163]

Although the need for members was so acute, standards of admission from a spiritual viewpoint seem to have been maintained well enough, but the standards of education and health seem to have been rather relaxed. On the other hand, the number of early deaths due to pulmonary diseases in the early years of the community may be no more than a reflection of the generally higher death rate from those diseases in that era. But particularly during the early years the education given the clerics was pitifully inadequate. Some, according to Abbot Innocent, were given but one year of philosophy and two years of theology.[164] In the nineties the norm was two years of philosophy and three years of theology, but even then some were being ordained after two years of theology because they were so badly needed.[165] At the same time these clerics were also putting in nearly a full day teaching and prefecting in the College. Not only were they given the bare fundamentals of theology, but, as the years were to prove, some of them lacked a solid spiritual foundation.

Meanwhile St. Vincent helped by sending such men as it could spare. They were an important contribution to St. Benedict's, but Abbot Innocent argued that as quickly as the community at Atchison gained one man, St. Vincent withdrew a man. Under those conditions the Abbot could not plan for the future. For that reason

---

[162] *Idem*, Mar. 6, 1893. (AM)
[163] Wolf an Wimmer, Atchison, July 15, 1887. (SVA)
[164] *Idem*, Apr. 13, 1885. (SVA)
[165] Wolf an Braunmueller, Atchison, Mar. 6; July 26, 1893. (AM)

Abbot Innocent asked Archabbot Wimmer to permit his priests to transfer their vows to St. Benedict's if they wished.[166] The Archabbot resented this suggestion and reminded Abbot Innocent that St. Vincent was not the whole Congregation and complained that St. John's had so many men that the Abbot there did not know what to do with them all.[167] The lack of man power in Kansas continued to be relieved by men on loan from St. Vincent until after the Archabbot's death. Many of them were fine monks and hard workers, but others, by holding themselves aloof, just waiting for the word to return to Pennsylvania, were problems.[168] Abbot Innocent once wrote that such men had given him "more heart burning than any other trouble."[169]

More Brothers were also needed in the community. The work on the farm and around the College was more than the few Brothers could handle. Even the Abbot sometimes helped to haul wood in order to encourage the overworked Brothers. The priests also helped them when possible, and the scholastics usually worked on their free afternoons.[170] The most difficult job to keep filled satisfactorily was that of cook. Archabbot Wimmer sent help, and the two abbots discussed the problem regularly until on April 22, 1884, St. Benedict's chapter decided to ask the Benedictine Sisters of St. Scholastica's Convent in Atchison to operate the kitchen. The Bishop had given permission for the arrangement,[171] but the Archabbot was fearful and very much opposed to it, although he admitted that he would do the same in case of extreme necessity.[172] Living quarters for the Sisters were arranged, and the meals at St. Benedict's underwent a wonderful change. Later, when Brother Joseph died, the Sisters took over

166 Wolf an Wimmer, Atchison, Apr. 13, 1885. (SVA)
167 Wimmer an Wolf, St. Vincent, Apr. 18, 1885.
168 Wolf an Wimmer, Atchison, Jan. 28, 1884; June 13, 1887. (SVA)
169 Wolf an Hintenach, Atchison, Sept. 4[?], 1891 draft.
170 Wolf an Wimmer, Atchison, Nov. 10, 1877. (SVA)
171 Idem, Apr. 24, 1884. (SVA)
172 Wimmer an Wolf, St. Vincent, Apr. 30, 1884.

the bakery as well, and Abbot Innocent wondered how St. Benedict's had ever managed without them.[173]

The Abbot sought candidates for the Brotherhood in Europe, and he wrote letters to the Catholic press. Such appeals, however, brought mostly the type that seems to make a career of sampling religious communities all over the globe. Plenty of that kind came without any particular encouragement.[174] From the time he took office until 1893, Abbot Innocent carefully entered the names of ninety-six candidates for the Brotherhood in the Abbey *Registrum*. Only sixteen of these became permanent members of the community. Fourteen came and went before one stayed. After most of the names the Abbot entered such notations as *non inveniens pacem* (not finding peace), or *nec orare nec laborare voluit* (he was unwilling either to pray or to work). So long as a man had the essential desire to serve God and live the religious life, other standards were not high. Speaking of a not-very-promising candidate, Abbot Innocent wrote, "I would try him for we are in great want, and we take persons. . . even fifty years old, whether cripples or not, if they are otherwise healthy and of good will."[175]

While the Abbot was in Europe in 1880, Father Boniface and Father Ambrose Huebner gave him a detailed picture of life at the Abbey and portrayed the Brothers and their work at that time. Brother Bernard Ball was "Chargé d'affaires on the farm," assisted by Brother Adam Gansen. Brother Clement Wirtz, of St. Vincent on loan as a cook and quite indispensable, was an old soldier who insisted on his periodical drop of whiskey for some mysterious illness incurred in service. Brother Joseph von Bragel was the baker at that time and "had improved his bread — thanks to a tramp baker. . . The bakery is kept clean and so is the baker." Brother Placidus Feser was the janitor and kept "everything as neat as a pin."

---

[173] Wolf an Wimmer, Atchison, Oct. 28, 1887. (SVA)
[174] *Idem*, Apr. 14, 1878. (SVA) Wolf to Edelbrock, Atchison, Aug. 31, 1889. (SJA)
[175] Wolf to Edelbrock, Atchison, Feb. 21, 1889. (SJA)

Brother Lawrence Egan was the dishwasher but was rather out of place in that job. Brother Thaddeus Weber was a teamster, but Father Ambrose wished him elsewhere. Brother Maurus Dobler found tailoring too confining, but he grew fat and happy on the farm. Father Boniface reported that Brother Andrew Allermann, as usual, was the man of all work, but Father Ambrose, the procurator, referred to him as "the same old one, I think you'll decapitate him when you come — I hope so." Brother Eugene Barry was a general handy man, and Father Ambrose wished he had "a few more like him."[176]

Since all the Brothers' common prayers were in German, Irish Brothers Eugene and Lawrence must have suffered — patiently or otherwise. Brother Eugene was an early citizen of Atchison, had bought a couple of lots, and became a citizen of the United States in 1861. Before entering the community he taught the boys in St. Benedict's parochial school and wrote a beautiful hand in English and Gaelic. He was intellectually active and kept notes on mathematical problems, the weather, the Boer War, and gave poke-berry ink a fair trial. He kept commonplace books of quotations, predominantly scriptural, but mercifully interspersed with such notes as "Monks and Lay Brothers, we assert, are one body with regard to the future life, but while on earth they are 'distinct' very. Disfranchised so to speak." And "I hope his soul enjoys eternal glory, for here on earth I was his purgatory." He recorded also some notable victories: "During the year 1906 I did not see a single bed-bug in the students' dormitory."[177]

Although Abbot Innocent in 1884 complained of the

[176] Verheyen to Wolf, Atchison, Nov. 3, 1880; Huebner to Wolf, Atchison, Nov. 4, 1880.
    Thaddeus (John) Weber was born in Cincinnati, Ohio, Dec. 18, 1845, professed Feb. 10, 1876, came to Kansas in 1879, died Nov. 23, 1908.—*Necrologium*, No. 370.
    Maurus (Frank) Dobler was born in Rascati, Russia, Apr. 19, 1855, professed Nov. 13, 1881, and died Nov. 8, 1889.—*Ibid.*, No. 165.
    Eugene Barry was born in Coolroe, Ireland, Dec. 21, 1838, professed Dec. 8, 1881, and died Nov. 29, 1909.—*Ibid.*, No. 382.
[177] Barry Diary, end 1906. Other items from his papers.

slow growth of his community, his monastic family was more than twice as large as it had been seven years before when he had taken over its direction. The community numbered fourteen priests, two deacons, eleven clerics, four choir novices, thirteen Brothers, and seven scholastics. Three priests from St. Vincent were on loan. About half the priests, eight, were stationed outside the Abbey and were engaged in the care of souls in eighteen stations. Three other stations were cared for from the Abbey.[178] The community was small but it was growing.

The problem of man power was to be solved but slowly, and it was the same with the problem of means. Abbot Innocent once wrote that if the Roman authorities had known the size of the debt in 1876, they would never have made St. Benedict's an abbey and that even then, in 1891, they would have him reporting every six months if they knew the debt was so large.[179]

On account of the new building the debt in 1885 increased to almost $70,000. Even then, owing to the growth of the community, the per capita debt was less than it had been earlier, but in the next five years the total was brought down to $48,000. Meanwhile income from the salaries and offerings received by the missionaries had increased from $1600 in 1877 when Abbot Innocent took office to $7000 in 1890. In the same period the College income rose from $5000 to $15,000, and the gross income from all sources increased from $15,000 to $35,000. Old debts were paid and new ones were made. Bad crops affected practically all of the community's sources of income — farm, missions, and College — but progress was steady. Credit for this must go first of all, of course, to the Abbot and community who worked and saved so hard, but they were aided by many good friends, such as Archabbot Wimmer, the other abbeys of the Congregation, the Ludwig-Missionsverein, the Leopoldinen Stiftung, the Abbey of Metten, and by good neighbors like William F. Dolan, on one of whose receipts the Abbot

[178] *Berichte der Leopoldinenstiftung*, LV (1885), 26.
[179] Wolf an Mueller, Atchison, Feb. 25, 1891. (SVA)

noted, "Mr. Dolan gave us groceries on credit and would not dun us."

Prior Oswald had succeeded in obtaining a loan of $20,000 at the low interest rate of six per cent from the Abbey of Metten in 1875 and had given a mortgage on the Priory and College. That mortgage was cancelled only thirty-two years later, on December 26, 1907. Half the loan was repaid in 1882, but the remainder was left with St. Benedict's as long as the community needed it. The interest rate was redeuced to five per cent in 1880 and to four per cent in 1884.[180] Most of the interest was paid by donations from the Ludwig-Missionsverein and by Mass stipends, of which Metten had a surplus, whereas a shortage of them existed among Benedictines in the United States. In several instances most of the Masses were offered by the monks of St. Vincent and St. John's abbeys, with St. Benedict's receiving the financial benefit of the offering.[181] Abbot Benedict Braunmueller of Metten in 1887 finally arranged that not only the interest but the remaining $10,000 principal should be repaid solely through the transfer of Mass intentions.[182] In expressing his appreciation for Metten's kindness to one of his abbeys, Archabbot Wimmer wrote, "Abbot Wolf has had hard times but they have been overcome and since the interest has been reduced substantially, the debt will be repaid rapidly. You have made an important contribution towards that."[183]

When shortly after his election Abbot Innocent decided to build so that the College might grow, Archabbot Wimmer wrote to the Ludwig-Missionsverein, asking them to give special consideration to St. Benedict's needs.[184] From 1877 to 1895 the Verein gave a total of

[180] Wimmer an Wolf, St. Vincent, Aug. 23, 1884.
[181] *Idem*, Mar. 5; Apr. 8, 1879; Mar. 30, 1881.
[182] Braunmueller an Wolf, Metten, Apr. 15, 1887.
    This plan, which should have been completed in 1900, was apparently amended when in 1893 St. Benedict's needed funds for building the monastery. —Wolf an Braunmueller, Atchison, Mar. 6, 1893. (AM)
[183] Wimmer an Braunmueller, St. Vincent, Mar. 12, 1887. (AM)
[184] Wimmer an LMV, St. Vincent, Dec. 19, 1879. (LMV Leav II 1/56)

about $5000 to St. Benedict's, particularly at those times when the need for new buildings increased the expenses of the community. The Leopoldinen Stiftung in Vienna also granted St. Benedict's a total of about $600 in three donations between 1878 and 1883. Archabbot Wimmer's support was of critical importance throughout this period. As he wrote to Abbot Innocent, "St. Vincent's and I owe you help, and I will do what I can. . . With God's help we will pull through."[185]   This support alone kept Abbot Innocent from sometimes succumbing to despair.

The relations between Archabbot Wimmer and Abbot Innocent, one of his favorite sons, were frank and friendly — those of a father and his adult son. Abbot Innocent proudly sent samples of the local wine for the Archabbot's nameday, and the Archabbot gave an altar for the chapel. Their correspondence covered every topic of interest to the Congregation and Benedictines generally, from advice on stopping runaway horses to the fourteenth centenary of St. Benedict, the need of a Vesperale, plans for the development of the Order in the United States, and the Archabbot's dreams of the mission to the Negro. They discussed their local problems with frankness, eager for each other's advice. Abbot Innocent was always grateful to the Archabbot for his aid to St. Benedict's, and dreaded the day when the Archabbot would no longer be there to help meet emergencies. "It sometimes frightens me," Abbot Innocent wrote, "to think what would happen to us if you were not there."[186]

They also had their differences. Abbot Innocent was sometimes irritated by the Archabbot's arbitrariness, but the irritation was always secondary to his love for the founder. Abbot Innocent complained to Abbot Alexius Edelbrock that suggesting improvements to the Archabbot was practically impossible even though he asked for suggestions, because he always took the most honest criticism as a personal affront and then proceeded to build

185 Wimmer an Wolf, St. Vincent, Apr. 8, 1878.
186 Wolf an Wimmer, Atchison, Nov. 11, 1881. (SVA)

backfires. An amusing instance of this was the issue of beefsteak for breakfast. At St. Benedict's the country custom of steak for breakfast had long been followed. Suddenly Archabbot Wimmer asked Abbot Innocent to discontinue the practice. Abbot Innocent answered that his men were outrageously overworked and needed a big breakfast, that St. Benedict permitted the abbot to introduce necessary changes of diet, that meat was often the cheapest food available in the West, and that furthermore the meals were simple and even Spartan. One of the Archabbot's arguments was that when his own monks then in Kansas returned, they would want the same at St. Vincent. Abbot Innocent was quick with a *reductio ad absurdum* and answered that they would also then demand the butter and eggs they had had at X, the fish, frogs, and eels that they had had at Y, etc., ad infinitum. As a remedy he suggested that those who complained that Kansans ate beefsteak for breakfast be sent either to the place they criticized or to the place they wished to imitate and see how they liked either. But the Archabbot was insistent, and Abbot Innocent was confident that his chapter would comply, but he asked that the Archabbot send him an official document that could be incorporated in the minutes.[187] The matter was so out of proportion that it was mysterious, but Abbot Innocent was convinced that it was the Archabbot's defense against the criticism by the visitators at St. Vincent in the preceding year. The visitators, Abbots Alexius and Innocent, had reported unfavorably on the discipline and the food at St. Vincent.[188]

Archabbot Wimmer suffered extremely during his last illness in 1887, but those days were brightened as one of his oldest and fondest dreams came true when Pope Leo XIII founded Sant' Anselmo as an international college for Benedictines. The old Archabbot's letters are full of a wonderfully youthful enthusiasm as he discussed every

[187] Wimmer to Wolf, St. Vincent, Jan. 31, 1885. Wolf an Wimmer, Atchison, Feb. 3, 1885. (SVA) Chapter Minutes, Dec. 22, 1885.
[188] Wolf to Edelbrock, Atchison, Apr. 15, 1885. (SJA)

detail of the new College, for which he had been working since 1855. *"Wie schoen, wie herrlich!"* he wrote, "wonderful things do happen in this world, and I am happy that I have lived long enough to see it."[189] Father Adalbert Mueller, Abbot Innocent's old Roman classmate, had received an invitation to join the faculty of the new College. Father Adalbert was most of the theology faculty at St. Benedict's at the time, but Abbot Innocent insisted that he be sent. The assignment would be a big honor for American Benedictines.[190] Archabbot Wimmer admitted that it would "tickle him to see an American filling a Roman chair."[191] Ultimately the necessary funds for Sant' Anselmo were collected, and Father Adalbert went on to become the first prior there.

The old Archabbot died on December 8 of that year, 1887. With his passing the first period in the history of the American Cassinese Congregation, the founder's era, came to an end. Conditions could never be quite the same, for in his day an intimate personal bond and a father-son relationship existed between him and the superiors of all the other monasteries in the Congregation. To put it another way, he had been the law. With his passing, law of the more impersonal kind had to be introduced. He had hoped that after his death the "spirit of brotherly love and mutual help [in the name of which he had done so much for St. Benedict's] will always remain in our Congregation."[192] This spirit did remain, but never again could it be founded on such close personal understanding.

189 Wimmer an Wolf, St. Vincent, Apr. 24, 1887.
190 Wolf an Wimmer, Atchison, June 13, 1887. (SVA)
191 Wimmer an Wolf, St. Vincent, June 8, 1887.
192 *Idem*, Jan. 14, 1887.

The Missions After 1877

The pioneer mission-circuits gradually grew into established rural parishes. No sharp line divides the two periods, but in the northeastern part of Kansas the change was well under way by 1880, and with that change arose the question of the compatibility of parochial work and the monastic life. By the end of the century Abbot Innocent, as president of the Congregation, was forced to defend the propriety of Benedictines continuing the work that had first brought them to the United States. Another change after 1870 was an increase in the number of immigrants direct from the old country. The Catholic settlers who had come into Kansas in the fifties and sixties were rarely direct immigrants. The majority had farmed or had done other work in more eastern parts of the United States or Canada before coming to Kansas. After 1870 greater numbers of Catholic immigrants came to the State, and a considerable proportion of them came directly from Europe.[1]

As the settlers thronged into Kansas in the seventies and eighties, the Benedictines at Atchison expanded the work of providing for their religious needs. With a temporary exception, the Atchison Benedictines did not expand their missionary territory, but more men were devoted to the care of souls as the number of Catholics increased and as one-time stations became parishes. As a matter of fact the needs grew faster than the community, and as fast as the Bishop could obtain priests he would send

[1] J. Neale Carman, "Continental Europeans in Rural Kansas, 1854-1861," *Territorial Kansas, Studies Commemorating the Centennial* (University of Kansas, 1954), 193 ff.

resident pastors to one after another of the old missions. By the end of the century the bishops of the surrounding territory still needed the Benedictines to help with parish work but not to the same degree nor with the same urgency as in the pioneer days. The work no longer provided a *raison d'etre* for the community.

The project of a new foundation in southwestern Kansas had been abandoned in 1876, but Bishop Fink was still intent on establishing religious communities as "Christian Forts" in the West. He asked Abbot Innocent to supply a priest for a big German settlement taking up land west of Great Bend. Abbot Innocent had no priest to send, and so the Bishop turned to Archabbot Wimmer. Since Abbot Innocent's older brother, Father Ferdinand Wolf, wished to go West, he was sent to Kansas to care for the new colony.[2]

After visits to Atchison and Leavenworth, Father Ferdinand arrived at Newton on May 14, 1878, and was introduced to his missions by the same Father Swembergh who had welcomed Prior Oswald Moosmueller and Father Boniface to the Southwest two years earlier.[3] Father Ferdinand's home base was to be Windhorst in Ford County, founded by the Cincinnati Colony.[4] His typical circuit started at Windhorst and at the Tennessee Colony, about twelve miles to the north; then Kinsley, Offerle, Windhorst again, then Larned, Fort Larned, Great Bend, Dodge City, Fort Dodge, and back to Kinsley at the end of the month. Between stations he offered Mass wherever he could find Catholics. He once said Mass at a water tank called Sherlock at four-thirty in the morning so that the three Irishmen on the section gang need not lose a minute's labor, but the men showed no appreciation and stayed in their blankets.[5]

[2] Fink an Wimmer, Leavenworth, Jan. 3, 1878. (SVA) Wimmer an Wolf, St. Vincent, Jan. 18, 1878.
   Ferdinand Wolf was born in Schmidheim, Rhenish Prussia, Jan. 29, 1834, professed July 11, 1858, ordained Dec. 22, 1860, and died Mar. 8, 1914.—*Necrologium*, No. 434.
[3] Ferdinand to Wolf, Newton, May 15, 1878.
[4] *Idem*, Cincinnati Colony, May 21, 1878.
[5] *Idem*, Sherlock, July 17, 1878.

That first year he spent Christmas at Great Bend. He had the traditional five o'clock Mass, but only two families lived near enough to attend it. The other Masses were better attended, and the Christmas collection totalled $5.40. On the feast of the Epiphany he spent twenty-four hours on a train stuck in the snow six miles east of Dodge City. January was very cold, and Father Ferdinand had to abandon his little frame house and take refuge in a sod-house to keep from freezing to death.[6]

In Dodge City Father Ferdinand found a welcome from friends who had welcomed Father Boniface two years before, particularly from Mayor Kelly, "a lively, generous, good-hearted man. I do hope and pray," wrote Father Ferdinand, "that in the course of time, he will also return to his duties and become a good Catholic. . . True, he is the soul of all sport; but just such smart men will also become *very* good, when they do turn to good." He also agreed that the city was much less sinful than reported, but he admitted that "things may become a little worse when more drovers come in, but the Catholic ladies tell me that no one gets hurt who minds his own business."[7] Father Ferdinand also continued the periodic visits to Camp Supply in the Indian Territory and to Fort Elliott in Texas. Almost three years had passed, and no priest had visited these posts since Father Boniface had been there.[8]

The colony at Windhorst offered St. Benedict's Abbey a quarter-section of land on condition that a monastery be built there, but the community had no men to spare for a new foundation, and so the offer was necessarily declined. Any regret was no doubt removed when at the same chapter all pastors were asked to encourage their parishioners to donate seed wheat to the Windhorst settlers, who had lost their crops on account of the drought.[9]

[6] *Idem*, Great Bend, Jan. 20, 1879.
[7] *Idem*, Dodge City, May 24, 1878.
[8] *Idem*, Great Bend, Jan. 20, 1879.
[9] Chapter Minutes, Aug. 22, 1879.

If no monastic foundation was to be made at Windhorst, there was no point in leaving Father Ferdinand in that distant mission if the Bishop had a priest to replace him. When the Bishop insisted that St. Patrick's parish south of Atchison must be given a resident pastor and no other priest was available, the chapter voted to recall Father Ferdinand.[10] The situation was embarrassing, however, for 1880 had been as bad a year for the settlers as 1879, and Father Ferdinand objected strongly to leaving under those circumstances.[11] The Bishop, however, was convinced that the settlement was too far west and advised the Abbot to withdraw Father Ferdinand and concentrate on the mission in northeastern Kansas.[12] Father Ferdinand was resigned to the change after Father Swembergh told him that the Cincinnati society had broken up and that the townsite and church land were to be sold.[13] The Bishop relieved Father Ferdinand in the autumn of 1881 and that ended the Benedictine adventures in western Kansas.[14] Their western mission was brief, but the Benedictines had been handy to fill temporary gaps and had done useful pioneer work.

When Abbot Innocent was elected in 1876, the Kansas monks divided their work of the care of souls among what were in effect four mission centers: Atchison, St. Benedict's in Doniphan County, Seneca, and Nebraska City. The first new growth appeared in the missions in the northern tier of counties. In the early 1870's Father Suitbert Demarteau had been sent to live with the pastor at Seneca to care for the missions both east and west of that town. Bishop Fink soon provided resident pastors at Irish Creek (1871) and Hanover (1873) to care for most of these missions, but the Benedictines continued to visit for a time St. Bridget's and St. Augustine's (Fidelity).

10 *Ibid.*, Dec. 9, 1880.
11 Ferdinand to Wolf, Fort Supply, Oct. 30, 1880.
12 Wolf an Wimmer, Bendena, Jan. 12, 1881. (SVA)
13 Ferdinand to Wolf, Spearville, May 11, 1881.
14 Fink to Wolf, Leavenworth, Oct. 18, 1881.

Father Timothy Luber was in charge of these two missions in 1878, and at the end of that year he built a residence at St. Bridget's.[15] Thereafter he lived at St. Bridget's and cared for the missions of Axtell and Capioma (Fidelity). But the Capioma parishioners began to clamor for a resident pastor in 1881.[16] Father Timothy supervised the building of a residence there in 1882-83, and another parish was erected.[17] The Benedictines were still short-handed, and when Father William Rettele, Father Timothy's successor as pastor, was stricken with tuberculosis, the Bishop was asked to take over Capioma.[18] The Bishop had provided a priest for St. Bridget's in the previous year but at the same time had asked the Benedictines to take charge of the parish at Effingham because it was near the Abbey.[19]

Of all the missions attended by the Benedictines, none grew so phenomenally as those in Nemaha County. A census of St. Mary's parish at Wildcat and Sts. Peter and Paul parish in Seneca taken in 1888 revealed 242 families in the two parishes, a total of 1273 souls, of whom 609 were at Wildcat and 664 at Seneca. Almost half the parents heading these families had come from Oldenburg, Hanover, Westphalia, and Rhenish Prussia. Another large group came from central and southern Germany, and about one-tenth of the families were of Irish extraction. About one-third of the families had come to Nemaha County from other parts of the United States or from Canada.[20] Both parishes had had schools taught by laymen since about 1870. The Benedictine Sisters in Atchison undertook their first missions in 1876, when Sisters were sent to teach the parochial school at Seneca

15 Luber to Wolf, Seneca, Nov. 12, 1878.
16 Wolf an Wimmer, Atchison, Nov. 11, 1881. (SVA)
17 Luber to Wolf, St. Bridget's, Nov. 13, 1882.
18 Fink to Wolf, Leavenworth, Aug. 18, 1885, and Wolf's notation.
William Rettele was born in Sheboygan County, Wisconsin, Feb. 13, 1855, professed July 25, 1879, ordained July 31, 1883, and died Oct. 3, 1885.—*Necrologium*, No. 129.
19 *Idem*, July 25, 1884.
20 Gilbert Wolters, O.S.B., *A Socio-Economic Analysis of Four Rural Parishes in Nemaha County, Kansas* (Washington, D.C., 1938), 16-17.

and the district school at Wildcat.[21]   In the following year sixty children attended the school at Seneca and forty-five at Wildcat.[22]

When Father Ferdinand Wolf returned from western Kansas at the end of 1881, he was assigned to take care of St. Mary's Church at Wildcat.   The Benedictine Sisters from Atchison who taught the school were already living there, and Father Ferdinand wanted permission to build a stable with a room for himself included.   He also wanted to build a new privy and gave his brother, the Abbot, a detailed report of the deficiencies of the old privy. But Abbot Innocent moved his brother to a smaller parish, Marak, and sent Father Timothy to build a residence at Wildcat.[23]

Meanwhile Father Emmanuel Hartig had been succeeded at Seneca by Father Thomas Bartl in 1881.   Four years later, when Father Thomas was incapacitated by illness, Father Suitbert Demarteau was sent to the parish.[24]   Father Suitbert had been one of the most active of the pioneer missionaries, caring for a wide area around Seneca during the early seventies.   He was a member of St. Vincent Abbey and was recalled from Kansas in 1875.[25] He was an able man and was made prior of St. Joseph's parish in Chicago, but, as Archabbot Wimmer wrote, Father Suitbert considered himself a *Kansatianer* and had long wished to return to Kansas.   He transferred his vows to St. Benedict's in January, 1885.[26]   By June he was installed as pastor at Seneca and promptly began erecting a proper church, which was blessed by Abbot Innocent on May 22, 1887.[27]   The church was completed free of debt, a feat which Abbot Innocent was convinced no other

[21] Kremmeter an LMV, Atchison, Oct. 31, 1876. (LMV Leav II 2/14)
[22] Hartig to Wolf, Seneca, Jan. 14, 1878.
[23] Wolf to Luber and Stader, Atchison, Aug. 24, 1883, copy; Luber to Wolf, Seneca, Oct. 11, 1883.
[24] Suitbert (Michael) Demarteau was born in Kripp, Rhenish Prussia, Sept. 1, 1834, professed Nov. 11, 1866, ordained Apr. 12, 1867, and died Jan. 16, 1901.—*Necrologium*, No. 281.
[25] Moosmueller to Wimmer, Atchison, Feb. 8, 1876. (SVA)
[26] Wimmer an Wolf, St. Vincent, Jan. 15, 1885.
[27] Wolf Diary, May 22, 1887.

of his monks could have duplicated.[28]   Father Suitbert's
ability was so impressive that after he had added a new
parish house at Seneca he was called back to the Abbey
in 1892 to be the community procurator.[29]

By the beginning of the twentieth century the two
pioneer Benedictine missions in Nemaha County had almost doubled in size.   According to a census made in
1903 the parish in Seneca numbered 1044 souls, and a
census of 1906-07 revealed 882 souls in St. Mary's parish
at Wildcat.[30]   The need of more farms for the younger
generation caused the formation of two new parishes, St.
Bede's at Kelly in 1902 and Sacred Heart at Baileyville
in 1909.

Another pioneer mission center was St. Benedict's
Colony in Doniphan County, today called from its nearest town and postoffice, Bendena.   It had been the residence of a pastor and a missionary since 1868.   In 1877,
in the age of eighty-acre family farms, the parish numbered about 500 souls, and twenty-nine children were baptized that year.[31]   The parish apparently reached its
greatest size in the 1870's when baptisms averaged slightly more than eighteen a year.   In the 1930's the average
was about five baptisms per year.

The missions attended from Bendena were given
resident pastors as quickly as they grew large enough.
The first of these was Wathena, for which the Bishop was
demanding a resident pastor as early as 1877.[32]   About
eighty families lived in the area, and since the Abbot had
no priest available, he asked the Bishop to send a priest
to take over the parish and its missions.[33]   The Bishop in
1886 sent a priest to reside in Troy, but since the people
could not support him, he left, and the Benedictines were

[28] Wolf to Mueller, Atchison, June 19, 1890. (SVA)
[29] Wolf Diary, July 2, 1892.
[30] Wolters, *op. cit.*, 20.
[31] Koumly to Wolf, St. Benedict's, Jan. 25, 1878.
[32] Fink to Wolf, Leavenworth, Feb. 27, 1877.
[33] Wolf Diary, Jan. 12, 1879.

asked to continue caring for the missions of Troy, Fanning, and White Cloud.[34]

Another group of missions, settled after the Civil War and visited at first from Bendena, were Marak and its neighbor and successor, Everest — both Bohemian groups — and a German settlement at Reserve, better known as Germantown (Mercier). These were being cared for by Father John Stader in 1882. The coming of the railroad and its shops at Hiawatha brought Catholics to that town, and so Father John added it to his circuit and began collecting to build a church. When Father Ferdinand took charge of these missions in 1883, he found churches at Marak and Reserve and a residence at Everest. Father Ferdinand protested that he was unable to carry a debt, could not collect money, could not run fairs, and so could not build a church in Hiawatha. Eccentric Father Ferdinand had his misadventures. A charming railroad man who did most of the collecting for him in Hiawatha absconded with a part of the fund. What was worse, he turned out to have been a drinker and a libertine. But in spite of all setbacks, churches were built at both Hiawatha and Everest.[35] However, a Bohemian-speaking priest was badly needed for Marak and Everest, and at the Abbot's request the Bishop sent Father Gaydousek, fresh from Louvain, in 1886.[36]

Of the missions cared for from Atchison, St. Patrick's, the oldest, was the first to receive a resident pastor. The parish had eighty-nine families in 1876, and a house was erected in the following year. The Bishop was already showing impatience at that time, but the Abbot was short

[34] Fink to Wolf, Leavenworth, Apr. 16, 1886, and Wolf's notation on *Idem*, Aug. 24, 1886.

A destructive cyclone caused a new church to be built at Bendena in 1895. —Wolf Diary, Aug. 10, 1895.

A church was erected at the nearby mission of Severance in 1884.—*Berichte der Leopoldinenstiftung*, I.V (1885), 31-32.

After the parish of Purcell had argued for three years about the location, Bishop Fink in disgust delegated Father Thomas Burk to lay the cornerstone for a new church in 1896.—Wolf Diary, June 16, 1896.

[35] Ferdinand to Wolf, 1883-1884, *passim*.

[36] Wolf to Fink, Atchison, June 18, 1886; Fink to Wolf, Leavenworth, Aug. 29, 1886.

190

of priests.[37] Four years later, after the Bishop had threatened to send a diocesan priest to the parish, Abbot Innocent finally assigned Father Adolph Wesseling as the first resident pastor of St. Patrick's.[38] In 1886 the Bishop was finally able to provide a resident pastor for Mooney Creek, which had long been visited from Atchison.[39] The congregation at Slattery's, formally named St. Louis but usually called Good Intent, built a church in 1880.[40]

The Abbey Church was awkwardly located for the parish in the days when most people walked to church. The arrival of the railroad age and the boom of the eighties in Atchison brought a new parish to the west part of town in 1882, when a combination school and chapel was built. The present Sacred Heart Church was dedicated in 1893 when Father Matthew Bradley was pastor. As early as 1871 a subscription list was circulated for a new church in the south part of town, but nothing came of it at that time. A partial solution to the problem was the erection of a new parish school in the central part of Atchison in 1889. After the fashion of the time and also because it was to offer commercial courses above the grade school level, the new school was called St. Louis College. Nevertheless, the Germans of St. Benedict's parish must have been dissatisfied, for in 1887 Bishop Fink had suggested giving them a separate church and school and made this an order in 1888.[41] Abbot Innocent's unwillingness to comply, particularly in view of his hope that the new central school would make such a development unnecessary, led to a temporary coolness between the Bishop and the Abbot. In the end no special church was built for the Germans.

The Abbey Church was gradually brought to completion by the efforts of the parish. One tower and a peal of bells were added at the time of the Abbot's jubilee in

37 Fink to Wolf, Leavenworth, Feb. 27, 1877.
38 Wolf Diary, Apr. 1, 1881.
39 Fink to Wolf, Leavenworth, Apr. 16, 1886.
40 Verheyen to Wolf, Atchison, Nov. 10, 1880.
41 Fink to Wolf, Leavenworth, Jan. 2, 1887; Mar. 25, 1888.

1891, and the other tower was completed in 1905. The marble and wood altar with its baldachin, a donation of William F. Dolan, was installed in 1895, and a year later the new organ was inaugurated with a "Grand Opening Concert." The church was beautifully decorated with religious paintings by Jacques V. Mueller in 1906.[42]

Missionary activity in Nebraska was limited to Nebraska City and its three small missions, which included only seventy-six families in 1877.[43] Bishop Bonacum asked Abbot Innocent to send a resident priest to Schmidt's Settlement in 1889, but the Abbot declined the invitation, stating that Benedictine help in the Nebraska missions was only temporary.[44] From time to time the chapter considered giving up Nebraska City, but Father Emmanuel would not have been happy anywhere else, and he was left there for the rest of his life, the sole relic of Benedictine activity on the Nebraska frontier.

The work of the Atchison Benedictines in Iowa originated, for the most part, with the mission to the German immigrant. The exception was Creston. St. Malachy's Priory was the dream of Father Augustine Burns.[45] Father Augustine had been a diocesan priest of Pittsburgh for seventeen years before he joined the Benedictines and became a member of St. John's Abbey in Minnesota. In 1873 he secured his Abbot's permission to found a new monastery particularly for Irish-Americans, though he had no wish to isolate himself from the German portion of the Order.[46] The site chosen was Creston, Iowa, an area where a notable Irish settlement already existed. Creston was also on the new railroad across Iowa. The Bishop of Davenport gave the new missionaries the care

[42] Gerard Heinz, O.S.B., *St. Benedict's Parish, an Historical Sketch* (Atchison, 1908).
[43] Bartl an Wolf, Nebraska City, Jan. 9, 1878.
[44] Bonacum to Wolf, Lincoln, Sept. 6, 1889; Wolf to Bonacum, Atchison, Sept. 9, 1889, draft.
[45] Augustine Burns was born in Tipperary, Ireland, Apr. 7, 1827, professed June 26, 1867, ordained May 14, 1850, died Aug. 12, 1874.—*Necrologium*, No. 68.
[46] Burns to Phelan, Mendota, June 8, 1874.

of souls in several counties. Father Augustine unfortunately died on August 12, 1874, at Burlington, Iowa, while collecting money for his new foundation. Father Eugene Phelan, originally a member of St. Vincent Abbey, was then made superior of the Priory and was joined by Father Placidus McKeever, who had originally made vows at Atchison.[47] The community was incorporated under the laws of Iowa on October 16, 1876, and land was acquired for the future monastery and college.

At the General Chapter in 1878 Archabbot Wimmer wished to give the Creston Priory the semi-independent status that he had found useful in earlier foundations. A faction in the General Chapter, however, denied that the Archabbot had the power to do so. The Archabbot agreed to submit the question to Abbot Pescetelli, the Congregation's Roman agent.[48] Without the Archabbot's knowledge Father James Zilliox, secretary of the General Chapter and representative of the dissidents, sent a petition to the Holy See through Abbot Pescetelli, insisting that Prior Phelan wanted canonical independence, that Bishop Hennessey of Dubuque wished it, that nearly everyone opposed the Archabbot's views, and demanding a decision of the Holy See instead of Abbot Pescetelli's opinion.[49] The Congregation of Propaganda obliged by making St. Malachy's Priory in Creston, with its two priests, canonically independent.[50]

Rome did not know it, but it had had a miscarriage. From a very modest beginning the house steadily declined. Prior Phelan was not very energetic, a school or scholasticate was not possible, and little attempt was made to attract vocations.[51] The only clerical candidates, a priest and a cleric, were disappointments. Archabbot Wimmer,

[47] Testimonial from Wimmer, St. Vincent, Feb. 10, 1875.
Eugene (Richard) Phelan was born in Dublin, Ireland, July 6, 1840, professed Nov. 13, 1862, ordained Apr. 12, 1867, and died May 6, 1903.—*Necrologium*, No. 304.
[48] Wimmer ad Pescetelli, St. Vincent, Aug. 3, 1878. (SPexM)
[49] Zilliox to Pescetelli, St. Vincent, Aug. 29; Sept. 18; Oct. 18, 1878. (SPexM)
[50] Dalla Prop., June 24, 1879, in Wimmer-Pescetelli papers. (SPexM)
[51] Wimmer to Phelan, St. Vincent, Oct. 13, 1879.

angered that canonical independence had been secured "behind [his] back," washed his hands of the whole project and offered only "advice. . . and. . . good will."[52] As the Priory did not grow, the ordinary, Bishop McMullen of Davenport, took several missions — a couple of counties — away from the community. Prior Phelan became seriously ill and finally resigned.[53]

Rome accepted the resignation and made Archabbot Wimmer responsible for the Priory.[54] He appointed Father Stephen Lyons to be its new prior. At a meeting of the abbots in Collegeville, Minnesota, Archabbot Wimmer delegated the direction of the Priory to Abbot Innocent Wolf because Atchison was the nearest Benedictine abbey.[55] After an official visitation in November, 1882, Abbot Innocent recommended that since no vocations were in sight and since the place was not suitable for a monastery, Rome be petitioned to suppress the independent priory.[56] But Archabbot Wimmer could not bring himself to send such a petition, fearing that the Roman officials would think he was trying to vindicate his original opinion.[57] Year after year the matter dragged on, with Abbot Innocent urging Archabbot Wimmer to write to Rome and settle the matter and with the Archabbot evading the unwelcome suggestion. Gradually he began to convince himself that the canonically independent priory of St. Malachy's was being held in a state of suspended animation until conditions would somehow improve and a small abbey would yet grace the Iowa prairies.[58]

The old Archabbot was quite out of touch with the facts of life at Creston. Father Placidus McKeever

[52] *Idem*, Sept. 26, 1880.
[53] Wolf an Wimmer, Atchison, July 20, 1882. (SVA) Wimmer an Wolf, St. Vincent, July 26, 1882.
[54] Wolf to McMullen, Atchison, Dec. 14, 1882, draft not sent.
[55] Agreement, Oct. 26, 1882.
[56] Wolf an Wimmer, Atchison, Nov. 24, 1882, copy.
[57] Wimmer an Wolf, St. Vincent, Dec. 27, 1882.
[58] Wimmer an Wolf, St. Vincent, June 22, 1886; Wimmer to Phelan, St. Vincent, Jan. 22, 1887.

transferred his vows back to St. Benedict's Abbey in 1887,[59] and the new Archabbot Andrew Hintenach in 1892 called Prior Stephen Lyons away from Creston to direct St. Bede College in Illinois.[60] A year later Father Eugene Phelan also transferred his vows to St. Benedict's. "Thus the Priory of Creston [becomes] extinct," wrote Abbot Innocent, "because Father Eugene was the last member."[61] On that point the Abbot's conscience was finally at rest.

Although St. Malachy's Priory had a sad constitutional history, nevertheless during the eighties and early nineties it was an active missionary center, staffed by monks sent from Atchison. In 1892 Father Bede Durham and an assistant cared for the Creston parish with 700 souls as well as for the missions of Afton (140), Orient (60), Thayer (40), and Murray (60). Father Dennis Murphy was stationed at Lenox with 330 souls and cared also for the missions of Bedford (30), Conway (40), Kent (16), Clearfield (16), and Gravity (20). Father Louis Flick was stationed at Massena, which numbered 60 Catholics, and cared for the missions of Reno (160), Bridgewater (100), and Cumberland.[62] Most of these missions were cared for by the Benedictines only until the Bishop could secure more priests, and in the next few years he supplied pastors for most of these places.[63]

In 1900 Bishop Cosgrove of Davenport and Abbot Innocent engaged in the following dialogue:

The Bishop: "I have been told that you wish to call home some of your priests. . . I can send a priest to Lenox. . ."

The Abbot: "I did not think of it at all. . ."

The Bishop: "I have on my hands, at present, several young priests."

The Abbot: "I thought all along, that we were to keep the places that we still attend in your diocese."

[59] Wimmer an Wolf, St. Vincent, Apr. 8, 1887.
[60] Wolf Diary, Aug. 8, 1892.
[61] Ibid., Sept. 2, 1893.
[62] Parish accounts, 1892.
[63] Wolf Diary, Aug. 7, 1894.

The Bishop: "I would be very sorry, indeed, that there should be any misunderstanding between us. . ."

The Abbot: "I would not do anything to keep a right in Lenox and missions, though we gave up much of the salary for years to build up the place. I will make arrangements to give it over."

The Bishop: "I will have a priest in Lenox on 21st of August. . ."[64]

In 1905 Bishop Davis, Bishop Cosgrove's coadjutor, decided that Creston needed a second parish and sent a diocesan priest to establish it. Abbot Innocent believed that the Bishop had been misinformed about the number of Catholics in Creston and that the new parish would do grave damage to the old parish. Consequently, on the advice of his chapter and particularly of such excitables as Father Thomas Burk, he appealed the case to Rome. The decision favored the Bishop.[65] With the chapter's decision in 1907 to sell the old farm at Creston, almost the last remnant of the dream of St. Malachy's Priory was gone.[66] A year later Abbot Innocent asked Bishop Davis to take over the parish at Afton since Father Alban Rudroff was no longer able to do the work there.[67]

The other Iowa parishes cared for by Atchison Benedictines were originally designed to provide for the religious needs of German immigrants, who showed an alarming tendency to drop the practice of their religion if they were not given German-speaking priests. In 1883 Bishop McMullen asked Abbot Innocent to send a priest to St. Mary's Church in Des Moines.[68] The Abbot sent Father Winfried Schmidt, who wrote that he needed Diogenes' lantern to find practical Catholics, but that a good spirit prevailed, and that he expected rapid improvement.[69] The Diocese of Davenport suffered from a sudden temporary

---

64 Cosgrove-Wolf correspondence, June 21 to Aug. 16, 1900.
65 Chapter Minutes, May 19, 1905.
66 *Ibid.*, Mar. 7, 1907.
67 Wolf to Davis, Atchison, Mar. 3, 1908, draft; Stahl to Wolf, Davenport, Mar. 11, 1908.
68 McMullen to Wolf, Davenport, May 30, 1883.
69 Schmidt an Wolf, Des Moines, July 17, 1883.

shortage of German-speaking priests in the late eighties, and Abbot Innocent sent Fathers Alban Rudroff and Placidus McKeever to help the Bishop for a couple of years.[70]

When in 1887 a new church became necessary in Council Bluffs, the Germans were permitted to form a parish. The Atchison community was asked to take charge of it.[71] Father McMenomy, of Council Bluffs, had been a particular friend of St. Benedict's since the sixties, and the Abbot agreed to accept the new parish only after assurance that Father McMenomy did not oppose the arrangement.[72] The Holy See on May 14, 1887, authorized the transfer of the parish to the Benedictines, and Father Adolph Wesseling was sent to Council Bluffs. Many of the local German Catholics had grown lax in the practice of their religion, but the new church was completed in the following spring. A frame school building was promptly added,[73] and the parish soon had forty families.[74] Unfortunately Father McMenomy's friendliness could not stand the strain of two priests simultaneously raising money for new churches in the same town.[75]

St. John's German parish in Burlington, Iowa, had been founded in 1855. For many years Jesuits from Germany had cared for the parish, but for reasons of policy they decided to give up the parish in 1889. A short time before, they had completed a rectory and an imposing church. Bishop Cosgrove asked the Atchison Benedictines to take over the parish.[76] The chapter welcomed the invitation and voted to accept the offer.[77] Abbot Innocent asked for such safeguards as would make possible the development of a priory.[78] Care of the parish was

[70] Cosgrove to Wolf, Davenport, Sept. 30, 1887; Trevis to Wolf, Davenport, July 26, 1887; Aug. 22, 1888.
[71] Trevis to Lyons, Davenport, Mar. 21, 1887.
[72] Wolf to Lyons, Atchison, Mar. 28, 1887, draft; Trevis to Lyons, Davenport, Apr. 13, 1887.
[73] Wesseling to Wolf, Council Bluffs, Feb. 10; Aug. 14, 1888.
[74] Wolf an Braunmueller, Atchison, July 1, 1890. (AM)
[75] Wesseling to Wolf, Council Bluffs, Aug. 19, 1887.
[76] Cosgrove to Wolf, Davenport, Dec. 6, 1889.
[77] Chapter Minutes, Dec. 11-12, 1889.
[78] Wolf to Cosgrove, Atchison, Dec. 22, 1889, copy.

given to the Benedictines by the Congregation of Propaganda on December 7, 1890.[79] The agreement with the Bishop provided that title to the church should remain in his hands, that the parish should not be divided for ten years (to facilitate payment of a debt of almost $10,000), and that policy concerning the use of German and English should be determined by the Bishop.[80] Abbot Innocent disliked a written agreement, though the terms were perfectly acceptable, and he only feared that English might not be used soon enough.[81]

Father Timothy Luber, who had been paying off debts at St. Patrick's, was sent to Burlington and given the honorific title of prior. He took charge of the parish on May 1, 1890. According to his estimate, the parish comprised 500 families, though little more than half of them were pewholders, and only about 100 attended church regularly. Of approximately 500 children about half attended the parish school.[82] Father Timothy was given one assistant and a Brother cook immediately, and later a second assistant was also assigned to Burlington for a while. So large a national parish, with its members scattered for miles around, was naturally troubled by periodic demands for a new German parish in this or that part of town.[83] It was a lively parish, and after paying the debt on the church, it erected a large new school in 1904.

By the nineties the parochial work of St. Benedict's Abbey was stabilized. In subsequent years only two new parishes were created, and a few more missions received resident pastors. In 1892 when the community numbered thirty-four priests, almost half of whom were engaged in parish work, the parishes and missions and the number of souls in each were as follows: St. Benedict's in Atchison about 1000; Sacred Heart in Atchison 300; Sts. Peter and

[79] Document enclosed in Cosgrove to Wolf, Davenport, Jan. 31, 1891.
[80] Mar. 6, 1891.
[81] Wolf to Cosgrove, Atchison, Feb. 9, 1891, draft not sent.
[82] Luber to Wolf, Burlington, Apr. 29, 1890.
[83] *Idem*, Aug. 30, 1897.

Paul in Seneca 500; St. Mary's at Wildcat 500; St. Benedict's near Bendena 250, with the missions of St. Mary's, Purcell 160, and Severance 48; St. Patrick's 400; and St. Anne's in Effingham 180, with its mission at Wetmore 25.

In Iowa St. John's parish in Burlington numbered about 1400; St. Mary's in Des Moines 500; St. Peter's in Council Bluffs 200, and its temporary mission at Mineola 40. St. Malachy's parish in Creston had about 700 members, with the missions of Afton 140, Orient 60, Thayer 40, and Murray 60. Lenox had about 330 members and its missions at Bedford 30, Conway 40, Kent 16, Clearfield 16, and Gravity 20. Massena had about 60 souls and its missions of Reno 160, and Bridgewater 100.

St. Benedict's parish in Nebraska City had about 200 members. The mission stations visited from the Abbey were Doniphan with 80 members, St. Louis at Good Intent 100, Troy 40, Fanning 60, White Cloud 15, Hiawatha 70, Avoca in Nebraska 60, and Perrin in Missouri 30.[84] At that time twelve parishes in northeastern Kansas with resident pastors from the diocesan clergy had at one time or other been part of the missionary circuits of the Atchison monks: Holton, Mooney Creek, Wathena, and Everest in the nearby counties; Strawberry (Upper Parsons Creek) and Hanover in Washington County; and Axtell, Frankfort, Lillis, Marysville, and St. Bridget's in Marshall County.

The Missionary Life

Particularly during the early years the missionary had to be a better horseman than a theologian. Those with scattered mission stations commonly rode at least a hundred miles a week, and sometimes, when their schedules were disrupted by sick calls, they got little rest from the saddle. The work could be hazardous, as the ebullient Father Timothy Luber found out in the winter of

[84] Parish accounts, 1892.

1878. He was struggling through snowdrifts to his mission and was within six miles of Capioma when his horse fell on him, badly twisting his left ankle. In the melee the horse ran away. Father Timothy hobbled for half a mile before catching him. He mounted painfully and necessarily from the wrong side. Then he had to return for his saddlebags, dismount, and mount again in agony. But he finally reached Mr. Rochelle's and from there wrote asking the Abbot to send a substitute for the next Sunday and Christmas.[85] Four months later Father Timothy could walk without a cane, but he could no longer go horseback and had to buy a team and a buggy.[86]

There were also unheroic hazards. Father Ferdinand once reported, "I got bilious diarrhea during Mass on Sunday; had to divest at the Offertory and run into the cornfield behind the church at the Reserve. I think it must have taken an hour before I could return. I finished Mass, had two baptisms, but when I came to the house I had to rush for the cornfield again."[87]

Father Herman Mengwasser described Sunday in a country parish in 1893. He reported to the Ludwig-Missionsverein that his parish of St. Mary's at Wildcat was building a new church and that all winter the farmers had been hauling sand, stone, and timber for its construction. He explained the system of renting pews and the special coal collection, both necessary for raising funds. He wrote that his country church was surrounded by hitching posts, because his parishioners came from as far as ten miles away. Sunday was quite strenuous for the pastor. Since few lived near the church, most of the parishioners went to confession on Sunday morning. According to Father Herman, sodalities were organized particularly to equalize these Sunday confessions. Each sodality had its particular Sunday of the month. Confessions preceded the eight o'clock Mass, and after that Mass the pastor taught Catechism to those children who

85 Luber to Wolf, near Capioma, Dec. 16, 1878.
86 Wolf an Wimmer, Atchison, Apr. 15, 1879. (SVA)
87 Ferdinand to Wolf, Everest, Oct. 16, 1883.

lived too far away to attend the local school. High Mass with sermon was at ten-thirty, followed by a conference for the sodality on their monthly Communion Sunday. Next came the pastor's busiest period of office hours and an attempt to eat a bite of breakfast. Meanwhile the parishioners had been visiting, and the women exchanged their eggs for groceries at the general store across the road. By one o'clock all were again on their way home. At two-thirty in the afternoon the pastor held catechetical instructions, followed by Vespers and Benediction for those who lived near the church.[88]

The documents fail to record some of the more wonderful tales of missionary life in the pioneer period, but oral tradition will keep them alive. One story, for example, has its setting in a parish where directly across the road from the church the men gathered on Sunday morning at the general store. There they could wash away the dust they had eaten on the drive to church and also with nice timing could miss the sermon but fulfill their Sunday obligation. One Sunday morning, however, the pastor intoned the *Asperges*, swept down the aisle, out the door, across the road and in among the startled stags, sprinkled them liberally with holy water, and herded them to church for the beginning of Mass.

The rise of the temperance movement in Kansas posed a serious threat to church picnics, particularly in German parishes. When the usually timid Father Ferdinand heard that the temperance people of Hiawatha intended "to catch the Catholics selling beer at their Picnic near Everest on the 4th of July and to make an example of them for breaking the law," he let it be known that he would bring a couple of kegs of beer to treat his friends and that the men of the parish would do the same.[89]

Father Ferdinand Wolf was a deeply religious man, but even the community at St. Benedict's considered him excessively eccentric, and he caused so many complaints

[88] Mengwasser an LMV, St. Benedict's, Feb. 12, 1893. (LMV Leav II 1/69-74)

[89] Ferdinand to Wolf, Everest, June 23, 1884.

from parishioners that the Abbot finally gave up trying to use him for parish work. The earliest record we have of Father Ferdinand portrays Archabbot Wimmer trying to make an administrator out of him, and when the experiment failed, concluding querulously that Father Ferdinand was merely being stubborn.[90] In the little frontier chapels with their makeshift curtained sacristies, he worried about having the congregation see him in his shirt-sleeves and about the cut of the altar boys' cassocks. At first he sang Sunday Vespers solo for his little congregations, but since the men and boys simply would not sing and since he did not want the women and girls to sing, he finally substituted the Rosary.[91]

When Father Ferdinand prayed, he prayed loudly; when he moved, whether on the street or in church, he ran. As one pastor complained, "It looks so bad, and endangers the limbs of the altar boys."[92] He was afraid of women, spoke to them curtly if at all, and so was reported as unmannerly. From the pulpit he waged war against the latest fashion — bangs. He was convinced that he was not alone in seeing the immorality of bangs, for they had been branded, he said, by men of high standing both in Europe and in America. His clincher was that Queen Victoria was also on record as being against bangs.[93] And so it went; each time a complaint was sent to the Abbot, the latter wrote to Father Ferdinand; he in turn was remorseful and promised amendment, and then the cycle was repeated. He finally became chaplain to a convent of Benedictine Sisters at Ridgely, Maryland.

Most of the monks who were engaged in pastoral care in this period have already been mentioned. However, Father Thomas Burk, who figures later in this story, was a very effective preacher.[94] Convinced that Catholics

[90] Wimmer to Wolf, St. Vincent, Nov. 17, 1868.
[91] Ferdinand to Wolf, Everest, Mar. 19, 1884.
[92] Luber to Wolf, Burlington, May 5, 1890.
[93] Ferdinand to Wolf, Everest, June 9, 1884.
[94] Thomas (Philip) Burk was born in New Orleans, La., Oct. 2, 1865, professed July 11, 1883, ordained Aug. 5, 1888, and died Aug. 23, 1926.—*Necrologium*, No. 626.

must unite if they were to have any influence in American life, he was an active organizer of the Federation of Catholic Societies. He is also credited with more than the usual success in persuading his parishioners to make the sacrifice of sending their children considerable distances to the parochial school.

One of the most popular pastors of the period was Father Charles Stoeckle.[95] Father Charles taught commercial courses in the College for ten years as a cleric and as a young priest but devoted the rest of his life to pastoral care. He was a particularly able pastor, guiding his flock with wisdom and, for example, helping the growing families of his Seneca parish find good farms as the colony expanded. He was noted for his civic-mindedness, a particularly useful virtue in view of the tendency for the German immigrant and his leaders to hold themselves aloof from the rest of the community and so to ghettoize themselves. When Father Charles died at Seneca, he was honored with memorial services in the Methodist church there, at which various clergymen spoke warmly of him as citizen and priest.

The story of the missionary was mostly a steady year in year out round of Masses, sermons, sacraments, and sick calls; of building and rebuilding churches, schools, and rectories; of repairs, bills and more bills, and the constant distasteful job of somehow securing the necessary money. The missionary's greatest happiness came in those moments when he realized that he was an instrument of God's grace for his people.

Bishop Fink and the Benedictine Missions

Louis Mary Fink was the only monk of St. Benedict's to become a bishop. The combination of good sense and sound spirituality that had made him a good monk and

[95] Charles (Ferdinand) Stoeckle was born in Bamberg, Ontario, Dec. 5, 1858, professed July 25, 1879, ordained Mar. 30, 1884, and died Apr. 14, 1903. —*Necrologium*, No. 303.

a good religious superior made him also a good bishop, particularly for a rural missionary diocese. W. J. Onahan characterized him as "one of the most active and zealous of the western prelates in encouraging colonization and providing for the wants and necessities of the Catholic settlers."[96] In time of hardship, such as the year of grasshoppers and drought, Bishop Fink begged for his people. His greatest task, however, was preventing the Catholic immigrants from scattering so widely that they could not be organized into viable parish groups. For this purpose he organized and aided Catholic colonies. His first step was to reach the prospective immigrant and inform him of existing Catholic settlements, the price of land in the various parts of the State, and the addresses of Catholic missionaries who could help him find a place in or near a Catholic community. The Bishop's chief means of contacting the prospective immigrant were the immigration societies and the press, including the Catholic Directories, railroad literature, and immigrant guide books. The Bishop's energies were devoted to the development of parish groups that could quickly afford a simple church and school and a resident pastor.

That some differences of opinion should arise between the Bishop and the community in regard to the missions was inevitable. Bishop Fink constantly pressed for the appointment of a resident pastor whenever a parish with a few missions could likely support him. He argued, quite rightly, that only thus could settlers be attracted to the neighborhood, backsliders be won back, and any real growth be made. St. Benedict's, however, was too short of men to fill all the Bishop's demands. When the Bishop sent a diocesan priest to take over a former Benedictine mission, the Abbot sometimes agreed that this was the normal process of growth, but more often he complained that as soon as a mission ceased being an economic liability, the Bishop took it.[97]

---

[96] W. J. Onahan, "Catholic Colonization of the West," *American Catholic Quarterly Review*, VI (1881), 442.
[97] Wolf an Wimmer, Atchison, Nov. 6, 1878. (SVA)

The Benedictines engaged in parish work unfortunately felt that the benefit of their pioneering work was lost to the Order if the Bishop appointed one of his clergy to live at a former mission.[98] Father Ferdinand was more typical than usual but as revealing as always when he wrote on this topic, "Of course, it is all for the honor of God and the salvation of souls, but the Order ought not to suffer thereby. After they have spent themselves, and others have worked hard, the Bishop, with a gracious smile for thanks, takes the parishes as soon as he sees that they bring some returns. Fine bishops! Very paternal, indeed!"[99]

As a matter of fact Bishop Fink was in an unenviable spot. He was happy when the Abbot could provide a resident pastor for a former mission in the old Benedictine district, but if the Abbot could not, the Bishop must. He urged Archabbot Wimmer to send more help because, as he wrote, "Poor Abbot Innocent has not members enough to do anything. . . The Fathers in Atchison try to do the best they can — but the heavy debts and lack of priests are a great impediment in their way."[100] Furthermore, as Abbot Innocent remarked after Bishop Fink's death, the Bishop "was ostracized or at least shunned" by other bishops because he was a religious, and in his own diocese he had to lean over backwards to avoid giving grounds for complaint that he was favoring the Benedictines. Abbot Innocent preferred to have no more bishops taken from the Order.[101]

To prevent misunderstandings and hard feelings, Bishop Fink once proposed giving the Benedictines "a certain district — for instance Doniphan, Brown, and Atchison counties — so that churches would be built as necessary and as directed by the Bishop — but that none but Benedictines should be made pastors."[102] This pro-

98 Luber to Wolf, Seneca, Dec. 10, 1878.
99 Ferdinand Wolf to Bartl, Hiawatha, Sept. 23, 1883.
100 Fink to Wimmer, Fort Scott, May 9, 1879. (SVA)
101 Wolf to Engel, Atchison, Feb. 17, 1910. (SJA)
102 Fink to Wolf, Seneca, Sept. 7, 1878.

posal was discussed for a number of years, but the community wanted to include Nemaha County.[103] The community probably wanted a district large enough to allow for future growth, whereas the Bishop had in mind a district tailored to current capacity. In any case Roman approval of such an arrangement was probably unlikely, and no attempt was made to establish such a district.

Later, when Abbot Innocent asked the Bishop to take over Marak and its missions, the Bishop expressed surprise that the Abbot had come around to a policy of giving up small parishes and agreed that "such little places are not what religious should have for the good of the community."[104] He then renewed a suggestion that he had made as early as 1879,[105] namely, that he give the community charge of a parish in Kansas City or one of the other larger towns of the Diocese and that the Abbey open a high school or college for day students in the same town.[106] But the Abbot had no men available for such an undertaking at that time.

The parish question became a problem because conditions had changed. In the early years parish work was imperative, and in carrying on the mission to the settlers the Benedictines were making an essential contribution to the Church in the West. Later on that condition was no longer true. Although the Bishop could not at any time have replaced the Benedictines on the parishes, the monks were no longer essential for the work. Conditions had changed, and, although parochial work is incompatible with the monastic way of life if not its ideals, the community never changed its policy regarding parishes. The Abbey had grown up in a pattern that devoted much man power to parochial work, and the habits of an institution tend to be rather more unchangeable than the habits of an individual. Furthermore, parochial work

103 Chapter Minutes, Aug. 25, 1882.
104 Fink to Wolf, Leavenworth, Aug. 29, 1886.
105 Chapter Minutes, June 25, 26, Nov. 30, 1879.
106 Fink to Wolf, Leavenworth, May 20, 1886; Jan. 2, 1887.

was traditional in the Bavarian Congregation from which the American Cassinese Congregation was founded. Until after 1900 at least, the majority at St. Benedict's probably considered parochial work the community's chief activity.

There were some scruples, of course, and General Chapters from an early date forbade accepting, except for a grave reason, parishes where only one priest could be stationed — an injunction which has been repeated for the better part of a century. From time to time Abbot Innocent resolved not to worry about trying to hold on to small places that would never need more than a pastor, for, as he wrote on one occasion, "if we trouble ourselves about little places we divide our forces, and will never be able to do any great work."[107] However, he never carried out this policy. After 1900, when the mission to the settlers was long past, Father Alban Rudroff complained that the policy of holding on "tenaciously to these little places. . . [was] bringing ridicule on the monastery for its isolated secularized monks."[108]

Archabbot Wimmer had performed wonders in promoting the Benedictine Order in the United States. He was completely American in his love of expansion and in his willingness to gamble. His Congregation grew and spread much more rapidly than anyone had a right to expect, but in his late years he seriously doubted whether this growth had been entirely healthy. On one occasion he wrote to Abbot Innocent, "I fear we hold to our Rule too little; therefore, God will withdraw His blessing bit by bit. . . There is too little spirit of the Order, etc., in most of the men. . . The small parishes are the graves of good discipline; we should take them only out of necessity."[109] On another occasion the old Archabbot feared that he had produced a "bogus kind of monks," adding that the older he became, the more he doubted about the direction the

---

[107] Wolf Diary, Jan. 1, 1879. Cf. Wolf memorandum, July 24, 1882; Wolf to Green, Carlsbad, June 7, 1897.
[108] Rudroff to Wolf, Des Moines, Oct. 1, 1912.
[109] Wimmer an Wolf, St. Vincent, Apr. 18, 1885.

Congregation had taken under his guidance. Finally, he consoled himself that his will had been good and that he had at least wished to do what was right.[110] Actually, of course, Archabbot Wimmer could hardly have built other than he did. He came to the United States to provide the German Catholic immigrants with missionaries, and he met that challenge well. The need was urgent, and he had to build fast. That some values should be neglected and that some evidences of hasty construction should appear, need surprise no one.

If Archabbot Wimmer had some doubts about the kind of monk he had developed, Oswald Moosmueller had none. He was convinced that the policy towards parochial work must be changed. Writing to Abbot Innocent about the new statutes for the Congregation proposed in the 1890's, he said: "I see you take a great deal of pain about the new Declarations or Statutes. In my humble opinion it is all the same whether we have the old Statutes or new ones... Whatever in a community is done or practised by a great majority like two-thirds, is to be considered as the *Rule*; and on the other hand whatever in a community is done by the great minority, say one-third, is considered the *exception*." His argument was that since so many of the monks lived outside the monastery, they were the rule. The young men "look upon the monastery more like a seminary in which they have to spend a few years than as their real home. Under these circumstances is it very natural that there are very, very few... who have a monastic spirit and who care much for a real monastery... I would not say that a Benedictine abbey should not have any parishes, and never let any of her priests be stationed outside on missions; such has been customary with many monasteries; but I mean at least, that such be the *exception* and not the Rule... If this fact must be acknowledged then we must also concede that the religious or monastic spirit cannot be restored... by new rules; the remedy must begin at the

<hr>

[110] Wimmer to Zilliox, St. Vincent, Jan. 12, 1886, sent to Abbot Innocent by Moosmueller in 1894.

root of the evil or else all other remedies that may be applied are merely palliatives."[111]

Abbot Innocent had always considered Prior Oswald as hopelessly doctrinaire. The Abbot was pained, however, when his old friend and classmate, Father Adalbert Mueller, turned out to be even less tolerant of parochial work for monks.[112] Abbot Innocent had to settle for a practical policy. He had to fit his ideals to the present needs of his community. In exhorting the St. John's monks after their abbatial election in 1890, he said: "Missions are not essential, as a College is not essential, but both can be carried on by religious. By and by we will be forced by Rome to give up the small missions, because Rome does not want so many religious to live alone and outside the monastery."[113] Convinced that small one-man missions were undesirable, unfortunately he was content to wait for Rome to force a change.

Abbot Innocent's most complete statement, or rationalization, of his policy regarding parishes was given to the Abbot Primate, who, he was convinced, "is against our having parishes."[114] The Abbot had two reasons for continuing parish work: first, the parishes were to develop into priories in the future, and secondly, the Abbey was dependent upon the salaries, honoraria, and Mass stipends sent in by the pastors. The Abbot Primate was looking closely into the American Cassinese Congregation at the end of the century because of a rash of requests for secularization. As Abbot Innocent explained to him:

Many single missions have been given up when the bishops could take them. It is the intention to establish priories in large towns with a parish attached; but men are still wanting. If we gave up those places, we would not be able to spread later when we have the men. The bishops are willing to admit religious and ask them to come when the secular priests are not numerous, but in those dioceses where they have enough priests, religious would not be admitted. Why, several bishops

111 Moosmueller to Wolf, Wetaug, Apr. 5, 1894.
112 Wolf to Haid, Atchison, Sept. 10, 1891, draft.
113 Wolf to Edelbrock, Atchison, June 23, 1890. (SJA)
114 Wolf to Engel, Atchison, July 15, 1905. (SJA)

called their dioceses virgin dioceses because they had no religious! So far we have our support from the parishes; if we give them up we must give up the monastery. This is the case in the majority of our monasteries. In fact I think only St. Vincent's could get along without parishes, but it could not do one-fourth of what it is doing now. We were thrown into this work and it will take years of patient labor and vigilance to direct all into the right channel.[115]

The idea of establishing small priories — mission houses combining parochial work and monastic life— seems to have died long ago. Income from the pastors' work, though never an enormous sum, was always *net* income.[116] Furthermore, since the College and other activities of the community did well merely to meet expenses, the income from the parishes was often the only real money available for paying debts or building costs. Finally, as Abbot Innocent also pointed out, history had put the Benedictines into parochial work, and continuing a tradition is always easier than changing it.

[115] Wolf to Abbot Primate, Atchison, Oct. 30, 1899. (SA)
[116] In 1892, for example, those monks engaged in parochial work, after paying their own expenses from their salaries and honoraria, were able to contribute $10,509.81 to the community income. This sum represented the savings of sixteen monks stationed on parishes and about ten with week-end missions.

CHAPTER VII

Seeds of the Future, 1888-1922

The St. Vincent Archabbey chapter assembled to elect a successor to Archabbot Wimmer on February 8, 1888. On that day Abbot Innocent in Atchison recorded the following in his diary:

After dinner I received a telegram from Father Michael [Hofmayer]: 'You are elected abbot. Please accept.' I went at once to my room and wrote back the answer: 'Give thanks to chapter for confidence, but cannot accept.' After I had written this, the thought came that this perhaps was a sign of God's will, and then I got very nervous, so that at that moment I could not have written a word. After a short prayer I rang for my confessor, confessed and then I was quiet again, and telephoned my answer to the Western Union.

Thereupon I went to the chapter room where all were anxiously waiting for news. I let them guess, and then told them that I had been elected. There was a pause of silence which I broke by saying: But I have answered already that I will not accept. Then there was an outburst of clapping and cheering. Afterwards I heard that there was much anxiety about my action, as there was also in St. Vincent's.

The monks of St. Benedict's had been worried. Abbot Innocent considered Father Adolph Wesseling a rather difficult subject; hence his attitude cannot have been that of a favorite but must be taken as typical. Writing after the election but before he knew that Abbot Innocent had declined, Father Adolph said, "Do stay with us, and abandon us not, dear Father; you have raised us, you know us, and we know you. For one or two ungrateful and incorrigible ones at Atchison you will find six in St. Vincent's. . ."[1]

[1] Wesseling to Wolf, Council Bluffs, Feb. 10, 1888.

211

Father Andrew Hintenach was elected archabbot of St. Vincent, and the history of the American-Cassinese Benedictines entered upon the post-Wimmer period. The St. Vincent monks on loan in Kansas were gradually withdrawn. Abbot Innocent had feared this turn of events, but his chief legitimate complaint was that the short notice of withdrawal caused grave inconvenience.[2] He called it cruelty,[3] but he need not have felt injured when the last of the St. Vincent men was recalled from Kansas in 1890,[4] because at this time he made two unsuccessful attempts at new foundations and had lent two men to the Bishop of Davenport.

Attempts at New Foundations

In 1888 and again in 1890 Abbot Innocent made weak attempts at possible new foundations. Since he considered his monastery overburdened with debt and so weak in numbers that he needed monks from other abbeys, his attempting new foundations is difficult to explain. Abbot Innocent left no clear-cut statement of what he had in mind, but apparently he was following Archabbot Wimmer's policies of expanding the Congregation from coast to coast and of carrying on truly missionary work, if not to the Negroes, then to the Indians.

In 1888 Bishop Mora, of Los Angeles, was looking for priests to supply southern California. Through Father R. F. Byrne, of Escondido, he offered the Benedictines fifty acres in the Pauma Valley in San Diego County. Abbot Innocent presented the offer to the General Chapter of the Congregation, but the offer was rejected. Bishop Mora was then informed by the Abbot that he could send two of his own monks to begin the project.[5]

[2] Wolf to Hintenach, Atchison, Dec. 28, 1888, draft.
[3] Wolf to Edelbrock, Atchison, Nov. 17, 1888. (SJA)
[4] Wolf to Mueller, Atchison, June 19, 1890. (SVA)
    Father Stephen Lyons, recalled in 1891, was the prior at Creston.
[5] Byrne to Wolf, San Diego, Feb. 27, 1888, and on it Wolf's notations of his answers to Mora, Mar. 7 and July 19.

Father Byrne came to Atchison in July, and in a memorandum the Benedictines were promised the following: fifty acres of land in the town site, free use of sixteen inches of water, and, to aid in building a college, one-tenth of the proceeds from the sale of town lots. Furthermore, $10,000 was said to be already available from such sales.[6]

Father Pirmin Koumly was sent to California to inaugurate the monastic foundation or at any rate to report on the prospects of the venture. His report was negative: the valley was very hot in comparison with other areas, it was too isolated for a college, only fifty scattered families of desperately poor Indians and Mexicans were in the vicinity, a priest could not be supported, the Indians would have to be driven away before white settlers could be attracted, and the Pauma Land and Irrigation Company did not seem to have water rights.[7] The Bishop, a true Californian, countered that the weather had been unusual, insisted that settlers would come, that nobody would drive the Indians away and that they occupied only sixty acres, and that since he held title to the water right, the company would have water rights. He was convinced that Father Pirmin had been victimized by a local enemy of the Bishop.[8]

Just at this juncture the Archabbot of St. Vincent recalled Father Henry Hohman, pastor of Sacred Heart Church in Atchison, and Abbot Innocent, again desperately in need of a priest, recalled Father Pirmin from California.[9] The Abbot was embarrassed, and he wrote to Abbot Alexius, "California was not much from the beginning, but in the end it would be best to have a hold there and prospects were not hopeless. Well, I gave it

[6] Memorandum, R. F. Byrne, n.d.
[7] Koumly an Wolf, Pauma, Sept. 16, 1888, and Los Angeles, Oct. 10, 1888. Wolf to Mora, Atchison, Oct. 10, 1888, draft.
[8] Mora to Wolf, Los Angeles, Oct. 16, 1888.
Father Ubach of San Diego, whom Father Boniface Verheyen had known, probably in Missouri, thought Pauma unpromising. He told Father Pirmin that the Bishop had sold the ranch to a syndicate and would not receive payment unless the land was settled. Father Ubach opposed the plan.—Koumly an Wolf, San Diego, Oct. 15, 1888.
[9] Wolf to Mora, Atchison, Nov. 3, 1888, draft.

up, and stand before the Bishop and clergy of Los Angeles as a fickle-minded man, or a simpleton, and it spoils much for any one else who may try to get in."[10]

The second attempted monastic foundation was also a fiasco. While Father Matthew Bradley was in Santa Fe for his health, he wrote that Archbishop Salpointe offered the community the direction of St. Catherine's Indian School, of which he had charge. With the government paying $125 a year for educating each of a hundred Indian boys, the school would pay its own way and need no financial support from the Abbey.[11] The Archbishop offered to give also the parish of Pena Blanca and its missions on a permanent basis, particularly to facilitate the supply of students to provide a link between the school and the boys' homes. The proposal was presented to the chapter and was accepted.[12] The necessary men were to be released by giving up some of the smaller parishes, like Effingham, "where there was no hope ever to locate two priests."[13] In writing to Archbishop Salpointe, Abbot Innocent agreed to take the school if the Archbishop would give Pena Blanca and its missions permanently. The Abbot insisted that there must be a basis for a future monastery,[14] although Father Matthew had emphasized from the beginning that the place was unsuitable for a monastery.

During April and May, 1889, Abbot Innocent accompanied Archabbot Andrew Hintenach on a tour of New Mexico, Arizona, and California to look at the Indian Missions. The Archabbot had been approached by the Catholic Indian Bureau and by Miss Katherine Drexel, the great benefactor of Negro and Indian missions. He sent monks to California but soon withdrew them. While making final arrangements with Archbishop Salpointe, Abbot Innocent, at the advice of Father Joseph A. Stephan, director of the Catholic Indian Bureau, asked that

10 Wolf to Edelbrock, Atchison, Nov. 17, 1888. (SJA)
11 Bradley to Wolf, Santa Fe, Jan. 14, 1889.
12 Chapter Minutes, Mar. 7 and 8, 1889.
13 Ibid., Mar. 7, 1889.
14 Wolf to Salpointe, Atchison, Mar. 24, 1889, draft.

the Archbishop give also a garden near the school for the purpose of raising vegetables.[15]   Apparently everything was arranged agreeably.

Upon his return to Atchison the Abbot sent Father Thomas Burk to take over St. Catherine's in Santa Fe. Father Thomas had been ordained less than a year, but he was a real go-getter. His sublime self confidence startles one the more because it had so little foundation. To staff the school the Abbot sent two clerics, a scholastic, and a Brother. Father Thomas persuaded two students to leave St. Benedict's and join him.[16]   Having arrived in Santa Fe, Father Thomas promptly began to aggravate the problems he had and to create new ones. The Sisters who cared for the kitchen and laundry were dismissed as a needless expense. He looked upon the Archbishop almost as an enemy and in general behaved like a boor.[17] Archbishop Salpointe thought Father Thomas "a splendid man for the management of the school, but not for material affairs," and considered his plans extravagant.[18]

With bad food and everything at sixes and sevens, the faculty began to quarrel with Father Thomas and with one another. By July everyone but Father Thomas besieged the Abbot with letters requesting permission to return to Kansas. By the time school was to open, most of them were ready to quit. Meanwhile Father Thomas had, almost literally, to round up his students. His chore was going from pueblo to pueblo and bringing in the reluctant Indian boys. The least that can be said for Father Thomas is that he was a very energetic worker. He drove himself relentlessly, but school opened with only thirty-one students, and ten soon left, whereas during the previous year they had numbered eighty-nine. By September Father Thomas was for the first time beginning to mention religious motives for his work.

---

[15] Wolf Diary, Apr. 16–May 11, 1889, *passim*; Wolf to Mueller, Atchison, June 29, 1890. (SVA)
[16] Wolf Diary, May 20–July 8, 1889, *passim*.
[17] Burk to Wolf, Santa Fe, May 22; June 18, 1889.
[18] Salpointe to Wolf, Santa Fe, June 16, 1889.

Meanwhile a monk from the Abbey was sent to Santa Fe on account of tuberculosis. His criticism aggravated the differences between the clerics and Father Thomas. In response to Father Thomas' impetuous invitation to leave if they did not like Santa Fe, they returned, unannounced, to St. Benedict's. The chapter deliberated on their fate and sent them back to Santa Fe, accompanied by the newly-ordained Father Alphonse Filian as a quasi abbatial legate and additional member of the faculty. Two weeks later Abbot Innocent was called to Santa Fe, and he achieved a measure of peace.

By the end of November Father Thomas had increased the student body to a respectable seventy. A government official inspected the school, and Father Thomas was certain that the report would be favorable, but it was not.[19] Furthermore, the Abbot complained that the Archbishop failed to give the community the promised missions and garden. Consequently, the community had nothing permanent on which to build a foundation, and at the end of October the Abbot informed the Archbishop that St. Benedict's would drop the project at the end of the current school year. Abbot Innocent's view was that the bishops wanted "the religious to go amongst the Indians, but don't want to give any aid whatever." But he feared that such failures would give the Congregation a bad name.[20] He could also have added that the project had been badly planned and badly led and that the staff chosen indicated the community's attitude toward school work at that time.

The New Monastery

The illusion that the community was large enough to undertake a new foundation was possibly due to the overcrowded conditions in the monastery. By 1891 the community had thirty-six priests, one-half of whom were liv-

---

[19] Wolf Diary; Wolf correspondence, *passim.*
[20] Wolf to Mueller, Atchison, June 29, 1890. (SVA)

ing in the College or Abbey. One deacon, three sub-deacons, nine clerics, seventeen Brothers, and a number of candidates made living conditions very crowded. Twenty of the priests were engaged in the care of souls in fourteen parishes and twenty-three missions. Further-more, six choir novices were at St. Vincent Archabbey.[21]

The fifty members of the community at home simply could not be fitted into the Old Priory. For years the visitators had complained that monastic life was impossible under such circumstances. The only part of the monastery that could be cloistered was the second floor, and so only the clerics and four priests lived within the cloister. Furthermore, the one chapel was shared by the community and the students.[22]

In June, 1891, Abbot Innocent first broached the subject of building a monastery.[23] The matter was taken up in earnest the following September. When the question of location arose, Father Herman Mengwasser asserted that no vote should be taken in the absence of the pastors.[24] The Abbot grudgingly consented but to protect the rights of his office stated that "in calling the Fathers from the mission to consult in the matter, he acted only by way of exception, that he need not have asked the consent of the chapter at all, but could have proceeded in the matter alone. He wished it understood therefore that this special summons was not to establish a precedent, nor should it

---

[21] Sittenauer an LMV, Atchison, Jan. 20, 1891. (LMV Leav II 1/63-65)

[22] Wolf an Kagerer, Atchison, Jan. 17, 1894. (LMV Leav II 1/77)

[23] Chapter Minutes, June 10, 1891.

[24] Herman (Peter) Mengwasser, born in Weckhoven, Rhenish Prussia, Nov. 13, 1855, professed July 25, 1879, ordained July 31, 1883, died Feb. 29, 1936. —Necrologium, No. 776.

Father Herman had come to St. Benedict's from the American College at Louvain. Abbot Innocent referred to him as his best and most useful cleric but too weak to be of much help in teaching. Nevertheless, he taught for a few years, mostly theology, but was never a very good teacher. His confreres considered him excessively opinionated, and he sometimes proposed unpopular motions in chapter, only to find himself left standing without a second. After 1888 he was assigned to parish duty, and his parishioners considered him an outstandingly good pastor. He was the best Latinist in the community, and after ill health had forced his retirement from pastoral work in the 1920's he taught Latin and devoted his leisure to producing a version of Juvencus and other exercises for students of Latin. As an exercise in technical virtuosity he did a version of the Rule of St. Benedict in Latin hexameters.

be looked upon as such."[25] The chapter discussed possible sites for the new monastery. One or two suggested the river bluff, Father Herman preferred the ball diamond, and others wanted the monastery south of the church. Still others wanted an addition to the College built first.[26] In the end they voted to build, and because practically no other site was available, to build north of the church.[27]

The architect of the new monastery was Alfred Meier of Atchison. Without ceremonial groundbreaking, excavation began promptly. Young Father Leo Aaron used the Abbey's new camera to record the growth of the heavy foundations with their intricate system of massive arches. The masonry work was contracted: the stone foundations to Adam Dilgert and the brickwork to Martin Hughes. The Brothers, aided by hired labor, did the carpenter work. Clerics and scholastics carried materials, and the Abbot recorded having spent a whole afternoon encouraging the boys in their labor of hoisting boards and joists.[28] The Abbot also warned the monks not to waste money by encouraging the paid workmen to stand around and chat.[29]

Even before the financial panic of 1893 the Abbot had difficulty in borrowing money for the new building, and this handicap slowed down construction. Money could be had for six per cent in the East but not for western projects. Locally the charge was seven and eight per cent.[30] In July, 1893, when banks were closing their doors, a promised large loan evaporated.[31] In August Abbot Innocent instructed Father Gerard Heinz, director of the College, to make no further purchases in Chicago. "We are dead-broke," he wrote. Several depositors, who had intended leaving their money indefinitely, suddenly had

[25] Chapter Minutes, Sept. 21, 1891.
[26] Wolf Diary, Sept. 21, 1891.
[27] Chapter Minutes, Sept. 21, 1891.
[28] Wolf to Luber, Atchison, Nov. 25, 1892.
[29] Chapter Minutes, Aug. 17, 1892.
[30] Wolf Diary, May 30, 1892; Wolf to Locnikar, Atchison, Apr. 15, 1892. (SJA)
[31] Wolf Diary, July 26, 1893.

to have it. The tinner, the plumbers — all wanted money. "Last week one time our cash balance was, I believe, a little over fifty cents."[32] But money was somehow borrowed, and the new monastery was finally completed in the summer of 1893. It had cost about $60,000. Consequently, the Abbey debt, which had been reduced to $48,000 in 1890, rose to some $95,000 in 1893. Ten years were needed to diminish it to the level of 1890.

The new monastery (now Freshman Hall) is a well-built and dignified brick building with Romanesque details, 204 by 58 feet, with four stories and a roomy basement. Its chief embellishment is a massive square tower, 143 feet high. For the first time since the creation of the Abbey the entire community could live within the cloister. Half the first floor was isolated from the cloister and devoted to parlors and guest rooms. In the south end of the building was an adequate sacristy for the church, and above the sacristy was a small chapel for the community.

Open house was held for a few days in July, and because many of the visitors had been reared on a diet of Maria Monk literature, some strange questions were asked. In August the monks began moving into their new home. On August 14 Abbot Innocent moved in, solemn Benediction was given in the new chapel, and community life in the new monastery began.[33]

A Period of Unrest and Change

After the monastery was completed in 1893 no further major building was undertaken until 1910. In some ways this period was one of trouble, but in other ways it was an

[32] Wolf to Heinz, Atchison, Aug. 11, 1893.
[33] Anthony Baar Diary, Aug. 12 and 14, 1893.
    Two years later St. Benedict's was a charter subscriber to Atchison's first electric company, contracting for fifty and ultimately 150 lamps at three-fourths of a cent a lamp per hour. The first lights went on in the College at six o'clock in the evening, Sept. 4, 1895. By November the Abbot was advocating that everybody go to bed at nine o'clock to reduce the light bill.—Wolf Diary, Sept. 4, 1895; Chapter Minutes, Nov. 7, 1895.

era of change that gave rise to the modern St. Benedict's. The trouble was twofold in that new vocations declined and an unusual number of monks left the community or at least wished to do so. The healthy element of change is seen in the growing consciousness of the meaning of liturgical prayer. Another positive advance was the new statutes, symbolic of the mature and independent existence of the American Cassinese Congregation. Finally, the gradual change in the school resulted in the modern St. Benedict's College. This last point will be discussed in a later chapter, but all of these developments were in the air simultaneously.

During this period Abbot Innocent was, on the one hand, distracted by illness and, on the other, was deeply engrossed in the affairs of the Congregation. He was elected president of the Congregation in 1896 and served until 1902. When elected president he was in such poor health that the other abbots advised him to go to Europe for treatment. He spent almost a year in various sanitaria and gradually overcame his extreme nervousness, intense headaches, and sleepless nights. He had never been away from his community for so long a period, and, naturally enough, monastic life did not run so smoothly as it did when he was directing it personally. That Father Andrew Green was a very reluctant prior did not improve matters. Father Andrew, ordained in 1890 and appointed prior in 1893, found the firmness necessary for the office quite uncongenial to his temperament.[34] Furthermore, the necessity of giving good example to the other monks was an intolerable burden. Abbot Innocent was constantly directing his young prior to stay in his room after Complin instead of visiting the Director of the College.[35] Toward the end of the Abbot's year in Europe Prior Andrew finally obtained the Abbot's permission to make some "necessary changes" and appointed, or rather at-

[34] Wolf Diary, Sept. 3, 1893.
    Andrew (Francis) Green was born Oct. 5, 1865 at Marak, Kansas, entered St. Benedict's in 1878, was professed July 16, 1885, ordained May 26, 1890, and died Jan. 2, 1950.
[35] e.g., Wolf to Green, Feb. 11; 18, 1897.

tempted to appoint, Father Gerard Heinz to the office of prior. The Abbot gave Prior Andrew some instruction in elementary canon law and the statutes of the Congregation, and on his return the Abbot appointed Father Joseph Sittenauer prior.[36]

That monastic problems in the 1890's were serious is evident when Abbot Innocent wrote that the year 1891 had been one of the worst in his career. Father Ambrose Rank had died, and two scholastics and two Brother candidates had left.[37] The Abbot had to make changes in personnel also that year, and in a religious community of such moderate size, talents and temperaments were a bare match for the positions to be filled, so that one change usually meant changing a large part of the team. As the Abbot wrote, "I prefer to make as few changes as possible, but if I start I have to keep on till the whole works well again."[38]

Since Abbot Innocent's coming in 1877, St. Benedict's had been growing at the rate of about one priest a year. An average of two priests had been ordained each year, but losses by death, incapacitating illness, or loss of vocation amounted to about half the gain. However, in the last four years of the 1890's five priests left the community for other monasteries or to join the diocesan clergy. And in the first decade of the twentieth century ordinations for the community totaled only twelve priests in contrast with twenty-one in the following decade. An occasional transfer is, of course, to be expected in a religious community, but the number in the late nineties was extraordinary. Furthermore, four others were so dissatisfied that they seriously considered transferring to other monasteries but ultimately remained at St. Benedict's. Very probably this unhappy development was primarily due to the rather haphazard spiritual and intellectual formation of the monks in previous years.

[36] Wolf to Green, "USMS Paris," July 22; St. Vincent, July 29, 1897; Chapter Minutes, Aug. 24, 1897.
[37] Wolf to Haid, Atchison, Sept. 10, 1891, draft.
[38] Wolf to Luber, Atchison, July 20, 1891.

The record on these problems indicates that the most serious pitfall for the monk is neither women nor drink but simple vanity. Most of these men felt that they were not appreciated and sought to take their talents elsewhere. Abbot Innocent's attitude probably was not very helpful: "We have a few here who thought that their work was not appreciated. I took occasion to speak of this publicly once, and said, that I would not dare to praise one to his face, for it might tempt him to pride, and I consider it flattery; . . that they should expect their reward from God, and as long as I did not complain, they should consider that I appreciated their work. Poor self!"[39]

The Abbot Primate, inquiring about the number of secularizations, apparently suggested that perhaps the state of the Church in America or the novitiate were at fault. Abbot Innocent, as president of the Congregation, did not agree with that analysis. He blamed American bishops for their willingness to accept ex-religious, thereby inviting dissatisfied monks to secularize. Furthermore, American abbots condoned securalization as preferable to keeping a discontented monk. In one sentence the Abbot wrote: "Some, when on parishes lose the religious spirit, and when they are taken back to the monastery find it difficult to get into order, and, when urged by the superiors, threaten to get secularized." But at the end of the same letter he denies "that our parishes introduce a bad spirit; I find that those in parishes make less trouble than some at home."[40] But a desire to leave the monastery for parish work was usually involved. The problem was a sad one, and the Abbot's only consolation was "that the body is vigorous enough to cast out bad blood, which, if it remained, would poison and paralyze the whole body.[41]

The early 1900's were also a difficult period. The older men were dying or were incapacitated by sickness, and replacements were not sufficient in number. No

39 Wolf to Engel, Atchison, Sept. 6, 1905. (SJA)
40 Wolf to Abbot Primate, Atchison, May 5, 1900. (SA)
41 Wolf to Engel, Atchison, Sept. 16, 1902. (SJA)

priests were ordained during the first three years of the decade. Fathers Suitbert Demarteau and Timothy Luber died, and three other priests were too sick to work.[42] The number of Brothers also declined. Candidates who applied were often discouraged by the unfriendliness of the older Brothers. German was adhered to strictly as the language of the Brotherhood, and furthermore, they were given too little spiritual direction. The scarcity of new vocations made the future look gloomy. Furthermore, the visitators complained that, "The opinion of the Fathers is that Father Abbot has not courage enough to correct and abolish abuses; hence they think it useless to advise him of shortcomings."[43]

Important measures were soon undertaken to remedy the situation, and the number of vocations was soon to increase. As was mentioned earlier, only twelve priests were added in the first decade of the century, but twenty-one were ordained in the second decade. Of the twelve priests ordained in the 1900's only four had been born in the United States and none of them in Kansas. Of the twenty-one ordained in the decade 1910-1919, however, only two were foreign born, fourteen had been born in Kansas, five of them in the Seneca-Wildcat area. The fundamental nature of the change is indicated by the decade of the twenties when thirty-four were ordained, of whom only three were foreign born. Twenty-four of them had been born in Kansas, nine in the Seneca-Wildcat area. These figures reveal that for an entire generation St. Benedict's had been so truly a frontier community that its vocations came largely from outside its own geographical area. After the turn of the century the children of the young families who had settled in Kansas in the seventies and eighties began to appear at St. Benedict's, and the community began to receive a dividend from the labor of the pioneer missionaries.

Furthermore, the establishment of a separate scholasticate was important. In 1907 the students intending

[42] *Idem*, Mar. 8, 1902. (SJA)
[43] Record of Visitation, Oct. 14-15, 1901.

to join the community were separated from the other priesthood students and given their own quarters in the monastery. Abbot Innocent took a fatherly interest in their welfare, and these youngsters became well acquainted with the monastic life. Their numbers increased. Father Lambert Burton was appointed their prefect in 1908 and rector of the scholasticate in 1912. He continued in that office until 1922. His intellectual and spiritual ideals were important in the formation of this new generation, who, aided by sympathetic older men, would make the new St. Benedict's College. This development depended upon a new attitude, namely, the monks' desire to devote themselves to community life— an attitude more apparent in this new group than in the majority of their predecessors.

Fundamental changes in the education of the younger members aided the development of this new outlook. The first real change occurred after young Father Joseph Sittenauer returned from Rome in 1895 with a doctorate in theology and took over the direction of the scholastics and clerics.[44] He added a fourth year of theology, and one of the monks wrote: "Clerics all doing well. One thing very noticeable among them is; they are all becoming good, thorough students. Joe undoubtedly deserves credit for his work among them."[45] However, apparently another result of the new regime and its tighter discipline was that five clerics quit in two years, an unusual number. Four of them became diocesan priests. And the Abbot, hardpressed as usual for priests, soon had the course in theology again reduced to three years.[46] Father Joseph championed better education for the clerics but he was not a very good teacher, and in 1912 he asked to do parish

[44] Joseph (Michael) Sittenauer, born in Walterkirchen, Bavaria, Sept. 24, 1863, was brought to the United States by Archabbot Wimmer, professed Nov. 28, 1884, volunteered for the Kansas mission in 1886, ordained June 28, 1889, studied at Sant' Anselmoin Rome 1891-1895, was prior of St. Benedict's 1898-99, transferred to St. Peter's Abbey, Muenster, Saskatchewan, Canada, in 1922, died Sept. 11, 1946.—*Necrologium*, No. 991.
[45] Weiffenbach to Wise, Atchison, Nov. 10, 1901.
[46] Chapter Minutes, Mar. 29, 1904.

work. He was appointed pastor of Sts. Peter and Paul's Church at Seneca. Nevertheless, he had been at least partially instrumental in introducing a change of direction that was of fundamental importance to St. Benedict's.

In spite of Father Joseph's policies, the root of the problem had remained untouched. The clerics were still doing double duty: prefecting all day and teaching a few hours in the school while supposedly studying for and attending regular classes in theology. As young Father Stephen Wise complained, the system prevented the clerics from acquiring an education, did an injustice to the college students, and damaged the community. He favored a central house of studies for the Congregation.[47] Agitation by the younger men, particularly Father Joseph, for a common house of studies, which Abbot Innocent at one time favored,[48] forced serious consideration of the problem.

The chapter could come to no agreement about the common house of studies, but all agreed that "our clerics are not getting proper attention, or rather have not opportunity to make a thorough course." The solution adopted was sending the two clerics then in philosophy, Fraters Sylvester Schmitz and Augustine Sklusacek, to St. John's Abbey for their theology.[49] For a few years the clerics were sent to St. Vincent or to St. John's for their philosophy and theology. In 1914 the chapter decided to resume training the clerics at home.[50] Those who had begun their courses at St. Vincent or St. John's completed them at those abbeys. Every Benedictine community prefers to train its young members within the family circle. Furthermore, since the novices were always trained at St. Vincent Archabbey except for a few years around the turn of the century, the clerics were needed for the proper celebration of the liturgy. The clerics also had various community chores during the school year, and during the summer months they were busy with repairs

47 Wise to Sittenauer, Atchison, Oct. 21, 1905.
48 Wolf to Edelbrock, Atchison, Jan. 9, 1889. (SJA)
49 Chapter Minutes, June 2; Sept. 9, 1908.
50 *Ibid.*, June 19, 1914.

or working on the farm. Working for the common good developed in them a good community spirit. The most important reason for training them at home was that the family was incomplete without its younger members. After their return the old system of double duty was carefully avoided. The vicious circle had been broken at last.

The new statutes of 1893 were another sign of healthy change and of growing maturity of the Congregation. When the American Cassinese Congregation had been created in 1855, it first used as far as applicable the Constitution and statutes of the Bavarian Congregation from which the new foundation sprang. But since this document dated from 1686, it had necessarily been interpreted rather broadly from the very beginning. Abbot Innocent was a gradualist with a built-in anchor, but he admitted that not one chapter of the Bavarian statutes was kept exactly[51] and that "it was demoralizing to have Statutes and have to hear always that the Abbots only keep what they like and find convenient."[52]

Abbot Innocent, however, was in no hurry for new statutes. To his mind the really important point about statutes was that they were in effect the constitution of the Congregation and gave it canonical immunity. Otherwise statutes were merely a general norm. For specific legislation he relied upon the decrees of the General Chapters, which he compared to the statute law of the states. He was in no hurry for change and was convinced that gradually improving on old laws was easier than concocting new ones. On the other hand, he liked the Beuronese idea of statutes in the form of a commentary on the Rule. "With us the Rule is buried under a mass of Statutes," he wrote.[53]

A decree of the 1885 General Chapter providing committees to propose new statutes failed to achieve results probably owing to Archabbot Wimmer's last illness and death. The 1890 General Chapter again decreed that

[51] Wolf to Edelbrock, Atchison, Apr. 4, 1884. (SJA)
[52] Wolf to Locnikar, Atchison, Sept. 7, 1894. (SJA)
[53] Wolf to Edelbrock, Atchison, Jan. 9, 1889. (SJA)

the statutes be revised, that the proposed articles be submitted before the end of the year, and that the form of the Declarations be Beuronese, that is, a commentary on the Rule. At St. Benedict's meeting after meeting of the chapter was held to work out proposed statutes. After about three weeks of such meetings a motion was made to refer the work to a committee. Abbot Innocent appointed to the committee all those who had voted aye, "for I thought they voted thus to avoid more chapter meetings."[54]

In making their proposals for new statutes in 1890, St. Benedict's capitulars tried to prohibit the wearing of beards.[55] The General Chapter of 1867 had decided that all monks should wear beards. Although Abbot Innocent insisted on conformity for many years, this rule soon became very unpopular and was not generally followed. Bishop Fink threatened to refuse ordination to monks with beards and wanted to argue the matter with the Abbot, but he told the Bishop that if he wanted a *Bartkrieg* (a beard war), he should take the matter to Rome.[56] The Abbot clung to his badge of monastic dignity to the grave.

The new statutes were approved on February 25, 1893, for a trial period of ten years. Abbot Innocent complained that they diminished the power of the abbot[57] and that Rome had given a vote to each of the delegates to the General Chapter.[58] In general he was satisfied, however, for, as he later confessed, he had had "the most to do in drawing up the statutes, because the work was simply put on me, so I know them and their origin pretty well."[59] He was satisfied that the statutes were practical, but he was happiest because "no one can cast up to the Superiors that they don't keep them themselves, so the ill-disposed

54 Wolf Diary, Nov. 18, 1890.
55 Chapter Minutes, Nov. 11; Dec. 16, 1890.
56 Wolf an Wimmer, Atchison, July 30, 1883. (SVA)
57 Wolf an Braunmueller, Atchison, Sept. 14, 1892. (AM)
58 *Idem*, May 12, 1893. (AM)
59 Wolf to Engel, Atchison, June 26, 1900. (SJA)

have no hold any more and must get into ranks and practice the Rule. The Rule was forgotten on account of the Statutes."[60]

More far-reaching than changes in the statutes were the gradual changes regarding the monk's prayerlife that began to appear at the turn of the century. Abbot Innocent and his monks were serious about their prayers, but the rediscovery of the spiritual riches of the liturgy and its central position in the monastic life by the men of Solesmes and Beuron was slow to affect St. Benedict's. The American Cassinese Congregation was heir to the Bavarian Benedictine tradition, and the Bavarians traditionally chanted the Divine Office in a small chapel not open to the public. In addition to this background a large proportion of the community was necessarily excused from choir, and so liturgical worship held a less central position than it does today.

Under these circumstances the Abbot's normal problem of having the monks attend early morning choir was even more difficult. In his second year at St. Benedict's Abbot Innocent could write that since only five monks were available for choir service, none dared absent himself with the assurance that there would be enough in chapel to carry on the Lord's service without him. It was fortunate that the Abbot could make that statement once, for he could never make it again. Men become monks because they believe in the corporate daily worship of God, and they know that it is their only essential work, but the old Adam is fertile in plausible excuses, especially around four o'clock in the morning. Consequently, abbots are constantly exchanging recipes for getting the monks to Matins and have been doing this, presumably, since St. Benedict's day. The Matins problem is one of the truly unchanging features of monasticism. Abbot Innocent tried one exhortation and penance after another

[60] Wolf to Schnerr, Atchison, Oct. 3, 1893. (SVA)
In 1890, in keeping with his determination to increase familiarity with the Holy Rule, Abbot Innocent had it read at table in English daily.—Wolf to Mueller, Atchison, June 29, 1890. (SVA)

and towards the end of the century confessed to his Prior, "I tried all ways already, but without permanent effect."[61]

The monastic order of the day remained as it had been in the earlier period. The Abbot experimented with the time of Vespers so that all could attend, but Vespers were sung only on the very greatest feastdays.[62] The Swiss-American Congregation of Benedictines was evidently much less backward in these matters, and in 1891 Fathers Andrew Green and Aloysius Bradley were sent to Conception Abbey in Missouri to learn choral singing.[63] From that time on Father Andrew, at least, let Abbot Innocent have no peace. Five monks attended a short course in Gregorian Chant at Conception in 1904. All were enthusiastic and urged the Abbot to introduce the Solesmes Vesperale at once. He raised the question of who had the authority to make the change. "I suppose," he complained, "each Superior has one or more prodding him with the *Motu Proprio* of Pius X on the Gregorian Chant."[64] Father Andrew wanted Conventual Mass sung daily, and at that time it was not even attended by the community. The Abbot retorted defensively, "Now, I do not believe that singing or the adoption of the traditional choral alone will make a good monk; neither that it is all that is required for a good monk." And he added that Father Andrew was certainly no model.[65]

St. Benedict's continued to use the Vesperale compiled by Father Conrad Ebert from available sources and printed by St. Vincent Archabbey in 1886 and 1897. A Caeremoniale, ordered by the General Chapter of 1893, was printed in 1907 by the Abbey Student Press in Atchison. Fathers Benno Feser, Stanislaus Altmann, and Abbot Innocent compiled this Caeremoniale.[66] The Abbot maintained that it had one great advantage since it provided

[61] Wolf to Green, Rome, Nov. 23, 1896.
[62] Wolf Diary, Oct. 30, 1890; Dec. 28, 1892.
[63] *Ibid.*, Aug. 18, 1891.
[64] Wolf to Engel, Atchison, Aug. 25, 1904. (SJA)
[65] *Idem*, Sept. 7, 1904. (SJA)
[66] *Idem*, Jan. 8, 1908. (SJA)

rules for choir, whereas none had been known or, at any rate, observed before.[67]

At a chapter in 1910 the Abbot finally announced that "with the beginning of vacation conventual Mass would be introduced."[68] As a matter of fact, the community as a whole was as suspicious of change as the Abbot. When proposals for the reform of the breviary, with fewer feasts and more ferias, were received in 1908, the chapter voted against the proposed revision.[69] Four years later when the proposals reappeared as the Holy Father's reform, the chapter voted to sustain the Pope's suggestions.[70] For the most part, consciousness of the possibilities of the liturgy in enriching monastic life would come later, but this first stirring of liturgical consciousness was another indication of the change that was beginning at St. Benedict's.

The 'New' St. Benedict's

The turn of the century was a period of grave problems at St. Benedict's Abbey, but it was also the period when those problems were solved. Income from the College and the missions had been stable since 1890, showing no significant signs of increase or decrease but merely dipping, as was to be expected, during the depression following 1893. College enrollment had fluctuated between 140 and 170 since 1888. Then quite suddenly 257 students enrolled in 1907, and just as suddenly vague ideas of building were changed to immediate plans.

The monastery had been completed in 1893, and during the next fifteen years the community concentrated on retiring the debt. By 1904 the net debt had been reduced to $30,000, and Abbot Innocent hoped to be free of debt and to build by 1908. The Abbot longed for the

[67] *Idem*, Feb. 6, 1908. (SJA)
A *Rituale et Caeremoniale Benedictinum* compiled by Rev. William Mackay and published by St. Vincent in 1868 was largely a collection of blessings.
[68] Chapter Minutes, Mar. 18, 1910.
[69] *Ibid.*, Oct. 16; Dec. 9, 1908.
[70] *Ibid.*, Apr. 19, 1912.

day when the community's savings could be used for new buildings rather than for interest payments.[71] In discussing a new college building, the chapter was immediately faced with a number of difficult problems, all centering round the question of location. In any case more land would probably be needed.

Abbot Innocent appointed a building committee consisting of Fathers Prior Leo Aaron, Andrew Green, and Matthias Stein, the procurator. To these were soon added Father Director Aloysius Bradley and Father Stephen Wise.[72] In its report the committee recommended building for a maximum of 250 students, proposed the adoption of an overall plan for future development, and submitted a long list of needed buildings.[73] In a separate report the committee considered the problem of whether to build adjacent to the buildings on Second Street or to develop an entirely new site on the river bluff.

To erect an entirely new complex of buildings on the bluff would be expensive, necessitating a separate heating plant, a water plant to supply water at adequate pressure, and long utility lines. On the other hand, the committee was rather scornful of the existing buildings and concluded that the college building (Bishop Fink Hall) would not last more than another twenty or thirty years. More important was the fact that the site near Second Street could not accommodate the needed buildings, and construction on the filled ground would be excessively expensive. The long-term advantages were with the hilltop site, and the committee concluded, "If we make the move, we will earn the benedictions of those that come after us."[74]

After much discussion the chapter voted to break with the past regarding both location and style of architecture. The new college building was to be on the river bluff, and plans for a Tudor-Gothic structure to cost about $120,000

[71] Wolf to Engel, Atchison, Feb. 17, 1907. (SJA)
[72] Chapter Minutes, Feb. 28; Mar. 31; Apr. 3, 1908.
[73] Ibid., Mar. 12, 1908.
[74] Ibid., loose inserts at the same date.

were accepted. The architects were Barnett, Haynes and Barnett of St. Louis. This building was to be the first in a projected open quadrangle, which was to include a student chapel, auditorium, and other buildings. The Procurator reported that $40,000 was available for construction.[75] The chapter then struck a snag, because "Difficulties arose on account of sewerage and lack of grounds."[76]

The sewer problem was an old one. The College was outside the city limits, but the College sewerage went south down a ravine through town. In 1896 the City Council decided that the College should construct a sewer to Riley Street or to the river if necessary. The College was obviously unable to afford such construction, and Abbot Innocent was convinced that the APA (American Protective Association), the nativist movement of that decade, was responsible for the demand. On that occasion a compromise was reached, and the College agreed to drill an artesian well of sufficient flow to flush the ravine.[77] The College installed septic tanks in 1905, but the City's unwillingness to lay a sewer and permit the College to make connection with it remained a problem.[78]

The other cause for delay was the matter of land. The College owned only a comparatively narrow strip of land from Second Street to the bluff. Breaking ground for a new group of buildings on the bluff was pointless unless more land could be obtained at a reasonable price. Meanwhile rumors began to circulate that St. Benedict's was going to move from Atchison. The rumor did include more than the usual amount of fact, for the community had seriously considered that possibility, but by 1908 it was already a burst bubble.

The idea of moving St. Benedict's College to Kansas City was the brainchild of Father Aloysius Bradley.[79]

[75] *Ibid.*, Apr. 14, 1908.
[76] *Ibid.*, Oct. 7, 1908.
[77] Wolf Diary, May 5–July 21, 1896, *passim.*
[78] Chapter Minutes, June 2, 1905.
[79] Aloysius Benedict (Francis) Bradley, born in Macon, Ill., Aug. 8, 1867, professed July 11, 1886, ordained June 29, 1891, transferred his vows to St.

He was an energetic man, progressive, refreshingly eager to try new ideas, and was an impressive speaker and a good public relations man. Unfortunately his ideas frequently tended towards the grandiose, his judgment was often guided more by imagination than by reason, and he evidently gave little consideration to the ideas and wishes of his co-workers. As a young priest he was a leader in college activities, but his personality clashed hopelessly with that of Father Gerard Heinz, then director of the College, and in 1897 Father Aloysius was loaned to St. Anselm's College in Manchester, New Hampshire, for a year or so. Back in Atchison in 1900, he again threw himself into the work of improving St. Benedict's. He was appointed director of the College in 1907, and his leadership is the only visible explanation for the phenomenal rise in the college enrollment that year. He was undoubtedly the dominant member of the building committee. He directed the College in lively fashion until 1910 when he was transferred to St. Benedict's Church, Kansas City, Kansas.

In 1904 Father Aloysius had become acquainted with William Kenefick and his wife of Kansas City. Mr. Kenefick was president of the Missouri, Oklahoma and Gulf Railway Company, which was a project rather than a completed railroad. The Keneficks would be millionaires if his railroad projects worked out properly. They proposed, at the suggestion of Father Aloysius, to found a college on land just south of Kansas City, Missouri, provide it with a modest endowment, and place the Atchison monks in charge of the institution. When this was presented to the chapter as a possibility in 1904, "the great majority expressed themselves in favor of moving."[80] Father Aloysius was permitted to accompany the Keneficks to Rome to secure the Pope's blessing on the project. The first $100,000 was earmarked for the venture, and the Kene-

Mary's Abbey, Newark, N.J., Aug. 2, 1915, where he was given the name of Benedict. He died Dec. 20, 1945.—*Necrologium*, No. 970.
  [80] Chapter Minutes, May 26, 1904.

ficks estimated that if all went well, they would be ready for their philanthropy in five years.[81] Then came the panic of 1907, and Mr. Kenefick suffered setbacks.[82] By 1908 the dream had been reduced to an offer of 250 acres of land, and the community would have to finance construction of the buildings.[83]

During the summer of 1908 the Kenefick project was still a faint possibility, and rumors multiplied in Atchison. When Abbot Innocent returned from a treatment at Monsignor Kneipp's water cure in Rome City, Indiana, he was met by a delegation from the Committee of Forty, a civic organization to promote the growth and prosperity of Atchison. The delegation asked the Abbot what St. Benedict's needed to remain in Atchison. The Abbot, according to his notes, listed sewer connections, more land at a reasonable price north of the existing campus, an outlet to Mound Street, and protection from excessively heavy blasting in a quarry near the site of the proposed new building. The delegation guaranteed sewer connections immediately.[84] Shortly thereafter the committee could assure the community that ten acres north of the campus as well as an unimproved block along the bluff giving access to Mound Street could both be purchased for $4500.[85]

The chapter considered both Mr. Kenefick's farm and the possibilities in Atchison and debated the matter for almost a month. Finally, the chapter voted to remain in Atchison, to erect a new building on the river bluff, and to build a house for the Sisters who operated the College kitchen.[86] The Committee of Forty ultimately donat-

[81] *Ibid.*, June 30, 1905; Bradley to Abbot Primate, Atchison, Aug. 14, 1905. (SA)
[82] Wolf to Abbot Primate, Atchison, Dec. 11, 1907. (SA)
[83] Kenefick to Bradley, Kansas City, Oct. 6, 1908.
[84] Wolf memorandum, Sept. 17, 1908.
The Spalding quarry used such heavy charges that the community considered them dangerous to the new building. Injunctions and a suit followed, but the matter was eventually settled out of court.—Chapter Minutes, Sept. 24, 25, 30, 1912.
[85] Chapter Minutes, Oct. 7, 1908.
[86] *Ibid.*, Nov. 4, 1908.

ed the land desired,[87] and the community bought also the adjacent block on Mound Street.[88]

Grading the hill for the new Administration Building began in the spring of 1909. A heating plant designed to supply the needs of all the proposed new buildings was erected about a hundred yards north of the new building, and alongside the heating plant was a water tower supplied from the spring near First and Riley Streets donated by P. J. Brown. The Administration Building cost $161, 588.37. When the students returned from their Christmas vacation in January, 1911, they moved into the new building.

Two-thirds of the cost of the Administration Building had been paid by 1912, and the community had planned to erect "Wolf Hall" in 1913. Wolf Hall was to have been an auditorium with a gymnasium in the basement. This hall was a project of the alumni, but at that time the fund had not yet reached $10,000.[89] The hope of building, however, was suddenly blasted when one pastor single-handedly doubled the community's indebtedness.[90]

Father Thomas Burk considered himself obligated to provide for the future of his sister's children, the victims of a broken marriage. He was not satisfied to have the community provide for their education but wished also to provide a home for them and set them up in business. He asked for secularization or at least for temporary dispensation from the vow of poverty. The Abbot, unwill-

[87] *Ibid.*, Apr. 5, 1909.
[88] *Ibid.*, Mar. 25, 1909.
[89] St. Benedict's alumni organization dates from 1898. Father Andrew Green was its director, aided locally by Patrick Hayes and W. P. Waggener. A delegation of clerical alumni had surprised St. Benedict's in 1907 by proposing to raise funds to build a memorial chapel. Father Boniface believed the movement had begun without stimulation from any college official.—Verheyen to Wolf, Atchison, Aug. 2, 1907. A year later, when the plan for a group of buildings on the river bluff was proposed, this group of alumni, joined by others and no doubt encouraged by Father Aloysius, began a campaign to raise $50,000 to build an auditorium in honor of Abbot Innocent on the occasion of the golden jubilee of the College.—*Champion*, Apr. 22, 1908; promotional literature for The New St. Benedict's. The approach of the Abbot's priestly jubilee in 1916 occasioned renewal of the project. After the building of the gymnasium in 1923-24 the aim was changed to a library and the project was ultimately superseded by the Centennial Expansion Program.
[90] Wolf an Schnerr, Atchison, June 9, 1913. (SVA)

ing to lose so useful a pastor, dissuaded him and assigned him to St. John's Church, Burlington, Iowa, where the family lived in the rectory. There Father Thomas set them up in business in a small organ factory and, with his accustomed vigor, tried to teach them the art of management, while at the same time he was the company's most effective salesman. In lieu of capital, Father Thomas used the credit of his parish and his office as pastor to prop up the little company. But the hoped-for financial stability never arrived. The Abbot was warned about financial irregularities,[91] but he accepted Father Thomas' assurance that he was helping the company only with his advice.[92] Two complaints from the Bishop failed to shake this confidence.[93] And so when the Abbot suddenly received a plea from Father Thomas to save him from imprisonment for bankruptcy, the Abbot was surprised. With some futile grumbling the community took the responsibility for another $60,000 worth of debt.[94]

This financial calamity was not the only instance of an overconfident pastor presenting the chapter with a nasty surprise. Some years later Abbot Innocent sent his "best businessman" to the same parish. The excitement of the war years and an excess of social Christianity cost the community $14,000.[95] But this later misfortune did not cripple community development. Abbot Innocent wrote of the organ-factory fiasco, "My ambition was to pay off the debt entirely and let my successor build. . . I did not succeed and must leave the burden to another. . . . I think we were punished for glorying in the new building on the hill too much. We are urged to build 'Wolf Hall' for which the alumni collected $10,000; if that debt had not been shouldered on us, we would have begun building. The alumni cannot see the cause of de-

[91] Rosenfeld to Wolf, Burlington, Aug. 16, 1911.
[92] Wolf's note of Sept. 23 on Burk to Wolf, Burlington, Sept. 20, 1912.
[93] Bishop Davis to Wolf, Davenport, Aug. 12, 1911; Stahl to Wolf, Davenport, May 17, 1912.
[94] Chapter Minutes, Sept. 30; Oct. 2, 1912.
[95] Ibid., Dec. 14, 1920.

lay."[96]   The Abbot's cup of bitterness was filled when his monks' complaints prompted the Abbot President of the Congregation to order the Prior to have each priest write to the President stating whether he thought Abbot Innocent should resign.[97]   All but two or three, however, strongly opposed the idea of the Abbot's resignation, and only one favored it.[98]

Though God might well have disclaimed responsibility for such catastrophies as the organ factory, Abbot Innocent accepted everything as from the hand of Divine Providence.   He maintained that he did not worry about the sudden increase in the debt, but a good bit of evidence shows the contrary.   "I don't worry," he wrote, "God knows our trouble, and has helped in the past when we were worse off, and He will help in the future."[99]   The Abbot's faith was evidently justified when St. Benedict's acquired the former Midland College in south Atchison. This Lutheran school had moved to Fremont, Nebraska, and in 1919 its campus and buildings were acquired by St. Benedict's through the friendly agency of Eugene Howe, W. P. Waggener, and Leo Nusbaum.   St. Benedict's purchased the buildings and campus of some twenty acres for the bargain price of $40,000.   In chapter, the Abbot wrote, "*All* Fathers agreed with *applause* to buy the place; there was only one negative and that was silent (mine)."[100]   With this acquisition St. Benedict's expanded by not one but by four useful buildings, the gymnasium being considered the great prize.   Maur Hill, as Abbot Innocent called the new school, began life as a boarding grade school with a good bit of confusion,[101] but its real importance lay in the future when it provided a separate campus and an individual life for the high school.

[96] Wolf to Engel, Atchison, Mar. 19, 1915. (SJA)
[97] Engel to Aaron, Collegeville, Jan. 27, 1913.
[98] *Idem*, Feb. 13, 1913.
[99] Wolf to Engel, Atchison, Oct. 30, 1913. (SJA)
[100] *Idem*, Jan. 8, 1920; Chapter Minutes, Oct. 7, 1919.
[101] Wolf to Engel, Atchison, Jan. 24, 1920. (SJA)

The outbreak of World War I troubled Abbot Innocent deeply. He had lived in the United States from infancy, but his background was solidly German. He was convinced that the war was solely the fault of the grasping British. He worried about unknown dangers to his community. "Somehow I fear troubles ahead, and I cannot put it out of my mind. Then I console myself again that God has helped so far in serious matters and that He will help again at the prayers of others."[102] He wrote to a cleric, "Let us all pray fervently for peace among the nations. If God does not interfere more will be drawn into war, and we in America will not escape. Pray especially during Mass for those who are dying and who died that day. Pius X granted a special indulgence for it."[103]

When the United States entered the war, six members of the community wished to volunteer as chaplains in the armed forces.[104] In July, 1918, Father Patrick O'Shea was commissioned a chaplain in the army and was promptly sent overseas. Father Henry Courtney went to Fort Sheridan for boot training that was to prepare him to handle a student training program at the College.[105] The Director of the College, Father Damian Lavery, was an effective patriotic speaker at bond rallies, and others also served as "Minute Men," making short speeches at informal rallies.[106]

The Abbot's greatest problem grew out of a couple of monks who viewed America's entry into the war as a terrible tragedy. They loved America, but they could not bring themselves to hate their fatherland, and so they were outspokenly pro-German. Their sympathy was readily understandable to their friends, but voicing their

[102] *Idem*, Jan. 6, 1915. (SJA)
[103] Wolf to Clement Nordhus, Atchison, Dec. 31, 1914.
[104] Chapter Minutes, Apr. 24, 1918.
[105] Henry (Edward) Courtney was born in Montrose, Mo., Dec. 30, 1888, professed July 2, 1910, ordained June 2, 1917, and died Dec. 1, 1955.
[106] Damian (Arthur) Lavery was born near Benson, Vt., Feb. 10, 1878, professed July 11, 1897, ordained June 14, 1903, and died July 31, 1943.—*Necrologium*, No. 927.

sentiments could do great damage to the College. The Abbot consequently drew up the following statement and had all members of the community sign it:

> Remarks must not be made before students or visitors about the President, about the war, about laws made by Congress in regard to war, about politics. If one of the community would be interned or arrested because of his remarks all will suffer and the College may even be closed. There is a motion before Congress, that the President appoint a day of prayer for the success of our army. If that passes, be absolutely sure that you say no word about it, and that your actions may not be reported as a disapproval.
>
> Let everyone sign this to show that they will obey the will of Father Abbot in a very serious matter.

Between the fanatics in his community and the fanatics outside, the Abbot had cause for worry. Father Edwin Kassens, pastor at Kelly, Kansas, reported, "Yesterday a U.S. Marshal came and looked in all corners of the church — looking for guns. Lately I received a new altar; it came in twelve large boxes and this had been reported to Washington. Someone had seen the lightning rod on the steeple and reported that we had a wireless plant. After looking through every nook and corner the Marshal left satisfied that the report had been false."[107]

But suddenly the war ended and St. Benedict's, like everything else, was never quite the same. Abbot Innocent had celebrated his sacerdotal golden jubilee in 1916 and on that occasion was given the honor of wearing the Cappa Magna, which he regarded with distaste as ostentatious. The end of the war found him a sick old man. He wrote to Abbot Peter Engel, the chief confidant of his later years, "I do not think that my health will get good again; the least exertion affects me, and my eyesight is getting less; rheumatism and cramps sometimes come on so suddenly that I may fall any time and any way, just as it catches me, even at the altar. I try to keep up to cheer all, and am thankful that I can attend Matins

[107] Edwin Kassens to Wolf, Kelly, June 5, 1918.

regularly. If I break down I would prefer that God take me, and let a better man take my place. That is my prayer, that I may not become a burden."[108]

The community necessarily suffered from the failing powers of the Abbot. The visitators of 1914 noted for the first time that "There is too much grumbling and murmuring."[109] The visitators of 1917 criticized the Prior, the master of clerics, the procurator, conditions in the College, neglect of the Brothers, and too much secrecy in handling community matters.[110] Finally, on October 27, 1921, Abbot Innocent informed the chapter that he had written a note for the Prior to read to them and then left the room. The note was as follows:

> For Chapter: The Rt. Rev. Abbot Ernest, Praeses, wrote that a petition of our Fathers was sent to him to have a co-adjutor Abbot elected here. At the advice of the Rt. Rev. Visitors he asked me, and I answered that I would consent to an election, although I preferred to resign. Then he applied to Rome and the petition was granted on September 14. Yesterday I received directions from the Rt. Rev. Praeses to appoint a day for the election. The Seniors advised to take November 10. The Praeses prescribes the *Oratio Imperata de Spiritu Sancto.*

Abbot Innocent did not take the initiative in laying down the burden of office, though his poor health would have made that reasonable years earlier, because he had developed a theory that resignation was usually contrary to the will of God. He had no illusions about the office of abbot, for he regarded it purely and simply as a cross that he hoped would earn him heaven. Accepting abbatial election, he once wrote, was "just like entering marriage with a wicked wife." He resented his having been urged so strongly to accept the office, but at the same time that circumstance guaranteed him that his acceptance was not his will but God's will.[111] Nevertheless, if

---

[108] Wolf to Engel, Atchison, Jan. 8, 1918. (SJA)
[109] Record of Visitation, May 11, 1914.
[110] *Ibid.*, May 8, 1917.
[111] Wolf to Edelbrock, Atchison, May 28, 1890. (SJA)

he had to make the same decision again, he wrote, "nothing would or could move me to accept."[112]

Abbot Innocent had considered resignation a number of times. He first entertained the thought after his disappointing European tour of 1880. That crushing experience was apparently the most serious crisis in his life. In 1907 the Abbot asked "that the chapter decide in secret ballot whether it objects to his resignation. The reason for taking this step is the state of his health which renders him unfit to perform the duties of his office." But the chapter decided "that the matter be represented to Father Abbot as a personal question on which the chapter does not consider it proper to express an opinion."[113] This answer could not have been very comforting. At the time of the organ factory catastrophe, some monk evidently suggested to the Abbot that he ought to resign. "I would gladly resign," the Abbot wrote, "but the Praeses will not hear of it, but tells me to carry my cross still farther. As God wills, I will be patient and work as best I can."[114]

Furthermore, from the cases he had known, he concluded that an abbot's resignation always had a bad effect upon the community — another proof that resignation was contrary to the will of God. On one occasion he explained his convictions on this subject to his old Roman classmate, Abbot Hilary Pfraengle:

If God calls an Abbot away, it's all right and He will provide, but if man tries to make the change there is no blessing in it. We are only weak tools in the hands of God and should not refuse to serve although we see better tools around us; if God selects, it's good. Hence I would advise all abbots to bear the burden as long as God wishes; if He wishes a change He will make it at the proper time; let us not force Him. . . We have now in our abbey forty priests and I have had trouble with nearly every one of them, yes, sometimes with the best, so that I thought seriously of resigning some ten years ago; I told this to no one except my confessor, who would not consent, and without this I would not act. . . I was in that state

112 *Idem*, Aug. 31, 1889. (SJA)
113 Chapter Minutes, June 25, 1907.
114 Wolf an Schnerr, Atchison, June 9, 1913. (SVA)

241

of mind for over a year and found the burden. . . almost un-bearable; then I made up my mind to go as long as God would permit.[115]

Whatever one's opinion of Abbot Innocent's reasoning, one cannot question the purity of his motives. After forty-five long years of service he accepted his retirement tranquilly. On October 14, 1922, he was called to his reward.

Abbot Innocent had suffered many disappointments in his life, but he had accomplished much. The little community of 1876 had grown into a sizeable family by 1921 — sixty-four priests, twenty clerics, eight Brothers, and five choir novices — and to all of them the Abbot had given something of his own piety, simplicity, loyalty, and affection. To the little brick Priory and the unfinished church had been added a large college building (Bishop Fink Hall), an imposing monastery (Freshman Hall), the Administration Building, and Maur Hill. Even more im-portant, the Administration Building was explicitly the beginning of a new St. Benedict's. Abbot Innocent's accomplishment was twofold: first, he took a financially and spiritually weak community and built it into a solid and permanent Benedictine family, and, secondly, he left a community full of promise for the future.

St. Benedict's was (and is) a working-class community. Its men, practically without exception, came from working class and farming homes; they had little tradition of cul-tural appreciation and rather scanty educations. They had to be taught everything from elementary manners to ascetical theology. The community did not have the necessary qualifications to assume real leadership in any-thing intellectual, cultural, or religious, but it did pro-duce able teachers and pastors. Abbot Innocent's typical sons were earnest and hardworking. Some of them were fine examples of intellectually and culturally selfmade men. Above all, they were marked by a simple, uncomplicated, but solid piety. They really lived close to God. Though

---

[115] Wolf to Pfraengle, Rome, Jan. 29, 1896. (SMA)

the old Abbot's concentration on accepting the will of God could sometimes take an odd turn, his faith in Divine Providence was probably his greatest legacy to his monks. This supernatural viewpoint kept lives and motives properly directed even though all during this pioneer period the community's debt played a large part in every choice of policy.

Abbot Innocent and his monks were the pioneers. St. Benedict's was not really a permanent monastic community until he came, and he and the men he inspired built that community. They knew that the unrelenting pressures of material needs unduly influenced their lives, and they worked to offset that influence, but the fact remained that theirs was the brick and mortar age. They had to lay the foundations and pay the interest.

CHAPTER VIII

Abbot Innocent's College, 1877-1910

St. Benedict's was truly Abbot Innocent's college from 1877 until at least 1910. Throughout that period Abbot Innocent's ideas of what the school should be were predominant. Minor changes, of course, were made even in the early years. As the enrollment increased, the curriculum was expanded modestly, and an experiment was made at including a full-fledged school of theology to accommodate neighboring bishops. By 1890 the faculty was becoming aware that American colleges had evolved away from the traditional classical school and that St. Benedict's would have to meet new standards to fill the needs of its students. And so began a process of change, tentative and at first timid, that resulted after some three decades in St. Benedict's evolving into a modern college. But the changes before 1910 in no way affected the essence of Abbot Innocent's educational policies.

Throughout his life Abbot Innocent firmly maintained that St. Benedict's first purpose was to educate men for the priesthood and, secondly, to educate young Catholic laymen.[1] He was convinced that the curriculum should be largely restricted to the essential tools: English, German, Latin, Greek, and mathematics. Expansion of the curriculum much beyond these essential tools, to his mind, merely fostered superficiality and prevented the development of thorough students.[2] The Abbot's ideas on banishing distractions, particularly athletics and all other forms of rivalry, carried him, as we shall see, into conflict with

---

[1] Wolf to Aaron, Newark, Apr. 4, 1910.
[2] Wolf to Greenwood, Nov. 17, 1913, draft.

244

the American boy's fundamental nature. But the students never really suffered very much from the Abbot's disapproval of their favorite activities, and the memory of the old Abbot that remains green in the minds of the oldest living alumni is of a kind, wise, and forgiving, though somewhat distant father.

Until 1883 Abbot Innocent was not only the president but also the director of the College. When the Abbot went to Europe in 1880, he appointed Father Peter Kassens the director.[3] But since Father Peter was needed to attend weekend missions regularly, the Abbot resumed the office shortly after his return from Europe.[4] But when school and faculty grew, Abbot Innocent in 1883 appointed Father Matthew Bradley vice-president of the College and accorded him the title of director in 1885. His duty was handling the correspondence and supervising the College. The Abbot, however, always kept quite a firm hand on policies and administration.

Father Matthew Bradley had joined the community under Prior Giles Christoph.[5] Father Matthew had no particular training as a teacher and usually taught the elementary classes. But he was even tempered, had good judgment and an impressive full, dark beard, and was successful in securing the cooperation of both students and teachers. Furthermore, he tempered the strict rules of the school with the humanity of rather liberal interpretation. He was director of the College until 1889 but on account of illness was not active in the administration of the school after 1887.[6] He was eventually assigned to parish work and became an able and popular pastor, continuing in that work until 1922.

Father Gerard Heinz was appointed to direct the College in 1889.[7] His appointment was not popular with the

[3] Board of Professors' Minutes, Jan. 28, 1880, Wolf's appended note.
[4] Wolf an Wimmer, Atchison, June 8, 1881. (SVA)
[5] Matthew (William) Bradley was born in St. Clair County, Ill., July 2, 1850, professed July 19, 1875, ordained May 10, 1880, and died May 23, 1923.—Necrologium, No. 580.
[6] Wolf an Wimmer, Atchison, July 15, 1887. (SVA)
[7] Gerard (John) Heinz was born in Chicago, Ill., July 11, 1864, professed July 11, 1883, ordained June 20, 1887, died Oct. 13, 1946.—Necrologium, No. 993.

younger members of the faculty, but the very reasons for their complaints were what recommended him to Abbot Innocent: he was conscientious, he would restore discipline, and he would carry out the Abbot's policies.[8] Although just ordained, Father Gerard had been practically acting director during Father Matthew's illness and at the Abbot's orders had proceeded to tighten the school discipline and consequently to increase the burden on the prefects. But Father Gerard had more than conscientiousness to recommend him. He had a sense of humor, and he was a thoroughly spiritual man. He usually taught the Third Classical course and was director of the College until the end of 1897. He then served as pastor of the Abbey Church for a quarter of a century until Abbot Martin appointed him prior in 1922. He served with notable wisdom for almost a quarter century in that office until his death.

Fathers Matthew and Gerard covered the long stable period of the old St. Benedict's College. The period of change at the end of the century brought a more rapid turnover in directors. Following Father Gerard, Father Charles Stoeckle was an interim appointee for one year. Father Matthias Stein, a man of infinite kindness and patience, was director from 1899 to 1904 when he was appointed the community procurator.[9] He was succeeded by Father Francis McDonald (1904-1907), a man of fine presence and an able speaker, who had previously taught the commercial courses in the College for eleven years.[10] The "new" St. Benedict's was the dream of Father Aloysius Bradley, who was director from 1907-1910. His administration will be discussed later in this chapter.

The faculty throughout these years until 1908, when the clerics were sent to other abbeys for their studies in philosophy and theology, was composed of about equal

[8] Wolf Diary, Aug. 21, 1889.

[9] Matthias (Wilhelm) Stein was born in Seneca, Kans., July 11, 1872, professed July 11, 1891, ordained June 28, 1896, died Jan. 26, 1951.—Registrum.

[10] Francis (Thomas) McDonald, born in Leavenworth, Kans., Feb. 22, 1872, professed July 11, 1891, ordained June 28, 1896, died Feb. 28, 1929.—*Necrologium*, No. 658.

numbers of priests and clerics. Furthermore, almost half the priests were newly ordained and not destined to remain in the teaching profession very long. As a consequence, the quality of the school depended largely on a nucleus of a few men who devoted most of their lives to teaching. Father Boniface Verheyen, with his wonderful intellectual curiosity, taught until 1915. Father Peter Kassens taught a little of everything until 1910 and consistently had a teaching schedule of thirty to forty hours a week in the early days. Father Matthew Bradley, the first director, taught the preparatory courses until 1887. These three pioneers formed the cornerstone of the institution. During the eighties Fathers Gerard Heinz, Joseph Sittenauer, and Aloysius Bradley, who have been previously mentioned, were added to the faculty. That decade also gave St. Benedict's three other men, Fathers Leo Aaron, Stanislaus Altmann, and Andrew Green, whose long careers in teaching — all taught into the 1920's — make them almost personify the College.

Father Leo Aaron was St. Benedict's first fulltime professor of chemistry and physics.[11] He was almost entirely self-taught in those fields, but he was a born tinkerer, and his unflagging interest made him a good teacher. Father Leo's mechanical skills and ingenuity produced much equipment that the poverty-stricken school could not buy for his laboratory. He was not especially polished, but his sturdy dependability was an important influence in both the College and the community, and he was Abbot Innocent's last prior, serving in that capacity from 1908 to 1922.

A classical school like St. Benedict's necessarily had many teachers of Latin and Greek, but none were so well remembered as Father Stanislaus Altmann.[12] He was a very able teacher, strict but kindly, carefully leading his

---

[11] Leo (Francis) Aaron was born in St. Nicholas, Pa., Apr. 27, 1863, professed July 11, 1883, ordained June 29, 1889, died May 11, 1927.—*Necrologium*, No. 632.

[12] Stanislaus (Joseph) Altmann was born in Rothenbaum, Bohemia, Aug. 4, 1866, professed July 16, 1885, ordained July 13, 1890, died Mar. 29, 1937. —*Necrologium*, No. 794.

students into the classics with the aid of his delightful personality and good humor. On the other hand, he was typical of St. Benedict's (and most schools of that period) in that he stressed the technical side of language rather than the literary and cultural values. He taught exactness and precision of expression and of thought. He was also a better than average musician and an enthusiastic and knowing philatelist. When he was stricken with paralysis on April 3, 1924, St. Benedict's lost a good Latin teacher, but Father Stanislaus did some of his finest teaching of the Christian virtues from his cheerful hospital bed during his remaining thirteen years.

The most effervescent personality of this trio of the eighties was Father Andrew Green, who has been mentioned previously as Abbot Innocent's reluctant prior in the nineties and as one of the first and most impatient promoters of the liturgical movement at St. Benedict's. He was not a good teacher, but he had a degree of creative ability and bubbling enthusiasm for the arts. His great love was music and his favorite instrument, the violin. He was a capable, if not distinguished, composer and produced not only compositions for the piano, vocal solos with piano accompaniment, marches for the band, and an operetta but also a symphony. He was also an accomplished amateur in poetry, and a collection of his verse, *The Bells of Atchison*, was published by the Abbey Student Press in 1908. After his retirement from teaching and as he approached and then passed the age of eighty, Father Andrew kept himself out of mischief by publishing two of his own retreats for religious as well as translations of two spiritual works.[13]

The nineties brought important additions to the faculty at St. Benedict's. Some have already been mentioned as directors, and others can best be considered later. But the pioneers and the men who began their teaching careers

[13] Green, *Retreat for Religious*, Herder, 1943.
— *The Love of God; Conferences to Religious*, Herder, 1946.
Wendelin Meyer, O.F.M., *The Pastoral Care of Souls*, Herder, 1944.
Joseph Pickl, *The Messias*, Herder, 1946.

in the eighties give a clear enough picture of the best of the faculty and consequently of the kind of school St. Benedict's was in the nineteenth century. Though still lacking in much formal education, they were nevertheless good teachers because they never stopped learning, were always interested and consequently interesting, worked hard, and consequently inspired their students to work. Perhaps the most important fact was that the students of St. Benedict's could see that solid Christian virtue could be an appealing and delightful possession and the secret of a happy life.

Early Growth

When Abbot Innocent took command in 1877, St. Benedict's College was a rather sickly youngster in its late 'teens. The troubles of the community were reflected and perhaps magnified in the school. Abbot Innocent found that "the old prejudices against the college are still alive and can hardly be laid to rest as long as Augustine Wirth's name is in the catalog. People think he is still here."[14] Abbot Innocent and his newly-inspired community slowly began to improve and enlarge the school. The beginnings were modest. In the school year of 1876-77 seventy-two students were enrolled (forty-one from Atchison County), of whom thirty were day students. But as was to be the case for the next few decades, many of the students came late and left early, so that only twenty-eight boarders remained when the school year was officially closed in June.[15]

The practice of sending representatives during the summer to interview prospective students was begun immediately, and the following year showed improvement.[16] At the opening of school nineteen boarders paid for their board and tuition. Fourteen additional boarders were scholastics studying for the Abbey or for the Creston

---

[14] Wolf an Wimmer, Atchison, Aug. 12, 1879. (SVA)
[15] Wolf to Bartl, Atchison, June 19, 1877.
[16] Wolf an Wimmer, Atchison, July 30, 1877. (SVA)

Priory — three of whom paid nothing, six paid incidentals, and five paid more than a hundred dollars toward their education. There were only six day students, but their numbers would swell after the farm work was finished in October. Thirty-three boarding students very nearly approached the capacity of the College at the time. Not more than thirty-eight could be crowded into the single dormitory. Similarly, all the students, large and small, classical and commercial, had to share one study hall, or "museum," as the Bavarians traditionally called it. Three classrooms and two dining rooms, sometimes also used for classrooms, completed the college accommodations.[17] The faculty numbered but six men. Fathers Boniface Verheyen, Peter Kassens, and Albert Robrecht of St. Vincent each taught about thirty-two hours a week and then usually took care of a weekend mission. Three clerics handled forty-eight hours of class among them and then followed their own studies in theology, practically limited to moral and dogma, taught by Abbot Innocent.[18]

The first problem was space, but since the community already had a larger debt than was healthy, the new building had to be modest. The first and south section of Bishop Fink Hall (the refectory building), forty-four by fifty-six feet, was the result. When it was occupied on November 4, 1878, the College had a new kitchen on the basement level, two 'large' dining halls and a telegraph office on the first floor, four classrooms on the second floor, and a dormitory and study hall on the third floor. Into the southeast corner of the building were built three stories of dry closets, very cleverly ventilated, as the college catalog proudly boasted. The new building was connected to the old by a corridor.[19]

The new building brought immediate improvement. The number of boarders rose to sixty, but competition from the Jesuits at St. Mary's, Kansas, forced some rate-cutting. Furthermore, the purchase of furniture, beds,

[17] *Idem*, Sept. 27, 1877. (SVA)
[18] *Idem*, Nov. 10, 1877. (SVA)
[19] *Catalog of St. Benedict's College*, 1879, 21.

250

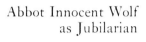
Abbot Innocent Wolf
as Jubilarian

he New Abbey
ewed from the East

The New Abbey
ewed from the Northwest

The Playground and Vineyard about 189[8]

The New Administration Building

Father Lambert Burton

The New Gymnasium and the Administration Building

A Study Hall in the Administration Building

The Clerics
Harvesting
Grapes

The Clerics'
"Jungle Band"
1913

Fr. Edmund, Fr. Louis, Fr. Leander, Fr. Leonard
Fr. Edgar, Fr. Henry, Fr. Pius, Fr. Isidor, Fr. Bonaventure,
Fr. Malachy.

The Sister Cooks 1900

The Abbey
Cemetery

The Mount
cheers St.
Benedict's
vs.
St. Mary's
1922

Football in the Twenties

Father Damian
and The Bus

Varsity Baseball Team. Back Row: Father Malachy, C. Stima?, D. O'Keefe, G. Burke. Se
Row: H. Smith, H. Merwick, Clar. Smith, John Senofsky, Leo Sander, Clement Voet. Front R
Frank Scherr, Anthony Mages, Tony Kilkenny, Norbert Wavada, Al Derada.

Varsity Basketball Team. Back Row: Tom Quigley, Clar. Smith, Malachy Sullivan, Leo Consid
J. H. Baker, John Senofsky. Front Row: Henry Grosdidier, John Green, H. Merwick, Ed C
didier, Leo Sander.

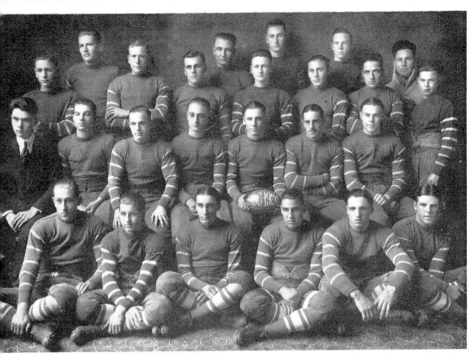

rsity Football Team. Back Row: Frank Nordhus, Jos. Puthoff, . . . Coupe, Leo A. Taylor,
.lachy Sullivan.   Second Row: E. Schwartz, Al Kelly, H. Smith, Lee Whitlock, John Green, L.
.ecal, Tom Curry.   Third Row: Leo Considine (Mgr.), Cecil Dorney, Leo Coakley, Leo Sander,
.H. Baker, Chas. Cragan, Gerard Nass.   Front Row: Leo Schwartz, G. Carlton, Hugo Marxer,
.e Bendon, Al Morley, Leo Nusbaum.

1905 Drama

"Pinafore" 1912

Brothers
1914
Top Row: Gabriel Fitzgerald, Raphael Scholz, Agatho Meyer, Andrew Allerman
Leonard Domen, Wolfgang Wolf, Anthony Eckstaller. Bottom Row: Fra
Daengeli, Clement Lehan, Lawrence Egan, Adam Gansen.

blankets, and strawticks was an additional expense. Abbot Innocent concluded that "the new students are no immediate material gain, but a moral gain. We become better known, and once here they are always glad to come back and to bring others."[20]

Continued growth made possible the completion of the new college building in 1883 with an addition twice the size of the original section. As the first section had made possible separate facilities for ecclesiastical and general students, the addition provided for the separation of the Seniors (older students) and the Juniors in each division. Furthermore, the basement of the new building provided the students with badly-needed recreational facilities in a rumpus room that served as theatre, skating rink, and gym. This room was formally labeled Society Hall. At the same time the campus was graded and improved.[21]

Throughout most of the eighties, St. Benedict's was a school with slightly more than a hundred boarding students and about twenty day students. In 1888, when Father Gerard Heinz took over the direction of the school, the number of boarding students suddenly rose to 170, and until 1907 the enrollment fluctuated between 150 and 180. One must remember, of course, that many students came late and left early. The official policy stated on the flyleaf of the 1881-1889 Student Register further qualifies the meaning of student enrollment: "Students who do not remain at least six full school days are not to be mentioned in the Annual Catalogue." But during the eighties the achievement of having one hundred students in actual attendance was marked not once but three times, and a freeday was given in January, 1881, on this account.[22]

The year 1884 marked the twenty-fifth anniversary of the College in Atchison. The community was notably optimistic that year. Although he did not share their optimism, Abbot Innocent could view the growth of the College with satisfaction. In seven years the faculty had

[20] Wolf an Wimmer, Atchison, Sept. 25, 1879. (SVA)
[21] *Catalog*, 1884, 43-44.
[22] *Catalog*, 1881, 30.

grown from six to seventeen, namely, eight priests (three of them on loan from St. Vincent) and nine clerics. The Abbot was confident that the community could soon staff the College without help from St. Vincent, particularly since the scholastics assured the steady growth of the community.[23] A faculty committee appointed to consider an alumni reunion and a proper celebration of the twenty-fifth anniversary of the College, however, cautiously recommended that "it be first ascertained how many of the former students in good social standing will probably attend the reunion."[24] Some months later the committee reported that it had sent sixty invitations to former students, that eight had accepted, and "of those who were willing to attend only a small fraction was desirable." They agreed, therefore, to postpone the celebration and the formation of an alumni association.[25] The past had little to offer as yet, but the future was promising.

The College had been founded primarily to educate prospective monks and thereby ensure the growth of the community. In Abbot Innocent's mind this primacy was enlarged but otherwise not changed. The fact that neither Prior Fink nor Prior Christoph had accepted scholastics had stunted the growth of the community for seven years, but by 1881 the youngsters gathered by Prior Moosmueller were clerics and the hope of the future.[26] Archabbot Wimmer's fundamental policy of furthering the mission to the immigrant by the creation of a self-sustaining school for priests, Benedictine and diocesan, was duplicated in Kansas. The new building afforded the ecclesiastical students their own study hall and dormitory. At the same time a fifth year of Latin, long in the catalog, was actually added to the curriculum.[27] The sixth year of the classical curriculum, philosophy, was for the clerics.

[23] Wolf an Wimmer, Atchison, July 10, 1884. (SVA)
[24] Board of Professors' Minutes, Oct. 29, 1884.
[25] Chapter Minutes, Mar. 6, 1885.
[26] Wolf an Wimmer, Atchison, Nov. 11, 1881. (SVA)
[27] Board of Professors' Minutes, Aug. 23, 1879.

Bishop Fink sent some of his prep-seminarians to St. Benedict's, happy "to be able to help the poor fellows a little,"[28] and recommended the Atchison Benedictines to the charity of the Ludwig-Missionsverein.[29] The Bishop considered a seminary the greatest need of his Diocese, and since the Benedictines were, after a fashion, teaching theology to their own clerics, he encouraged the community to fill out the curriculum and open a seminary.[30]

The experiment was made in 1882. Bishop Fink sent six theologians, namely, Thomas Lillis, who became successively Bishop of Leavenworth and of Kansas City, Missouri, Michael Harrigan, Alexander Jennings, Nicholas Neusius, J. J. O'Brien, and F. J. Neuhoffer.[31] Abbot Innocent taught moral theology; Father Winfried Schmidt taught dogma, introduction to Holy Scripture, philosophy and Hebrew; and Prior Boniface Verheyen taught homiletics, physics, and chemistry.[32] But the experiment was discontinued after one year because the faculty found teaching in both college and seminary too strenuous, and adequate space was not available. The addition to the college building had not yet been completed, and even before the seminary was attempted, classes were being held in the community chapter room.[33] To accommodate the seminarians, the Brothers' dormitory had to be moved to the attic of the old Priory.[34]

Although he had to send his students of theology elsewhere, Bishop Fink continued to send his minor seminarians to St. Benedict's. Since a knowledge of both German and English was needed by priests in a majority of his parishes, the Bishop insisted that his students speak German in recreation two or three times a week. Furthermore, he expected Abbot Innocent to enforce this policy. On one occasion after a number of exchanges on this topic,

[28] Fink to Wimmer, Leavenworth, July 15, 1879. (SVA)
[29] Fink an LMV, Leavenworth, Dec. 21, 1879. (LMV Leav I 6/8)
[30] Fink an Kagerer, Leavenworth, Nov. 24, 1883. (LMV Leav I 6/12) Fink to Wolf, Leavenworth, Dec. 29, 1882.
[31] Report an Leopoldinenstiftung, Feb. 28, 1883, draft; *Catalog*, 1883, 7.
[32] Wolf to Edelbrock, Atchison, Sept. 22, 1882. (SJA)
[33] Wolf an Wimmer, Atchison, Nov. 11, 1881. (SVA)
[34] Report an Leopoldinenstiftung, Feb. 28, 1883, draft.

the Bishop wrote, "You will please enforce the rule I laid down."[35]   Poor Abbot Innocent expressed his anguish by jotting the following notation on this communique: "Jan. 11: Will start with the Juniors this evening, but those that don't want to learn will sit there dumb. *They* ought to get the scolding."

The training of men for the priesthood continued uninterruptedly through the years. Abbot Innocent proudly reported that at the end of the school year of 1881-82 nine students had finished their studies at St. Benedict's and were ready for the seminary. Only two of them could pay the full cost of their education. Henry Tihen, later to become successively the Bishop of Lincoln and of Denver, had been accepted by the Archbishop of St. Louis; two belonged to the Diocese of Leavenworth; one to the Diocese of Kansas City; and one had been accepted by the Archbishop of Boston. The remaining four entered the community.[36]   By 1894 there were eighty minor seminarians studying at St. Benedict's. None of them could pay the full cost of their education, although the charges at that time were "Board, Lodging, Tuition, and Washing, for five months, $100."[37]   More than half of these students were on full scholarships. This large percentage of scholarships was double the usual number and was undoubtedly attributable to the depression following 1893, which at the same time caused a decrease in enrollment and income. Abbot Innocent explained to his benefactors that he was afraid to refuse a boy when God had sent him. Of the previous year's graduates, seven had gone on to diocesan seminaries, and two had joined the community. The Abbot happily added that students from St. Benedict's did well at Innsbruck, Louvain, and in American seminaries.[38]

[35] Fink to Wolf, Leavenworth, Dec. 23, 1888.
[36] Wolf an LMV, Atchison, Mar. 5, 1883. (Leav II 1/59-60)
[37] *Catalog*, 1895, 26.
[38] Wolf an Kagerer, Atchison, Jan. 17, 1895; Wolf an Brueckl, Atchison, Feb. 3, 1895[6]. (LMV Leav II 1/78-79)
  A note on proportions: In 1891 of about 150 students, 69 were studying for the priesthood. Of these 69, 13 were clerics and 18 were scholastics, a total

With such a large proportion of the students educated at the expense of the community, the College did not have a net income even in good times.[39] On the other hand, the scholastics repaid the gift in part by doing chores around the school and, one one occasion, by whipping up fifty crudely made quilts in two days.[40] They particularly looked forward to occasional jobs on the farm, such as picking apples, because this often meant no class and always meant a lunch and a lark.

Secondary only to training priests was preparing young men for "public civil life." These students were offered a three-year course, including English, arithmetic and mathematics, commercial law, and bookkeeping. Although these students were sometimes a minority of the boarders, they were always in the majority when reinforced by the day students. To the end of the century a large proportion of these general students could attend school only during the slack season on the farm. The college catalogs of the seventies and eighties harped constantly on the trouble caused by those who arrived late. Perhaps to minimize this evil, the expressed policy was that all students should remain at the College even during Christmas vacation. As the catalog explained, "An absence from college for a few days is, as a rule, productive of no good results. This is a lesson taught by experience, the exceptions to which are but few. Several days come and go before outside impressions are wiped away and the student can apply his mind without distracting thoughts." And the result? "Dec. 23. . . The majority of the students left to rejoin their friends and relatives at home."[41]

Some of the students who needed very elementary instruction were already well developed physical specimens.

of 31 Benedictine students, whereas 38 were diocesan students. As to national varieties the 69 were classified by Father Joseph into 24 German-Americans, 23 Americans, 9 Bohemians, 8 Germans, 4 Poles, and one Frenchman.—Sittenauer an LMV. Atchison, Jan. 20, 1891. (LMV Leav II 1/63-65)

[39] Wolf to Mueller, Atchison, Dec. 29, 1891. (SVA)

[40] Report an Leopoldinenstiftung, Feb. 28, 1883, draft.

[41] Catalog, 1888, 21 and 57.

The Abbot once asked the faculty whether another class "for such scholars as have not the knowledge requisite to enter our first class and are too large to be sent to the elementary course, should be introduced."[42] Another result of this situation was what might be called a Prefects' Protective Association. Thus Father Ignatius Stein gave greenhorn prefect Frater Gabriel Vonderstein "several *practical points* about keeping the coast clear and how to signal to his fellow-comrades in arms, when in danger of being overpowered by some disloyal citizen."[43]

Student Life

The order of the day at St. Benedict's during the nineteenth century was clearly based on the principle that at least where boys are concerned leisure leads only to mischief. When Jimmy Rank, later Father Ambrose, rode in from Doniphan County with his father on a load of wheat to enter St. Benedict's in 1876, he found that the students arose, with encouragement from the prefects, at five-thirty in the morning and after their ablutions attended morning prayers and Mass. After breakfast the hours from seven to noon were devoted to study and classes, except for a fifteen-minute recess in mid-morning. After dinner the students were free until one-thirty when they had study hour and class until four. They were free until five when they again studied for an hour before supper. After supper they were permitted recreation until seven-thirty, when they studied for an hour, then said night prayers and went to bed. The routine was broken by long walks, accompanied by a prefect, on Wednesday and Saturday afternoons. On Sunday the students were up as usual, attended High Mass at ten-thirty, and wrote letters or held their various club meetings before dinner. After dinner they might walk to West Atchison, but they

[42] Minutes of Professors' Meetings, Dec. 19, 1882.
[43] Ignatius Stein to Wise, Atchison, Dec. 20, 1900.

were back by three for Vespers. Study hour and the week's work began again at five.[44]

This general pattern changed very little for decades. In 1894 the *Abbey Student* reported, "Of the many new privileges this year none are appreciated more than the extra half hour sleep in the morning, and the dispensing with reading in the refectory."[45] Classes then began at eight instead of at seven-thirty. Through the years, of course, St. Benedict's has stressed the ideal opportunity offered for a full Christian life among its students, and so attendance at Mass, prayers in common, and student retreats all date from the earliest years.

The "General Regulations" of the College in 1877 also remained essentially unchanged until World War I. The day students' private studies,

to which two or three hours ought to be devoted every evening, should be watched with great solicitude. . . No one will be allowed to leave the precincts of the College except in company with a Tutor or a Prefect. All letters, papers, books, etc., sent or received by students, are subject to the inspection of the President or his substitute. The use of tobacco is positively prohibited; such as cannot discontinue the use of it will not be admitted. Violations of the established discipline of the College are suppressed in a mild but effective manner. Should any student prove refractory or immoral, in spite of all efforts to correct him, he will be sent back to his parents or guardians. Students whose parents live in the vicinity of the College are allowed to visit them but once a month.[46]

Two decades later the rules for receiving visitors and for leaving the precincts had been relaxed a bit. Furthermore, politeness was encouraged, and students were urged to write home but only on Saturday or Sunday. Tobacco was still frowned upon, and strict silence was imposed "during study and class-hours, when going to and coming from the chapel and dining room, in the dormitories, washrooms, and closets."[47]

[44] Ambrose Rank Diaries, *passim.*
[45] *Abbey Student*, IV (Oct., 1894), 21.
[46] *Catalog*, 1878, 6-7.
[47] *Catalog*, 1895, 24-25.

Life at St. Benedict's was, of course, never as grim as the picture painted by the "General Regulations." The application of the rules was tempered with humanity, but freedom was sometimes abused. For example, Frater Ambrose Rank recorded that on April 9, 1883, the following plaintive notice was posted in both study halls:

> On account of the manner in which some have abused the confidence placed in them by entering forbidden places (which are Saloons, Billiard or Pool Halls, the Skating Rink and all dwelling houses) when permitted to go to town; by not coming home at the appointed time; by coming back sick &c., I feel compelled to make the following rule, viz.: In future anyone permitted to go to town and guilty of the above offences shall be punished.
> P.S. No one will be permitted to go to town unless he has a reasonable excuse.
>
> Matthew Bradley, O.S.B.[48]

Tobacco was, of course, a constant problem. Although most of the faculty at St. Benedict's were inveterate smokers, it was common knowledge that the habit was harmful to youth, and St. Benedict's warred on the weed for half a century. In 1895, for example, Abbot Innocent "reprobated the practice that had crept in of allowing students to smoke at certain times and places."[49] By 1908 the College had been forced to retreat to a degree of toleration except for those new-fangled cigarettes. In that year one of the staff of the *Abbey Student*, Henry Courtney, reported:

> Our Reverend Director, in his initiatory remarks to the students at the opening of school, stated in firm, lucid, and telling tones that the smoking of cigarettes would absolutely not be tolerated by the College Faculty and declared that anyone found breaking this rule would be immediately expelled from the institution. The decisive stand of the Faculty on this disgusting and deteriorating habit is certainly an admirable one. Statistics show most conclusively that more young men ruin their health, reputation, and character by the use of the 'coffin nail' than in any other way.[50]

[48] Ambrose Rank Diary, 1883-1884, end.
[49] Chapter Minutes, Jan. 10, 1895.
[50] XVIII (Oct., 1908), 26.

Although one might suppose that corporal punishment was rather freely dispensed in those days, Abbot Innocent forbade prefects and professors to strike or whip a boy, "no matter how much they may have been provoked."[51] Corporal punishment was reserved to the President (the Abbot) or the Director, but in most cases the Abbot preferred to expel a student rather than whip him.[52] The school discipline was, of course, influenced by local circumstances, but it was molded essentially by centuries of Benedictine educational experience.

At St. Benedict's this tradition was codified in a manuscript volume, *Regulae pro Officialibus Collegii* (Rules for the College officials), which each prefect was required to read at the beginning of the school year. These rules show the touch of Abbot Innocent's hand, but basically they embody the Benedictine tradition as practiced in St. Vincent, Metten, and in other Benedictine schools back through the centuries. The regulations were based on the Holy Rule and on common sense. In the spirit of St. Benedict's Rule, for example, the prefects were admonished that,

> Those having charge of the young should try to follow the example of a good, kind and prudent father. *Meekness* and *patience* should predominate. Whether speaking or acting these virtues should control. A mild and resolute temper wins far more than harsh words or punishments... If we have once gained the confidence and love of those under our care, then the respect and affection they bear us will be sufficient to control them. Pnishments will rarely be necessary.

Young prefects were given the excellent advice to avoid harsh and cutting words and to avoid humiliating the culprit who must be punished. Furthermore, the prefects were to see that their students practiced cleanliness. The added injunction to "avoid pulling the ears; it disfigures that organ," was undoubtedly authored by Abbot Innocent.

---

[51] Chapter Minutes, Apr. 23, 1907.
[52] Minutes of Professors' Meetings, Dec. 4, 1883.

School spirit depended largely upon the prefects, who, besides being disciplinarians, were as fathers or big brothers to their charges. The prefect slept in the same dorm with his group of students, supervised their study hours, accompanied them in their prayers, at Mass, at meals, and at recreation. The prefect helped his students organize their games, repair the backstop, sew baseballs, and patch bats. The prefect found a place for every student in the school athletic leagues and was ferociously loyal to his teams. As a consequence the most unchanging and prominent feature in student accounts of life at St. Benedict's through the decades is the family spirit. In a class history, for example, C. P. O'Neill, '94, recounts the joys of being tapped to help harvest the apples, the outdoor and indoor sports enjoyed, his pride in the Shakespeare Society — which did actually stage Shakespeare as well as farces — and the lively class rivalry in sports and clubs. Through the whole account runs the bright thread of the warmth and joy to be found in this family of monks and young men.[53]

Some departments were better handled by women, however, and it was a happy day for St. Benedict's when the Sisters of Mount St. Scholastica agreed to take charge of the kitchen in 1884. Before that date the students sometimes had grounds for complaints beyond the usual griping that merely indicates good health. On one occasion Abbot Innocent noted that the meat for breakfast had not been properly cooked but was nearly raw. And the old ditty about the inedibility of dried-apple pie came to life. The students refused to eat the pie, insisting that in it they had found even coal.[54]

The dormitories continued to be infamously cold during the worst nights of winter, and "F. A.," a member of the zoology class, contributed to the *Abbey Student* a long scientific essay on the bedbug, including personal observations. The morning dash out of doors was no longer

[53] *Abbey Student*, III (June, 1894), 111-116.
[54] Wolf Diary, Jan. 8, 1883.

necessary after the new college building was completed in 1878, and water closets were installed in 1905.[55] This advance of civilization had been preceded by the bathroom. In a chapter of 1894 Abbot Innocent had explained that the Director requested permission to install a bathroom "as many parents want their sons to bathe."[56] In the following April the *Abbey Student* announced: "The bath rooms are opened every Monday and Thursday afternoon. Strict silence prevails there at all times."[57]

Although frequent bathing might have seemed a novelty, the colleges of the time were rather careful about sanitation. It was an age of regular epidemics, and that threat caused the greatest fear in the minds of college authorities. Students entering school or returning from vacation were carefully scrutinized for signs of measles or worse. At least one house physician was always on the roster. Twice in the early years the school doctors had to deny rumors of epidemic and affirm that sanitary conditions at the College were good.[58] All in all, St. Benedict's was fortunate, but it did not survive the years unscathed. Mumps or measles sometimes went the rounds, disrupting the school for weeks or even months. Diptheria and the poxes, possible killers, were the real source of dread.

The first outbreak of an epidemic came in March, 1884, when forty boys caught scarlet fever. When that had been cleared up, twenty students developed mumps, just to keep the school disrupted, while at the same time Father Boniface, one of the most essential professors, was completely incapacitated by a severe attack of inflammatory rheumatism.[59] The most unhappy period in the history of sickness in the College was around the turn of the century. The climax was reached in the winter of 1900-1901 when diptheria appeared, and so many students were

[55] Wolf to Engel, Atchison, Sept. 6, 1905. (SJA)
[56] Wolf Diary, Sept. 13, 1894.
[57] IV (Apr., 1895), 107.
[58] *Champion*, Jan. 15, 1870; Feb. 11, 1872.
[59] Wolf to Edelbrock, Atchison, Apr. 4, 1884. (SJA)

stricken that the monastery guest rooms were turned into a sick bay. Two Sisters from Mount St. Scholastica stayed in quarantine there to nurse St. Benedict's sick students for seventy days.[60] That experience appears to have been St. Benedict's worst nightmare.

Fortunately, sickness was the exception. A more constant problem for the College authorities was providing outlets for healthy youthful exuberance. Special facilities for recreation were few, of course, but that condition was normal, and for some years no more than a playing field with a makeshift ball diamond was expected. When the weather was bad, the students played the popular indoor games of the day. They always played cards, although Abbot Innocent was still forbidding this practice in 1911.[61] In 1897 the *Abbey Student* reported that "the most popular games during the evening recreation are Crokinole and Archarena," and "Our Mandolin club . . . has made a decided hit."[62] The nineties saw also the first period of the popular camera fad, and the golden age of the bicycle did not leave the College unchanged. Some of the mounts were alleged to be ferris wheels.[63]

Nevertheless, student morale sometimes reached dismally low ebbs, particularly during prolonged periods of bad weather. Runaways were quite rare, Abbot Innocent in 1882 reporting the first since his coming.[64] But on January 16, 1889, the Director, Father Gerard Heinz, noted in his diary: "The students are very wild and blue ever since Christmas. It is so muddy outside that they cannot enjoy a good game; they have not been taken walking; and many [were] refused [permission] to go visiting so often and to go to town on small pretense, v.g., to get a bath. Some few dissastified persons are leaving and others intend to."[65] As a cure for the situation the Abbot promptly ordered weekly walks. Cold winter

[60] Mother Aloysia to Wolf, Atchison, Nov. 16, 1901, and Wolf's note.
[61] Instructions to faculty, Sept., 1911.
[62] VII (Nov., 1897), 141, 143.
[63] *Ibid.*, IV, (Oct., 1894), 19.
[64] Wolf Diary, Jan. 11, 1882.
[65] Director's Diary, 1885-1896.

days were better. The most popular outing was skating on Doniphan Lake, with a roaring fire on the shore and trips to the general store for cigars, salami, and candy.

Student life in the nineteenth century, as in the twentieth, depended less on haphazard incidental games for fun than on organized activities, holidays, and other events calling for celebration. In early years a prominent part of special celebrations was firing salutes. An anniversary of Pope Pius IX was celebrated with a salute of fifty guns and an illumination of the College. The gun was a heavy piece borrowed from Seaton's foundry for the occasion.[66] Being needed for the parade, only the band was permitted to attend Atchison's first Corn Carnival in 1895. The other students staged their own parade on the campus. They successfully demanded a freeday, raided a nearby cornfield, and decorated themselves appropriately. They also made floats out of the Minims' donkey cart, a wheelbarrow, and similar wheeled implements. The order of the parade was the Minim Cadet Corps, the Volunteer Fire Brigade, the various clubs, and a fife and drum corps without fifes. The favorite songs used on the occasion were "Chain the Lion Down" and "Marching through Georgia." The major point, of course, was the free day.[67] After 1900 St. Benedict's students were lively participants in the annual Corn Carnival.

Freedays were casual and frequent occurrences. September 21, the nameday of Father Director Matthew Bradley, was always a freeday. On this day in 1885 the students spent the morning hunting pawpaws, devoted the afternoon to baseball, and decided to have a short band concert outdoors after supper.[68] St. Patrick's Day was usually devoted to field events and other sports. The best day of all was May Day. It was always supposed to be a big surprise, for the exact day was unknown to the stu-

---

[66] *Catalog*, 1877, 12.
[67] *Abbey Student*, V (Oct., 1895), 20.
[68] Director's Diary, 1885-1896.

dents, and half the enjoyment was in the tingle of anticipation. Before 1900 this big day was most frequently held at Sugar Lake where boating, naval battles, swimming (perforce), fishing, and other sports of the day could be combined with the picnic dinner. Sometimes May Day was held at the College farm south of town. Occasionally the day included a ride on a train, once to Fort Leavenworth;[69] on another occasion a special train was taken to Ashcraft's Grove on Independence Creek. By that time, 1895, the big event of the day was the Senior-Junior championship ball game. The many prizes for the field events included a mustache cup for the winner of the Senior Jump.[70] In 1896 the students were transported to Mt. Pleasant Grove, nine miles south of the College, in "ice-wagons." Since the students had not arrived until noon, they asked Father Director Gerard Heinz to let them stay all night, and "gazing upon the determined crowd before him he concluded that it was the only alternative." Although a large hall was on the grounds, very few slept because the singing and speech-making continued into the wee hours of the morning. Somebody began a base-ball game at four o'clock in the morning, but "during the last half of the third inning, the umpire observing seven of the outside nine asleep, standing up in his wrath, called the game." Mass was offered at five o'clock (presumably this was at St. Patrick's), breakfast was served, the students walked home and slept all afternoon.[71]

Much of the students' extracurricular activity, although not ceasing to be recreation, was an important part of their education. Biographies of prominent figures in American political life at the turn of the century lead one to conclude that the most important part of college education was elocution and debate. These disciplines were emphasized by St. Benedict's at the same time. The Philomathic Society, organized by Father Boniface Ver-

[69] *Abbey Student*, VII (June, 1898), 587.
[70] *Ibid.*, IV (June, 1895), 125-6.
[71] *Ibid.*, V (June, 1896), 180-1.

heyen, held its first meeting November 21, 1869. The last meeting is dated November 4, 1908. The object of the Philomathic Society, according to its Rules and Regulations, engrossed in a fine flourishing hand, "shall be to prepare its members for public speaking and to furnish their minds with facts and arguments relating to the various branches of science."[72] At one of the society's early meetings, "Rev. Peter descanted largely on the advantages derived from a debating Society, showing that men of otherwise small pretensions rise to distinction by a facility in the art of oratory."[73] At first the meetings were completely controlled by the faculty moderator, who chose the topics and judged the debates, but before the year was out the faculty member's role was reduced to that of a moderator properly speaking, and the students conducted their own society.

The first topic debated was whether the reading of novels should be encouraged. Other topics concerned the comparative blessings of city and country life, of riches and education, of agriculture and commerce, and the comparative destructiveness of war and intemperance. The same topics recurred for the first few years, but a number of topics on historical figures appeared in the seventies. Woman suffrage came up for discussion in 1872, and the eighties introduced genuine problems of the day, strictly local as well as national. After 1885 topics debated were the tariff, Chinese immigration, the value of strikes, baseball, Kansas prohibition, the Mills Bill (tariff), and Cleveland vs. Harrison as possible presidents. In debates on the proposition that smoking is injurious, vice was always triumphant. Among the topics debated during the nineties were government control of the railroads, the annexation of Cuba, the benefits of Socialism, the value of direct election of senators and of presidents, and the value of organized labor to society. Although the Rules and Regulations forbade it, personal animus sometimes enlivened the meetings. The important point was

[72] Records and Minutes, I, 29.
[73] Ibid., Dec. 5, 1869.

that the old Philomathic undoubtedly tricked a great number of students into finding out more about the world they lived in and into developing their talents for self-expression and persuasion.

The older students were avid followers of current political issues, and even in 1884 six students were old enough to vote in the presidential election. Two of them supported Blaine. Father Director Matthew Bradley reported: "All the students appeared to be much interested in political matters and were quite jubilant when the news of Cleveland's election was announced."[74] When William Jennings Bryan was in Atchison to give a lecture in 1897, the students invited him to call at the College, where they received him with great jubilation. As the *Abbey Student* explained: "In the political circles of the College, Bryan is a beloved idol."[75]

The annual oratory contest was a highlight of the school year. Most of the contestants evidently relied heavily on the emotional power of the current melodramatic temperance pieces. The contest of 1892, for example, included interpretations of "The Death Struggle," "A Drunkard's Death," and "Rum's Ruin."[76] During the nineties the standards of oratory improved, and student interest in oratory increased notably. Abbot Innocent once noted in his diary: "At the Professors' meeting this evening there was much dispute about elocution; it seems the younger Professors put too much stress on dramatic art."[77]

The younger professor most responsible for this activity was Father Philip Williams, who with the aid of a cleric, Frater Celestine Sullivan, was compiling the first book published by the young Abbey Student Press: *Elements of Expression, Vocal and Physical.*[78] As the title

74 Bradley to Wolf, Atchison, Nov. 28, 1884.
75 VII (Oct., 1897), 47.
76 *Abbey Student*, I (June, 1892), 107.
77 May 8, 1894.
78 Philip (William) Williams was born in Leavenworth, Kans., Apr. 22, 1869, professed July 11, 1889, ordained July 26, 1893, died Aug. 20, 1920. —*Necrologium*, No. 541.

indicates, the volume followed the Laws of Francois Delsarte, "the great Catholic philosopher of expression," and his intricate system of formal gestures. Many selections were chosen from Catholic authors not "to depreciate any of the noble names of literature" but simply "to remove writers of merit from cobwebbed shelves, where their beauties have too long been obscured."[79] Father Philip was responsible also for the appearance at St. Benedict's of some of the great professional actors.[80]

In some ways Father Philip was very similar to Father Andrew. Much more reserved than Father Andrew, he had a real appreciation for literature, which enriched his own life and that of his students. He was a man of more refined sensibility than the average at St. Benedict's. Beginning in 1890, he taught only eight years and then entered upon parish work because of weak health. While on the faculty, however, he did much to improve St. Benedict's, and his successful stimulation of interest in oratory and dramatics was carried on to another generation by his students, particularly by Fathers Ignatius Stein and Damian Lavery. Father Philip was the first pastor of St. Benedict's Church in Kansas City, Kansas, but after a few years was obliged to go to California on account of tuberculosis. His ability and charm as well as his all-embracing charity gave him extraordinary influence for good over souls both as teacher and as pastor.

A number of other societies were organized for the fulfillment of the student's spiritual and artistic needs. The Sodality of the Blessed Virgin began in 1875 and was quickly followed by an altar society, for the care of the students' chapel, and an acolytes' society. A Reading and Literary Association was reported in the catalog of 1881 and became the St. Thomas Aquinas Library Association in 1888. The dramatics society and the band were both sub-

[79] Second revised edition, 1896, 111.
[80] The tragedian Keane did readings at St. Benedict's, Apr. 1, 1896.—Wolf Diary. Ward and Skinner had also been presented from the tiny stage of Society Hall.—*Abbey Student*, X (Nov., 1900), 63.

ject to rather regular reorganization, but both played a great role in student life. The band was an essential ingredient of any celebration, and school could not close without it. In the catalog of 1887 the student choir was added to the roster, joined in the following year by a glee club and a quartette. The College acquired three more pianos at this time.[81] This burst of musical activity is traceable to the ability and enthusiasm of Father Alexius Grass, on loan from St. Vincent, who was an excellent music instructor. He built well, and after he left St. Benedict's the student choir continued to be well trained and sang polyphonic Masses and hymns excellently. Father Andrew began the first class in plain chant for students in 1901,[82] but four years passed before students and clerics sang the first Mass in Gregorian chant "a la Solesmes" on St. Benedict's Day, March 21, 1905.[83] Throughout these years the College had not only a band but also usually an orchestra. Abbot Innocent wanted everyone to acquire an appreciation for music, and he always encouraged some kind of community orchestra for the training of the clerics and for sheer enjoyment. On the other hand, Abbot Innocent had his doubts about popular music and forbade the playing of the "Guitarre, Mandolin, and Zither" by either monks or students.[84]

No year passed without some student effort in the field of drama. In lean years the students were satisfied with variety shows. When the College was particularly crowded before Bishop Fink Hall was completed, productions were presented with difficulty. In order to stage a show celebrating St. Patrick's Day in 1882, for example, a stage was erected in a dormitory and the beds stacked to the sides.[85] In 1877 a production of *Major André*, by Father Leo Haid, O.S.B., of St. Vincent, was considered good enough to stage for the townspeople in Corinthian Hall.[86]

---

[81] Wolf Diary, Aug. 24, 1888.
[82] *Abbey Student*, XI (Oct., 1901), 67.
[83] *Ibid.*, XIV (Apr., 1905), 255.
[84] Chapter Minutes, June 30, 1899.
[85] Wolf Diary, Mar. 17, 1882.
[86] *Ibid.*, Dec. 26, 1877; Jan. 1, 1878.

The Drama Association of the eighties gave way to the Shakespeare Club in 1893 and marks the dawning recognition that drama was literature and art. Even though thoroughly mutilated by the omission of all feminine parts, Shakespeare was staged and apparently enjoyed by the students.

Activities at St. Benedict's were tailored to fit the aims of the school, and the aims were always realistically chosen to fit the needs of the people the school served. The school's first purpose was to train priests who were to care for largely immigrant parishes, and the candidates for the priesthood came from the same immigrant groups. Furthermore, the school provided general and business training, again primarily to immigrants who were in the process of setting foot on the lower rungs of the economic ladder in their new homeland. Consequently, the practical and useful were always stressed more than the strictly cultural. Nevertheless, the need of cultural development was recognized, and Abbot Innocent in particular always tried to find time and occasion to fill this gap in the background of his community and its students. A course in drawing was offered, but at first it won little student interest. In the nineties, however, the art classes, though small, were active and had a studio on the second floor of the Old Priory. The crayon portraits and drawings popular at the time formed the bulk of the production, but some painting was done as well.[87] However, music, literature, drama, and oratory always provided the bulk of the cultural content of education.

Every student community naturally needs some kind of publication to chronicle its activities, attitudes, and private jokes. The usual bulletin board news sheets were short-lived, and like any other college, St. Benedict's needed also a journal to encourage serious thought and expression among its students. Towards the end of 1891 the suggestion was made to publish a quarterly to be

[87] *Abbey Student*, V (Oct., 1895), 17; (June, 1896), 153.

called the *Abbey Student.*[88] The first number, which appeared in December, was both a literary journal and a report of school life. At first the contents were composed largely of carefully corrected themes done for the various classes, but this practice was quickly abandoned for the usual earnest articles in the fields of literature, science, social problems, religion, and do-it-yourself verse. For some years the editorials, unsigned, were written by faculty members. The short squibs labelled "Locals" reflected college life, chronicling the fads of the day and the eternal esoteric joke. Through the ages, evidently, boys on discovering that their language possesses a greater wealth of vocabulary than they had first suspected, have found words more funny than useful, for example, "Who has discarded his efflorescent mustache? Come forward, H."[89] Intimate minutiae that later form the stuff of memory were also recorded:

> "—5 A.M. Newcomer—Hark! oh, I hear a wall falling!
> Old Timer—Shut up; it's only those punctual Minims."[90]

The Minims' donkey, Shakespeare, better known as Shake, was always good for a line, most often by being unfairly blamed for noises produced by snoring students. The *Abbey Student* continued to fill the dual role of literary publication and commentator on school life until the *Rambler* appeared in the autumn of 1921 to fill the need for a school newspaper.

After two years of operation the *Abbey Student* decided on vertical integration. Peter Boesen, a student at the time, was a typesetter and job printer of some experience. Income from subscriptions and the money reserved to print the next few issues in a commercial shop were used instead by buy second-hand type and a press. Father Luke Blahnik became director of the printing press— squeezed into a small room and hallway of the chemistry wing — and Boesen was foreman, assisted by an assort-

---

[88] Minutes of Professors' Meetings, Nov. 7, 1891.
[89] *Abbey Student*, I (June, 1892), 105.
[90] *Ibid.*, II (Dec., 1892), 53.

ment of amateurs: priests, clerics, and students.[91]   For some time the substitution of enthusiasm for experience was quite obvious in their productions, but such was the beginning of the present Abbey Student Press.   Better equipment and greater competence were both acquired in time; for example, a monotype caster was added in 1905 when Father Athanasius Koenn was manager of the Press. Abbot Innocent was quite proud of the *Abbey Student*, so completely the work of the students and school, and he was convinced that the publication was practically unique.[92]

Nineteenth-century athletics at St. Benedict's shows the strong influence of Abbot Innocent.   If he could have enforced his ideas, college life would have suffered some serious amputations, because on this point he completely lacked understanding not only of American boys but of boys.   His attitude is probably explained by his extreme nervousness and chronically bad health.   Sports gained but the barest toleration from him.   All forms of rivalry were to him but strife, faction, and a source of cliques. He opposed even class colors on this account and forbade printing photographs of persons, games, or clubs in the college catalog.[93]   He was appalled by college yells.   One wonders what the students thought when the following inspired editorial, unsigned, but written by Father Aloysius Bradley, appeared in their journal:

Any attempt to start a college yell will meet with the opposition of all respectable students.   The more the hoodlum and the rowdy are kept in the background, the more conspicuous will the gentleman appear.   Recognition purchased at the price of such barbarity cannot reflect credit on the college.   It should be the boast of this institution that her students are everywhere recognized by their cultured gentlemanly conduct. Any attempt to bring discredit upon us as students, let us resent with righteous indignation.[94]

[91] *Ibid.*, III (Feb., 1894), 77; Wolf Diary, Jan. 23, 1894.
[92] Wolf an Braunmueller, Atchison, Feb. 22, 1894. (AM)
[93] Wolf Diary, Feb. 27, 1896; Minutes of Professors' Meetings, Mar. 27, 1896; Board of Professors' Minutes, Apr. 7, 1910.
[94] *Abbey Student*, IV (Dec., 1894), 52.

Abbot Innocent maintained his low opinion of athletics to the end of his life. In 1910 he instructed his Prior, Father Leo Aaron:

I would also object to having reports in the Catalogue about baseball or any. . . other games. I know that some want to use such matter as an advertisement. Our aim should be to advertise our College by the advancement or progress of the students. If. . . sport is our forte we lose our purpose, to educate first of all young men for the priesthood, and then others for public civil life, and for that purpose hard study is required, which is not done by students who dream only of sports. Professors, who think sport should be as important as study, do not teach well either.[95]

Nevertheless, on this front the Abbot fought a steadily losing battle, for sports were always an important part of student life. From an early date intramural teams were rather well organized. The students needed little assistance in that department. On one occasion quite a crisis arose when a prefect appointed a Classical-Hall committee to organize the nines for a baseball league. The Commercial students went on strike against this loss of voice in the arrangements, the Director had to call a meeting, Abbot Innocent was called in to address it, and as a result the students elected their own committee to make up the teams.[96]

The College catalog of 1876 listed the Base Ball Club with other student organizations, but after Abbot Innocent took charge of the College, sports received no such recognition until 1887 when the College Athletic Association appeared with other student clubs. "Its competitive rehearsals are held on recreation days," explained the catalog. Nevertheless, the intramural season in baseball was always closed with an all-star or championship game. In 1892 the contending teams in the championship game were the Commercials and the Classics. For a number of years the opposing teams were the Seniors and the Juniors, and in the years around 1910 they were the World vs. Kansas.

[95] Wolf to Aaron, Newark, Apr. 4, 1910.
[96] Wolf to Heinz, Atchison, Apr. 12, 1891.

Baseball was the most popular sport, but football of one kind or other regularly put in its appearance, although it was periodically forbidden on account of its "unusual brutality."[97] Ultimately Abbot Innocent compromised and permitted football games if they were chaperoned by a prefect whose duty it was to prevent the rougher boys from joining in the game.[98]

The creation of playing fields had accompanied the completion of Bishop Fink Hall in 1883, and larger fields were completed in 1890.[99] Tennis courts and handball alleys were added gradually. Until comparatively recent times the most popular outdoor sport at St. Benedict's was handball. "Behind the handball alleys" is a nostalgic phrase implying either stolen smokes or the settlement of personal differences.

"Society Hall," which was a theatre, rumpus room, and skating rink in the basement of Bishop Fink Hall, was inadequate for recreation in bad weather. In 1898 the chapter decided to build a gymnasium at the end of the vineyard north of Bishop Fink Hall. The budget allotted for the construction of the gymnasium was $450.[100] In the *Abbey Student* Editor James Salmon (later Father Robert) opened the new school year with a long article on the benefits of athletics and demolished all objections. The gym had been completed, and the grateful student described this sixty-by-forty foot building:

Framed of solid timber, resting on a foundation of sturdy oak, crisscrossed and ribbed with heavy scantlings, well boarded and tightly shingled, stands our new gymnasium. Unpretentious in regard to beauty and style of architecture, it stands forth as a neat, spacious building, which will accommodate all or most of our students. The western interior is fitted out for handball, while the south is designed for a bowling alley. The north and eastern walls will be equipped with all manner of pulleys, weights and machines. Bars, traveling rings, trapeze, etc.,

[97] *Abbey Student,* IV (Dec., 1894), 61.
[98] Wolf to Engel, Atchison, Dec. 4, 1907. (SJA)
[99] Moved 5666 cubic yards at a cost of $670.—Director's Diary, Apr. 22, May 14, 1890.
[100] Chapter Minutes, Sept. 16, 1898.

will be attached to the transverse beams twenty feet from the floor.[101]

This barn-like gym was an eloquent symbol of the place of athletics in the College, but it did provide improved recreational facilities, and the students became rather fond of it.

The story of athletics at St. Benedict's — of the attitude towards sports and of the facilities provided — is similar to that of any other small college at the time. St. Benedict's simply moved with the times. By the end of the century discussion began regarding intercollegiate sports. Somewhat earlier the American abbots had begun informal discussions of their school problems in order to promote uniformity in curriculum and discipline. In 1894 these abbots agreed not to permit intercollegiate sports.[102] This decision was entered in the Corporation Minutes of St. Benedict's College, and Abbot Innocent continued to fight off attempts at change until after World War I.[103]

The students of course dissented, and the first "intercollegiate" game actually was played clandestinely in 1898. The Atchison *Globe* reported that football teams from St. Benedict's and the Atchison business colleges had played a practice game at Forest Park on November 16. The game consisted of two ten-minute halves, and St. Benedict's won 12-0. The reporter stated that this was St. Benedict's first game with an outside team and remarked that, given experience, the students from St. Benedict's should do well against other colleges. But the reporter added: "It is not probable, however, that the faculty will allow them to play with outside colleges."[104]

The official policy of the College was primly stated in a publicity release of 1909. Admitting to a lively program in intramural baseball, the author hastened to reassure the public:

[101] *Abbey Student,* VIII (Oct., 1898), 61.
[102] Wolf memorandum, Apr. 22, 1894.
[103] May 10, 1894.
[104] Nov. 17, 1898.

St. Benedict's allows no games with outsiders. Her ambition is to develop home athletics. . . St. Benedict's does not covet a reputation for athletics, believing that in an institution of higher education athletics should be relegated to the lowest place in the order of importance. She encourages athletics only for the good of it — the recreation and physical development. Her students are forever reminded that their parents send them to College to get an education — to work, not to learn to play.[105]

But Abbot Innocent was ultimately forced to give way on this point. When the reorganization of the school was under way in 1919, the new body of deans recommended that under proper regulations intercollegiate games be permitted. The faculty was not confident of securing this change because only a few years earlier a committee of the prefects, Fathers Sebastian Weissenberger and Sylvester Schmitz, had asked the Abbot to permit a few basketball games with outside teams. The old Abbot had answered with finality, "I would rather let you take my head off than grant such a permission."[106] But by 1919 Abbot Innocent was resigned to the inevitable and finally capitulated.[107]

In the spring of 1920 St. Benedict's fielded a varsity baseball team.[108] In the following autumn the deans were faced with the problem of providing suitable periods for varsity football practice. After due consideration they set aside the hours from four to six on Tuesdays, Wednesdays, and Thursdays for this purpose.[109] St. Benedict's was not rushing headlong into an overemphasis of athletics.

The Curriculum

The present St. Benedict's College is a product of evolution, largely determined by two forces, the demands

---

[105] *Catholic Tribune*, St. Joseph, Mo., Oct. 9, 1909, in Scrapbook 3, 65.
[106] Sylvester Schmitz, O.S.B., The Development of the Curriculum of St. Benedict's College, 1915-1945, unpublished manuscript, 79.
[107] Minutes of Deans' Meetings, Dec. 14, 1919.
[108] *Ibid.*, Apr. 20, 1920.
[109] *Ibid.*, Sept. 30, 1920.

of contemporary society as well as the needs and dreams of the students and faculty who are the College. The process is traceable mostly in the work of committees. They are to a college what the vital organs are to the human body. Year after year the committees churn away, revising and rebuilding, often under the illusion that their creations are permanent, only to continue the endless discussions, proposals, and changes in the future. At St. Benedict's these life processes are recorded in the Minutes of the Board of Professors (1877-1927) and the Minutes of Professors' Meetings (1882-1907). The first recorded meeting of the Board of Professors was held on January 17, 1877, shortly after Abbot Innocent became superior in Atchison. Little more than five years later it was decided that since the young and inexperienced clerics were normally at least half the faculty, two faculty bodies were necessary. The Professors' Meetings, which included the clerics, discussed the affairs of the College but were supposed primarily to aid in training these young clerics as teachers. The Board of Professors, on the other hand, was thereafter attended only by chapter members, who had a consultative vote on questions concerning college policy.[110]

Until 1885 the College catalog announced three curricula, namely, a six-year classical, a three-year commercial, and a preparatory. The six years of the classical curriculum were traditionally labelled Grammar, Syntax, Humanities, Poetry, Rhetoric, and Philosophy. The complete curriculum was actually taught only after the growth of the faculty and the student body made the program practical. The fifth year was added in 1879, and no algebra, geometry, or Greek had been taught prior to that time. A year of philosophy was of course always taught for the clerics.[111] Class periods had been reduced to three-quarters of an hour in 1878 to permit a greater number of courses in the curriculum.[112]

---

110 Board of Professors' Minutes, note in Abbot Innocent's hand, Oct. 19, 1882.
111 Wolf an Wimmer, Atchison, Apr. 15, 1879. (SVA)
112 Wolf Diary, Sept. 8, 1878.

The first notable change in the curriculum occurred in 1886. The Third Plenary Council of Baltimore had recommended an extended curriculum for the classical divisions of Catholic colleges engaged in training students for the priesthood. The major change was extending the study of the classics to six years.[113] The notable differences in the St. Benedict's catalog were the addition of a specific description of courses and textbooks, the study of German or French as well as vocal music was made mandatory for each year, geography was deemphasized, and introductory courses in the natural sciences appeared in the last four years. The only complete change was in the sixth year, which had previously attempted to cover the whole of philosophy, but was now devoted to the usual courses in language, mathematics, and history, plus an introduction to bookkeeping for future pastors. Seventh and eighth years, devoted to philosophy, were added in the catalog in 1887. Actually the faculty was unable to teach the sixth year of classical studies until 1895, and it was dropped again in 1904.[114]

In the 1890's a student following the classical curriculum was required to take five-year courses in each of the following subjects: mathematics, English, history, Latin, religion, and vocal music. A modern language was also mandatory, a student having the choice between German and French. In addition he studied Greek and natural science during his final three years. During his first two years he had been taught penmanship. His courses in mathematics included arithmetic, algebra, geometry, and trigonometry. His English courses had taught him grammar, reading, spelling, rhetoric, composition, literature, and elocution. He had been introduced to ancient, medieval, modern, and American history. Latin grammar was studied throughout the five years, and the student read Nepos, Ovid's *Metamorphoses*, Livy's *De Urbe Condita*, Virgil's *Aeneid*, Horace's *Odes, Epistles, and Satires*, and

[113] Minutes of Professors' Meetings, Mar. 30, 1886.
[114] Board of Professors' Minutes, Apr. 8, 1895; Minutes of Professors' Meetings, May 16, 1905.

Cicero's *Orations*. In Greek, besides a firm grounding in grammar, a student delved into Xenophon's *Anabasis* and *Cyropaedia* and into Homer's *Odyssey*. Science courses introduced a student to botany, zoology, chemistry, and "natural philosophy."

The commercial curriculum continued to cover three years of study. A student following this curriculum in the 1890's studied English, arithmetic or algebra, book-keeping, penmanship, religion, and history or geography during each of his three years. In his final year he followed courses also in shorthand, commercial law, political economy, and civil government. The curriculum was designed "to impart a thorough commercial or business education."

Examinations at St. Benedict's were oral until the end of the century. Oral examinations had their disadvantages, and Abbot Innocent once issued a circular reminding the faculty that at the examinations "the scholars should speak more than the Professors."[115] In 1900 the faculty finally decided that the examinations should be written, but the change was not welcomed by many of the professors.[116]

St. Benedict's in 1873 began to grant diplomas certifying the graduates of the commercial curriculum to be "Masters of Accounts." In the 1890's the annual number of such graduates sometimes reached ten. The College catalog announced Bachelor of Arts and even Master of Arts degrees until 1886 when the faculty decided that since philosophy was not being offered, the degrees should no longer be announced in the catalog.[117] The offer of the Bachelor of Arts degree was restored in the catalog of 1895. The College granted a few A.B.'s before 1910 but only to priests or on one or two occasions to doctors of medicine who successfully completed a course in philosophy either at St. Benedict's or elsewhere.[118] The first

---

[115] Wolf Diary, Jan. 26, 1882.
[116] Minutes of Professors' Meetings, June 7, 1900.
[117] Board of Professors' Minutes, May 25, 1886.
[118] *Ibid.*, June 4, 1883; Oct. 16, 1894; June 10, 1902.

A.B. was awarded to Reverend Nicholas Neusius on June 4, 1883.

Abbot Innocent disliked secular ceremonies, which always made him nervous, and when he became president of St. Benedict's College, he reduced the annual commencement exercises to the minimum of formality. As he wrote at the end of his first school year, he decided "to skip the spectacle" and had completed the awarding of prizes in half an hour.[119] Furthermore, as the students were eager to catch early trains, this academic ceremony was held immediately after breakfast. By 1900 the school reputation demanded slightly more respect for the traditional closing of the scholastic year, but even then the Abbot had given but little ground. As was typical of him, he stressed the religious aspects of the ceremony, and in that year, for example, school was closed with a Solemn High Mass and Te Deum. In Society Hall after breakfast the Abbot awarded the degree of Master of Accounts to four graduates, presented the coveted gold or silver medals to the scholastic leaders in each class, and announced the winners of 142 premiums. The reading of an even larger number of 'distinctions' was omitted for lack of time. John Neu delivered a brief valedictory, and the shouting students were released to dash for their trains.[120]

Abbot Innocent usually gave the boys a brief and intensely practical talk on these occasions. Among his papers are the notes for one of these farewell addresses, delivered in June, 1881:

My young friends:

During the past year you have studied hard, or if not, have taken on yourselves punishments whether willingly or unwillingly. For what purpose? Most of you have had a purpose, an aim, an end, which you wished to obtain. Some have studied to graduate, others to become priests, to become bookkeepers, tradesmen; others had no purpose. Those who had a purpose generally applied their time very well; those who had no

[119] Wolf an Bartl, Atchison, June 19, 1877.
[120] *Abbey Student*, IX (July, 1900), 609.

purpose, or were undetermined, lost a great many hours by idling. The purpose of life is, as we have learned in catechism, to know God, love and serve Him in this world, and to be happy with Him in the next. This general purpose every one must have, but it allows us to select among the particular states, and this is called vocation. Purpose gives us prudence and fortitude, while the lack of it makes us imprudent and weak. . .

The Abbot then went on to remind the students that when they left the supervised college life, they were guarded and watched by God and His Holy Angels. He admonished them not to be ashamed to do good. He dwelt on this point at some length, probably feeling that human respect was a temptation that loomed large in children of immigrants. After admonishing the students to avoid bad company, not to be idle, and to receive the Sacraments as often as they had at school, he sent them on their way with his blessing.

More important changes than those indicated in the catalog were slowly taking place. During the nineteenth century St. Benedict's had two libraries, a theological library for the monks and a general library for the students. Abbot Innocent was careful to acquire the essential theological works and a few most needed items for the College, but no more was possible for some time. During the early years annual library expenses fluctuated from a low of $36.50 in 1878 to a high of $753.53 in 1885. At the same time the annual laundry bill was about $400, and the operating expenses of the stable were about the same.[121]

The students' circulating library was increased by fifty "select volumes" bought with students' contributions in 1876-77, and eighty-six volumes were added in the following year.[122] Most small-college libraries were inadequate in those days, but by the 1890's growth was more promising. By 1895 the faculty voted to abandon the "readers" that had supplied the literature portion of

---

121 Annual Statements, *passim.*
122 Wolf Diary, Sept. 15, 1877; June 17, 1879.

all English courses until that time and to introduce instead complete masterpieces from standard authors. The wily professors added that "Some reading could be for enjoyment, with the element of understanding allowed to lie out of sight."[123]   In 1892 the monastic library numbered 7500 books and 700 pamphlets, and the student library contained 1829 volumes.[124]   By 1900 Abbot Innocent was spending two thousand dollars a year for books for both libraries.   His first concern was to obtain the standard theological collections, and he considered St. Benedict's collection of canon law at that time to be superior to that of any other library in the United States.   Before he died Abbot Innocent had built up a wisely-selected theological library at St. Benedict's.

The natural sciences received more sympathetic attention than might have been expected in a school devoted primarily to the classics.   But the wonders of science, with their promise of a new era, were beginning to command universal admiration.   And besides, Father Boniface had an indefatigable interest in the wonders of nature. Furthermore, no college could convince the public of its right to the name unless it had a museum.

When Father James Defouri, one of the earliest pioneers in the Vicariate, left the Diocese of Leavenworth and moved to Santa Fe, he donated his collection of minerals and mounted animals to St. Benedict's.[125]   Students and friends began to send rocks and plants from far and near.   The donations of course included such items as an alleged petrified elephant tooth and "a very perfect alcoholic specimen of a double-headed rattlesnake."[126] But they included also 130 birds, all, with one exception, taken in Atchison County.[127]   By 1885 the museum had also an herbarium of 1500 specimens.   Both Father Boniface and Father Pirmin Koumly were avid collectors and bird-watchers.   Father Pirmin, at that time pastor in

[123] Minutes of Professors' Meetings, Oct. 22, 1895.
[124] Report to U.S. Bureau of Education, Mar. 31, 1892, draft.
[125] Wolf Diary, Aug., 1877.
[126] Catalog, 1890, 69.
[127] Catalog, 1879, 23.

Seneca, was elected a member of the American Ornithologists' Union in 1892.[128]

During the eighties, Father Boniface, who had acquired a magic lantern, gave numerous illustrated lectures on geology and geography as well as lectures on magnetism and electricity. Of the first classes in the natural sciences, the college catalog reported: "Several informal volunteer classes were also formed during the Second Session [of 1878-1879] in the Departments of Botany, Geology, Paleontology, and Entomology. The classes will be continued, but must be conducted in this informal way, separate from the regular curriculum, till the growing demand for these pursuits shall justify their adoption in the regular course." The recommendations of the Council of Baltimore helped to stimulate interest in the sciences, and formal courses were announced in the catalog of 1885-1886, but even before that St. Benedict's had a "physical laboratory." Its origin is unrecorded, but by 1885 it was "being added to right along, in order to make its appointments complete. Among the larger pieces quite recently added may be mentioned a new plunge battery, an inclination and declination compass, and a dissected Ruhmkorff coil." The science courses taught were elementary, but after Father Leo Aaron was ordained in 1899, St. Benedict's had at least a full time teacher for the courses, though he had no professional training. No doubt the one who journeyed to the Columbian Exposition in Chicago in 1893 was Father Leo, accompanied perhaps by Father Boniface. From the wealth of exhibits at the exposition were selected a number of pieces of scientific apparatus, including "Queen's Patent Triple Plate Toepler-Holtz Electrical Machine with twenty inch revolving plates."[129]

Towards the end of the century academic standards came into greater prominence. Bishops of course had always demanded adequate classical preparation for their

128 *Abbey Student*, II (Dec., 1892), 49.
129 *Ibid.*, III (Feb., 1894), 83.

minor seminarians. The essential features of a respectable academy were traditional and well understood, but the appearance of courses in natural science was only one indication that times were changing. As Abbot Innocent explained to the Abbot of Metten:

We are not molested by the government about studies, but we are much bound by *public opinion*, which is often blind and tyrannical. We are subject to it because our livelihood depends on it, but even such institutions as are independent in this respect cannot [ignore public opinion] unless they want to get the reputation of being old-fashioned and out of date. Still we see to it that in our schools, in spite of public opinion, the classic studies are taught well, and the results show that our students in higher institutions are among the first.[130]

Abbot Innocent was confident that compared with other Catholic colleges St. Benedict's was not substandard. As he wrote to the Director, Father Gerard Heinz, in 1891:

I am glad that you see other Colleges. Three years ago, I believe, you thought we were not progressive enough; that other Colleges were ahead. Considering the pay I think we do very much. If we wouldn't have the heavy debt and could use the savings for improvements we would soon be ahead of others. Besides, we educate more *poor* ones for the priesthood than half a dozen Jesuit Colleges.[131]

A few years later, however, the professors, after comparing standards in academic grading with those of other colleges, decided that St. Benedict's had better raise the passing grade to seventy per cent in the classical courses, although the old standard (sixty per cent?) was retained for the commercial courses.[132]

By that time the small classical colleges were looking up to see that the larger schools were growing away from them and that the term college was beginning to have a different meaning. The greatest pressure for change came from the need to provide students with a curriculum that would make them acceptable to professional schools. Agitation on standards in Catholic colleges began largely

130 Wolf an Braunmueller, Atchison, Apr. 11, 1888. (AM)
131 Wolf to Heinz, Atchison, Feb. 24, 1891.
132 Minutes of Professors' Meetings, July 24, 1894.

as a result of the work of Rev. Thomas J. Conaty, the rector of the Catholic University of America. The University constitution provided for the affiliation of seminaries and colleges, and the Rector first moved to bring to closer agreement the standards of his University and the seminaries. He next raised the question of standards in the colleges. The Association of Catholic Colleges held its first meeting in Chicago on April 12-13, 1899.[133] Abbot Innocent attended this first meeting as the representative of St. Benedict's.

Probably impressed by the united front the Jesuits displayed, the Archabbot of St. Vincent suggested that the Benedictines assemble to discuss educational matters before the next meeting of the Association.[134] Consequently a preliminary meeting was held at St. John's Abbey immediately after a General Chapter in 1899. The following year Abbot Innocent, as president of the Congregation, issued a circular announcing a meeting of delegates from the various colleges of the Congregation with instructions that the delegates were not to adjourn before completing a schedule of a full classical curriculum. Furthermore, each delegate was instructed to sign this schedule. Any minority report was similarly to be signed. The purpose of this determination was not to introduce a new curriculum immediately but to have a uniform plan ready for the next meeting of the Association of Catholic Colleges.[135] The delegates' report included a curriculum that devoted half the hours to Latin and Greek, dividing the other half among English, history, mathematics, and religion. Introductory courses in the natural sciences were postponed to the two-year course in philosophy.[136] The report produced some debate at St. Benedict's but no essential change in the curriculum. The Association of Catholic Colleges never succeeded in uniting the colleges

---

[133] Peter E. Hogan, S.S.J., *Catholic University of America, 1896-1903, Rectorship of Thomas J. Conaty* (Washington, 1949), 63-70.
[134] Wolf to Engel, Atchison, May 25; June 8, 1899. (SJA)
[135] *Idem*, June 7, 1900. (SJA)
[136] *Report of the Delegates of the Benedictine Colleges of the American-Cassinese Congregation, July 11, 1900.*

for purposes of standardization, but it did cause them to get acquainted with the idea.

Meanwhile the faculty continued to debate what kind of school they wished to develop, and this discussion soon led to attempts by at least one group to secure more voice in making school policies. At first Abbot Innocent had been president, director, board of discipline, treasurer—everything. Since the eighties the College had had a director, whose powers were undefined and practically depended on the Abbot's approval. The priests on the faculty had a consultative vote on issues concerning the College. Until 1910 the director, with the Abbot's concurrence, was predominant in fixing the policies of the College so long as the faculty was not so strongly opposed that accomplishment was made impractical. This arrangement worked well enough until grave differences of opinion arose regarding the curriculum.

In the midst of this debate about the curriculum, Abbot Innocent in 1907 was suffering a severe attack of erysipelas. With his approval and on the advice of the Seniors, Prior Boniface Verheyen made several changes in personnel. Father Philip Williams had been ordered to California by his doctor, and a good administrator was needed to replace him in building St. Benedict's parish in Kansas City. Father Francis McDonald, who had been director of the College since 1904, was chosen for this task. Father Aloysius Bradley, the imaginative and energetic leader of the group pressing for what Father Aloysius termed the "New" St. Benedict's, was appointed director of the College. At the same time, in the first serious move to secure professional training outside the fields of theology, philosophy, and the arts, Fathers Vincent Kreis, Lambert Burton, Felix Nolte, and Justin Sion were sent to summer school at the University of Chicago.[137]

When Father Aloysius was appointed director, the enrollment jumped from 183 to 257. In the next three years he obviously had a large part in developing the

[137] Wolf Diary, June 28, 1907.

285

"New" St. Benedict's, particularly the plans for an entirely new group of buildings on the river bluff. He was a man of many valuable qualities, but unfortunately he was arbitrary in determining the policies of the College, and this trait was naturally resented by at least a part of the faculty. This personal tension, in addition to the existing debate regarding the lines along which the College should develop, finally resulted in the sudden appearance in 1910 of a proposal for a Standing Committee on Studies and Discipline.

The committee was to include the Prior, the Director, the Rector of the scholasticate, one prefect chosen by the Abbot, a member chosen by the Abbot from each board of examiners, and one member chosen by the chapter. The Abbot was to delegate management of the College to this committee, and both the Abbot and the committee could take the initiative in college affairs. The committee was to ensure uniformity and stability in the management of the College and the scholasticate.[138]

Father Joseph Sittenauer, rector of the scholasticate, read this proposal to the chapter on March 18, 1910. In two following meetings the chapter discussed the question in rather lively fashion. Father Lambert Burton, who was to devote years of hard work to Benedictine education, insisted that the proposal was both practical and necessary in view of the growth of the College. Fathers Damian Lavery, Benedict Kappler, and Aloysius Bradley, the director, attacked the proposal as unsound and unjust. Father Benedict considered it a menace to the Director's freedom of action, which was precisely the purpose of the proposal. Father Aloysius protested that "if Father Abbot was not competent to exercise his authority in matters of studies and discipline under present arrangements with one Director, he would not be competent to exercise such authority with a committee of seven constituted to manage the college."[139] The question never came to a vote, but the incident marks the end of Abbot Innocent's

138 Printed proposal, dated by Wolf, Mar. 22, 1910.
139 Chapter Minutes, Mar. 29, 1910.

college, for the next few years saw important changes in St. Benedict's.

St. Benedict's remained essentially an academy until after World War I. Moving the study halls and dormitories to the new Administration Building on the bluff in 1911, however, was a symbolic change from a pattern of life that for half a century had been followed in the narrower confines of the old buildings. Since 1883, when Bishop Fink Hall had been completed, the only increase in space for the school had occurred when the monastery was built in 1893. The College of 1910, therefore, was physically very similar to that of the 1880's. In Bishop Fink Hall the kitchen and Society Hall were in the basement; the dining rooms, museum, and library on the first floor; the Director's office and study halls on the second floor; class rooms on the third floor; and dormitories in the attic. The old Priory had showers in the basement; parlors and some private rooms on the main floor; lockers and private rooms on the second floor; and a dormitory for thirty-three persons in the attic. Lemke Hall (the present chemistry wing) had a lavatory in the basement; the science laboratory and the Abbey Student Press on the first floor; the infirmary, toilets, and bathtubs on the second floor; and a chapel on the third floor.[140]

The battle over the proposed Standing Committee on Studies and Discipline was more conclusive than the minutes of the chapter indicate. Changes began immediately, according to Abbot Innocent's diary of 1910:

June 23: Chapter at which officers resigned.
June 27: Told Father Aloysius to be pastor of St. Benedict's, Kansas City.
July 3: Appointed Father Damian Director.[141]

Father Damian Lavery was to be director for the next twelve years. His solid virtue, fraternal charity, sound common sense, and good humor provided stability in the midst of the changes that were to come.

[140] Wolf to Owen Doyle, Atchison, Dec. 31, 1909, draft.
[141] Abbot Innocent kept a microscopic diary in his Ordo at this time. The chapter of June 23 must have been informal, for it is unrecorded. Annual resignation of officials is traditional in monastic communities, but this is the only time Abbot Innocent made note of it.

CHAPTER IX

Abbot Martin Veth

The Right Reverend Martin Veth, second abbot of St. Benedict's, was the second child and the only son of John and Ottilia (Fick) Veth. He had four sisters, one of whom died in infancy. Martin was born September 25, 1874, in Dettelbach, Bavaria, and was baptized two days later. His father was a miller, and in 1884 he decided, like so many of his countrymen, to improve his economic condition by emigrating to America. The year 1884 was one of depression and a bad year for all laboring men. After a few months' hardship in Buffalo, New York, the impoverished Veths moved on to Atchison where Charles Goodrich helped them. The families remained life-long friends.

According to his brief autobiography, Martin acquired a newspaper route and soon developed it to the point that he needed a pony to carry the papers. The money he thus earned was sufficient, he wrote, to pay for the modest family home. He was serious and hard-working, and he never enjoyed a real boyhood. In later years he could never understand the necessity of play, and even his notions of a hobby were very restricted — his own was the study of Dante.

Martin completed the grades at St. Benedict's parochial school and entered the academy division of St. Benedict's College as a first-year Latin student in 1888. Two years later he entered the scholasticate and became a boarding student. He entered the novitiate in 1893. The monastery on Second Street had just been completed, and Abbot Innocent decided that he could now train his novices at home. Father Martin always deplored the haphazard training that resulted. He and his class (Ignatius Stein and George Keim) received the cowl on St. Benedict's Day in July but had no novice master until Father Boniface Verheyen's appointment in September. The three novices received little spiritual training since most of their time was devoted to manual labor. Even so, Father Boniface must have been a helpful novice master, for young Frater Martin recorded a number of conferences with him, and the novice's diary indicates a beginning of good self-knowledge. Martin Veth was by nature timid and indecisive, and these traits stand out in his novitiate diary. For example, after a conference with Father Boniface, Frater Martin exhorted himself, "Be bold and you will be generous. . . get over sensitiveness. . . doubt. Act boldly. . . ignore all uneasiness, doubts, etc."[1] But he never really succeeded in altering these characteristics, and they would be the root of many difficulties throughout his life.

In 1897 Frater Martin was sent to Sant' Anselmo, the international Benedictine college in Rome, to complete his studies in theology. At the end of his second year he was dissatisfied with his grades, but Abbot Innocent reassured him, "I must say that I was not disappointed. I see you were. Well, that comes from the different way of looking at it. I judge from the side of your talent, and you from your diligence. . . You could not expect to be as good as brilliant students are. So don't let that trouble you, since it does not trouble your Abbot."[2] Frater Martin passed his licentiate, but even before his ordination he had worked himself into a state of sleeplessness and continual headaches. He was ordained at the Abbey of Einsiedeln on July 16, 1899, and a week later offered his first Mass there at Our Lady's pilgrimage altar.

In later years when discussing the value of an education at Sant' Anselmo, Abbot Martin wrote that he placed more hope in the students' opportunities for developing

[1] Veth Diary, Apr. 23, 1894.
[2] Wolf to Veth, Atchison, July 24, 1899

religious spirit than in their intellectual attainments. He wanted his monks to return from Sant' Anselmo with high monastic ideals and to take the lead in promoting those ideals in their home monastery.[3] That Sant' Anselmo students became acquainted with the ideals and trends of Benedictine life throughout the world was a notable advantage of the school, but Abbot Martin was also stating what Rome had meant to him. During his years as a student there he had the opportunity of visiting most of the European monasteries. He was privileged to make a retreat at Maredsous under Dom Columba Marmion, then prior of Mont César. He preferred the chant and the recitation of the divine office as carried out at Maredsous, because he thought it more masculine and less nervous than that at Beuron and Maria Laach.[4]

Furthermore, he formed friendships that were kept alive by correspondence through the years. These friendships were not very intimate, for as a student he wrote rather formal letters even to his family and signed them stiffly, P. Martin Veth, O.S.B. At Sant' Anselmo he came to know and admire Alcuin Deutsch, later abbot of St. John's; Lawrence Zeller, eventually the abbot of St. Matthias in Trier and finally an archbishop in South America; and particularly Fidelis von Stotzingen, later Abbot Primate. These were the men, among his correspondents at any rate, whose ideals and ideas he valued, and his relationship to them was always more that of the disciple than of the friend.

Back in Atchison in 1901 Father Martin taught most of the courses in theology. His services as a trained theologian were sought in revising the diocesan statutes. He was the abbey librarian from 1912 to 1921 and master of the clerics from 1914 to 1920. From 1906 to 1921 he was chaplain of Mount St. Scholastica Convent, and throughout his life he found this type of work most congenial.

[3] Veth to von Stotzingen, Atchison, Feb. 25, 1924. (SA)
[4] Veth Diary, Aug. 10; Sept. 16, 1900.

In 1921 the Abbot Primate, Fidelis von Stotzingen, Father Martin's old Roman friend, asked Abbot Innocent for Father Martin as *Magister Alumnorum* (master of students) at Sant' Anselmo. Abbot Innocent replied that although Father Martin was a good religious and gave perfect example in observing the Rule, he had been a failure as master of the clerics. He had found leading young people very difficult, was constantly running for advice to the Prior and the Abbot but then could not carry out the advice. The young priests, Abbot Innocent added, said that Father Martin lacked prudence and patience; that he was severe on small faults; and that he kept everyone unhappy. The Abbot concluded that if Father Martin could not keep order at home, he certainly could not do so at Sant' Anselmo.[5]

Father Martin's experiences with the clerics are necessary to understand some of his problems as abbot, since four months after Abbot Innocent's letter to the Abbot Primate, Father Martin was elected second abbot of St. Benedict's. In the election of November 10, 1921, Father Martin was a compromise candidate. The younger men idolized Father Lambert Burton, for years rector of the scholasticate, who had been a powerful influence in their formation and had given so many of them the monastic and educational ideals that are notable in that generation. The older men preferred Father Francis McDonald, who had been director of the college years earlier, was currently an outstanding pastor, and who was a man of impressive presence. Although Father Martin was a compromise candidate, the quality that recommended him to the community was uncompromising, for he was almost universally respected as a truly spiritual man. Father Martin was elected on the third ballot by little more than the necessary two-third majority. His election was confirmed by the Holy See on November 15, and he was blessed on December 27, 1921.

Physically the new Abbot was delicately built, five

[5] Wolf an von Stotzingen, Atchison, July 7, 1921. (SA)

feet, eight inches tall and had small features and a fair complexion. He had a high forehead, blue eyes, a small mouth, and his brown hair had turned grey before he was elected abbot at the age of forty-seven. He chose as his motto the words *Oculis ac manibus in coelum* from the antiphon of the office of his patron saint. He himself was a man of prayer and an ascetic. In his view his task as abbot was to lead his community to a deeper spirituality. He wanted to make St. Benedict's a spiritual center comparable to the famous European abbeys.

Abbot Martin was determined that his monks should be first and foremost men of prayer. He taught this religious principle in every conference, in almost every chapter, and most of all by his own life. His belief that men of prayer was the community's greatest need was reinforced by the ideas of Abbot Zeller and the Abbot Primate. Abbot Lawrence Zeller believed that the broader fields of Benedictine work in America had been providential but that the time was ripe to "build up the inner, more normal Benedictine life in the cloister, with prayer, etc.," and that American Benedictinism was "poor in ideals."[6]

The Abbot Primate's thoughts were very similar. Commenting on the undesirability of the Atchison monks taking charge of an Amarillo high school, he wrote, "It is of the greatest importance that our abbeys in America should develop the inner cloistral life more and more and place the greatest importance on that. There is great danger that 'the pioneer stage' will last too long, at least in its effects."[7]

Abbots Zeller and Von Stotzingen were doubtless correct, but the American Benedictines were not without ideals, although they were not the ideals of the Beuronese Congregation from which both abbots came. Archabbot Wimmer's model of monasticism was the missionary monks of the centuries immediately following St. Benedict. He

---

[6] Notes of a conversation held in September, 1925, in Veth Mass-intention record, 1924-26.

[7] Von Stotzingen an Veth, Rome, Dec. 27, 1934.

saw an analogy between immigrant America and the early mission to the Germanic tribes. The ideals of his foundation, in other words, were drawn from history, while the ideals of the Beuronese and French congregations had more literary roots. The missionary era, or pioneer stage, had passed, of course, but what the American monks lacked was not so much ideals as a theory or theology of monasticism. Abbot Martin proceeded to supply this lack in his own community.

He did succeed in promoting a richer interior life, and the accomplishment is the more remarkable since he achieved this spiritual goal in spite of lacking most of the qualities of natural leadership. He tended to be suspicious and narrow minded, and his usual reaction to any new proposal or question was negative, apparently on the assumption that he could always say yes later if really necessary or desirable. Every slightest sign of human weakness raising its ugly head in his own life was met with a prompt penance. But applying the same principle to his monks merely made him appear harsh and petty. Sometimes the results were comic. The clerics once asked him for permission to go ice-skating on a Sunday afternoon. He explained his refusal by asking, "What would the Protestants say if you broke through the ice and drowned *on Sunday?*"

Abbot Martin really lived St. Benedict's Rule, and he realized intensely that he was the father of the community, but his concept of a father stressed duty and obedience, with all signs of affection being rather strictly limited to the spiritual realm. He never seemed completely at ease with his monks, and his greatest effort at bonhommie was to puff rather ineffectually on a cigar on St. Benedict's Day, Christmas, and Easter. Finally, Abbot Martin never learned to tolerate honest and open difference of opinion. He tended to avoid friction by avoiding advice.

These were the natural handicaps under which Abbot Martin labored, but in many ways he was an outstandingly successful abbot. His contradictions were summarized in his spiritual conferences. He was not a commanding figure, his voice was thin and rather irritating, his manner of speaking, nervous and distracting — he bounced on his toes and toyed with his pectoral cross — but what he had to say was impressively solid. Numerous retreatants had the same strangely impressive experience, for after he became abbot he gave more than thirty-six retreats, eight in one year, an unusually large number for one in his position. That most retreatants considered him an unusually good retreat master is not surprising, since the spiritual life was so thoroughly real to him.

During the school year Abbot Martin normally gave the community a spiritual conference weekly. When he visited Maria Laach in 1925, he was much impressed by the Abbot's role as the spiritual director and teacher of that community. He notes that the Abbot of Maria Laach gave three conferences a week on the "Holy Rule in its application to modern times and needs — not so much its historical side, nor even its moral or ascetical, but more its psychology, religious principles, philosophy."[8] Abbot Martin pursued this ideal throughout his regime at St. Benedict's. He was concerned for the spiritual welfare also of the monks engaged in parochial work, encouraging them in their parish school duties and in preaching, as well as unlocking the treasures of the liturgy for their parishioners. His spirituality made him useful also to the Congregation, and he served for many years as one of its official visitators.

After his election Abbot Martin continued giving spiritual conferences to the Sisters of Mount St. Scholastica Convent and was spiritual director to individual Sisters, some even half across the globe. A Benedictine nun of the St. Ottilien missionary congregation had studied English at Mount St. Scholastica's and was then sent to a post in the Philippines. Through the years she secured her spiritual direction by mail from Abbot Martin. "When I was in trouble or needed advice," she writes, "I used to call on Abbot Martin, and I always received help."[9]

[8] Veth Mass-intention record, 1924-26.
[9] Sister M. P., O.S.B., to Beckman, Maasin, Nov. 4, 1953.

His advice to this Sister probably reflected what Abbot Martin himself was striving for. On one occasion he wrote:

You ask for a recipe for cheerfulness. It is not an easy thing to suggest a short way to acquire this beautiful virtue. . . The secret of cheerfulness lies in resignation to God's holy will, both in doing and in suffering. I am glad you feel the need of it; it shows that you are trying to acquire it. Natural cheerfulness as a disposition is a blessed gift, but better still and more meritorious is that supernatural cheerfulness which is acquired by hard labor in resisting the tendency to bitterness and discouragement and sadness. Cheerfulness is on the outside; as a virtue it has its roots in humility and selfdenial, and is a result of the mortification of our sensitive self-love. Try, for love of God to make others happy around you and to forget your own petty feelings and grievances. Humble yourself nicely to our Lord when you have shown or given way to your feelings. Don't *be* cross because you *have been* cross; in other words, bear your infirmities patiently and keep on trying to resist your sensitiveness. Pray for cheerfulness — and pray for me.

On another occasion Sister asked him to advise her how to be a good superior. The Abbot stressed prayer first and then:

Have a compassionate, mild and loving heart for all; have God in view and when you must correct, let it be with the aim to bring others nearer to God. Learn to be patient and to wait, and do not be surprised at the many infirmities in others, and do not get upset at the opposition you meet with in your efforts for their welfare.

St. Bernard says: "You owe your subjects three things: word, example, and prayer; the greatest of these is prayer." And St. Augustine: "We warn others that they may avoid evil; we teach them that they may be instructed; but to convert them we must pray for them." It is wonderful how suddenly God often steps in when we pray for others. Do not give way to worry and anxiety. Take reasonable care, do quietly what you clearly see you can and ought to do for others, and then leave everything completely and entirely to the disposal and guidance of Divine Providence. Speak less to your subjects and more to God about them.

Although Abbot Martin could be almost intolerably irritating about small points, these ideals for a good shepherd help to explain why he was a most kind and loving father to any monk with really serious trouble.

Shortly after his election Abbot Martin wrote that "there is on the whole a good spirit, and I must say I was edified and agreeably surprised at the unity, the charity, the faith which the circumstances of the election brought to light in our community."[10] And for almost a year the community rejoiced in the progress made under the new Abbot. He appreciated the need of bringing the College up to date, and so in rapid succession he arranged for faculty graduate study, employed the first lay athletic coach, and approved plans for a gymnasium. But Abbot Martin soon began to fear that the school discipline was becoming too liberal, and he had difficulty selecting a suitable director of the College. At the same time he moved too vigorously in tightening monastic discipline particularly by being excessively severe about small matters. In trying to spiritualize his monks, Abbot Martin tended to take the joy out of monastic life.[11]

The canonical visitators of 1923 found the community tending to divide into factions, the College and the Abbey, with consequent damage to fraternal charity. Conditions in the clericate were unsatisfactory, and the Abbot was sometimes injudicious in his corrections. As a consequence, the visitators observed that some lacked respect for the Abbot.[12] Abbot Martin, on the other hand, was faced with peculiarly difficult problems. The College, the community, and the whole world were all in a period of transition. Problems of personnel were also particularly difficult to solve. The Abbot wrote that he expected much good of this first canonical visitation in his adminis-

[10] Veth to von Stotzingen, Atchison, Jan. 9, 1922. (SA)
[11] A note from the council minutes (ten years later) will suffice to illustrate: "Father Abbot said a radio set was available. There is none in the monastery and Fathers and clerics that wish to listen in at the Catholic Hour must go to radios in the rooms of the pastors or various prefects or even of students. The set is to be kept in Father Prior's room, and to be taken to the chapter-room [community recreation room] for extra occasions." Feb. 21, 1936.
[12] Record of Visitation, Apr. 27, 1923.

tration and added, "My great difficulty is to steer a safe course between two extreme elements: the young and the old; unfortunately [on account of the decline in the number of vocations in the nineties], we have very few middle-aged members in the community to preserve a proper balance."[13] And as he had remarked earlier, "No fewer than five of our Fathers out on parishes are sick or growing feeble and must soon be relieved of their work. Then too, our College curriculum is undergoing a change. . . This calls for professors with degrees recognized by secular universities and State schools. The problem of preparing such professors without too great a loss of time, without injury to their ecclesiastical education and religious training is often a very knotty one."[14]

In view of all the difficulties inherent in this transition period, it was particularly fortunate that Abbot Martin made such wise appointments to the various monastic offices. He delayed a general change of monastic officials until the summer of 1922, when he appointed Father Gerard Heinz his prior and Father Edmund Pusch his procurator. Since the prior is an executive officer charged with the immediate administration of the details of life within the community, Prior Gerard's well-known calm good judgment was invaluable. He had been director of the College in the eighties and nineties and since that time had been pastor of the Abbey Church. He was Abbot Martin's only prior and died in office two years after the Abbot's death. His years as prior were probably the most fruitful of Father Gerard's life. He was an excellent teacher of moral theology, and his advice on difficult moral problems was sought by both bishops and priests from a wide area. When troubled by doubts about vocation or any other problem, most of the younger members of the community took their troubles to good Father Prior. He had a puckish sense of humor, and his quiet but irresistable laugh was a sort of breathless chuckle that made

[13] Veth to von Stotzingen, Atchison, May 9, 1923. (SA)
[14] *Idem*, Jan. 9, 1922. (SA)

every muscle right down to his toes quiver with joy. He had strict but rather individual notions of monastic propriety. He once appeared at a faculty picnic in the jungles of the Missouri River bottoms attired in pants, hat, undershirt, and Roman collar. Spiritually Prior Gerard was a true son of Abbot Innocent. The Prior made a daily pilgrimage to the community cemetery to say a prayer for his confreres. He had no doubt whatsoever about Abbot Innocent's saintliness, and knowing that no one in heaven could have more interest in the community's welfare, he put the acute needs of the community straight into Abbot Innocent's hands. Prior Gerard's piety was deep, solid, and simple. At the same time he appreciated the new richness of religious and spiritual life unveiled by Abbot Martin's conferences to the community. The Prior's life and teaching in and out of the classroom had a profound influence on most of the present-day members of the community.

Father Edmund Pusch as procurator or business manager of the community carefully husbanded the Abbey's resources, especially during the difficult times of the depression. A particularly important contribution was his success in piecing together bits of land on the bluffs and in the river bottoms so that the Abbey now has a farm adjoining it to the north to help sustain the community and its schools. He was Abbot Martin's only procurator.

Abbot Martin entrusted the formation of the clerics— the youngest professed members of the community — to Father Subprior Bonaventure Schwinn, a man with a keen appreciation for quality in matters spiritual and intellectual. Father Bonaventure has been editor of the *American Benedictine Review* since its foundation.

Father Gerard Heinz, prior; Father Bonaventure Schwinn, subprior and master of the clerics; Father Edmund Pusch, procurator; and Father Sylvester Schmitz, dean of the College — these four lieutenants of Abbot Martin contributed greatly to the welfare and the growth of St. Benedict's.

Abbot Martin Veth
1921-1944

The Abbot's Chapel

Top Row: Edmund Pusch, Malachy Sullivan, Benedict Kappler, Sylvester Schmitz, Patrick O'Shea, Claude Enslein, Damian Lavery, Sebastian Weissenberger, Cosmas Schneider, Felix Nolte, Cyril Bayer, Justin Sion, Henry Courtney, Victor Gellhaus, Louis Baska, Clement Nordhus, Dominic Weber, Bonaventure Schwinn, Raymond Woydziak. Second Row: Lambert Burton, Anthony Baar, Leonard Schwinn, Odilo Otott, Andrew Green, Gregory Neumayr, Adalbert Blahnik, Lawrence Theis, Robert Salmon, Stephen Wise, Francis McDonald, Matthias Stein, Ignatius Stein, Gabriel Vonderstein, Paul Berens, Adrian Stallbaumer, James Burns. Third Row: Alphonse Filian, Thomas Burk, Gerard Heinz, Matthew Bradley, Alban Rudroff, Athanasius Koenn, Abbot President Ernest Helmstetter, Abbot Martin Veth, Abbot Innocent Wolf, Prior Leo Aaron, Boniface Verheyen, Herman Mengwasser, Denis Murphy, Edwin Kassens, Hilary Rosenfeld. Bottom Row: Edgar Schmiedeler, Romuald Fox, Leander Scheier, Isidor Smith, Paschal Pretz, Edward Schmitz, Cuthbert McDonald, Pius Pretz, Callistus Kramer, Mark Merwick, Albert Haverkamp.

Chapter Members 1922

Prior Gerard Heinz 1935
(at Abbot Innocent's old desk)

The Abbey

Father Sylvester Schmitz
Dean of the College 1927-1945

"Sweethearts" 1936

A Student
Room in
the 1930's

Maur Hill Administration Building and Gymnasium

Maur Hill Refectory Building

The Novices' Study Hall

The Monastic Chapel 1929-1957

Memorial Hall 1950

NAIA Champions 1954

Abbot Cuthbert McDonald and the New Abbey Church

VITA ET PAX

The magnificent new Abbey on the bluff overlooking the Missouri River dominated Abbot Martin's administration for good and for ill. At the time of his election the entire community realized that the need for new buildings was urgent, and the Abbot hoped that an abbey, Abbey Church, and library would be the first new buildings.[15] After discussing which new building was needed first, however, the chapter voted to build a gymnasium. Having won their point on the gymnasium, the chapter at the same meeting, without too much care in the choice of words, authorized the Abbot also to "go ahead with preparations for the erection of the new Abbey."[16] These words of authorization the Abbot significantly entered on the first page of his personal memorandum book. He added notes from Butler's *Benedictine Monachism* wherein the author states that the council and the chapter are to advise an abbot but not to control him and that the powers of the chapter are negative but never positive.

Consequently, Abbot Martin engaged the architectural firm of Brielmaier and Sons, of Milwaukee, and began developing plans for the new Abbey. By 1926, after consulting various abbots and architects, Abbot Martin and the Brielmaiers had completed plans for the new Abbey. The Abbot then brought the plans before the chapter and suggested that construction begin at once. Some capitulars, however, thought that the decision should be deferred until all members, including those residing outside the monastery, could be consulted.[17]

The chapter held after the annual retreat, when practically all capitulars were present, clearly showed objection to being presented with a finished plan to accept or reject. After making their feelings plain, the chapter finally approved a loan of $300,000 so that construction could begin.[18] As the canonical visitators of that year noted, the entire community agreed that a new Abbey

---

15 *Idem*, Apr. 4, 1922. (SA)
16 Chapter Minutes, June 30, 1922.
17 *Ibid.*, Mar. 8, 1926.
18 *Ibid.*, June 18, 1926.

was badly needed but objected to having no voice in the plans. Furthermore, the Abbot had been proceeding without the advice even of his council, for no Seniors — the elected members of the council — had been chosen for two years.[19]

Ground for the new Abbey was ceremonially broken by the Abbot Primate, Fidelis von Stotzingen, who had attended the Eucharistic Congress in Chicago and was visiting the American abbeys. As Abbot Martin's old friend of student days at Sant' Anselmo, the Abbot Primate agreed to celebrate at Atchison the silver jubilee of his abbatial blessing and to break ground for the new Abbey. The ceremony took place on St. Martin's Day, November 11, 1926, but actual work on the new building was delayed until the following spring.

Like almost all churchmen of that day, Abbot Martin would have scoffed at the idea that contemporary architects could produce anything better or more appropriate for religious buildings than the classic ecclesiastical styles developed in the Middle Ages. He believed that Gothic was the perfect expression of religion in stone and that this style was consequently timeless. Therefore his new Abbey would be Gothic. The *Rambler* reported that "Leigh Hunt of Milwaukee has been appointed by the College authorities to see personally that the new monastery is built strictly along the best lines of Gothic architecture. He was formerly a lecturer in the Chicago Art Institute and also former Assistant State Architect in Illinois."[20] No general contract was let because construction was directed by superintendents employed by Father Edmund, the procurator. Stone for the walls was secured from the local Kerford quarries. The trim-stone came from Carthage, Missouri, and all stone was shaped on the site.

The new Abbey rose from the bluff stone by stone. Construction costs were considerably greater than the

[19] Record of Visitation, May 1, 1926.
   In 1929 Abbot Martin was still being criticized for not holding meetings of his council.—*Ibid.*, May 3, 1929.
[20] Nov. 1, 1927.

300

architect's estimates, however, so construction of the Abbey Church was postponed.[21] The interior of only the two lower floors of the Abbey were completed. To finish even this much required borrowing an additional $100,000. By the time it was ready for occupancy, the new Abbey had cost $780,000.

Abbot Martin blessed the new Abbey on August 5, 1929, and the monastic life of prayer, work, and study began in the new home. The Abbey is a noble building on a noble site. The lovely broad valley of the Missouri, viewed from the Abbey high on the bluffs, is a constant reminder of the beauty and goodness of God. The new Abbey had caused Abbot Martin many heartaches, and the worst was yet to come, but it is a building worth sacrifices. The new monastic home was the necessary physical equipment for the deeper religious life that Abbot Martin hoped to give his community. He regretted deeply that the most important part, the Abbey Church, could not be built, but he hoped that it could be added soon.[22]

Unfortunately, the stock-market panic that announced the great depression occurred only two months after the community had moved into its new Abbey. The hope of rapidly paying off the indebtedness disappeared, and soon the community was struggling mightily merely to prevent the debt from increasing. By 1931 the situation seemed desperate. Extraordinary effort kept the college enrollment from shrinking radically, but college income nevertheless declined. To the loss of jobs and low prices during the depression was added the drought on the farms. As in the past, salaries from monks in parish work sometimes provided the only money for paying interest, but now, owing to the depression, the pastors could not be certain of collecting their salaries. Furthermore, in spite of its own difficulties the community did its share in pro-

---

[21] "Our new building. . . will cost so much more than we anticipated." —Veth to Esser, Atchison, May 26, 1929, copy.

In 1934 Abbot Martin complained to Leo Brielmaier that costs had been more than double the architect's estimates.—Feb. 13, 1934, copy.

[22] Veth to Esser, Atchison, May 26, 1929, copy.

viding financial aid for another abbey in even worse distress. The most crushing blow of all, however, was a financial adventure by several monks that cost the community approximately $100,000. The chapter at which that was announced closed fittingly "with the recitation of the *De Profundis*."[23] By that time the community's debt had gone past the half-million dollar mark, but with everyone cooperating in severe retrenchment and with Father Edmund's talent for saving, they held the line.[24]

Meanwhile the common endeavor and the spiritual life helped to pull the community together. By 1935 the canonical visitators reported "a distinct upward movement in the community, a closer knitting together of its parts, a stronger desire for its development along the line of finer Benedictine tradition."[25] Three years later the large debt still caused some pessimism concerning the development of the College, but the progress being made was too evident to be ignored.[26]

Abbot Martin made no new monastic foundation during his administration. Circumstances were hardly propitious for such a development, and the growing College as well as the parishes and chaplaincies absorbed all available manpower. From time to time Abbot Martin was offered various Catholic high schools, but he always refused because he considered such projects unsuitable for Benedictines. According to him experience had proved that monks teaching in city high schools could not maintain a proper community and religious life.[27]

In the last year of his administration Abbot Martin agreed to supply one or two monks to aid Father Alcuin Heibel, O.S.B., of Mt. Angel Abbey in Oregon, in his agricultural missionary project in Sahuayo, Michoacan,

[23] Chapter Minutes, Dec. 29, 1931.
[24] Until 1931 St. Benedict's was a single corporation — St. Benedict's College — but the large debt incurred in building the new Abbey endangered the standing of the College with accrediting agencies. Consequently, in that year the monastic community was chartered as a separate corporation, and the debt was transferred to St. Benedict's Abbey.
[25] Record of Visitation, Feb. 2, 1935.
[26] *Ibid.*, Jan. 29, 1938.
[27] Veth to von Stotzingen, Atchison, Nov. 25, 1924, copy.

Mexico. This experiment was a failure but led to the community's accepting for a period of three years the management of a private school in Tepeyac, a suburb of Mexico City.[28] In 1946, at the end of the three years, St. Benedict's was confronted with a post-war mushrooming student enrollment and with associated building plans, so the chapter declined to continue the project at Tepeyac.[29] Sisters from Mount St. Scholastica, Atchison, had taken charge of the girls' school in Tepeyac, and these Sisters remained. The boys' school was accepted by the monks of St. John's Abbey, and both schools have been developed successfully. Father Lambert Dehner remained in Mexico as chaplain to the Sisters and to continue his uniquely American apostolate as coach of the Politechnico football team, thereby revising the inheritance of anticlericalism among Mexican youth.

Most of St. Benedict's energy went into the development and improvement of its college and high school, which are discussed later. Two Atchison monks became abbots of other communities, namely, Abbot Lambert Burton, of St. Martin's Abbey, Olympia, Washington, and Abbot Leonard Schwinn of Holy Cross Abbey, Canon City, Colorado. Father Alfred Koestner was sent to aid the Benedictines at San Beda school, Manila, in the spring of 1940. After Pearl Harbor he was interned by the Japanese. He was in the notorious Los Banos prison camp from July, 1944, until his release by American troops on February 23, 1945.

Abbot Martin allowed some of his monks to take part in general public service as well. Father Edmund Pusch, for example, for a number of years served on the Kansas State Commission for Crippled Children. Similarly Father Louis Baska represented the public interest on the War Labor Board of Kansas City in 1943. Father Gilbert Wolters in the summer of 1941 directed a ten-day Rural Life School under the auspices of the National Catholic Rural Life Conference. The lectures by government and

[28] Chapter Minutes, Oct. 29, 1943.
[29] *Ibid.*, June 5, 1946.

religious leaders were attended by priests from twelve dioceses. Similar rural life schools were held in 1942 and 1944, but wartime conditions made their continuance difficult.

The community's activities continued to expand particularly in religious fields. The first laymen's retreats at St. Benedict's were offered in the summer of 1921. Father Henry Courtney, who was particularly interested in mission and retreat work, was primarily responsible for this development. Other members of the community also took up the work. With the exception of the war years this program has been steadily expanded, and in 1956 the first retreats for married couples were given at St. Benedict's. Father Edgar Schmiedeler had been the first to introduce this kind of retreat in the United States. In cooperation with other Benedictine communities, St. Benedict's has encouraged the union of prayer of Benedictine Oblates since 1925. The *Abbey News* began publication in the interests of the Abbey Guild in 1928. The paper's growing importance in publishing alumni news was reflected in the change of its name in 1945 to the *Raven Review*. Father Bernard Sause has contributed a number of guides on various features of Catholic life. His synthesis of Benedictine spiritual thought, *The School of the Lord's Service*, appeared in three volumes, 1947-1951.

Every Benedictine community prefers, when possible, to train its young members at home. Ideally each Benedictine community should have its own novitiate. When Abbot Innocent completed his monastery in 1893, he promptly began to train his novices at home. The conditions were less than ideal and in 1908 the novices were again sent to St. Vincent Archabbey in Pennsylvania. When Abbot Martin completed his new Abbey, facilities for a novitiate on the top floor of the refectory wing had been in the plans from the beginning. In July, 1930, St. Benedict's again opened its own novitiate. Since then the novitiate quarters, which at first seemed so large, have frequently been overcrowded, particularly since novices from one or the other community help swell the numbers.

Some clerics from other monasteries are usually studying in St. Benedict's College. Over the years these student monks have come from various abbeys, because as Benedictine communities have their own faculties trained and their colleges accredited, they no longer need to send their clerics to St. Benedict's for recognized degrees. The first large group that came to St. Benedict's were clerics of St. Martin's Abbey in 1928. Since then clerics have come from the abbeys of Conception in Missouri, Holy Cross in Colorado, St. Bernard's in Alabama, Belmont in North Carolina, St. Leo in Florida, St. Gregory's in Oklahoma, St. Bede in Illinois, Assumption in North Dakota, St. Mary's in New Jersey, St. Andrew's in Ohio, St. Sylvester's in Detroit, and St. Anselm's in New Hampshire. In 1931 the community played host to a group of twenty-four young Augustinian Recollects who were refugees from the Spanish civil war. A year later half of them left for England where they had procured a monastery. The last of the Basques were ordained when St. Augustine's Monastery in Kansas City, Kansas, was opened in 1935.

Abbot Martin's desire to enrich his community's spiritual life necessarily involved increased stress on liturgical prayer. But the Abbot also had a tendency to introduce extra devotions and to urge his community to private prayer by making it public. These devotions tended to multiply over the years until the canonical visitators finally advised the Abbot to reduce their number.[30] Year by year Abbot Martin sought to give the divine office in choir greater richness and an ever greater importance in the life of the community. Father Lambert Burton in the summer of 1925 was given the opportunity to attend the Pius X school of music in Sacred Heart College in New York. Thereafter he taught Gregorian chant not only to the clerics but also to college students, particularly those preparing for the priesthood, since chant courses were added to the curriculum at that time. This work was supplemented by Father Sylvester Fangman, of St.

[30] Record of Visitation, Jan. 29, 1938; Nov. 18, 1940.

Bernard's Abbey in Alabama, who directed summer classes in chant and choir recitation for the clerics in 1932 and subsequent years.

In the first year of his administration Abbot Martin reintroduced the singing of Complin, the official evening prayer.[31] Beginning two years later conventual Mass was sung on all Sundays and holydays of obligation.[32] Adjusting the demands of daily community worship and the demands of teaching without slighting either has been a continuing problem through the years. What some of his monks called hardship Abbot Martin viewed merely as an opportunity to practice mortification. Until 1942 the community arose at four o'clock and spent three hours in chapel before breakfast. But in that year, when the comnunity began to sing Vespers as well as the conventual Mass daily, the schedule was necessarily revised drastically. In the new schedule the time for arising was at twenty minutes to five, and minor hours and conventual Mass now followed breakfast. The teaching schedule was rearranged for classes to begin at eight-thirty.[33]

Subtle changes in theory, practice, and above all in spirit have taken place in adapting the institution of the lay Brotherhood to modern times. The need for change was first frankly faced in Abbot Martin's administration. The Abbot hoped to introduce in a small way the craft-school system successfully developed in some European abbeys. He never succeeded in putting this policy into practice, but during his administration greater unity was achieved through the liturgy. Originally only priests and clerics chanted the divine office, whereas Brothers daily recited fifteen decades of the Rosary. The Brothers did not join the choir monks in prayer except at conventual Mass. Under Abbot Martin's administration in 1935 the Brothers joined the rest of the community in singing

[31] The singing of Complin had been discontinued years earlier when all the clerics went to St. Vincent and St. John's for their studies.—Annales, Sept. 27, 1922.
[32] Ibid., Dec. 7, 1924.
[33] Ibid., Oct. 31, 1942.

Complin.[34] Their participation in the divine office has expanded since that date, and the net gain has been an increase in the real unity of the community. A better understanding of the central role of the liturgy had begun before Abbot Martin's administration, but it was he who brought the ideal to life, and it was no doubt his greatest contribution to St. Benedict's.

Abbot Martin suffered his first severe illness in 1940, and suddenly he felt very old.[35] Fatigued by the long Christmas services, he contracted pneumonia, December 27, 1940. He recovered but slowly and so in October 1941, went to St. John's Abbey to consult with Abbot President Alcuin Deutsch about the advisability of resigning. While there he contracted a cold and entered St. Mary's Hospital in Minneapolis where doctors discovered he had cancer. He hoped that the operation would restore his health, but when the Abbot learned otherwise, he asked permission for a coadjutor. He announced his retirement at a chapter meeting, May 31, 1943. Prior Gerard, secretary of the chapter, made the following entry in the minutes:

The unusual nature of the meeting of this day was sensed by all who entered the chapter room, and was evident from the presence of most of our priests on Kansas parishes.

Father Abbot opened the Chapter with prayer, followed by the reading of the minutes. He then read to the astonished community the attached lengthy communication in which he stated that the Holy See had authorized the election of an Abbot-Coadjutor. On finishing the masterfully constructed manuscript Father Abbot spoke informally for a few minutes expressing his best wishes for his successor and for the community, and the hope that the remaining debt of $115,000 may soon be cleared. He also recommended that future building be not undertaken beyond the means on hand.

In the statement alluded to by Father Prior, the Abbot announced that owing to his age (sixty-eight) and illness he had on the preceding December 14 asked for a coadjutor. He went on to say that he had reached his decision only

[34] *Ibid.*, Oct. 1, 1935.
[35] Veth to Deutsch, St. Leo, Fla., Feb. 11, 1941. (SJA)

after much prayer but still with trepidation, because on the one hand he feared the possibility of cowardice, but on the other hand he feared more the possible damage to the community that could result from the disparity between his responsibilities and his physical vigor. His words of farewell were memorable:

Now I realize that by taking this step I am making myself a temporary exile from my monastery. This is not a pleasant situation to contemplate for me, but I feel and know from what has happened in similar cases elsewhere, that I shall be in the way, and that my presence will not always be agreeable. At least for a time, a year or two, if God lets me live that long, I ought to be out of the house, so as to give my successor a free hand. I shall miss the Divine Office and the Conventual Mass. It will be fifty years in July since I entered the novitiate, began the Divine Office and the Religious Life; and I can say that they have been happy years. I thank God for them. The Divine Office has been a joy in my youth, and it is a greater joy and consolation in my old age. The time has come, I think, when I can do more for you by praying for you than I can by trying to rule you.

The next few weeks will be a critical period for the community. Naturally, you will be full of misgivings about the election to be made, full of hopeful and fearful anticipations of the changes that must follow. Let me ask you to fall back on prayer. This is God's house, and He is more interested and concerned about what takes place here than you are; He knows what is for its greater welfare. Pray much from now on, that God may guide the electors and direct the destinies of the community aright. . .

May God protect and prosper the community, and sanctify all its members; May He bless and assist my successor, so that he may accomplish much more for the good of the community than I have been able to do. I humbly beg pardon for the bad example given you in the past twenty-two years, and for all the offenses and negligences against the community and its members. *Orate Pro Me.*

Abbot Martin was in his last illness, and except for two months at St. Mary's Convent, Leavenworth, he left the Abbey only to go to the hospital. The next eighteen months brought out all that was best in him. With relief from the nagging details of administration and from the responsibilities of his office, which had always weighed too heavily upon him, suffering the cross of his illness and left alone with God, all the beauty of his personal sanctity bloomed forth. After months of patient suffering he died in the Atchison Hospital, December 12, 1944.

He was a strange man to have governed the Kansas monks. His entire career as abbot was marked by a certain lack of harmony between him and his community. Yet during his administration the community increased in size by two-thirds, and the College developed into a modern institution of higher learning. Abbot Martin had made himself unnecessary difficulties with college problems and with college administrators, but it cannot be said that the College was modernized in spite of him, for the final decisions on policy were his, and he sincerely favored the creation of a sound liberal arts curriculum. In his own mind his greatest task was to enrich the spiritual life of his community, and in accomplishing this aim he undoubtedly made his greatest contribution. Abbot Martin will grow in stature with the passage of time, for the spiritual difference between the community whose direction he accepted in 1921 and the one he relinquished in 1943 is subtle but nonetheless real.

His achievements are the more remarkable because he was severely handicapped by not having the natural gifts of the born leader. His monks respected Abbot Martin, but probably none of them loved him. Abbot Innocent had been like a potter molding clay — none too gently at times — whereas it was Abbot Martin's destiny in God's providence to be given a rasp to continue work on the hardened pieces. Exactly like Abbot Innocent, however, Abbot Martin had the firm conviction that in the last analysis the work all rested in the hands of God:

It is God's community and we are only God's instruments and ministers. If we do our duty to the best of our power, give a good example and put our trust in prayer, He will have care of us and of ours. Building up a good community is slow and tedious work, and much of the fruit of our labors will turn up only after we are dead. Be patient therefore and trust in God![36]

[36] Veth to Burton, Atchison, Jan. 22, 1934. (St. Martin's Abbey)

309

CHAPTER X

St. Benedict's Becomes
A Modern College

From 1876 to 1910 St. Benedict's College, with its five-year classical academy and its three-year commercial course, underwent only gradual and minor change. The dispute in 1910 on appointing a standing committee on studies and discipline was left undecided, but the dispute heralded change. The new generation of young monks felt that if St. Benedict's was to serve its students adequately, it must develop into a college according to the pattern of other American colleges. The youngsters failed to effect a distribution of the director's powers, but the appointment of Father Damian Lavery as director in 1910 was nevertheless a concession to their viewpoint because he was known to be in sympathy with their aims.

Between 1915 and 1927 St. Benedict's abandoned the traditional academy, greatly enlarged the curriculum, and became an accredited liberal arts college. The development was by no means painless, for it was dotted with minor crises. Some of the consequences, furthermore, were a surprise to the faculty. The evolution was completed in three main steps, taken one at a time. First, the curriculum was modernized and a beginning was made at providing professional training for the faculty, then intercollegiate athletics was introduced, and, finally, after a few years of confusion, the basic disciplinary policy was revamped to fit men of college age.

After the Christmas holidays of 1910 some two hundred returning students, with the exception of the scholastics, moved into new quarters on the bluff in the first building of the "New St. Benedict's." The wings of the H-shaped Tudor Gothic Administration Building held study halls, common dormitories, and locker rooms that seemed magnificent in size after years in the crowded old college building in the valley. Some of the older students were not so sure that the change was entirely for the better. Since classrooms and dining halls remained in the old building, a student could no longer go through his day without ever setting foot out of doors. Abbot Innocent was convinced that the health of the students had noticeably improved since they were forced to go out each day, rain or shine, if they wanted to eat.[1] Another problem was that the students had been removed from their old haunts, where the corners considered safe for sneaking a smoke were not only familiar but traditional. Students had not yet achieved similar rapport with their new building.[2] The Director who moved into the new offices was Father Damian Lavery. His academic field was oratory and dramatics, and his pronouncements as director tended to be flowery. He was not a trained educator, but he wanted to see St. Benedict's modernized. His cooperation was essential to the young monks who made St. Benedict's a college.

Although the *Abbey Student* first referred to the upper classmen as Freshmen and Sophomores in 1914,[3] the first real curriculum change was in the academy. As prefect of St. Edward's Hall (for the older general students) Father Sylvester Schmitz had observed that many of his charges were repeating courses already completed successfully in other schools. Students entering St. Benedict's after a year or more of high school elsewhere were classified according to their knowledge of Latin. This academic requirement usually set them back a year since no provision was made, for example, for a boy to take first-year Latin and second-year English. Consequently, students

[1] Wolf to Novices, Atchison, Apr. 24, 1911.
[2] Wolf to Engel, Atchison, Jan. 21, 1911. (SJA)
[3] The May issue was edited by the Freshmen, and the June issue was, for the first time, a kind of yearbook for the graduating Sophomores, including an essay by each graduate, together with his portrait.

sometimes repeated many courses. Furthermore, in the summer of 1915 when Father Sylvester attended the University of Wisconsin to study mathematics, he was shocked at learning that the university officials considered St. Benedict's curriculum inadequate in mathematics and the natural sciences. With the approval of Father Damian, Fathers Sylvester and Louis Baska began studying school catalogs and made their first acquaintance with high-school units and credits. They did not dare advocate such a complete break with the European plan as the introduction of electives, they did not think it tactful even to use the unit terminology, but they did work out a broader and more flexible curriculum. The Board of Professors in 1916 approved this revised curriculum, and it went into operation in the school year of 1916-17.[4] To provide facilities for the new science courses the former dormitories in the attic of Bishop Fink Hall were remodeled and converted into laboratories for botany and zoology.[5]

At that point World War I intervened. The alumni service men's Roll of Honor in the *Abbey Student* grew to 285 names by November, 1918. Seven of these alumni were wounded, Leo McGuire won the American Service Cross, and Captain Edwin E. Schwien won the French War Cross. Three gold stars were on the College service flag for Harry A. Fleming, Francis Howe, and Alvin C. Beasley.[6]

Back at the College students bought War Savings Stamps and collected money to buy Liberty Bonds for the Wolf Hall Fund. A band concert benefit for the Red Cross was distinguished by patriotic songs that Fathers Andrew Green and Damian Lavery composed especially for the occasion.[7] Father Damian was frequently invited to "exercise his well-known power of eloquence in the interest of Liberty Bonds, Food Conservation, and other

[4] Sylvester Schmitz, O.S.B., "The Development of the Curriculum of St. Benedict's College, 1915-1945," unpublished manuscript, 4-15.
[5] *Abbey Student*, XXVI (Oct., 1916), 48.
[6] *Ibid.*, XXVIII (Dec., 1918), 134.
[7] *Ibid.*, (Jan., 1918), 247.

312

patriotic enterprises. His stirring orations are becoming famous in this section of Kansas and elsewhere."[8]

The war had little effect on St. Benedict's enrollment because only twenty-one college students were enrolled before the United States entered the war.[9] Father Sylvester and his confreres meanwhile continued modernizing St. Benedict's. In 1918 work began on setting up a true college curriculum. The system of grouping fields of study and other details were mostly borrowed from the University of Kansas catalog. The new plan even included requirements for A.M. and Ph.D. degrees. In later years Father Sylvester was convinced that the faculty's blissful ignorance in plunging into curriculum revision was fortunate. In Father Sylvester's opinion, if the faculty had known what labor and expense were to be necessary for expanding the library and laboratory facilities and for training the faculty, he thought they might not have accepted such a tremendous task.[10]

Another feature of the 1918-19 revisions was the organization of a Board of Deans, who were to have full responsibility for academic matters. Father Martin Veth became dean of the School of Theology; Leonard Schwinn, dean of the College; Lambert Burton, principal of the Academy of Commerce; Sylvester Schmitz, principal of the Academy of Arts and Sciences; and Claude Enslein, principal of the Grade School.[11] The Board of Deans continued from 1919 to 1927, and its influence was at first paramount in determining academic policies.

Meanwhile St. Benedict's continued to grow. College enrollment increased from twenty-seven in 1919 to fifty-

[8] *Ibid.*, (Nov., 1917), 111.
[9] Schmitz, "Curriculum," 84.
[10] *Ibid.*, 34-45.
[11] Minutes of Deans' Meetings, Feb. 8; Mar. 19, 1919.
After Father Lambert Burton was appointed director in January, 1922, the Board of Deans had the following members: Father Bonaventure Schwinn, dean of the School of Theology; Father Malachy Sullivan, dean of the College; Father Louis Baska, principal of the High School; and Father James Burns, dean of the School of Commerce and Economics. After Father Louis Baska was appointed director in 1924, Father Victor Gellhaus became the principal of the High School. These men took the lead in executing the program of modernization.

seven in 1920, bringing the total enrollment of college, high school, and grade school for that year to 310. Fortunately, in 1919 St. Benedict's had purchased the Midland College campus and buildings in south Atchison. In January, 1920, the grade-school boys moved from the College to St. Benedict's Maur Hill, the new name given the recently-acquired institution. Father Cyril Bayer became principal of the school, and Fathers Gabriel Vonderstein, Claude Enslein, Leander Scheier, and Edward Schmitz formed its first faculty. When Maur Hill was solemnly dedicated, January 15, 1920, the religious services were followed by "two fast basketball games."[12] With a modern gymnasium at Maur Hill, college authorities purchased a bus, and St. Benedict's students were transported across town to play basketball and use the indoor swimming pool. The old barn-like gym at the College was converted into a garage to house the new bus.

While the faculty was revising the curriculum during the years 1916 to 1918, it also decided to seek formal recognition as an accredited college from the University of Kansas.[13] However, since the faculty's first enquiries were made shortly after the United States entered World War I, the university officials could not formally inspect the College until after the war. The Board of Deans reopened the matter late in 1919.[14] University committees visited St. Benedict's twice during 1920,[15] and the Uni-

[12] *Abbey Student*, XXIX (Feb., 1920), 271, 255.
[13] Board of Professors' Minutes, May 16, 1917.
Father Aloysius Bradley might have begun a similar move much earlier. In 1909 he proposed that the catalog be revised to coordinate courses with university requirements.—Board of Professors' Minutes, Sept. 24, 1909. Three months later Chancellor Frank Strong of the University wrote to Abbot Innocent, referred to a visit made two years earlier, expressed a wish to visit St. Benedict's again, and mentioned that four professors were assigned to the visit.—Strong to Wolf, Lawrence, Dec. 2, 1909. This was evidently a surprise to the Abbot. In a note he says that at first he was inclined to ask what the matter was all about, but "Father Director thought we should try to have the good will of the University, for so far it has accepted our testimonials of proficiency without any examination."—Wolf note, Dec. 4, 1909. The Abbot wrote, welcoming the committee, but no record exists showing that the committee came or that any consequences followed.
[14] Minutes of Deans' Meetings, Dec. 14, 1919.
[15] Board of Professors' Minutes, Jan. 26, 1920; Minutes of Deans' Meetings, Nov. 16, 1920.

314

versity Senate admitted St. Benedict's to the list of fully accredited colleges in January, 1921.[16] The college administration next sought academic recognition from the State of Kansas, and at its meeting on January 31, 1922, the State Board of Education approved St. Benedict's as a senior college.[17] In July of the same year the High School received similar recognition.[18] As soon as state approval seemed assured, the faculty aspired to regional academic recognition and decided to apply for membership in the North Central Association of Colleges. The Board of Deans and Father Director Louis Baska finally achieved this goal in 1927.[19]

Meeting the standards for admission to the North Central Association, however, had proved difficult. Father Sylvester considered the Board of Professors' meeting on January 25, 1923, of key importance. At this meeting Father Director Lambert Burton outlined what the College needed, presumably for admission to the North Central Association. To round out the necessary eight academic departments, the College would have to offer more courses in physics and biology. Furthermore, since a professor with at least a Master of Arts degree was required to head each department, faculty members needed graduate training. Finally, the college laboratories would have to be expanded and better equipped, and the library would have to be enlarged and made more accessible to the students.[20] This appraisal by Father Lambert had a sobering effect on the Board of Professors. Years later Father Sylvester was of the opinion that "this meeting more than anything else helped to remove from our minds the feelings of self-complacency and self-satisfaction" in which many had indulged after receiving recognition from the State Board of Education.[21]

---

[16] F. W. Blackmar to Lavery, Lawrence, Feb. 19, 1921.
[17] Euna M. Arrasmith to Burton, Topeka, Mar. 10, 1922.
[18] Claire W. Mitchell to Burton, Topeka, July 26, 1922.
[19] Minutes of Deans' Meetings, May 3, 1927; *Rambler*, Apr. 1, 1927.
[20] Board of Professors' Minutes, Jan. 25, 1923.
[21] Schmitz, "Curriculum," 123-4.

The problems listed by Father Lambert in 1923 were promptly attacked and solved (at least for the time being) in the next few years. During this period the college curriculum was undergoing fundamental changes. When the modern high school went into effect in 1916, a college curriculum was also drawn up for the catalog. In most respects, however, this curriculum resembled an advanced high-school curriculum. The college students had class schedules of twenty-five or even thirty hours a week. Each English class read groups of authors presumably graded for difficulty but otherwise unrelated. The authors read in Latin and Greek classes were greatly increased in number, however, and mathematics was extended to calculus. The only completely new additions were geology and astronomy in the sciences as well as one course each in economics and journalism.

The influence of the suggestions from the University of Kansas committee is evident in the catalog of 1919 (printed in the spring of 1920). The curriculum was divided into eleven groups, each with a chairman, but as yet the chairmen's names carried no academic degrees. Student class-schedules were reduced to between fifteen and twenty hours a week. Degrees of A.B. or B.S., without specification of a major, were offered, and pre-medical, pre-legal, and civil engineering curricula were outlined. Several courses in social science and one course in education were added. More important, however, all the courses lost their high school characteristics. English now included, for example, Nineteenth-Century Poetry and Prose, and history included a course in the French Revolution.

The catalog of 1921 announced that St. Benedict's was "fully accredited to the University of Kansas." At the same time the group chairmen were listed with their academic degrees ranging from A.B. to Ph.D. These degrees, however, had all been awarded in philosophy or theology by St. Benedict's or by other Benedictine schools attended by the various chairmen. In most cases the degree had no direct relation to the field of study headed by the chairman. These degrees were a temporary expedient until degrees in the necessary fields of study could be earned. Each summer a large part of the faculty was busily engaged in graduate study. As each faculty member progressed in his special field and approached a master's degree, the fact was reflected in the catalog by the increased number of courses offered in that field. Chemistry and education courses were increased, and sociology was added in the 1921 catalog. Economics, physics, biology, and then other departments showed the same development in the following years.

The degrees actually granted by St. Benedict's also depended on the development here summarized. In 1922 the College offered an A.B. in language and philosophy, a Ph.B., a B.S. in chemistry, and a B.S. in mathematics. An A.B. in economics was added in 1923. However, before 1928 the only bachelor degrees awarded were A.B.'s without any specification of a major. The confusion in the early part of this period is evident in the degrees granted at the 1920 commencement. Three A.B.'s were granted, and three A.M.'s were granted, presumably for advanced work in philosophy, to Fraters Mark Merwick, Paschal Pretz, and Victor Gellhaus. Furthermore, a Ph.D. was granted to Rev. H. C. Hengel, who needed status as student chaplain at the University of Wisconsin, on his submission of a thesis entitled "Are You an Ape?"[22] The most critical portion of this period of change had been passed by 1927 when St. Benedict's was accredited by the North Central Association of Colleges. The organization of the curriculum at that time will be discussed later.

Developing the science laboratories depended closely on the progress of faculty training, but year by year the laboratories were expanded and equipped. The library was in some ways an even more difficult problem. The abbey library was a good collection, strong in classics, philosophy, and theology but not accessible to students. The college library had some standard works in English

<hr>

[22] Board of Professors' Minutes, Jan. 26; Apr. 9, 1920.

and American literature, approved novels for recreational reading, very little reference material, and was open for but a few short periods each week. Luckily one of the clerics, Frater Colman Farrell, was interested in the libraries and began studying modern methods, receiving inspiration particularly from Father Paul Foik, C.S.C., at the University of Notre Dame. A small reference library was first arranged, and as soon as Father Colman was ordained in 1925 he became librarian and opened the reference room afternoons and evenings.[23] The gradual transfer of the high school to Maur Hill gave the library additional space in the Administration Building, so the abbey library was transferred to the new quarters, and the collections were united. Work now began on recataloging according to the Library of Congress system. A trained librarian, Mr. Charles Flack, was employed to begin the cataloging while Father Colman studied at the University of Michigan and became the first priest in the United States to earn a degree of Master of Arts in Library Science.[24]

The most difficult problem of all was that of graduate training for the faculty. The training involved not only very considerable expense but also the juggling of personnel as well as finding and employing lay teachers when juggling was inadequate. Before 1900 faculty members rarely had any training beyond their seminary courses in classics, philosophy, and theology. With rare exceptions the need for further training was felt only in the arts, commerce, and graduate training in theology. A definite policy of graduate training for faculty members dates from the curriculum revision period of 1915 to 1918. The number of monks attending summer school in various universities increased, and by the time St. Benedict's was seeking recognition from the State of Kansas at least a dozen were so engaged each summer. And in 1922 a dozen meant two-thirds of the college faculty. In earn-

[23] *Rambler*, Oct. 1, 1925.
[24] *Ibid.*, May 15, 1926.

ing his master of science degree in chemistry from the University of Chicago in 1923, Father Adrian Stallbaumer was the first to receive an advanced degree from a recognized graduate school.

At the important Board of Professors' meeting in January, 1923, as Father Sylvester pointed out, the faculty for the first time became aware that summer school training alone would not solve their problem, and they recommended that leaves of absence be given so that the monks could complete their graduate training much earlier. Abbot Martin remonstrated that he had just lost seven monks, but he nevertheless began planning a schedule. In September, 1925, Fathers Edgar Schmiedeler and Sylvester Schmitz enrolled in the Catholic University of America to study, respectively, sociology and education. Two years later they returned with doctorates, and other faculty members received the same opportunity. By 1934, besides those who had attended summer schools, twenty-three faculty members had received leaves of absence to study in ten universities.[25]

Another recommendation of the North Central Association was to separate the High School from the College. This separation was completed in 1934. Membership in the North Central Association marked a turning point for St. Benedict's, and the numerous evidences of this advance will appear elsewhere in this chapter. One immediate result was that College officials could now counter Abbot Martin's distrust of change by pointing to objective standards to maintain the College regional accreditation.

Intercollegiate Athletics

Before full academic recognition had been received, the faculty had taken the second major step in moderniz-

[25] *Ibid.*, Aug. 18, 1934.
Since the beginning of the program faculty members have received graduate training in the following universities: Sant' Anselmo, Collegio Angelico, Studio della Sacra Congregazione del Concilio, and Pontificium Institutum Biblicum — all in Rome — Catholic University of America, Chicago, Colorado, Columbia, Cornell, Florence (Italy), Fordham, Fribourg, Harvard, Illinois, Iowa, Iowa State, Johns Hopkins, Kansas, Kansas State, Laval, Louvain,

ing the College. Introducing intercollegiate athletics was the sign of progress most joyfully hailed by the students and by at least the younger faculty members. The younger generation now on the faculty had a greater appreciation than their elders for the value of organized athletics in school life. These younger monks expended comparable effort upon the various sports programs. Basketball, for example, had been introduced to St. Benedict's in 1903, only to languish because no one knew how to play the game properly.[26] When Frater Sylvester Schmitz returned from St. John's Abbey, where he had been studying theology and incidentally learning a good bit about indoor and outdoor winter sports, he converted the old barn-gym to an indoor court, and the game received "a new impetus."[27]

By 1919 Fathers Sylvester, Malachy Sullivan, and Isidor Smith had organized the intramural football teams into two leagues, with three teams in each league. They secured expert advice and aid in refereeing from Mr. Henderson, the Atchison High School coach. At the end of the season they feted the winning teams with a banquet.[28] Next they wanted to test their mettle against teams of other schools, and, as was said earlier, Abbot Innocent was finally induced to consent to this innovation. The role of intercollegiate athletics during this period of change can hardly be exaggerated. It was desired not only because it provided healthy interests and a better-rounded program for young men, but in the minds of students and faculty alike intercollegiate athletics was above all the symbol of progress and of status as a college. More fundamental changes, such as a new concept of student social life and student participation in school government, followed in the wake of intercollegiate athletics.

St. Benedict's first varsity coach was Father Malachy

Michigan, Minnesota, Montreal, Munich, North Carolina, Northwestern, Notre Dame, Ohio, Ottawa, Oxford, Paris, College de France, Toronto, Wisconsin, and Yale.

[26] *Abbey Student*, XIII (Dec., 1903), 123.
[27] *Ibid.*, XX (Feb., 1911), 204.
[28] *Ibid.*, XXIX (Dec., 1919), 158-9.

Sullivan. The first varsity team under the new dispensation was actually the basketball team of 1919-1920, but owing to the influenza epidemic, its schedule was cancelled after the team had lost its debut, 32-37, to the Carroll Club of the local parish.[29] The baseball team of 1920 played a schedule of six games, losing to Haskell 6-10, and winning from Rockhurst 7-0. The other games were with Knights of Columbus and similar club teams.[30]

At the beginning of the 1920-21 school year the St. Benedict's College Athletic Association was formed with James H. Baker as president and Leo Coakley as vice-president. The football schedule for that year included a mixture of colleges, special training schools, and high schools: Wesleyan College, of Cameron, Mo. (the state champions); Lawrence High School; the State Training School, of Buckner, Mo.; the Olathe School for the Deaf; Rockhurst; the Kansas State School of Agriculture; the Washburn Freshmen; and Graceland College, of Lamoni, Iowa. To meet this schedule St. Benedict's had both a college varsity and an academy varsity. The Academy played the high schools and other schools of that level, and the College played the others. However, St. Benedict's did not have enough college men to make up a team, and so the larger and abler high-school boys played on both teams. St. Benedict's enjoyed a first season "far surpassing expectations," with the Purple and White (the contemporary College colors) winning five and losing two. Leon A. McNeill was the school's first official cheerleader.[31]

[29] The squad: Jim Baker (captain), Henry Merwick, Clem Voet, Norbert Wavada, Bernard Flaherty, Tom Quigley, Ed Grosdidier, Gervase Burke, Leo Sander, Leo Schwartz, John Senofsky.—*Abbey Student*, XXIX (Feb., 1920), 261; (Apr., 1920), 362.
[30] The squad: Henry Merwick, Charles Stimac, Harold Smith, Clarence Smith, Frank J. Scherr, John J. Senofsky, Norbert Wavada, Daniel C. O'Keefe, William Aldrete, Leo Coakley, Clement Voet, Tony Kilkenny, Wilfred Mages, Gervase Burke, Frederick J. Trapp.—*Ibid.*, XXIX (May, 1920), 429; (June, 1920), 493-5.
[31] *Ibid.*, XXX, *passim.*
College varsity: H. Smith, L. Nusbaum, A. Kelly, A. Morley, G. Nass, L. Schwartz, H. Marxer, L. Sander, C. Creagan, J. Baker (captain), L. Coakley. Substitutes: T. Quigley, L. Senecal, E. Schwartz.
Academy varsity: G. Carlton, L. Nusbaum, A. Kelly, A. Morley, J. Put-

The basketball team of 1920-21 played a variety of colleges, academies, clubs, and business house teams, winning six and losing seven.[32] The schedule must have been particularly difficult to arrange because Coach Father Malachy could get permission to play games away from home only after the election of Abbot Martin.[33] Other and more important changes quickly followed the election of Abbot Martin. On March 7, 1922, the monastic chapter, with little debate, approved the recommendation to engage a lay professional coach. A few days later Larry Quigley, "noted Missouri Valley Official and Trainer" and a disciple of Zupke of Illinois in 1915, was signed to a two-year contract and began working with the baseball squad on March 13.[34] Two months later St. Benedict's became a member of the Kansas Conference.[35] St. Benedict's first Homecoming was on September 28, 1922, and, according to the *Rambler*, was satisfyingly successful.[36]

The climax to these first years of intercollegiate athletics was building the gymnasium in 1923-24. When completed it was one of the largest and best equipped in the Middle West and symbolizes better than anything else the importance of intercollegiate athletics to both faculty and students. In February, 1922, the monastic chapter had debated whether to build a residence hall, abbey, or a gymnasium and finally decided that a gymnasium was the more essential.[37] The building was designed by E. Brielmaier and Sons, and the contract was let to the Immel

hoff, L. Senecal, G. Nass, C. Creagan, J. Baker, H. Marxer, T. Quigley. Substitutes: Green, Coupe, L. Schwartz.
Baker was captain of both teams.
[32] *Ibid.*, (Jan., 1921), 225.
The squad: Henry Merwick (captain), Thomas Quigley, John Senofsky, John Green, Edward Grosdidier, Clarence Smith, Henry Grosdidier, Leo Sander, James Baker, Harold Smith, Bernard Flaherty, Aloysius Morley.
[33] Abbot Martin at first permitted three games in each sport to be played away. Apparently the first was in basketball, St. Benedict's vs. St. Joseph Veterinary College, 53-8—*Rambler*, Jan. 1, 1922.
[34] *Ibid.*, Mar. 15, 1922.
[35] *Abbey Student*, XXXI (June, 1922), 524.
The Kansas Conference was reorganized without St. Benedict's at the end of 1928.—*Rambler*, Jan. 8, 1929.
[36] Oct. 1, 1922.
[37] Chapter Minutes, Feb. 21, 1922.

Construction Company, of Fond du Lac, Wisconsin. The basketball floor was generously proportioned to permit three intramural games at one time. The building included also a swimming pool of standard size as well as other gymnastic and recreational facilities. When completed the gymnasium had cost a little more than $240,000. St. Benedict's proudly showed its new gymnasium at the formal opening on January 13-14, 1924. The first basketball game on the new court was a loss to Baker University, 19-41.[38] A few weeks later Father Isidor Smith's students offered the first play, *Julius Caesar*, from the new stage.[39]

Intercollegiate athletics was brought under the control of a special faculty board in 1924, and for some years the College was satisfied with its athletic program. During the early years the big football game of the season was often that with St. Mary's College, of St. Marys, Kansas.[40] Coach Quigley's football teams usually broke even on the season, but the team of 1925 had an undefeated season with six wins and one tie. The basketball teams during these years usually suffered a few more defeats than victories. The road conditions and consequent transportation problems sometimes contributed extra hazards to athletics. In 1926 the *Rambler* reported:

The team that met the Kirksville Osteopaths Thursday afternoon, Oct. 14, and went down to a 14-7 defeat was simply overtrained. Twenty-four hours of pushing a two-ton bus hubdeep in Missouri mud from St. Joseph to Chillicothe, of chasing on foot up the Missouri mountains with half the State's real estate clinging to their heels, merely to harden muscles, and of dieting on chili and hamburger to help breathing, proved excellent training for the Hillites.[41]

38 *Rambler*, Jan. 15, 1924.
39 *Ibid.*, Feb. 15, 1924.
40 Father Director Lambert Burton's diary has the following: "Sept. 25, [1922] — Heard today that the Academy girls and, of course, several Sisters with them, will attend the S.B.C.-St. Mary's foot-ball game. This is the first time in history that this occurs." The girls, accompanied by several nuns, sat demurely on the grass on the steep bank west of the Administration Building, where they were joined by Father Abbot. This game is the only one known to have been attended by Sisters.
41 *Rambler*, Nov. 1, 1926.
Until 1927 St. Benedict's teams had no generally recognized nickname, and hardpressed reporters tried various possibilities, such as Saints, Irish,

Discipline and Student Government

Abbot Martin, in his first six months of administration, had permitted the completion of an intercollegiate athletics program and the plan for building a gymnasium, but then his natural hesitation asserted itself. He feared that intercollegiate athletics was an excuse to break down school discipline. At the same time the Abbot saw the threat of change from another quarter. Father Lambert Burton and others were enthusiastic participants in the National Benedictine Educational Association. This association had been organized in 1918 by representatives of the various American Benedictine schools, and the members were busily studying problems and making recommendations concerning curricula, standards, and faculty training. Abbot Martin viewed these activities with his usual caution. He expressed his own ideas to Abbot Alcuin Deutsch, of St. John's Abbey:

> Is it not advisable to work out a common "Benedictine" standard of discipline for our educational institutions? This, it seems to me, is far more important than a common course of studies. As Benedictines, standing, in name at least, for the oldest and best-tried educational institution within the Church, we ought to have some definite and uniform ideals to offer our Catholic people. Are we not rather granting our young men what they want instead of offering them what they ought to have; in other words, are we not becoming their obliging servants instead of their educators?[42]

When Abbot Martin was elected, the College was at an awkward stage in its development. These would have been tumultuous years in any case, because St. Benedict's was in the throes of change. The faculty was trying to fit old and treasured values, and some new values, with contemporary forms. The majority of the faculty agreed that traditional Benedictine educational values need not depend on the traditional classical curriculum. The faculty's disagreements were rather over questions of form

Hillites, Purples, and Purple and White. Finally the *Rambler* asked for suggestions, and 'The Ravens' became the official title.—*Ibid.*, Dec. 20, 1927.
[42] Veth to Deutsch, Atchison, Oct. 3, 1922. (SJA)

than of substance, namely, how to modernize the curriculum without losing the traditional values of educating the will as well as the intellect. Equally important was the problem of modernizing the disciplinary system, because an important but subtle educational influence in any boarding school is its residence life. The faculty debate, in other words, concerned not so much irreconcilable differences of policy but rather the questions of how fast and how far St. Benedict's should go.

Abbot Martin had had little experience in the College. In his autobiographical notes he remarks that after a year of prefecting he was happy to return to the less nerve racking life in the Abbey. His teaching experience was limited almost exclusively to the clerics. Furthermore, Abbot Martin was out of sympathy with the convictions of the majority of the faculty, and he learned to delegate authority only after some troubled experiences.[43] A general change of officials was made in 1922. In January of that year Father Damian, who had been director of the College since 1910, was relieved of the office and Father Lambert Burton was appointed. Father Lambert had been engaged in training the scholastics since 1908, as principal of the Academy of Commerce had been a member of the Board of Deans, had represented St. Benedict's at meetings of the National Catholic Educational Association, and had been secretary and an enthusiastic promoter of the National Benedictine Educational Association since its organization. Abbot Martin and Father Lambert agreed on but few points regarding St. Benedict's College, and, after three semesters as director, Father Lambert asked to be relieved and "to be sent out on a parish as far away as possible."[44]

Abbot Martin next appointed Father Henry Courtney director of the College. He presumably reflected the

[43] The canonical visitations of 1923 and 1926 drew attention to this problem. The visitators on the latter occasion advised the Abbot: "The ordinary routine work of the college should be left to those whom you have placed in charge. Failing to do this you will never get wholehearted service."—Record of Visitation, May 1, 1926.
[44] Burton to Veth, Atchison, May 10, 1923.

Abbot's ideas more faithfully, but Father Henry's methods were dictatorial, and he had rather harsh ideas on student discipline. Within two months Abbot Martin convened a faculty meeting which he hoped would be a peace conference. Instead, he found that he had a near-mutiny on his hands. The faculty put on record its "deep dissatisfaction with recent official statements and with current policies," but the Abbot could only support his appointed officials.[45] Conditions did not improve much, and at the end of that school year Father Louis Baska, principal of the high school, was appointed director and continued in that office until 1928.

Curriculum revision and intercollegiate athletics were followed some years later by a degree of student government and a new concept of student life. Before World War I there was little change in the pattern of student life. Movies replaced lantern-slide lectures in 1913, when films on educational and sometimes comic subjects were shown weekly. Father George Keim and his musicians entertained between reels. In 1912 Father George also produced the first operetta at St. Benedict's. Gilbert and Sullivan's *Pinafore* featured Dan Fletcher in the role of Dick Deadeye, S. Carroll as Sir Joseph Porter, K.C.B., J. E. Dyer as Bill Bobstay, J. Urbany as Captain Corcoran, and J. Garvey as Ralph Rackstraw.[46] But Father George was extremely temperamental, and this attempt at operetta was the last for many years. The old system of student discipline, including even chaperoned shopping trips to town, continued for a few years following World War I.

St. Benedict's had always been known as a strict school, but until the early 1920's its discipline had never been seriously out of touch with what was considered proper for a school of its type. Disciplinary policies that had been developed in the nineteenth century for a school made up almost entirely of seminarians and high-school

---

[45] Board of Professors' Minutes, Nov. 20, 1923.
[46] *Abbey Student*, XXI (Apr., 1912), 260-2.

boys simply did not fit college men. Furthermore, some of the post-war students were veterans, and the students sponsored by the Extension Society from 1923 to 1928 were for the most part older than the average college student.

To provide priests for the home missions, Monsignor Francis Kelley (later Bishop of Oklahoma City-Tulsa), of the Catholic Church Extension Society, developed a plan for belated vocations and for young men without funds to study for the priesthood. These students' training was to be predominantly in Latin, philosophy, and theology. The Extension Society recruited and sponsored these students, but they were to seek adoption by the bishop of a missionary diocese as soon as possible. Since a full range of courses from high school to theology was offered at St. Benedict's, it seemed a suitable center for such a program, and late in 1922, Archbishop Mundelein, president of the Society, approached Abbot Martin. He and the chapter accepted the project, and twenty-one Extension students enrolled in St. Benedict's in September, 1923. Their ages ranged from eighteen to thirty-five, and their classes ranged from high school to theology. Within a few years their numbers rose to about a hundred. For the second time in its history St. Benedict's was operating a general seminary.

After the school year of 1927-28 the program was discontinued because the Holy See insisted that acceptance and training of diocesan priesthood students was the responsibility of individual bishops and not the proper field for the Extension Society. Some of these students remained a number of years to complete their courses at St. Benedict's under the direction of their bishops. Though the program was of short duration, it had affected St. Benedict's and for the most part beneficially. Since mature theologians could not be asked to follow St. Benedict's traditional disciplinary system, special rules were made for them. This modification tended to break down the old system. Secondly, although the Extension students with their outrageous mixture of classes were the bane of the Dean's existence, nevertheless many of them were college students, and they helped bring the college enrollment to the magic number of one hundred, the minimum necessary for admission to the North Central Association.

Another post-war discovery was that college men preferred semi-private rooms rather than the old-fashioned common dormitories and study halls. St. Benedict's could offer a few private rooms in 1920, when the rooms on the second floor of the Administration Building (originally intended as guest rooms or music rooms) were converted to the use of college men. But only twenty or so could enjoy the luxury of living in what its inhabitants called "Demerit Alley."[47] One of the needs stressed by Father Director Lambert Burton in 1923 was rooms for college men. Since no funds were available for an elaborate residence hall, the administration resorted to an intended temporary expedient, St. Joseph Hall. The procurator had built a series of concrete garages into the side hill in the southwest corner of the campus. Later it was decided to use the garages as the foundation for a building, to be erected cheaply, to house the print shop, and temporarily, student rooms. When a proper residence hall could be built, the plan was to remove the partitions in St. Joseph Hall and use the vacated area for a book bindery. St. Joseph Hall was first occupied in September, 1924, by thirty-five lucky students, who promptly christened it the "Muehlebach."[48]

Publication of a school paper, the *Rambler*, had begun in November, 1921, with the enthusiastic support of Father Bonaventure Schwinn. The faculty adviser did much of the writing for a time, but the students soon caught on and were able to express some of their own opinions. For some time news of intercollegiate athletics dominated the paper, but intramural sports never lost their healthy liveliness. The golf course was also opened

[47] *Ibid.*, XXX (Oct., 1920), 40.
[48] *Rambler*, Mar. 1; Oct. 1, 1924.
The cost including furnishing was $36,842.91.

in 1921 and the *Abbey Student* reported that the prefects took up the game enthusiastically.[49] Elocution, oratory, drama, and music continued to be popular extracurricular activities. Intercollegiate debate was introduced in 1926 when John Bachofer and Kenneth Spurlock defeated a team from Park College, debating the child labor amendment. Father Isidor Smith continued to stage a good bit of Shakespeare, and the only complaint was that not enough students were given an opportunity to participate.[50]

By 1924 St. Benedict's had more than a hundred college students. It was the age of Harding and Coolidge and permanent prosperity, it was the jazz age, and college men at St. Benedict's tried to conform as best they could to the contemporary fashions for collegians, but they were severely handicapped. In the columns of the *Rambler*, references were made to the Charleston and even to flappers, and the ukelele craze rose and subsided in the "Muehlebach,"[51] but the social life of the college man at St. Benedict's was still largely limited to a Smoker, with speeches, songs, and a lunch.[52]

The first changes in social life are found, as might be expected, as exceptional permissions granted to the college men of St. Joseph's Hall. In 1925 "a number of St. Joseph's Hall students saw the splendid musical comedy, 'Ghosts of Hilo', staged by the academy girls in the Mount St. Scholastica auditorium, Tuesday evening, March 17."[53] A year later the denizens of the "Muehlebach" received, by way of exception, permission to attend a movie at night. They were to be back by ten o'clock.[54]

Development of a larger social life and increased participation of the students in school government went hand in hand but slowly. On April 1, 1925, a smoker was held

[49] *Abbey Student*, XXXI (Dec., 1921), 164.
[50] *Rambler*, Feb. 15, 1926.
[51] *Ibid.*, Mar. 15, 1925.
[52] *Ibid.*, Feb. 15, 1924.
[53] *Ibid.*, Apr. 1, 1925.
[54] *Ibid.*, May 1, 1926.

to promote the idea of a Student Council.[55]   A constitution was formed and adopted by unanimous vote of the students on May 18.   Student Council officers were selected by school authorities from among the class officers.[56] The new Student Council published St. Benedict's first yearbook, the *Raven*, in 1926, but otherwise student expectations were disappointed, because the hoped-for liberalization of student privileges was not forthcoming in the next two years.

Father Louis Baska, director of the College, was caught between the Abbot, whose directives Father Louis was obliged to execute, and on the other hand the faculty, who almost completely disagreed with the Abbot's views on student privileges.[57]   Abbot Martin in September, 1927, ordered Father Louis to have minutes kept of prefects' meetings and to secure the Abbot's approval for any change in school policy.   Evidently the prefects had been trying to change it quietly.   The prefects consequently reported their recommendations to the Abbot on December 4, 1927.   They urged the need of a fundamental change of policy: "Our attitude toward the students has so often been colored by our struggles to control the misconduct of a few.   The reform-school days of St. Benedict's seem to be over."   They suggested increased student participation in school government and more liberal student privileges, with, for example, one evening a week off campus for freshmen and any evenings for seniors, on condition of good conduct and passing grades.[58]

Abbot Martin did not immediately approve these recommendations.   The *Rambler's* enquiring reporter found that "Student criticisms may be summarized under three heads: the lack of sufficient privileges, the lack of sufficient variety in food, and the lack of representation of high

[55] *Ibid.*, Apr. 15, 1925.
[56] *Ibid.*, June 1; 15, 1925.
   The first officers were President John Bachofer, president of the Senior class of 1926; Secretary John Burke, president of the Junior class; and Treasurer Robert Nusbaum, vice-president of the Sophomore class.
[57] The visitators of 1926 advised Abbot Martin to be more liberal on this point.—Record of Visitation, May 1, 1926.
[58] First Report of Prefects' Committee, Dec. 4, 1927, Veth papers.

school students in the Student Council. . . When the student speaks of privileges, he refers to being released from the premises both in the afternoon and evening. This point is reasonable, because the necessity of social education is being recognized more and more by college authorities throughout the country."[59]

Dissatisfaction with the Student Council went beyond the exclusion of high school students, for a Diet meeting on March 11, 1928, took under consideration the "noticeable agitation for a new government." Two days later at a three-hour meeting of the students, a wide-open discussion revealed student dissatisfaction with the manner of voting and with representation on the Diet.[60] The students approved a new constitution on April 20. Thereafter Student Council officers were elected directly by the students.[61] One result of the airing of grievances in March was that on April 23 the faculty officially approved plans for the first student dance. The 'B' Club, with Tom Dorney as chairman, sponsored the dance. It was held at the Elk's Club and was considered a big success.[62]

The year 1928 marked the turning point. The old position of director of the College was replaced with that of dean of men. Father Louis Baska went to the Catholic University of America to do graduate work in economics, and Father Lambert Burton was appointed the first dean of men. When he was elected abbot of St. Martin's Abbey, two months later, Father Richard Burns was appointed dean of men. A degree of student government and more liberal privileges for college men were established officially with the publication of the Student Handbook the following October.[63] The sophomores proceeded with

[59] *Rambler*, Mar. 1, 1928.
[60] *Ibid.*, Mar. 15, 1928.
[61] *Ibid.*, May 1, 1928.
   The first officers elected were John Koerperich, president; Vincent Gorman, vice-president; and Harold Greif, treasurer. Greif did not return to St. Benedict's the following year, and Francis Knaup was elected treasurer.
[62] *Ibid.*, May 1; 15, 1928.
   The previous Thanksgiving a dinner given by townspeople for the football squad at Memorial Hall had been followed by an informal and spontaneous dance. As a result Father Louis was severely reprimanded by Abbot Martin.
[63] *Ibid.*, Oct. 11, 1928.

the first freshman initiation. The first student trip was to the Raven-Rockhurst game, November 3, 1928.[64]

Social relations between St. Benedict's and Mount St. Scholastica students were introduced gradually. There is no indication that Mount St. Scholastica students attended St. Benedict's first dance. In January, 1930, however, Abbot Martin consulted his council on the advisability of social gatherings for the two colleges. He presumably approved the innovation. The first Junior-Senior Prom was announced for May, 1930, but Mount St. Scholastica authorities were apparently not yet ready for individual dating. The college men then substituted a dance to be held in St. Benedict's parish hall, and the entire student body of Mount St. Scholastica College, then comprising only the Freshmen and Sophomores, was invited *en bloc*.[65] The girls invited the boys to a dance in the same parish hall the following November — the Mount's first dance.[66] The complexities of social relations were ironed out bit by bit, and, according to C. J. McNeill, '33, one of the first committeemen, the Intercollegiate Social Committee was organized in 1931-32. During that year the first prom, a rather ambitious undertaking with a dinner, was held in the Hotel Whitelaw (now Hotel Atchison). The second annual prom was the first dance held in St. Benedict's gymnasium.[67]

Growing Pains

The years 1928 to 1936 were a period of development and vigorous activity, some of it sane, and some of it not so sane. It was as though the College were going through a period of adolescence, which reached a climax in 1935-36 before achieving maturity. Intercollegiate athletics again symbolized the hopes of the College. Coach Quigley resigned in February, 1928, and was replaced by Robert Schmidt. At this time night football was introduced at

[64] *Ibid.*, Oct. 22; Nov. 15, 1928.
[65] *Ibid.*, May 1; June 4, 1930.
[66] *Ibid.*, Dec. 1, 1930.
[67] *Ibid.*, Apr. 1, 1933.

332

St. Benedict's. Coach Schmidt was succeeded by Larry ('Moon') Mullins in 1932, and soon the *Rambler* was hailing St. Benedict's entry into "Big Time Football."[68] Those were the days when little Center College won national fame by the prowess of its football team, and many small colleges tried Jack-the-Giant-Killer's road to success. St. Benedict's scheduled the University of Kansas with unhappy results.

This adolescent period's climactic year, 1935-36, opened with a football game with the University of Kansas, which was marred by unsportsmanlike conduct and ended in a 0-42 defeat for St. Benedict's. The *Rambler* summed up the general reaction with its headline, "K. U. Game Remains A Horrid Nightmare."[69] Homecoming, however, was big and successful that year, and the students declared themselves a holiday. Disciplinary action followed. The *Rambler* ended a long and sarcastic editorial, "It is certainly lucky that homecoming comes but once a year to disturb our placid, serene, and thoughtless existence."[70] The Associated Collegiate Press wrote the *Rambler's* editorials for the next few issues.

It was a turbulent year, and on February 10, 1936, the faculty met with the senior-college men in an unusual joint session "to bring about a better understanding between students and faculty." The *Rambler* reported a "general opinion among the students that the college was lacking in scholastic atmosphere, and that the prevailing spirit was hardly conducive to any sort of serious study."[71] As is usual in such cases, the spokesman for the student body on this occasion was not notorious for his love of study. The protest did not necessarily mean that the students wanted to study harder but merely that they were dissatisfied.

The climax of the year came at the Junior Prom in February. Although a working social arrangement with

68 *Ibid.*, Dec. 1, 1934.
69 *Ibid.*, Oct. 15, 1935.
70 *Ibid.*, Nov. 1, 1935.
71 *Ibid.*, Feb. 15, 1936.

333

Mount St. Scholastica had been achieved only a few years earlier, the college men, in a desire to show their male independence or perhaps impelled by the mysterious forces that move young men in springtime, elected a Prom Queen, not from the Mount, but from the rival St. Mary College in Leavenworth. The Mount countered by cancelling all dates for the Prom. The impasse was dissolved and diplomatic relations restored by the decision to crown no queen that year. Came the prom and St. Benedict's Junior-Class President introduced the charming cause of the crisis as the All-American Girl. He was called before the board of discipline and "admitted that his action was contrary to the expressed orders of the Dean of Residence, the Officers of the Student Council, and the agreement of the Junior Class made in class meeting." He was requested to withdraw from school for the balance of the year.[72] Unless some alumnus can supply the deficiency, the name of St. Benedict's own Helen of Troy is lost to history.

Although the faculty breathed a sigh of relief when that school year was over, this period was productive of much more than the antics just summarized. In the field of athletics Coach Mullins' teams were consistently good. The football team enjoyed an undefeated season in 1936, and the two preceding seasons were marred only by the losses to the University of Kansas. William (Bud) O'Neal, Leo Deutsch, and Leo Danaher were named on All-American teams. The basketball teams also had good records. The teams were outfitted in black and white suits in 1930, and three years later, at the suggestion of the 'B' Club, these colors were adopted as the College colors. Boxing was introduced in 1930 and became an intercollegiate sport at St. Benedict's in 1933. For some years a tumbling team, introduced by Father Maurus Kennedy with the support of J. B. Gatson and C. J. McNeill, produced some lively shows. In 1938, a year after Marty Peters was engaged as coach, St. Benedict's entered the Central Intercollegiate Athletic Conference of

[72] Board of Discipline Minutes, Feb. 26, 1936.

334

Kansas. A lively program of intramural sports continued throughout this period. The men of St. Joseph's Hall introduced touch football in the fall of 1930, and intramural softball leagues were added the following spring.[73]

These same years saw significant advance in music and drama. The two men most responsible for this were Father Albert Haverkamp and Mr. John McKenzie, who made the years 1935-1938 memorable.[74] But the beginning of this trend goes back to the Extension Society students at St. Benedict's. Charles M. Schneider, one of the seminarians, organized a glee club in 1927. Meanwhile Mr. McKenzie succeeded in rebuilding the orchestra, and three soloists of the Glee Club, Crowley, Early, and Rack, closed the year by singing a wonderfully hilarious *Cox and Box*. An operetta was the next step, and the first was *Pickles*, produced in 1930. Father Isidor Smith had to recruit his feminine leads and chorus from town, except for a group of ten dancers added as an afterthought by the Mount. With this production the *Rambler* hailed "A New Era Of Activities," for *Pickles* was the first St. Benedict's stage production that included women.

For some years the operetta was an annual event. The hectic year 1935-36 brought *Tulip Time*, the first operetta produced by the joint efforts of St. Benedict's and Mount St. Scholastica. In the following spring Father Albert and Mr. McKenzie produced Haydn's *Creation* and wound up the year with a three-day music festival. A year later, in the spring of 1937, the Twin College Players was organized and produced *Death Takes a Holiday*. So much enthusiasm developed that students began trying their hands at writing and producing one-act plays. And for

[73] Lack of specific activities for high-school students was. their complaint in the early 1920's, but they were needed to fill out the college teams. In 1928 the high-school basketball team topped two very successful seasons (twenty-one successive victories) by winning the Catholic State High School championship at St. Marys. At the National tournament in Chicago they were eliminated in the first round by Elder High of Cincinnati.—*Rambler*, Mar. 15; Apr. 1, 1928. They were State Catholic champions again in 1929 and in a state tournament lost to Lawrence in the third round.—*Ibid.*, Mar. 15; Apr. 4, 1929.

[74] Mr. McKenzie was a well-trained musician with a sparkling personality. He was a member of St. Benedict's faculty from 1927 until his death, August 30, 1942.

a time in 1939 the students of the two colleges produced weekly programs over the local radio station, KVAK. Father Albert staged a production of *The Upper Room* with such success that with the aid of Bill Bannon,'94, it was taken to the Kansas City Music Hall for Lenten audiences. Unfortunately, Father Albert expended more nervous energy in this work than he could spare, and so he asked to be relieved in 1938. Abbot Martin reluctantly acceded to his request and appointed him pastor of St. Benedict's Church, Atchison. In time other men were found to carry on and develop this tradition of dramatics just as Father Albert had developed the work that can be traced back through Fathers Isidor Smith, Damian Lavery, Ignatius Stein, and Philip Williams.

During this same period other extracurricular activities had been developing steadily. Father Edgar Schmiedeler, the first trained sociologist at the College, arranged a series of lectures on social questions and organized a Social Study Club back in 1922. Two years later he was instrumental in introducing the St. Vincent de Paul Society to St. Benedict's. At first a conference unit for the senior sociology class was formed to study the social work of the Society. Probably nothing at St. Benedict's has had as much influence in teaching practical sociology and Christian charity to succeeding generations of students. The sixth annual meeting of the Catholic Rural Life Conference, held at St. Benedict's in 1928, stimulated interest in rural problems. Father Charles Aziere promoted study clubs, particularly regarding the cooperative movement. Father Victor Gellhaus organized a Round Table Club for discussing problems of domestic and international politics. This organization ultimately became the International Relations Club. In keeping with this trend scholars and leaders in various fields were invited to lecture at St. Benedict's. Again using the hectic year 1935-36 as an example, students heard Christopher Hollis, the noted historian, and went to Mount St. Scholastica to hear Dorothy Day, co-founder of the Catholic Worker Movement.

These adolescent years of the College also brought notable progress in the development of the curriculum and in training the faculty. The Board of Deans in its first years had been the most influential voice in developing a new college policy, but by the middle 1920's the deans complained that they were not permitted to make necessary changes even in their own departments. In the summer of 1927 the Dean of the College, Father Malachy Sullivan, and the Principal of the High School, Father Victor Gellhaus, asked to be relieved. Father Sylvester Schmitz had just won his doctorate in education from the Catholic University of America and had intended spending the summer in Columbia University for a firsthand look at progressive education. He was hurriedly recalled to become dean. In taking over his new position he observed that the administrative conflict had destroyed faculty esprit-de-corps. "The conclusion was rather clear that some other organization which would break completely with tradition would have to be established."[75]

Father Sylvester's immediate solution was establishing a new administrative body, the College Faculty, which would meet under the chairmanship of the Dean of the College instead of the Abbot and was to be under the direct jurisdiction of the Abbot instead of the Director. The faculty was given control over all academic matters, including the arrangement and equipment of classrooms. Under Father Sylvester's leadership the faculty quickly recovered its spirit, solved its problems by committee study, and made steady advances. It promptly appointed a Committee on Organization, which proposed that the position of Director be discontinued and that the office of Dean of Residence (later changed to Dean of Men) be substituted. This change was adopted the following year. College policy in the last analysis remained the responsibility of the Abbot, but the Committee on Organization proposed a special group of advisers, the School Council. The Abbot accepted this proposal. The School Council

[75] Schmitz, "Curriculum," 201.

included the Abbot's monastic council, the officials of the seminary, college, scholasticate, and high school, as well as elected representatives of the prefects and of the college and high school faculties. This organization has been amended and polished but is basically still the college administrative board.

The program of faculty graduate training soon began to bear fruit. As quickly as one monk completed his studies, another was given a leave of absence. With a growing number of professors qualified to head departments according to current academic standards, the faculty in 1928 felt justified in offering majors in history, English, economics, philosophy, education, sociology, Latin, and chemistry.[76] A year later a major was introduced in music. A journalism school was added in 1930 but was soon discontinued because it had too few students and was considered a step away from the liberal arts ideal that the College sought to preserve. Within the next few years the faculty took steps both to secure better knowledge of its students' educational background and abilities and to demand more mature thought of its graduates. Placement tests for Freshmen and comprehensive examinations for Seniors were inaugurated in 1934.

College facilities were greatly expanded when the new Abbey was completed in 1929. When the monks moved into their new quarters, the old abbey was gradually remodeled to provide rooms for 150 students, tripling private-room facilities previously available. Most of the dormitories in the Administration Building were partitioned into classrooms or were used for an expanded library. The new classrooms in turn made possible the expansion of the science laboratories in Bishop Fink Hall. The chemistry laboratories took over another floor in Lemke Hall. In 1934 the last two years of high school were transferred to Maur Hill, and the space gained by that move sufficed until after World War II.

[76] Faculty Minutes, May 3, 1928.

St. Benedict's had increased its residence facilities just in time to welcome the depression. In 1932 the Abbey debt was more than half a million dollars, the drought years put farmers in an almost hopeless position, and the College was faced with the likelihood of a serious decline in enrollment. Father Sylvester and other monks recruited students in metropolitan Chicago with such success that in two years Chicago-area students made up one-fifth of the College enrollment. Father Sylvester felt that a serious setback had been averted, for the enrollment did not decline but even increased in those difficult years.[77] In 1925 College enrollment (excluding theology students) was 112. Only four years later the figure was 222 and remained substantially stable until 1933. In 1934 enrollment went up to 241, and from that year until 1937 St. Benedict's had about 250 college students each year. In 1938 the figure rose to 279, and from the following year until the country's entry into the war enrollment was around 300.

Growth implied increased administrative complexity. For almost as long as the oldest faculty member could remember, periodic suggestions had been made to appoint a policy committee to study College needs, to draw up a suitable statement of policy, and to define the functions of each department and official. Father Sylvester was convinced that had such a policy been introduced years earlier, the faculty might have been spared much grief. However, only "after nearly twenty years of experimentation," he wrote, did Abbot Martin finally appoint a policy committee. The members were Fathers Bonaventure Schwinn, chairman, Sylvester Schmitz, Florian Demmer, Anthony Reilman, Victor Gellhaus, Malachy Sullivan, and Gervase Burke. This committee first met on April 13, 1937 and it submitted its report on May 20, 1939. This report formed the basis for the faculty handbook printed in 1940.[78] The handbook marked the conclusion of the argument that had begun in the monastic chapter in 1910.

[77] Schmitz, "Curriculum," 300-303.
[78] Ibid., 353-8.

The metamorphosis that St. Benedict's College went through between about 1920 and 1936 was productive of many things, some in retrospect comic, and some admirable. This period was definitely one of intense activity and change. Even the pioneers had not lived through anything quite like it. By 1940 the character of the College had to a large extent jelled. When in 1945 Father Sylvester looked back at the development of St. Benedict's curriculum, he was satisfied that the community had made a notable record, sometimes at great sacrifice, in providing opportunity for its monks' graduate training. During the thirty years from 1915 to 1945 monks had accumulated 119 years of graduate training. Nevertheless, Father Sylvester was convinced that only a beginning had been made. "In spite of this," he wrote, "the community now has only fourteen members with the Ph.D. degree, seven with two years of graduate work, and seventeen with the master's degree or its equivalent."[79] Nonetheless, as more monks became qualified in the various fields of study, by 1946 the curriculum was rounded out with recognized majors in philosophy, history, sociology, economics, business, English, Latin, German, mathematics, chemistry, biology, and music. The process Father Sylvester had so ably encouraged continues to contribute new blood to the college faculty and to broaden and deepen the scope of its educational offerings.

Father Sylvester also found other indications of real progress. He noted particularly that by 1930 the faculty had begun serious discussion of the aims and organization of liberal education and that for the first time some faculty members had won professional recognition nationally. Discussion of the aims and meaning of liberal education promises never to end, of course, but is quite essential to St. Benedict's welfare and progress. The professional recognition accorded faculty members indicated the intellectual progress achieved in so short a time. Father Colman Farrell, among others, taught in the Catholic Uni-

[79] *Ibid.*, 404-5.

versity of America several summers. In 1932-33 he also received an American Library Association fellowship with a Carnegie Corporation grant-in-aid to catalog and classify religious literature in the Library of Congress. He did this work under the direction of the University of Chicago graduate school.

Father Edgar Schmiedeler, head of the department of sociology, in 1922 introduced marriage and family courses that were the first offered for credit in any college or university in the country. His *Introductory Study of the Family* (1930) was the first Catholic textbook published on this subject in the United States. In 1931 Father Edgar was named director of the Rural Life Bureau of the National Catholic Welfare Conference in Washington, D.C. He later organized the Family Life Bureau and became its first director. He paralleled twenty-five years of strenuous organization work with vigorous activity as a writer, editor, and lecturer. During those years he published five books on family problems, filled a number of editorial assignments, and wrote innumerable articles and columns. When he retired in 1956, his co-workers in Washington presented him with a silver plaque, saluting him as "priest, publicist and scholar. . . in grateful recognition of his tireless zeal in furthering the cause of Christian Family Life as first director of the NCWC Family Life Bureau." He received further recognition when the Catholic University of America in the same year awarded him an honorary degree of Doctor of Laws.

Father Sylvester Schmitz was another recognized leader in Catholic educational circles. He was active in the National Catholic Educational Association, the National Benedictine Educational Association, and in the various educational organizations of the State. He was active also in the North Central Association. He fought to help "save Catholic college accreditation when in the late 1920's a move was on foot to withdraw recognition if colleges lacked a large financial endowment. He supported other Catholic leaders in successfully obtaining a new policy whereby the contributed services of religious

teachers became the equivalent of a financial endowment."[80] Father Sylvester contributed articles to a number of educational journals and published a number of
monographs, especially in educational psychology. After
he retired as dean of the College he wrote the history on
which much of this chapter is based: "The Development
of the Curriculum of St. Benedict's College, 1915-1945."
This sober account of the critical period in the development of the College, written with remarkable objectivity
by the principal architect, is an invaluable contribution
to the history of St. Benedict's.

No one man, of course, made St. Benedict's College,
but no man contributed more to its development than
Father Sylvester. To the students and to the young
faculty members whom he had helped train, Father Sylvester personified St. Benedict's. He was born of sturdy
German and Bohemian immigrant stock at Seneca, Kansas, on July 13, 1888. He enrolled at St. Benedict's in
September, 1901, among a group of promising youngsters
who entered the scholasticate just after the turn of the
century. Father Sylvester made vows as a Benedictine
July 11, 1907, studied philosophy and theology in St.
John's at Collegeville, and was ordained June 28, 1912.
At St. Benedict's he was at various times principal of the
high school, registrar, and from 1927 to 1945, dean of the
College.

He was an intense and energetic man. As a young professor, deeply involved in pushing through the modernization of the curriculum, he drove himself too hard. He was
such a stern taskmaster that his students called him 'The
Bear.' The tension grew greater, and in 1921 he had a
nervous breakdown. This misfortune was possibly a
blessing in disguise, for after eighteen months of rest he
returned to a light teaching assignment, then went to
the Catholic University of America for graduate study,
and returned to become the dean of the college. He was
sometimes still called 'The Bear,' but now affectionately,

[80] *Raven Review*, Jan., 1954.

342

for he was as kindly and understanding a guide as any student could ask. As a professor he taught with all his old intensity and enthusiasm but with an extraordinary interest in the individual student. Father Sylvester was a man who quite simply and naturally left a deep impression on those who came under his influence. Students who missed this influence in the classroom could come under his spell at the bridge table, on a bobsled, or on the Missouri River. After his breakdown Father Sylvester had learned to relax. He always had energy to spare, and he let it spill over into a variety of hobbies. As a youth he had been an able athlete — one of the best pitchers ever developed at St. Benedict's and an enthusiastic basketball player. As Dean of the College he introduced students to the joys of roaring down the bluff on a bobsled. In warmer months they could sail with him on the Missouri. He acquired a large, clumsy skiff and rigged it with a sail. A good stiff gale brought out the sail, but if there were merely a breeze, Father Sylvester put his back to the oars. He built a concrete blockhouse for his equipment, and the dedication of Father Sylvester's Oar House in 1936 initiated the annual faculty picnic. He loved picnics. For indoor sport Father Sylvester turned to bridge, which he played with laughing vigor and with scorn for orthodoxy. He also spent many happy relaxed hours playing the zither. And then, quite typically, just to see if he could do it, he built a zither. Throughout his life, at work and at play, Father Sylvester was a deeply spiritual man, a man of prayer. He was among the wisest guides of souls that St. Benedict's has ever had.

By 1945 Father Sylvester was tired and ready to be relieved of his position as dean. In his last years he returned by preference to the subject he had taught in his youth — elementary Latin. He had always insisted upon the importance of a good beginning in fundamentals. He died December 18, 1953, at the age of sixty-five. Such a man, so soundly spiritual, so professionally competent, and so humanly interesting, necessarily had a great influence on the community and on the College. Father

Sylvester guided St. Benedict's out of the days of the old academy into the world of the modern college. He planned, he taught, he persuaded, and he worked. He guided young monks to graduate studies in the best universities in Europe, Canada, and the United States. Some forty priests received advanced degrees during his eighteen years as dean of the College. More important than everything else, St. Benedict's College still breathes the spirit and traditions built into it by Father Sylvester.

Since The War

On July 6, 1943, the monastic chapter elected Father Cuthbert McDonald the third abbot of St. Benedict's. By virtue of special powers granted by the Holy See during World War II, the President of the Congregation, Abbot Alcuin Deutsch, confirmed the election immediately. The new Abbot was born in Dublin, Ireland, July 6, 1894. He made vows as a Benedictine July 2, 1915, and received ordination June 27, 1921. He had been professor of Greek and College treasurer for many years and since 1940 had been also dean of men. He was solemnly blessed as abbot by the Most Reverend Paul C. Schulte, bishop of Leavenworth, on September 8, 1943.

Abbot Cuthbert was faced with all the problems of a school in wartime. Shortly after Pearl Harbor St. Benedict's assessed its possibilities and applied for a government technical training program. Federal officials, however, did not grant the program. Consequently, the College offered what services it could to the government, such as the Naval Reserve programs. Enrollment, which had been slightly more than 300 before the war, declined until it reached a low of seventy-five at one time in 1944. Intercollegiate football was suspended in 1943 for the duration of the war. The College of course maintained the essentials of its liberal arts and sciences program, released as many monks as possible for military chaplaincies and other temporary assignments, and began to plan for the postwar period.

Fathers Paschal Pretz and Romuald Fox were released to teach electronics at the University of Kansas. Father

Romuald taught later also in the University of Notre Dame. At the request of the Bishop of Davenport, Fathers Bonaventure Schwinn and Mark Merwick organized a Catholic Student Center at the University of Iowa. Father Mark and Father Walter Vollmar taught in St. Ambrose College, Davenport, Iowa, and Father Edward Schmitz taught in St. Bede College, Peru, Illinois. Meanwhile ten monks were released to serve as military chaplains: Fathers Fabian Harshaw, Otho Sullivan, Raphael O'Malley, Jerome Merwick, Boniface Moll, Gervase Burke, Philip O'Connor, George Spiegelhalter, Peter Beckman, and Maurus Kennedy.

While Abbot Martin was still in office he had appointed a policy committee to plan for the future of the College. The members of the committee were Father Bonaventure Schwinn, chairman, Fathers Sylvester Schmitz, Cuthbert McDonald, Anthony Reilman, Aloysius Kropp, Malachy Sullivan, Victor Gellhaus, and Gervase Burke. The faculty, under the committee's guidance, began studying contemporary experiments in liberal arts education with the intent of developing a clearcut policy for the postwar St. Benedict's. No change in the fundamental aims of the College was thought necessary, but the faculty generally agreed that new buildings would be among the first needs. Meanwhile the *Rambler* and the *Abbey News* published news of the many alumni in the armed forces and naturally provided closer contact with alumni everywhere. They responded enthusiastically to Abbot Cuthbert's proposal of building a new residence hall as a memorial to St. Benedict's alumni who had given their lives in the war. The Centennial Expansion Committee was organized October 29, 1944, with Mr. Leo Nusbaum as its general chairman. He volunteered full-time service without salary. Mr. Nusbaum's energetic leadership has been invaluable, because he is an experienced business man, having retired from managing a wholesale grocery shortly before accepting his new position at St. Benedict's. He had been active in Catholic action long before the Pope had given it a name. He had aided the Kansas bishops in safeguarding the parochial school system and had long given active and personal support to St. Benedict's College. With the Centennial Expansion Program organized, the monastic chapter decided that the first goal would be a new residence hall.

Expecting an immediate rush of students following the war, the monks could not wait for the time and funds needed to build a new residence hall. So the administration began modernizing the interior of Freshman Hall several months before the war ended. This improvement provided rooms for thirty-five additional students. The increased living accommodations, however, were far from sufficient to house the rapidly growing number of veterans who enrolled immediately following the war. The enrollment increased to 400 a year after the war, and the number soon rose to 515. Consequently, 135 out-of-town students were forced to live off campus. Furthermore, the increased enrollment demanded additional classrooms, and so space in the Administration Building was realigned for a net gain of five classrooms. Two more classrooms were acquired by obtaining a former military barracks and locating it northeast of St. Joseph's Hall.

Other physical improvements achieved during this immediate postwar period were renovating the interior of St. Joseph's Hall and the gymnasium. With the increased number of vocations to the Brotherhood and with an expanding clericate, more living accommodations were needed also in the Abbey. The top floor of the Abbey, most of which had remained unfinished since 1929, was completed in 1947. The clericate was then moved to the newly-furnished quarters, and the Brothers have since lived on the ground floor vacated by the clerics. Other improvements within the Abbey soon followed, and in 1950 the monastic refectory, used but unfinished since 1929, was finally decorated. During this period also the plant of the Abbey Student Press was expanded, a recreational center was built at Maur Hill, the farm in the Missouri River bottoms was enlarged, and the College dairy farm was developed as a demonstration unit for the agricultural courses now offered in the College. Mr. Herbert Funk, instructor in agriculture, has supervised a great improvement in the dairy farm and the herd, and the dairy now has a Grade-A rating. The backlog of essential physical improvements had been due to the large debt on the Abbey, the economic depression of the 1930's, and the impossibility of procuring building materials during World War II. The debt had been liquidated in 1944, the war ended in 1945, and so the monks undertook and completed a major physical improvement program during the five years following the war.

Operating and maintaining St. Benedict's demands great man power and many talents. Today's Brothers exhibit a wonderful variety of skills as farmers, gardeners, viticulturists, truck and tractor drivers, welders and mechanics, carpenters, plumbers, electricians, printers, secretaries, and college professors. Fortunately, vocations to the Brotherhood have in part, at least, kept pace with St. Benedict's postwar growth. The policies introduced in Abbot Martin's administration have been further developed into a well-rounded monastic life.

While the postwar improvement program was in progress the Expansion Program Committee had been successfully soliciting funds from alumni and other friends. Furthermore, the well-known architect, Mr. Barry Byrne, had presented a master campus plan for the long-range future development of St. Benedict's, and a building committee was ready with plans for a new residence hall designed by the architects' firm of Carroll and Dean, of Kansas City, Missouri. On April 24, 1950, the ceremonial ground-breaking for this new building took place, and in September, 1951, it was filled to capacity by 104 students and three prefects. On October 20, as part of the Homecoming festivities, the new building was blessed and dedicated. Special guests for the occasion were the parents of the fifty alumni memorialized on the plaque in the reception room and individually on the doors of the students' rooms. Memorial Hall includes a chapel, dedicated to St. Martin, and a comfortable lounge. This new residence hall was erected at a cost of $363,000 and is the first St. Benedict's building totally paid for by alumni and other friends.

The expanded residence facilities on campus gave rise to new problems. The greatly increased number of boarding students created difficulties in the dining rooms and kitchens. More Sisters were obtained for the kitchen, and in 1955 their house was enlarged. Much new kitchen equipment was added, and the kitchen itself was expanded and thoroughly modernized. Finally, in September, 1956, the century-old practice of serving students family style gave way to a cafeteria.

With the graduation of the veterans, the enrollment declined slightly but not for long. By 1957 the students numbered more than 600, and once again more than a hundred students were forced to live off campus. When the pastors of St. Benedict's Church moved to a new rectory west of the church in 1956, their former quarters in the Old Priory became the students' infirmary. The old infirmary was converted to rooms for ten students, a negligible number compared with facilities needed. St. Benedict's consequently applied to the Housing and Home Finance Agency of the federal government for a loan to build another residence hall to house 150 students. The designs of the architects, Shaughnessy, Bower, and Grimaldi, of Kansas City, were approved, and the contract was awarded to F. P. Gehring of Atchison. On February 22, 1957, ground was broken for this latest addition to the College.

Those exciting student days of St. Benedict's adolescent period prior to World War II will presumably never come again, but college students being what they are and the educative process being what it is, life at the College continues to be interesting and never quite predictable. The delightful madness that envelops a boarding college with a championship team still occurs, most notably in 1954 when the Ravens won the National Association of Intercollegiate Athletics basketball championship.

Since the war other extracurricular activities, particularly student study groups, have also benefitted from intercollegiate contacts. St. Benedict's joined the National Federation of Catholic College Students at the end of 1940, and three years later St. Benedict's students helped organize the Central Mid-West Region of the NFCCS. Older clubs have been stimulated by contact with like-minded students in other colleges, and the Federation has added richness to college life by encouraging, through its numerous commissions, the study of some fundamental problems facing the young Catholic citizen.

In the past ten years the program of courses has been revised and enlarged, and at present degrees are offered in fourteen major fields. To enable all students to secure at least two years of Catholic college education, special curricula are offered in preparation for the various professional schools. Courses in agriculture have been the latest addition in this program. A new feature in recent years is the arrangement of the pre-agricultural and pre-engineering curricula in cooperation with certain professional schools. A physical education major has been reintroduced, particularly to supply Catholic teachers and coaches for high schools. The latest addition to the curriculum has been courses in fine arts. The deliberations of the policy committee set up during the war have resulted in increased stress on general education and less specialization, providing the student with a broader background. To help students integrate various fields of knowledge and enquire into the philosophical and theological implications of some concrete modern problems, the faculty has been offering a seminar since 1948.

St. Benedict's history clearly shows that the College has simply grown with the people it serves. The purpose for which the College was founded, namely, to help educate a native clergy, has never been abandoned. In its first century St. Benedict's has played a part in educating 895 priests. Of this number 189 joined St. Benedict's Abbey, 223 were educated for other Benedictine abbeys, and 77 were members of other religious orders. Of the 895 priests, 416 were ordained for sixty dioceses in the United States, and approximately a fifth of these priests were ordained for the Archdiocese of Kansas City in Kansas. St. Benedict's takes particular pride that eight alumni have been consecrated bishops and seven have become abbots.

In its earliest years St. Benedict's gave a classical education to youngsters who later became priests or, in some cases, became lawyers, doctors, or farmers, but the majority of the immigrants' sons wanted a commercial education for better prospects in the business world. With the passage of the years the educational needs of the immigrants' grandsons and greatgrandsons have grown, greater numbers prepare for professions, and at last some are going on to graduate schools. St. Benedict's has never lost sight of the liberal arts ideal and has always endeavored to help the student develop his faculties so that he can enjoy a richer life as a human being and as a child of God.

Maur Hill, the preparatory school for St. Benedict's College, first opened its doors in January, 1920, as a boarding grade school for Catholic boys. Forty-three "Minims" had been transferred from St. Benedict's, and in the following year the enrollment rose to eighty-four. To improve the school's facilities, the Administration Building (old Atchison Hall) was completely rebuilt, made fireproof, and was given another story. The student chapel in the added story was decorated with paintings by a Cincinnati artist, Theodore Brasch.

Demand for a boarding grade school was not great, however, and by 1923 enrollment had declined to fifty. At the same time St. Benedict's College was growing, more space was needed for library expansion, and accrediting agencies favored separating the college from the high school. Consequently, the first two years of high school were successively transferred from St. Benedict's to Maur Hill in 1925 and 1926. Maur Hill discontinued the lower grades and operated as a junior high school (seventh to tenth grades) until 1934. In September, 1934, Maur Hill absorbed the senior high school at St. Benedict's, discontinued the grades, and became a standard four-year high school. Enrollment rose to 157 in the following year, slipped back to 126 in 1941 but thereafter rose steadily. Since 1950 the enrollment of Maur Hill has been approximately 225, its present capacity. Of this number between eighty and ninety are day students.

Alumni remember with affection the early principals of Maur Hill, Fathers Cyril Bayer, Claude Enslein, and Mark Merwick. A school's eccentricities usually form the stuff of alumni memories, and, in the interest of body tone and posture, the first two principals required drill and calisthenics before breakfast each morning. Another rule called for wearing house slippers to preserve the gleaming floors of the newly-remodeled Administration Building.

One of the greatest contributors to Maur Hill's success was Father Albert Haverkamp. He was assigned to Maur Hill in 1920 and remained there until 1932. His great talent for producing music and drama soon enriched the life of Maur Hill students. His choruses were favorite entertainers and broadcast over radio stations in neighboring towns. By 1928, under Father Albert's direction, Maur Hill students were staging creditable productions of Gilbert and Sullivan.

The *Tatler* began publication in 1926 when Maur Hill was a junior high school. Until 1934, when Maur Hill became a four-year high school, the *Tatler* was a mimeographed paper. Back in the days when it was only a grade school, Maur Hill had ferociously-named teams of very small boys vigorously competing in basketball and baseball. The school had a lively intramural program and a varsity that played all available neighboring schools. Moving the high school to Maur Hill protected the lives of the high school students from being overshadowed by college sports and other activities. On the athletic field Maur Hill has usually given a good account of itself.

Camp St. Maur was opened in the summer of 1937. This summer camp for boys on the campus of Maur Hill is staffed by young priests and clerics from St. Benedict's

Abbey and has proved popular with both boys and their parents. In its first quarter century Maur Hill School has developed a rich boarding-school life and traditions of its own. Its faculty of enthusiastic young monks has kept pace with the growing enrollment and now numbers eleven priests and two lay instructors. Maur Hill has also expanded its curriculum without, however, departing from its purpose as a preparatory school for St. Benedict's.

As a result of the mission to the settlers, twenty-seven monks still provide pastoral care for twenty-one parishes. Some of the early missions grew into large parishes with parochial schools. Sts. Peter and Paul Parish in Seneca has even its own high school. Three of the old mission stations, Hiawatha, Troy, and Wetmore, received resident pastors only in recent years. Some country parishes, however, reached their prime in the days of the small family farm before the end of the last century. The increasing size of individual farms and the consequent decline in the number of farmers has reduced the number of souls in these parishes. The 1955 report for parishes served by St. Benedict's Abbey is as follows:

CHURCH	CITY	No. of families	No. of children in parochial school (or religion classes)	No. of Baptisms	No. of Marriages
St. Benedict's	Atchison, Kans.	412	180	50	14
Sacred Heart	Atchison, Kans.	220	118	39	5
St. Joseph's	Atchison, Kans.	225	195	73	26
St. Patrick's	Atchison, Kans., RR	42	38	7	2
St. Louis (Good Intent)	Atchison, Kans., RR	56	47	6	2
St. John Baptist	Doniphan, Kans.	24	(30)	3	1
St. Benedict's	Bendena, Kans.	39	(58)	4	–
St. Vincent's	Severance, Kans.	29		3	–
St. Mary's	Purcell, Kans.	44	23	7	–
St. Benedict's	Kansas City, Kans.	428	254	64	21
Sts. Peter and Paul	Seneca, Kans.	510	429	83	24
St. Mary's	Seneca, Kans., RR (Wildcat)	115	178	14	8
St. Ann's	Effingham, Kans.	63	23	7	3

Immac. Conception	Valley Falls, Kans.	61	57	7	4
St. James	Wetmore, Kans.	57	27	14	1
St. Bede's	Kelly, Kans.	117	155	14	4
St. Ann's	Hiawatha, Kans.	77	(67)	19	5
St. Charles	Troy, Kans.	60	(46)	11	3
St. Malachy's	Creston, Iowa	204	122	12	10
St. John's	Burlington, Iowa	661	417	97	23
St. Mary's	Des Moines, Iowa	33	–	6	1
St. Peter's	Council Bluffs, Iowa	136	156	36	9

Eleven members of the community are chaplains at Mount St. Scholastica College and Convent, Atchison; St. Scholastica Convent, Chicago, Ill.; St. Mary's Convent, Nauvoo, Ill.; St. Benedict's Convent, Waunakee, Wis.; St. Lucy's Priory, Glendora, Calif.; St. Mary Convent, Xavier, Kans.; Ursuline College, Paola, Kans.; Lillis High School, Kansas City, Mo.; St. Mary's Hospital, Manhattan, Kans.; and Winter General Hospital, Topeka, Kans. Two monks are chaplains in the armed forces.

The first centenary of St. Benedict's Abbey is best symbolized in the new Abbey Church. It is the second built by the community but the first to have adequate accommodations for the only really essential work of the monk, worshipping God in the monastic choir. Prior Augustine Wirth's Abbey Church, without a proper monastic choir, could not be remedied. A new Abbey Church was the very heart of Abbot Martin's hopes for his community, but the depression prevented the realization of his plan. After World War II Abbot Cuthbert pressed in earnest for this fulfillment of the community's dreams. The project began to take definite form by 1950, and the firm of Barry Byrne and Parks was chosen to design the church. Since repeating the Gothic style of the monastery was neither practical nor desirable, the architect was faced with the difficult task of designing the church in a contemporary style that would nevertheless blend with the monastery. The contract was awarded to the Lippert Construction Company, of Oklahoma City, and ground was broken on March 31, 1955.

The new Abbey Church with its massive tower seems to soar into the western sky. The choir accommodates

160 monks, and the nave seats more than 600 persons. The vast crypt contains a large chapel for the Brothers, an Our Lady chapel particularly suitable for retreats, and twenty-six other altars for the monks' private Masses. This new Abbey Church, dedicated in the centennial year, is a fitting crown to a century of monastic life in Kansas.

The community that began monastic life in Father Henry Lemke's shack in Doniphan now numbers 168 members: 121 priests, 17 clerics, 27 Brothers and 3 Oblate Brothers. The bonds that unite today's big monastic family to the handful of pioneers who made the first community are very real. No one is more vividly conscious of his debt to past generations than the monk, because the present was built by the past, and the ideals of the first generation remain the ideals of the last. St. Benedict's has not merely the buildings hallowed by the sacrifices and lives of its pioneers but also a rich complex of family tradition built from their devotion, their piety, and their very human peculiarities. The external works of the community, such as the missions and the schools, have been byproducts of the essential monastic vocation, namely, community life for the purpose of seeking God through prayer and work.

U. I. O. G. D.

INDEX

Aaron, Father Leo, 231, 247, 282
Abbey Church (1957), 354 f.
Abbey News, 304
Abbey Student, 269 ff.
Abbey Student Press, 270 f., 347
Academic Standards, 282 ff.
Accreditation, 314 ff.
Administration Building, 231 ff., 310 f., 338, 347
Afton, Iowa, 195, 199
Allermann, Brother Andrew, 100, 145 f., 177
Altmann, Father Stanislaus, 247 f.
Alumni, 235, 252, 346, 349
Arago, Nebr., 125
Art, 269
Aspinwall, Nebr., 125
Association of Catholic Colleges, 284
Atchison, Kans., 38, 45 ff., 77 f., 129
Athletics, 57, 271 ff.
Athletics, intercollegiate, 274 f., 319 ff., 332 ff.
Athletics, intramural, 272 f., 320, 335
Augustinian Recollects, 305
Avoca, Nebr., 199
Axtell, Kans., 187
Aziere, Father Charles, 336
Baileyville, Kans., 189
Baker, James H., 321 f.
Ball, Brother Bernard, 145, 176
Baltimore, Third Plenary Council, 277
Barry, Brother Eugene, 177
Bartl, Father Thomas, 62 f., 76, 78, 87, 112, 120 ff., 126, 142 f., 188
Baska, Father Louis, 303, 312 f., 326, 330

Bath rooms, 261
Bavarian Congregation, 2, 85, 207
Bayer, Father Cyril, 314, 352
Bayer, Father Urban, 93
Beasley, Alvin C., 312
Bellemont, Kans., 121
Bendena, Kans., 36, 45, 117, 120 ff., 133, 189 f., 199, 353
Benedictine Sisters, Mount St. Scholastica, 76, 82, 175, 187 f., 260, 262, 294, 303
Benedictine Sisters, Nebraska City, 124
Benedictine Sister, St. Ottilien, 294 f.
Bishop Fink Hall, 163 f., 169 f.. 250 f., 287
Blahnik, Father Luke, 270
Bliemel, Brother Lambert, 145 f.
Board of Deans, 313, 337
Board of Education, Kansas State, 315
Board of Professors, 276
Bode, Father Eugene, 66, 87, 112, 141 f.
Boesen, Peter, 270
Bradley, Father Aloysius, 229, 231 ff., 285, f., 314
Bradley, Father Matthew, 214, 245, 247, 258
Braunmueller, Abbot Benedict, 179
Brielmaier and Sons, 299 ff.
Brothers, 145, 175 ff., 223, 306 f., 347 f.
Brown and Bier, 82, 106.
Brown Spring, 235
Brownsville, Nebr., 118, 125
Bryan, W. J., 266
Burk, Father Thomas, 155, 196, 202 f., 215 f., 235 f.

356

357

Rotter, Father Severin, 62, 119 f.
Rudroff, Father Alban (Casimir),
66, 87, 113, 196 f.
Rulo, Nebr., 118, 125

Sacred Heart Church, Atchison, 191,
198, 353
Sahuayo, Mexico, 302 f.
St. Augustine's Hall, 349
St. Augustine's Settlement, see Fi-
delity
St. Bede's School Society, 108 f.
St. Benedict's Abbey, 109 ff.
St. Benedict's Church, Atchison, 47,
76 ff., 82, 87, 93 f., 96, 117, 164 f.,
191 f., 198, 349, 353
St. Benedict's Church, Kansas City,
Kans., 353
St. Benedict's College, 47 ff., 76 ff.,
88, 96, 102 f., 104
St. Benedict's College, General Re-
gulations, 55, 257 f.
St. Benedict's Colony, see Bendena
St. Benedict's Priory, 44
St. Boniface Abbey, Munich, 108
St. Bridget's, Kans., 118 ff., 126,
186 f.
St. Catherine's Indian School, Santa
Fe, 214 ff.
St. John's Abbey, 15, 44, 111, 179,
303
St. Joseph, Mo., 117
St. Joseph's Church, Atchison, 353
St. Joseph's Convent, Atchison, 76
St. Joseph's Hall, 328 f.
St. Louis College, 191
St. Malachy's Priory, Creston, 192ff.
St. Mary's Church, St. Benedict,
see Wildcat
St. Patrick's Church, 38, 117, 120,
126, 190 f., 199, 353
St. Vincent Archabbey, 12, 91, 107,
179, 211
St. Vincent de Paul Society, 336
Salmon, Father Robert, 273
Salpointe, Archbishop J. B., 214 f.
Sand's Settlement, Nebr., 38

Sant' Anselmo, 181 f., 289 f.
Santa Fe, N.M., 214 ff.
Sause, Father Bernard, 304
Scheier, Father Leander, 314
Schmidt, Robert, 332 f.
Schmidt, Father Winfried, 112, 168,
196, 253
Schmiedeler, Father Edgar, 304,
319, 336, 341
Schmitz, Father Edward, 314, 346
Schmitz, Father Sylvester, 275, 311
ff., 319 f., 337 ff., 341 ff.
Schneider, Charles M., 335
Scholarships, 254
Scholasticate, 105, 173, 223 f., 252
School Council, 337 f.
Schools, parochial, 75, 108 f., 187 f.,
191
Schwinn, Father Bonaventure, 313,
328, 346
Schwinn, Abbot Leonard, 298, 303,
313
Science courses, beginnings, 281 f.
Secularization, 221 f.
Seidenbusch, Bishop Rupert, 82, 111
Seitz, Father Casimir, 30 ff., 50,
59 f., 135
Seneca, Kans., 122 f., 187 f., 199,
353
Severance, Kans., 190, 199, 353
Sewer problem, 232, 234
Sion, Father Justin, 285
Sisters cooks, 234, 349
Sittenauer, Father Joseph, 221, 224,
f., 286
Slavery, 23.
Smith, Father Isidor, 320, 329, 335
Social life, student, 329 ff.
Society for the Propagation of the
Faith, 68, 71
Society Hall, 251
Society of Jesus, missions in Kansas,
17 f.
Sodality B.V.M., 267
Sonora, Mo., 38, 118, 125
Spiegelhalter, Father George, 346
Stader, Father John, 113, 144, 190